P9-EGC-197

RECORDS OF CIVILIZATION

SOURCES AND STUDIES

EDITED UNDER THE AUSPICES OF THE

DEPARTMENT OF HISTORY, COLUMBIA UNIVERSITY

NUMBER XXII

CONCERNING HERETICS

Sebastian Castellio

Concerning Heretics

Whether they are to be persecuted and
How they are to be treated
A collection of the opinions of learned men
Both ancient and modern

An anonymous work attributed to

Sebastian Castellio

Now first done into English, together with excerpts
From other works of Sebastian Castellio and David Joris
On religious liberty

by

Roland H. Bainton

New York: Morningside Heights
Columbia University Press
A. D. Mcmxxxv

Published 1935

PRINTED IN THE UNITED STATES OF AMERICA
QUINN & BODEN COMPANY, INC., RAHWAY, NEW JERSEY

1965

To My Father

Acknowledgments

I wish to express my indebtedness to the John Simon Guggenheim Memorial Foundation for a fellowship in 1926. To Professor George L. Burr of Cornell I am grateful for an incomparable correspondence course extending over a period of more than ten years. From the staffs of the following libraries I have received unfailing courtesies: the University of Basel, in particular Carl Roth; the Zentralbibliothek, Zürich; the Doopsgezinde Bibliotheek, Amsterdam; the Schwenckfelder Historical Library, Pennsburg, Pa.; the Gardner Sage Library, New Brunswick, New Jersey; the New York Public Library; the libraries of the Union Theological Seminary, New York City, the Hartford Theological Seminary, and the universities of Cornell, Columbia, Harvard, and especially my own university—Yale.

The financial difficulties of publication have been eased by the courtesy of the Columbia University Press, the treasurer of Yale University, and the General Education Board Fund for Research in Language and Literature.

The careful supervision of Professor Evans is not adequately acknowledged by the formal printing of his name as the general editor of the series. To work with him is an education in book making.

I have been helped in the preparation and checking of the index by my wife, Ruth Woodruff Bainton, our children, Olive and Herbert, and our friend, John Moore.

ROLAND H. BAINTON

New Haven, Conn.
July 20, 1935

Contents

Illustrations

John Calvin 68

Reproduced from a drawing discovered by M. A. C. Coppier in 1930 in an account book commenced in 1565. There is universal agreement that the paper and the leads belong to the sixteenth century. In view of the queries raised as to whether the drawing has not been touched up, an examination was made by M. Cellerier, Directeur du Laboratoire des arts et métiers at Paris (September 22, 1931) and by M. Wolff, an expert chemist (September 28, 1931), who could discover no trace of any difference in the pencils. This information was kindly supplied by M. Coppier with whose permission the likeness is reproduced.

Caspar Hedio 80

From the drawing by Hans Baldung Grien (1543) in Baldungs so-called "*Skizzenbuch*" in the Kupferstichkabinett of the Badische Kunsthalle, Karlsruhe i. Baden.

Otto Brunfels 86

From the woodcut of Hans Weiditz on the reverse of the title-page of *Annotationes Othonis Brunfelsii, rei medices doctoris peritissimi, theologiae, trium linguarum variarumque artium insignite eruditi, in quatuor evangelii et Acta Apostolorum.* Argentorati, Georgio Ulrichero Andelano Impressore, An. MDXXXV, Mense Septembri, reproduced without the superscription by Johannes Ficker, *Bildnisse der strassburger Reformation* (Strassburg, 1914), Tafel 11.

Duke Christoph of Württemberg 132

Surrounded by dignitaries of the Catholic Church in the guise of animals who seek to devour him, reproduced from the original by courtesy of the Württembergische Landesbibliothek, Stuttgart.

John Brenz 154

The verse below recounts the posts which he filled until his death in 1570. The cut is taken from Reusner's *Contrafakturbuch* (1587), by courtesy of the Sächsische Landesbibliothek, Dresden.

The Book Sealed with Seven Seals, by Sebastian Franck . . 184

Conrad Pellican 204

From the lithograph printed in the *Neujahrsblatt*, herausgegeben von der Staatbibliothek in Zürich auf das Jahr 1871 (Zürich), based on the oil painting by Hans Asper in the Zentralbibliothek, Zürich, which is reproduced in color in *Ulrich Zwingli; zum Gedächtnis der zürcher Reformation, 1519-1919* (Zürich, 1919), Tafel 8, opposite col. 114. For an account of the painting see pp. 230-31, where the ascription to Holbein is corrected.

How to Recognize and Seize the False Prophets, by Urbanus Rhegius 258

Abbreviations and Symbols

AHR: American Historical Review (New York, 1895-).

ANF: Ante-Nicene Fathers. 10 vols. (Vols. 1-8, Buffalo, 1885-86; Vols. 9-10, New York, 1896-99).

ARG: Archiv für Reformationsgeschichte (Leipzig, 1903/4-).

Bossert Quellen: Quellen zur Geschichte der Wiedertäufer. Vol. I. Herzogtum Württemberg von Gustav Bossert, hrsg. von seinem Sohne Gustav Bossert (Leipzig, 1930). Quellen und Forschungen zur Reformationsgeschichte, XIII.

BSHPF: Bulletin de la Société de l'histoire du protestantisme français (Paris, 1852-).

BWKG: Blätter für württembergische Kirchengeschichte (Stuttgart 1-5, 1886-90, N.S., Vol. I, 1897-).

Codex Iust.: Codex Iustinianus, Corpus iuris civilis, 3 vols. (Berlin, 1912-28), Vol. 2, Codex Iustinianus, 9th ed. Paul Krüger (1915).

Codex Theod.: Theodosiani libri xvi . . . ed. Th. Mommsen et Paulus M. Mayer, 3 vols. (Berlin, 1905).

CR: Corpus reformatorum, including Philippi Melanthonis opera (28 vols., Halle, 1834-60); Calvini opera (59 vols., Brunswick and Berlin, 1863-97); Huldreich Zwinglis sämtliche Werke (Berlin and Leipzig, 1905-).

CSEL: Corpus scriptorum ecclesiasticorum Latinorum (Vienna, 1866-).

Friedberg: Corpus iuris canonici, ed. Aemilius Friedberg, 2 vols. (Leipzig, 1922).

HE: Historia ecclesiastica, referring to the work of Eusebius in Greek in Die griechischen christlichen Schriftsteller der ersten drei Jahrhunderte. 3 vols. (Leipzig, 1903-9), in English translation in PNF [2] I; referring also to the work of Socrates and Sozomen, PG LXVII, English PNF [2] II.

Migne, PG: Migne Patrologia Graeca, 161 vols., plus index (Paris, 1857-79).

Migne, PL: Migne Patrologia Latina, 221 vols. (Paris, 1844-64).

PNF [1]: Nicene and Post-Nicene Fathers, series 1, Vols. 1-8, Augustine (Vols. 1-4, Buffalo, 1886-87; Vols. 5-8, New York, 1887-88). Vols. 9-14, Chrysostom (New York, 1889-90).

PNF [2]: Nicene and Post-Nicene Fathers, series 2, 14 vols. (New York, 1889-90).

RE [3]: Realencyclopädie für protestantische Theologie und Kirche, 24 vols., 3d ed. (Leipzig, 1896-1913).

SVRG: Schriften des Vereins für Reformationsgeschichte (Leipzig, 1883-).

WA: Dr. Martin Luthers Werke (Weimer, 1883-).

ZKG: Zeitschrift für Kirchengeschichte (Gotha and Tübingen, 1876-).

In the translation, single brackets connote passages which Castellio has inserted in his sources; double brackets indicate material which the translator has supplied.

Introduction

The Occasion and Authorship of the Book

THE work here translated, to which I shall frequently refer by the first words of the Latin title *De haereticis*,[1] was a protest against the execution of Michael Servetus for heresy. He was burned at the stake at Geneva on October 23, 1553. The counts on which he was convicted were the rejection of infant baptism and the denial of the doctrine of the Trinity as held by the reformers. The arrest of Servetus was occasioned by the denunciation of John Calvin; the conviction and execution were at the hands of the town council of Geneva, who sentenced the heretic in the name of the Father, Son, and Holy Ghost.[2]

The present protest against his treatment appeared in two simultaneous Latin editions, as well as in French and German translations. The Latin versions differ only in that in one Luther and Brenz appear under their own names, in the other under the pseudonyms "Aretius Catharus" and "Witlingius," respectively. This pseudonym for Brenz had been used before in a commentary on some of the Psalms which he composed during the period of his

[1] *De haereticis, an sint perseqvendi, & omnino quomodo sit cum eis agendum, doctorum uirorum tum ueterum, tum recentiorum sententiae. Liber hoc tam turbulentio tempore pernecessarius, & cum omnibus, tum potissimum principibus & magistratibus utilissimus, ad discendum, quodnam sit eorum in re tam controuersa, tamque periculosa, officium.* At the end: Magdebvrgi, per Georgium Rausch, Anno Domini 1554. Mense Martio. 173 pages + 2 unnumbered.

[2] The only full account in English of the trial is that of Robert Willis, *Servetus and Calvin* (London, 1877). On Servetus, the man, consult Alexander Gordon, "Michael Servetus," in *Addresses Biographical and Historical* (London, 1922). The first two works of Servetus are now available in English translation by Earl Morse Wilbur, *The Two Treatises of Servetus on the Trinity* (Cambridge, Mass., 1932). Harvard Theological Studies, XVI. For the literature on Servetus see my article, "The Present State of Servetus Studies," *Journal of Modern History*, IV, Pt. I (March, 1932).

exile at the fortress of Wittlingen.[3] Both of the Latin editions of the *De haereticis* were printed ostensibly at Magdeburg in 1554. The French translation was printed ostensibly at Rouen in the same year. The French differs from the Latin, not only in minor details, but in the addition of an extra dedication to William of Hesse, of another passage from Luther, and of excerpts from Hedio, Agricola, Schenck, and Hoffmann. A passage from the *Historia tripartita* is omitted. This French version is available in a modern reprint.[4] The German translation is without date and place. Luther, Brenz, and Franck are reproduced directly from the original. An extra passage is included from Luther, but not the same one as is in the French. The dedication to William of Hesse does not appear, nor the passages from Schenck and Hoffmann, al-

[3] Walther Köhler, *Bibliographia Brentiana* (Berlin, 1904), No. 163; Julius Hartmann und Karl Jäger, *Johann Brenz nach gedruckten und ungedruckten Quellen* (Hamburg, 1840), II, 181.

[4] *Traité des hérétiques, à savoir, si on les doit persécuter, et comment on se doit conduire avec eux, selon l'avis, opinion, et sentence de plusieurs auteurs, tant anciens, que modernes, par Sébastien Castellion*, édition nouvelle publiée par les soins de A. Olivet . . . préface de E. Choisy (Genève, 1913). Attention was called to a number of misprints in this reprint by Charles Bost, "Sébastian Castellion et l'opposition protestante contre Calvin," *Revue de théologie et de philosophie*, N.S. (Lausanne, July 10, 1914), 301-21, but he was not in a position to say whether the mistakes were also in the original. Carl Roth of the library of the University of Basel has compared the reprint with the original and gives me the following report:

Page	*Lines from top*	*Lines from bottom*	*Reprint*	*Original*
33		4	fuyant	suyuant
37		4	en fassent	confessent
46		6	qui s'hérésie	que d'hérésie
72	2		entendu	entendu (for attendu)
80		5	prit avec foi	print auec soy
82	6		pourvoit	pouruoye
86		6	pour	pour (for pas)
105	4		saints	faints
122	1		Hosman	Hosman (for Hoffmann)
140	7		pertes	pestes
141	14		sainte	faincte
196	4		de guerre	des coeurs

though the citations from Hedio and Agricola are included.[5]

Calvin and his associates were not slow to recognize the source of this attack. Beza wrote to Bullinger, "Unless I am mistaken this Magdeburg is on the Rhine," [6] and he hints very broadly that Oporinus was the printer.[7] He was. The first posthumous list of Oporinus's works frankly listed the *De haereticis* among them.[8] The French, Beza believed to have been printed at Lyons by Castellio's brother.[9] Of the accuracy of this surmise we cannot be so confident.

As to the authors, suspicion attached itself most immediately and persistently to Sebastian Castellio, professor of Greek at Basel. Beza sensed the same blasphemous spirit in the preface to Castellio's Latin Bible as in the dedicatory epistle of Basil Montfort.[10] In addition to Castellio, Beza named Lelio Sozini, the migratory Italian exile,[11] and Coelius Secundus Curio, professor of rhetoric at Basel.[12] Calvin laid the blame also at the door of Martin Borrhaus,

[5] The only copy of the *Von Ketzeren* in this country is at Cornell. Buisson was unable to locate a copy abroad. I am indebted to George L. Burr for the above description.

[6] *Calvini opera*, XV, Ep. 1936, p. 97, no date.

[7] *Ibid.*, Ep. 1973, p. 167, no date.

[8] Ferdinand Buisson, *Sébastien Castellion*, 2 vols. (Paris, 1892), II, 2, n. 1, citing the *Oratio de ortu, vita, et obitu Joannis Oporini Basiliensis, typographicorum Germaniae principis . . . authore Andrea Jocisco Silesio* (Strassburg, 1569). There is a copy at Cornell of which George L. Burr writes me: "The list given by Jociscus has no dates, and this title appears in its alphabetical order: '*De haereticis, an sint persequendi, diversorum tam veterum quam recentiorum doctorum sententiae.* 8.' (The '8' of course means octavo.) The list must have been one prepared by Oporinus himself and while he was in the full tide of his activity; for at its end one reads: '*Unà cum multis aliis, quæ Divina juvante gratia, et vitam nobis prorogante, . . . in lucem dabimus.*' "

[9] *Calvini opera*, XV, Ep. 1973, p. 166, n. 4.

[10] *Calvini opera*, XV, Ep. 1936, p. 97. Beza wrote to Grataroli for confirmation of his suspicion, but could not obtain absolute proof. Neither could he establish his assertion that Castellio had denied the paternity. For the evidence on these points see Buisson, *op. cit.*, II, 13.

[11] *Calvini opera*, XV, Ep. 1973, p. 166, where he is indicated, but not named. He is named in the "Vita Calvini," *Calvini opera*, XXI, 149.

[12] *Calvini opera*, XV, Ep. 1973, p. 166. On Curio see Carl Schmidt, "Celio Secundo Curioni," *Zeitschrift für die historische Theologie*, XXX (1860), 571-634.

professor of the Old Testament at the University of Basel.[13]

Contemporaries, of course, were guessing; we are somewhat better informed. In the case of Borrhaus we have a suppressed portion of the *Contra libellum Calvini* preserved in manuscript in the hand of Castellio. The passage reads:

> At Basel there are three professors whom the Calvinists openly regard as followers of Servetus. They are Martin Cellarius or Borrhaus, head professor of theology, Coelius Secundus, and Sebastian Castellio, both professors of the liberal arts. The last two, as we said above, have written against persecution. . . . As for Borrhaus, Servetus submitted his book in manuscript to his judgment before publication. Borrhaus replied in a friendly way that he approved of some parts, as he had indicated in annotations, that he disapproved of others, and that some he did not understand.[14] The degree to which this same Borrhaus agreed with Servetus appears from a careful reading of the *De operibus Dei.* As for persecution, he told many that he thought no one should be persecuted for the faith, that he had never consented to the death of Servetus and "thanked God that he had never passed sentence on any one." [15]

One would like to take this statement at its face value, but unfortunately Capito informed Zwingli that Borrhaus vigorously defended him against the charge of cruelty to the Anabaptists in the execution of their leader Felix Manz.[16] The motive was perhaps the desire to avoid controversy with colleagues at Strassburg, for

[13] Not by name, but he said that De la Vau appealed, in addition to Castellio, to two other professors at Basel, and that the three agreed with each other as cats and dogs. One will have been Curio and the other Borrhaus, who had a vigorous controversy with Castellio over predestination. *Calvini opera,* XV, Ep. 2118 (Feb. 20, 1555), p. 441. On Borrhaus see Bernhard Riggenbach, "Martin Borrhaus," *Basler Jahrbuch* (1900), pp. 47-84.

[14] Borrhaus, whose first name was Martin, has been identified with the Marrin of Basel to whom Servetus wrote with reference to the publication of the *Restitutio.* For opinion pro and con see *Calvini opera,* XIV, Ep. 1617, p. 309; cf. VIII, 835.

[15] Buisson, *op. cit.,* II, 479 and 10-12. The last statement is made also in the "Historia de morte Mich. Serveti" published at the end of the *Contra libellum Calvini* and reprinted in Johann Lorenz von Mosheim, *Anderweitiger Versuch einer vollständigen und unpartheyischen Ketzergeschichte* (Helmstaedt, 1748), p. 449.

[16] *Huldreich Zwinglis sämtliche Werke,* IX, "Briefwechsel," III (Leipzig, 1925), Ep. 643 (Aug. 18, 1527), p. 193. CR XCVI.

Capito wrote again: "Cellarius [Borrhaus] is of such a nature and spirit that he speaks ill of no one and reproves revilers in a friendly way. This disposition has prompted him to make a strong defense of your reputation." [17]

Such a man might perhaps participate in a clandestine protest against persecution. But his liberalism was certainly not far-reaching. In the very year of the publication of *De haereticis* he had as censor suppressed portions of Castellio's annotation on Romans 9, and in 1557 he had the effrontery to ask Castellio for his arguments against predestination in private while denying him an opportunity to bring them out in public.[18] As for the similarity of Borrhaus's book to that of Servetus I am not in a position to judge, but neither the summary of Schweizer,[19] nor of Borrhaus himself,[20] betrays any likeness. All in all, I feel inclined to doubt whether Borrhaus can have been very active in his collaboration. Perhaps he may have prepared the German translation.

Curio also may very well have had a hand in the production. An excerpt from his work against Anthony Florebell is included under his name. Although he protested that he did not share the views of Servetus,[21] there is extant an apology for Servetus by a certain Alphonsus Lyncurius Tarraconensis with manuscript notes said to be in Curio's hand.[22] It is also not without interest that Curio's son

[17] *Ibid.*, Ep. 655 (Sept. 24, 1527), p. 221.

[18] Buisson, *op. cit.*, II, 113.

[19] Alexander Schweizer, *Die protestantischen Centraldogmen*, 2 vols. (Zürich, 1854-56), I, 134-38.

[20] *Zwinglis sämtliche Werke*, IX, Ep. 649 (Aug. 31, 1527), p. 207.

[21] *Calvini opera*, XV, Ep. 1938 (1554), pp. 101-3.

[22] "Alphonsi Lyncurii Tarraconensis apologia pro M. Serveto," published in *Calvini opera*, XV, Ep. 1918, pp. 52-63. Note on p. 60 the comparison with Phalaris and the appeal to the parable of the tares, as in Basil Montfort. The editors say *In margine additur hanc Apologiam manu Curionis correctam esse.* Buisson (*op. cit.*, II, 9) has no doubt of the annotation by Curio. Carl Roth of the library of the University of Basel writes me that the manuscript is numbered Mscr. Ki. Ar. 26a. "Die Schrift ist nicht von Secundus Curio. Hingegen zeigen sich Correctureinträge, die eine Randbemerkung des 19. Jahrhunderts der Hand Curios zuschreibt. Die nämliche Hand bezeichnet am Rande den Namen 'Alphonsus Lyncurius Tarraconensis' als Pseudonymus." This apology has been used all too confidently as the work of Curio. Jules Bonnet

Horatius possessed the manuscript of Servetus's *Restitutio Christianismi,*[23] composed probably in 1546. Nevertheless, on stylistic grounds I find it impossible to identify Curio with Basil Montfort,[24] whose peroration exhibits not the florid Ciceronianism of Curio, but the prophetic outburst of a Castellio. Curio's position as to religious liberty will be discussed later in connection with the excerpt from his work cited in the *De haereticis*.

The suspicion that Lelio Sozini had a hand in the work is highly plausible. He was in Basel at the time, and he was not averse to saying publicly that he disapproved of the execution of Servetus. When accused of entertaining the opinions of Servetus he replied,

> I do not know whether I ever gave any occasion for regarding me as a follower of Servetus or an Anabaptist, unless that when I was at Geneva I expressed regret at the hasty execution of Servetus. And this I said not because I utterly disapprove of the coercion of heretics and blasphemers nor because I favor the doctrine of Servetus, which I should like to see extinct, but precisely because I reject his depraved teaching I should have preferred to see him freed from it than to see it burned in him.[25]

That Lelio, entertaining these opinions, should have been at least privy to the publication, is almost certain, but that he took a prominent part in the composition I should be inclined to doubt. He was

in his *Récits du seizième siècle* (Paris, 1864), p. 257, translates a portion (*Calvini opera*, XV, 61) as from Curio's manuscript at Basel; Francesco Ruffini in his *La libertà religiosa* (Torino, 1901), p. 81, asserted, "Celio Secondo Curione di Moncalieri scrisse una violenta Apologia di Serveto, che poi non pubblicò. . . . Si conserva in Basilea nello stesso volume, ove e il residuo manoscritto del Castellion contro Calvino." W. K. Jordan, *The Development of Religious Toleration in England from the Beginning of the English Reformation to the Death of Queen Elisabeth* (Cambridge, Mass., 1932), pp. 308-9, says, "Curio, a friend of Acontius, is said to have written a violent apology for Servetus which he apparently did not publish."

[23] See my article "The Smaller Circulation: Servetus and Colombo," *Sudhoffs Archiv für Geschichte der Medizin*, XXIV, 3/4 (1931), pp. 371-74.

[24] As Beza did, *Calvini opera*, XV, Ep. 1973, p. 166. Later Beza was not so confident (*ibid.*, n. 7). Jacques Pannier has made the same identification. "Quelques remarques bibliographiques sur le Traité des hérétiques à propos d'une nouvelle édition," BSHPF LXII (1913), pp. 551-56.

[25] Joh. Henricus Hottingerus, *Historiae ecclesiasticae Novi Testamenti*, IX, Seculi XVI, Pars V (Zürich, 1667), p. 419; *Bullingers Korrespondenz mit*

too urbane for the prophetic flare which characterizes all the portions of the work which cannot be traced to known authors.

The responsibility for the *De haereticis* attached itself most persistently to Sebastian Castellio,[26] and I think correctly. He was a native of Savoy, and in French was called Châteillon. A refugee from the Inquisition, he had become a school teacher at Geneva. At the outset of his career an aversion to persecution betrayed itself in his dramatization of the stories of the exposure of Moses for fear of Pharaoh and of the sale of Joseph at the hands of his brethren.[27] Castellio, seeking ordination at Geneva, was rejected because of his repudiation of the inspiration of the Song of Songs of Solomon and of Calvin's interpretation of the descent of Christ into hell. In consequence of this rebuff Castellio went to Basel and supported his family by odd tasks, while devoting his spare time to Biblical scholarship. The notes in the *Moses Latinus* contain a protest against capital punishment for theft, and the rendering of Jonah into Homeric Greek betrays a predilection for this Old Testament story of latitude. The prefaces to the Latin Bible of 1551 and the French Bible of 1555 (the preface was circulating in manuscript as early as 1553) [28] were both protests against persecution. As a result of this work Castellio became professor of Greek at the University of Basel and prepared to settle down to a life of literary labor, when the execution of Servetus plunged him into a life-long controversy.

---

den Graubündnern, hrsg. Traugott Schiess, I Teil (Basel, 1904), No. 290 (Juli 1555), 411. Quellen z. schweizer Geschichte, XXIII. For a fuller discussion see Buisson, *op. cit.*, II, 3-7.

[26] On him see Buisson, *op. cit.*; Etienne Giran, *Sébastien Castellion* (Haarlem, 1914); Rufus M. Jones, *Spiritual Reformers in the Sixteenth and Seventeenth Centuries* (London, 1914); Roland H. Bainton, "Sebastian Castellio and the Toleration Controversy of the Sixteenth Century," in *Persecution and Liberty: Essays in Honor of George Lincoln Burr* (New York, 1931), pp. 183-209.

[27] We have now a facsimile reproduction of the edition of 1543, *Dialogues sacrés par Sébastien Castellion* (Fischbacher, Paris, 1932). The title-page of the work itself reads, *Dialogi sacri, Latino Gallici, ad Linguas, moresque puerorum formandos. Liber primus. Authore Sebastiano Castalione. M.D.LIII.* This date is an error for 1543. Cf. Buisson, *op. cit.*, II, 341.

[28] *Calvini opera*, XIV, Ep. 1769 (Aug. 6, 1553), p. 586, n. 7. Cf. Ep. 1889, p. 727.

He was at length brought to trial for his own heresies, but died during the proceedings in 1564.

I am inclined to see his hand not only in the sections which appear under the pseudonyms "Martin Bellius" and "Basil Montfort," but also "George Kleinberg." Buisson suggested that this name might represent David Joris (or George), the Dutch Anabaptist who lived in Basel under the assumed name "Johann van Brugge." That he should have contributed to the *De haereticis* is entirely within the range of probability. We know that Castellio submitted to his judgment the preface to the Bible, probably the French version, for we have Joris's reply. "I have gone through the preface to your Bible," he wrote, "and I like it greatly. God grant that it may be accepted. I have made a few suggestions and have toned down a word here and there or a name where it seemed to me too hard. I hope you will take it in good part. I could not do otherwise." [29] Nevertheless, the George Kleinberg passage, as Kühn has rightly discerned,[30] bears all the marks of Castellio's ethical and rational piety and pointed style and in no way resembles the formless mystical disquisitions of Joris, in whose writings a touch of rationalism is extremely rare.[31] Joris's thought and style appear in characteristic fashion in his plea for Servetus, which is translated in part at the close of the present work.

In a word, Castellio, I think, edited the entire work and himself composed all of the sections which cannot be assigned to known sources. Throughout I shall refer to him as author and editor. In compilation and translation he may well have had the assistance of

[29] *Sendbrieven*, I, III, 45. The greater part of the letter is translated into German by Friedrich Nippold, "David Joris von Delft," *Zeitschrift für die historische Theologie*, XXXIV (1864), 587-89. See my article, "Wylliam Postell and the Netherlands," *Nederlandsch Archief voor Kerkgeschiedenis*, XXIV/II (1931), 161-72, for the way in which Joris or some member of his circle worked over Postell's plea for tolerance.

[30] Johannes Kühn, *Toleranz und Offenbarung* (Leipzig, 1923), p. 274; note.

[31] I have read, I think, practically everything of Joris for a forthcoming work and have discovered only this example in the second edition of the *Wonderboeck* (1551), Pt. II, Chap. VI, f. 15. On the Trinity, he says, we do not have "perfect light and assurance of the truth."

Lelio Sozini, Coelius Secundus Curio, Martin Borrhaus, and perhaps David Joris.

The excerpts which appear in the *De haereticis* are culled from the early fathers and contemporaries, with nothing directly from the Middle Ages. The material included is sometimes from genuine liberals, sometimes from persecutors, who were to be embarrassed by a reminder of the rash utterances of their youth. Commentary upon this material must be the more detailed because the selections thus frequently went counter to the mature opinion of their authors. Castellio's translations are essentially faithful, but provocative expressions are omitted or recast, classical allusions are introduced, place names are changed, involved sentences condensed, and portions of the originals omitted with no bridging of the gaps. My initial intention of translating directly from the sources broke down in the face of these discrepancies. I found it necessary to translate the translations and to call attention in footnotes to deviations from the originals. The marginalia of the *De haereticis*, consisting sometimes of indications of the content, sometimes of references to sources, have been either dropped or incorporated in footnotes.

The following discussion of the excerpts begins in chronological fashion with pre-Reformation writers; then follow the Protestant persecutors in a roughly ascending scale of severity; next come the liberals classified as "Erasmians" and "Independents." The introduction is closed by a brief account of the influence of the book.

Pre-Reformation Writers

LACTANTIUS, CHRYSOSTOM, AND JEROME

THE earliest writer cited in our compilation is Lactantius. His *Divine Institutes* were composed between A.D. 305 and 311 in the early days of Constantine's successes. Nearly three centuries of Christian development lay behind Lactantius, and certain attitudes with regard to persecution had come to be fairly well defined. To persecute, a man must believe that he is right, that the point in question is important, and that coercion is effective. On the first two points the early Church was not dubious.

The conviction of certitude is inherent in Christianity at the outset. "I know him whom I have believed." [1] The skepticism of the late Academy was met by the ringing affirmation, *credo*. The content of that credo became ever more precise. The contest with the Gnostics led to the formulation of dogma, the closing of the canon, and the restriction of interpretation to the custodians of the tradition, namely, the bishops of the apostolic sees.

Nor was there any reservation on the second point that Christian certitude applied to a matter of great importance, since salvation was regarded as dependent upon right belief and upon membership in the organized Church, which came to be regarded as a Noah's ark outside of which there is no salvation.[2] The Church was prepared, therefore, to tolerate the moral offender within, who could not be saved were he cast out. The primitive Christian view of the Church as a congregation of the saints was abandoned to the Montanists, Novatianists, and Donatists.[3] The next step, though not yet

[1] II Tim. 1: 12.

[2] Anton Seitz, *Die Heilsnotwendigkeit der Kirche nach der altchristlichen Literatur bis zur Zeit Augustinus* (Freiburg i. B., 1903). Teil 1 was published separately as a "Habilitationsschrift" (Freiburg i. B., 1902).

[3] Erich Altendorf, *Einheit und Heiligkeit der Kirche* (Berlin & Leipzig, 1932). Arbeiten zur Kirchengeschichte, XX.

taken, was to urge that the heretic on the outside be compelled to come in.

The key to these two conceptions of the Church is to be found in the interpretation of the parable of the tares, which comes up over and over again in our compilation. Those who thought of the Church as a congregation of the saints, identified the tares with the heretics without, not with the moral offenders within. The heretics are not to be brought in, the delinquents are to be cast out, lest the society be sullied. Those who thought of the Church as an ark of salvation reversed the interpretation.

Further emphases in later exegesis may be noted here. The liberals sometimes adduced rationalistic grounds—we do not know enough to effect a separation; sometimes eschatological grounds—God will burn the tares at the harvest; sometimes legalistic grounds—Christ has commanded us to leave the tares. The persecutors avoided the liberal implications, not only by identifying the tares with the moral offenders, but also by equating the servants in the parable with ministers only, not with magistrates. Further, it was pointed out that Christ's concern was for the wheat only, and when the separation could be effected without danger of mistake, as when the heretics voluntarily separated themselves, then there was no reason why they should not be destroyed.[4]

But to return. The Church came to regard heresy as a most serious offense, because rejection of the creed and withdrawal from the organization spelled damnation. For that reason, even in the ante-Nicene period, the heretic was described as a spiritual adulterer, a ravager of the bride of Christ, a counterfeiter of divine truth, the first born of Satan, Antichrist, and a murderer of souls.[5]

On the third prerequisite for persecution, belief in the efficacy of coercion, the Church had no occasion to formulate a theory in the period when it was itself a persecuted body. Except, of course, that all of the apologies are full of protests against the coercion of

[4] The subject is more fully discussed in my article, "The Parable of the Tares as the Proof Text for Religious Liberty to the End of the Sixteenth Century," *Church History*, I (June, 1932), 67-89.

[5] Abundant illustrations in the work of Anton Seitz listed above.

Christianity. Tertullian did use more universal terms when he asserted that, "It is not in the nature of religion to coerce religion, which must be adopted freely and not by force." [6]

But although the Church was not in a position to coerce the heretic, certain predispositions to persecution were forming. The Old Testament penalties lay at hand for the offenses of idolatry, blasphemy, and apostasy, waiting to be transferred to heresy. And there was the New Testament injunction, "A man that is a heretic after the first and second admonition reject." [7] The seriousness with which this admonition was taken may be seen from the story of Irenaeus, that John, the Lord's disciple, fled from the bathhouse without bathing on discovering the heretic Cerinthus within.[8] The Montanists were repulsed like wolves from the orthodox churches and stigmatized their opponents as "slayers of the prophets." When the two groups came to die in the arena for the same Lord they separated themselves to opposite corners unwilling to be eaten by the same beasts.[9]

Whether the ante-Nicene fathers would have gone beyond this, had the secular arm been at their disposal, is seriously open to question. Even if we must relinquish the liberal saying attributed to Clement of Alexandria,[10] we have the statement of Origen, who when confronted with the jibe of Celsus that the Christians hate one another with a perfect hatred, replied that those who hold different opinions and will not be convinced, after a first and

[6] "Ad Scapulam," II: Migne, PL I, 699; ANF III, 105. Cf. "Apologeticus," XXIV and XXVIII: Migne, PL I, 418, 435-36; ANF III, 39, 41.

[7] Titus 3: 10.

[8] "Adv. Haer.," III, 4: Migne, PG VII, 853-54; ANF I, 416.

[9] Eusebius, HE V, xvi, 12, 17, 22. *Die griechischen christlichen Schriftsteller der ersten drei Jahrhunderte: Eusebius* II, I (whole series IX, I), 464, 466, 468; PNF [2] I, 232-33.

[10] "It ill befits Christians of all men to correct the mistakes of the erring by constraint. God crowns those who refrain from evil by choice not by necessity." The saying is attributed to Clement in the "Sacra parallela" of John of Damascus (Migne, PG XCV, 1285) and on this authority by Theodor Zahn, *Forschungen zur Geschichte des neutestamentlichen Kanons,* III (Erlangen, 1884), 54, n. 17. The passage was used as an illustration of Ante-Nicene opinion by Otto Schilling, *Die Staats- und Soziallehre des hl. Augustinus*

second admonition, are indeed to be rejected (Titus 3: 10), but the corrupters of Christianity are not to be regarded with hatred and called bad names.[11] The penalties of burning and stoning for transgression of the Mosaic law are no longer in force.[12] "For Christ conquers no one who is unwilling." [13]

There are passages, however, in Cyprian and Tertullian which have been construed as implying something more severe. Both were urging that Christians should endure martyrdom rather than commit idolatry, against which God had prescribed such frightful penalties in Deuteronomy. Cyprian argued that if these precepts were valid before Christ, how much more after Christ. He was talking, be it observed, about the precepts against idolatry, and not about the penalties,[14] which he tells us elsewhere are abrogated under the new dispensation.[15] Likewise Tertullian was pleading against Christians who would escape martyrdom by compliance. They are not to be reasoned with, he says, but squelched by the divine injunctions against idolatry. This is, I think, a fair rendering of his meaning, but his words are ominous, "Heretics may properly be compelled, not enticed to duty. Obstinacy must be corrected, not coaxed." [16] By the end of the ante-Nicene period there were those who were not unwilling to give concrete expression to such sentiments. In A.D. 272 at the request of the orthodox, the Emperor Aurelian ejected Paul of Samosata from his see.[17]

(Freiburg i. B., 1910), p. 134. But S. Haidacher ("Chrysostomos-Fragmente," *Byzantinische Zeitschrift*, XVI (1907), pp. 170-71) pointed out that the passage is from Chrysostom's "De sacerdotio," II, III (Migne, PG XLVIII, 634), and Otto Stählin in consequence listed the passage among the spuria of Clement (*Die griechischen christlichen Schriftsteller: Clemens Alexandrinus* III, Leipzig, 1909, p. lxxiii).

[11] "Contra Celsum," V, LXIII: *Die griechischen christlichen Schriftsteller: Origenes* II (whole series III), 67; ANF IV, 571.

[12] "Contra Celsum," VII, XXVI: *loc. cit.*, II, 177. 6-10; ANF IV, 621.

[13] "Selecta in Psalmos" (Ps. IV): Migne, PG XII, 1133.

[14] "Ad Fortunatum," V: CSEL III, I, 326; ANF V, 499.

[15] Ep. IV, 4: CSEL III, II, 476. 18-477. 5; ANF V, Ep. LXI, 4, p. 358.

[16] "Scorpiace," II: CSEL XX, 147. 3-8; ANF III, 634.

[17] Eusebius, HE, VII, XXX, 18-19: *Die griechischen christlichen Schriftsteller*, II, 2 (whole series IX, 2), 714; PNF [2] I, 316.

The passages in Lactantius against coercion are entirely in line with the previous protests of the apologists against the persecution of the Christians. But his paean over the victory of Constantine presages the church-state.[18]

By that victory an anti-imperial cult became the religious bulwark of the State, and the State was naturally concerned for the stability of the Church. Constantine had hoped that Christianity would serve to unify the Empire and was aghast that the Church itself was divided by the Donatist controvery in the West and the Arian, in the East.[19] Constraint was used in both cases. The edict against the Arians threatened capital punishment against those who refused to surrender a book composed by Arius.[20]

Under the sons of Constantine the situation was reversed. When Constantius overcame his brother, Arianism was in the saddle and the supporters of the Nicene position, including Hosius of Cordova, Athanasius, and Hilary of Poitiers, were sent into exile. All three protested. Hosius called for a sharp division of Church and State. The clergy should not bear rule on earth, the emperor should not burn incense.[21] Athanasius declared that persecution is of the devil.[22] "Truth is not proclaimed by swords and missiles, nor by means of soldiers, but by persuasion and counsel." [23] The Arians have recourse to stripes and imprisonment because they cannot convince by argument.[24] Hilary of Poitiers remonstrated

[18] "De mortibus persecutorum," LII: Migne, PL VII, 274; ANF VII, 321-22.

[19] For a succinct review of the imperial legislation from Constantine to Theodosius see Otto Schilling, *Die Staats- und Soziallehre des hl. Augustinus* (Freiburg i. B., 1910), pp. 8-17.

[20] Socrates, HE I, 9: Migne, PG LXVII, 89; PNF[2] II, 14.

[21] Letter to Constantius preserved in Athanasius, "Historia Arianorum," XLIV: Migne, PG XXV, 745-48; PNF[2] IV, 286; also in Shotwell and Loomis, *The See of Peter* (New York, 1927), pp. 577-80; and B. J. Kidd, *Documents Illustrative of the History of the Church*, II (London, 1923), § 23.

[22] "Apologia de fuga sua," § 23: Migne, PG XXV, 674 (cf. § 8, 654B); PNF[2] IV, 263 and 257.

[23] "Historia Arianorum," § 33: Migne, PG XXV, 732A; PNF[2] IV, 281.

[24] *Ibid.*, § 67: Migne, PG XXV, 773; PNF[2] IV, 295.

with the emperor that "God does not need forced obedience, nor does He require obligatory confession." [25] To Auxentius, the Arian bishop of Milan, he pointed out that Christ and the apostles were not supported by the State. This passage is reproduced in the *De haereticis* in one of the excerpts from Sebastian Franck.[26]

From the time of Constantine on legislation against the pagans became increasingly rigorous. Julius Firmicius Maternus could refer Constans and Constantius to Deuteronomy 13 without reservation as a warrant for the suppression of pagan idolatry.[27] Against such intolerance there were protests from three distinguished pagans, the orator Libanius, the statesman Symmachus, and the philosopher Themistius. Libanius complained to Theodosius of the illegal iconoclasm of the monks and reminded the Christians that their own laws commend persuasion and condemn force.[28] Symmachus urged that there is more than one path to truth.[29] Themistius pointed out to Emperor Jovian that coercion can produce only a hypocritical subservience to the purple, and that God, the author of nature, must prefer diversity because He has implanted in nature a tendency to variety. The king, therefore, although the incarnation of the divine law, must recognize a limitation to his authority in the sphere of religion.[30] Themistius also addressed a protest to the Arian Emperor Valens against the persecution of the Nicene party. A fragment of this oration is pre-

[25] "Ad Const. Aug.," I, § 6: Migne, PL X, 561; B. J. Kidd, *Documents*, II, § 24.

[26] See pp. 194-95, below.

[27] "Julii Firmici Materni de errore profanarum religionum," XXX: Migne, PL XII, 1048; cf. cap. XXI, *loc. cit.*, p. 1029, and cap. XXIX, *loc. cit.*, p. 1045.

[28] "Oratio pro templis," XXX (XXVIIIR), *Libanii opera*, ed. Richardus Foerster, III (Leipzig, 1906). Sections of the oration are translated by Nathaniel Lardner, *A Large Collection of Ancient Jewish and Heathen Testimonies to the Truth of the Christian Religion*, IV (London, 1766), XLIX.

[29] "Relatio Symmachii urbis praefecti," § 10, in *Ambrosii epistolarum classis I:* Migne PL XVI, 969; PNF ² X, 415; also in B. J. Kidd, *Documents*, II, § 72.

[30] *Themistii orationes* . . . emendatae a Guilielmo Dindorfio (Leipzig, 1832), No. V.

served by Socrates,[31] and is incorporated in the *De haereticis* in the section by Basil Montfort.[32] The oration itself is lost, unless it be extant in a Latin translation made by Dudith in the sixteenth century.[33] This, however, is probably a forgery; doubt as to its genuineness is awakened by the fact that the inappropriate praise of Valens for his tolerance seems to have been borrowed from the extant oration to Jovian, from which also whole sections have been incorporated bodily in Dudith's version.[34] On the other hand, it is odd that Dudith did not make his forgery plausible by including all of the fragment from Socrates. The statement there made that the pagans have more sects than the Christians does not appear in Dudith at all.

Throughout the fourth century the legislation against heresy was growing increasingly severe. The first instance of the infliction of the death penalty occurred under the usurper Maximus in the West in A.D. 385 against Priscillian and his followers in Spain. Martin of Tours and Ambrose of Milan were thoroughly shocked and refused to communicate with the ecclesiastics responsible for the condemnation.[35] Of this unequivocal stand no use is made in the *De haereticis*, although it would have been very much to the

[31] HE IV, 32: Migne, PG LXVII, 552; PNF [2] II, 115. Cf. Sozomen, HE VI, 36: Migne, PG LXVII, 1401-02; PNF [2] II, 372.

[32] See pp. 237-38, below.

[33] Reproduced with a Greek translation in *Themistii orationes*, No. XII.

[34] These objections were first raised by Benj. Friedrich Schmieder, *De Themistio tolerantiae patrono* (Halle, 1789). The case against the genuineness is worked out in greater detail by Richard Foerster, "Andreas Dudith und die zwölfte Rede des Themistius." *Neue Jahrbücher für das klassische Altertum*, VI (Leipzig, 1900), 74-93. The article contains an excellent brief biography of Dudith and a collection of his utterances on religious liberty.

[35] There is an excellent account of the whole affair by E. Ch. Babut, *Priscillien et le Priscillianisme* (Paris, 1909). Bibliothèque de l'École des hautes études, CLXIX. A brief account is given in English by B. J. Kidd, *A History of the Christian Church to A.D. 461*, II (Oxford, 1922), 299-310. Our information as to Martin is derived from Sulpicius Severus, "Hist. sacra" II, 50 (Migne, PL XX, 157-58; PNF [2] XI, 121), and "Dialogus," III, XI-XIII (Migne, PL XX, 217-19; PNF [2] XI, 50-52). Ambrose refers to his protests in Epp. XXIV, § 12, and XXVI, § 3; Migne, PL XVI, 1039 and 1042.

point, especially since Ambrose had no objection to the suppression of heretical assemblies.[36]

To the end of the fourth and the beginning of the fifth century belong Chrysostom and Jerome, who are both cited in our compilation. Chrysostom took the position of Ambrose that capital punishment is not to be inflicted, but freedom of assembly may be denied. This view is clearly stated in the excerpt in the *De haereticis* from Homily 47 on the parable of the tares. A further illustration of the extent of his intolerance toward paganism is furnished by his rejoicing over the forcible abolition of heathen altars, temples, feasts, and sacrifices.[37] His iconoclastic zeal led him even to organize bands of monks for the demolition of pagan temples in Phoenicia.[38] His attitude to the heretic appears in that some regarded his misfortunes at Constantinople as a retribution for the violence which he had exercised in depriving the Novatians and the Quartodecimans of their churches in Asia and Lydia.[39] He threatened, also, to silence the preaching of the Novatianist bishop at Constantinople, but was mollified by a clever piece of repartee.[40]

In the main the above statements are made, not by Chrysostom, but about him. One would like to regard them as exaggerations in the light of the two following pleas for tolerance. In the twenty-ninth Homily on Matthew, Chrysostom wrote:[41]

There are those who indulge their passions under the guise of vindicating God, whereas they ought to proceed with clemency. God, the

[36] Ep. X, § 12: Migne, PL XVI, 944.

[37] "Expositio in Ps. 109: 5": Migne, PG LV, 273.

[38] Theodoret, HE V, 29: *Die griechischen christlichen Schriftsteller*, XIX, 330; PNF [2] III, 152. The accuracy of Theodoret at this point has been impugned by Chrysostomus Baur (*Der heilige Johannes Chrysostomus u. seine Zeit*, II, München, 1930, p. 331) on the ground that in letters CXXVI (Migne, PG LII, 685-87) and CXXIII (*Ibid.*, 676-78) Chrysostom merely urged the monks to endure with patience the trials which had come upon them. True, but in Ep. LIV (*Ibid.*, p. 639) he writes to Gerontius in Phoenicia that funds are not lacking for the *destruction of edifices.*

[39] Socrates, HE VI, 19: Migne, PG LXVII, 724; PNF [2] II, 151.

[40] Socrates, HE VI, 22: Migne, PG LXVII, 729B; PNF [2] II, 152.

[41] "In Matthaeum Homil., XXIX" (al. XXX), § 3: Migne, PG LVII, 361-62; PNF [1] X, 197-98.

Lord of all, who can hurl His bolts against blasphemers, sends rather His sun and His showers and supplies all other bounties. We should imitate Him and beseech, advise, and instruct with humility, without wrath and enmity. No one can hurt God by his blasphemy that you should be so incensed, but the blasphemer himself receives the wound. Therefore groan and weep for the offense is worthy of tears, and there is no better cure than gentleness which is more powerful than any constraint. . . . We must, then, use gentleness to remove a disease. He who is cured by the fear of men speedily relapses. . . . [Then follows an appeal to the parable of the tares.] When, then, you see an enemy of the truth, cure him, care for him, bring him to a better way through the example of an excellent life and irreproachable speech. . . . Imitate a good doctor who uses not one medicine only, but when an ulcer does not succumb to the first drug, tries another and another. Now he cuts and now he binds. So may you be a physician of souls, using every means of cure according to the laws of Christ. . . .

The following excerpt is from the tract *On the Priesthood:* [42]

It ill befits Christians of all men to correct the mistakes of the erring by constraint. Judges without the Christian fold may exercise coercion against those who are legally convicted, but in our case such men must be brought to a better fruit, by persuasion rather than compulsion. The laws do not confer upon us authority of this sort for coercing the delinquent, nor if they did could we use it, because God crowns those who refrain from evil by choice and not by necessity. . . . The priest has much to do also in gathering up the scattered members of the Church. The shepherd can recall a wandering sheep with a shout, but if a man errs from the true faith, the pastor has need of great effort, perseverance, and patience. The wanderer cannot be dragged by force or constrained by fear. Only persuasion can restore him to the truth from which he has fallen away.[43]

The excerpt from Jerome in the *De haereticis* is also a commentary on the parable of the tares. Here he identifies them with the heretics. Elsewhere he sees in them moral offenders.[44] Both

[42] "De sacerdotio," II, §§ 3, 4: Migne, PG XLVIII, 634-35; PNF [1] IX, 41.

[43] Other passages in which Chrysostom says that he opposes heresy, not the heretic, are collected by Anton Seitz, *Die Heilsnotwendigkeit der Kirche*, p. 202.

[44] "Dialogus adversus Luciferianos" XXII: Migne, PL XXIII, 177; PNF [2] VI, 331-32.

are to be let alone, yet not entirely alone. In this passage we are told to reserve judgment "where the case is dubious." [45] What if we think it clear? In any case the consolation is offered to us that some heretics and hypocrites are sure of hell in the end. In another passage Jerome applies the slaughter of the priests of Baal by Elijah and of a great multitude by Jehu to the treatment of heretics, but the penalties are spiritualized. "God kills the prophets of the heretics when he threatens them with eternal punishment and deprives them of true life by abandoning them to the death of sin." [46] Yet the javelin of Phineas, the harshness of Elijah, the zeal of Simon the Zealot, the severity of Peter against Ananias and Sapphira, and the firmness of Paul in blinding Elymas the sorcerer, all serve as justification for the virulence of Jerome's polemic against Vigilantius. "Zeal for God is not cruelty. 'If thy brother or thy friend or the wife of thy bosom entice thee from the truth, thy hand shall be upon them, and thou shalt shed their blood; and so shalt thou put the evil away from the midst of Israel.' " [47] Jerome does not say that the heretics are to be treated literally in this fashion, but the inference is not remote. The following passage is still more precise. "A spark should be extinguished, fermentation removed, a putrid limb amputated, an infected animal segregated. Arius was but a spark, but because he was not immediately put out the whole world caught fire." [48] The length to which Jerome might have gone is suggested by the statement that the "punishment of murder, *sacrilege,* and poisoning is not bloodshed, but merely execution of the law." [49]

AUGUSTINE

In the matter of persecution and liberty, Augustine was as usual the father of both sides. The advocates of liberty, Erasmus, Franck,

[45] "Comment. in Evang. Matth.," II, XIII: Migne, PL XXVI, 93-94.

[46] "Comment. in Osee," Lib. II, Cap. VI, Vers. 4, 5: Migne, PL XXV, 869. The passage is used in our compilation by Urbanus Rhegius.

[47] Deut. 13: 5. Ep. CIX, § 3; Migne, PL XXII, 908; PNF [2] VI, 213.

[48] "Comment. in Ep. ad Gal." III, v, 9: Migne, PL XXVI, 403.

[49] "Comment. in Jeremiam Prophet.," IV, XXII: Migne, PL XXIV, 811D, italics mine.

and Castellio, appealed to him. So also did the apologists for the massacre of St. Bartholomew and for the revocation of the Edict of Nantes.[50]

The explanation is not simply that Augustine changed his mind. Both parties drew their arguments from the works of his later period when he defended persecution. The liberals pointed out that at his worst he was far removed from the practice of their own day. The persecutors extended his arguments, not improperly, to cover much more than he would have been prepared to admit.

He did change his mind. Up to A.D. 404 he was unwilling to appeal to the State.[51] He would not receive an unwilling convert,[52] reproved a Donatist for constraining his vassals,[53] and sympathized with the request of the Catholic clergy for the remission of fines imposed upon their opponents.[54]

Nevertheless, two of the requisites for persecution Augustine carried over from the early Church. He believed that the Church was right and that heresy was serious.

That the Church was right and that her authority was to be accepted he confessed when he submitted to baptism. No matter how much he might continue to wrestle with the problems raised by Neoplatonism, all dubiousness on this score had been eliminated before the Donatist schism raised the issue of persecution.[55]

On the second point, also, Augustine was clear. Heresy and schism are of grave moment because destruction awaits the

[50] Saint-René Taillandrier, "St. Augustin et la liberté de conscience," *Rev. des deux mondes*, 2me periode XXXII (Juillet 15, 1862), 503-12.

[51] Ep. XXIII, 7: CSEL XXXIV, 71; PNF [1] I, 244. CSEL XXXIV is in two parts bound separately and with separate pagination. This reference is to Part I. All subsequent references are to Part II.

[52] Ep. XXXV, 4: CSEL XXXIV, 30; PNF [1] I, 265.

[53] Ep. LXVI, 2: CSEL XXXIV, 236; PNF [1] I, 323.

[54] Ep. LXXXVIII, 7: CSEL XXXIV, 413; PNF [1] I, 371.

[55] I am following the excellent chapter of Jens Nörregaard, *Augustins Bekehrung* (Tübingen, 1923), Kap. 13, "Das Christentum als Autorität," against Wilhelm Thimme, *Augustins geistige Entwicklung in den ersten Jahren nach seiner "Bekehrung"* (Berlin, 1908), pp. 386-91. The controversy, however, is immaterial here because Thimme would not extend the dubious period beyond A.D. 391.

branches cut off from the Lord's vine.[56] The endurance of persecution brings no reward to heretics and schismatics,[57] since "outside of the Church there is no salvation." [58] By "the Church" Augustine meant the visible organization. To be sure some of those outside of this society might be of the elect. Nevertheless, hope could scarcely be entertained for those who deliberately left the ark of Noah or spurned an invitation to return.[59]

On what ground other than that of expediency could a man convinced on these two points object to persecution? Augustine had already come to feel that suppression is legitimate, though unwise.[60] The Donatists helped to break down his lingering reservations by their failure to repudiate unequivocally the Circumcellions, a party of social malcontents, who committed acts of lawlessness against the Catholics. Suppression of these ruffians could be regarded not as constraint of conscience, but as preservation of the peace.[61]

[56] Ep. XXIII, 6: CSEL XXXIV, 71; PNF [1] I, 244 (A.D. 392).

[57] "De sermone Domini in monte," V (13): Migne, PL XXXIV, 1236; PNF [1] VI, 7 (A.D. 393).

[58] Augustine quotes with approval the famous dictum of Cyprian. "De baptismo," IV, 17 (24): Migne, PL XLIII, 170; PNF [1] IV, Chap. 17 (25), p. 458 (A.D. 400). In later years he added nothing to these statements save tartness. *See* Ep. CLXXIII, 6: CSEL XLIV, 644; PNF [1] I, 545 (A.D. 416).

[59] Capistran Romeis, "Das Heil der Christen ausserhalb der wahren Kirche nach der Lehre des hl. Augustins," *Forschungen zur christlichen Literatur- und Dogmengeschichte*, VIII, 4 (Paderborn, 1908), 1-155.

[60] Ep. LI: CSEL XXXIV, 144-49; PNF [1] I, 296-97 (A.D. 399/400); "Contra Ep. Parmeniani": CSEL LI (A.D. 400); "Contra litteras Petiliani": CSEL LII; PNF IV (A.D. 401/3). There is an excellent review of Augustine's development by Gustave Combès, *La Doctrine politique de Saint Augustin* (Paris, 1927), pp. 352-409. The letters are well analyzed by Wilhelm Thimme, *Augustin: ein Lebens- und Charakterbild auf Grund seiner Briefe* (Göttingen, 1910), § IV, "Augustin als Kämpfer gegen Haeresie und Heidentum," pp. 138-83. The political background is well covered by Edward F. Humphrey, *Politics and Religion in the Days of Augustine* (Diss. Columbia, New York, 1912). Of value is the article by W. B. O'Dowd, "The Development of St. Augustine's Opinions on Religious Toleration," *Irish Theological Quarterly*, XIV (Oct., 1919), 337-48.

[61] "Contra litteras Petiliani," II, 83 (184): CSEL LII, 112-15; PNF [1] IV, 572-73 (A.D. 401/3). Cf. Ep. LXXXVII, 8: CSEL XXXIV, 404; PNF [1] I, 368 (A.D. 405).

The decisive step was occasioned by the testimony of events. In A.D. 404 the Catholic bishops of Africa proposed to invite imperial intervention. Augustine persuaded them to ask that the fine be imposed only in those districts where violence actually occurred, but the government, on its own motion, inflicted fines upon all the Donatist laity and banishment upon the clergy.[62]

The result was that Donatist congregations came over wholesale to the Catholic side, declaring that they had not been so much coerced as liberated from intimidation.[63] Augustine capitulated:

> I have succumbed [he wrote] to the evidence presented by my colleagues. I was formerly of the opinion that no one should be forced to the unity of Christ, that we should agitate with the word, fight with disputation, conquer by reason, lest we substitute feigned Catholics for avowed heretics. This opinion of mine was changed, not by the words of critics, but by the logic of events. My own town rose up to convict me. It had been entirely devoted to the Donatist party, but now was brought to Catholic unity by fear of the imperial laws.[64]

Once convinced, Augustine was too sensitive to the force of his former objections to accept the change of front complacently. Precisely because he was more alive than his colleagues to the discrepancy between religious persecution and the spirit of Jesus, he now essayed a harmonization and became the first theorist of the Inquisition.

The corner stone of his theory was love. The Christian must be his brother's keeper. How can genuine affection suffer a loved one to die a death more tragic and more real than that in the flesh? [65] How can it permit him to commit a crime worse than murder, which destroys only the body, whereas schism and heresy shed spiritual blood? [66] In face of such peril, can love be scrupulous about

[62] Ep. LXXXVIII, 7: CSEL XXXIV, 414; PNF [1] I, 371; Ep. CLXXXV, VII, 25-26: CSEL LVII, 23-25; PNF [1] IV, 643.

[63] Ep. CV, II, 5: CSEL XXXIV, 598; Ep. XCIII, V, 16: CSEL XXXIV, 461; PNF [1] I, 388.

[64] Ep. XCIII, V, 17: CSEL XXXIV, 461-62; PNF [1] I, 388.

[65] "Contra Ep. Parmeniani," VIII, 14: CSEL LI, 34-35.

[66] "Contra Cresconium" IV, LII, 62: CSEL LII, 559. Cf. Ep. XLIV, IV, 8: CSEL XXXIV, 116; PNF [1] I, 288. Cf. also Romeis, *op. cit.*, p. 72.

methods? Christianity calls not for an absolute nonresistance, but for a benevolent disposition which makes its own choice of means.[67] Constraint and love are not incompatible. In support of this contention Augustine introduced two analogies which for him pointed in the same direction, but are capable of divergent applications. The first looks only to the individual. The persecutor, said Augustine, is like a kind father who disciplines a wayward son, or like a dutiful son restraining a crazy father from destroying himself.[68] In each case the concern is to save the erring. Such analogies are irrelevant as justification for burning heretics at the stake. But there is another comparison which is susceptible of wider application, namely, that of the physician who amputates a diseased member for the sake of the rest of the body.[69] So long as the death penalty is not admitted, so long as the State is not personified,[70] this simile is innocuous. But the moment the diseased body is identified with the social group, then the individual becomes the rotten member to be destroyed for the sake of the larger good. Then the imagery swiftly shifts; the heretic becomes the wolf, the fox, the serpent, the thief, and the robber, epithets which themselves suggest the proper treatment. All of these terms are found in Augustine,[71] as in his predecessors, waiting to be used as justification for a policy more rigorous than any he would countenance.

Yet he did occasionally verge on a severer attitude with the suggestion that the few might be sacrificed for the many. Some of the Donatists were killing themselves rather than submit to the coercive measures. In the light of this circumstance, asked Augustine, what is the function of brotherly love? And he answered

[67] Ep. CXXXVIII, II, 13: CSEL XLIV, 138; PNF[1] I, 485.

[68] Ep. CXXXVIII, II, 14: CSEL XLIV, 140; PNF[1] I, 485; Ep. CLXXIII, 3: CSEL XLIV, 642; PNF[1] I, 544; Ep. CLXXXV, II, 7: CSEL LVII, 6; PNF[1] IV, 635.

[69] Ep. XCIII, II, 8: CSEL XXXIV, 452; PNF[1] I, 385; Ep. CIV, II, 7: CSEL XXXIV, 587; PNF[1] I, 429; Ep. CLXXXV, II, 7: CSEL LVII, 6; PNF[1] IV, 635; "Contra Gaudentium" I, v, 6: CSEL LIII, 203; "Contra Cresconium" LI, 61: CSEL LII, 558.

[70] Offergelt contends that Augustine does not personify the State. Franz Offergelt, *Die Staatslehre des hl. Augustinus* (Diss., Bonn, 1914), p. 25.

[71] Romeis, *op. cit.*, pp. 71-72.

with the query, Shall we through fear of the transitory fires of the furnace for the few commit all to the eternal fires of hell? [72] And again he abandoned love as a ground of persecution when he introduced predestination. He was willing that the many should be saved by the loss of the few, "whom God has predestined to extreme penalties." [73] God has no concern for the number of the damned.[74]

To justify the persecution of heresy Augustine turned for authority to the Bible. The Old Testament supplied abundant material on penalties, though nothing on heresy. Hezekiah destroyed the idols,[75] and Nebuchadnezzar issued a decree against those who should blaspheme the God of Shadrach, Meshach, and Abednego.[76] When Gaudentius very pertinently asked, "What does a man who defends God by violence, think of Him if not that He cannot take care of Himself?" Augustine evaded the problem by simply pointing to the example of Moses, who was more concerned to vindicate the divine honor than his own.[77] In the case of Elijah's slaughter of the priests of Baal, Augustine ran upon a snag. One of the Donatists pointed out to him that the prophet was authorized by a special commission which is no longer valid.[78] Let an example be produced from the New Testament.[79]

[72] "Contra Gaudentium" XXII, 25: CSEL LIII, 224; Ep. CCIV, 2: CSEL LVII, 318. Cf. Karl Holl, "Augustins innere Entwicklung," *Gesammelte Aufsätze* III (Tübingen, 1928), p. 90, n. 4. It does not seem to me that Augustine inadvertently reveals his real state of mind when he says that teaching and affection are to be preferred to fear as means of correction. He does not admit that the teacher who appeals to fear is not himself actuated by love.

[73] Ep. CCIV, 2: CSEL LVII, 318.

[74] Ep. CXC, III, 12: CSEL LVII, 146.

[75] Ep. CLXXXV, v, 19: CSEL LVII, 17; PNF [1] IV, 640.

[76] Ep. XCIII, III, 9: CSEL, XXXIV, 453; PNF [1] I, 385; "Contra litteras Petiliani" II, 92 (212): CSEL LII, 137-38; PNF [1] IV, 584; "Contra Gaudentium" I, 19 (20): CSEL LIII, 216.

[77] *Ibid.*

[78] This solution of the difficulty has played a large rôle in the history of exegesis. See my article, "The Immoralities of the Patriarchs According to the Exegesis of the Late Middle Ages and of the Reformation," *Harvard Theological Review*, XXIII, 1 (Jan., 1930), 39-49.

[79] Ep. XLIV, IV, 9: CSEL XXXIV, 117; PNF [1] I, 288.

Here there was mention of heresy, though little about penalties, but Augustine was ingenious. He was the first to introduce the fateful text, "Compel them to come in," [80] and could point out that Paul coupled fornicators, idolators, poisoners, heretics, and drunkards,[81] implying that all are subject to the civil power.[82]

This appeal to the State to maintain the faith required a theory of Church and State. The problem would have been simple if Augustine had regarded religion as a department of the State, but against this position the tradition of spiritual independence and even anti-imperialism was too deeply intrenched in early Christianity, and nowhere more so than in Africa, where it was now represented by Augustine's opponents, the Donatists. Yet he, too, shared this African hostility to the State,[83] and found it very useful in the solution of another problem as to why divine providence should permit the sack of Rome. The answer was in part that large states, like the Roman Empire, *without justice*, are but piracy on a big scale.[84]

The bridge from the hostile to the friendly attitude toward the State is found in that word "justice." For Augustine, this is not mere equity. There can be no genuine justice apart from the Christian faith.[85] If then the State promotes the faith, let her sway be extended.[86] This is the point at which Augustine attains the greatest clarity, and at which he most markedly anticipates the Middle Ages. However much the *Civitas terrena* and the *Civitas*

[80] Luke 14:21-23. Ep. CLXXIII, 10: CSEL XLIV, 647; PNF [1] I, 547; Ep. XCIII, II, 5: CSEL XXXIV, 449; PNF [1] I, 383; "Contra Gaudentium," I, xxv, 28: CSEL LIII, 227.

[81] Gal. 5:19-21.

[82] "Contra Ep. Parmeniani" I, 10 (16): CSEL LI, 37.

[83] Cf. Christopher Dawson, "St. Augustine and His Age," in *A Monument to Saint Augustine* (London, 1930), pp. 52-57.

[84] "De civitate Dei," IV, 4: CSEL XL, I, 166; PNF [1] II, 66.

[85] "De civitate Dei," II, 21: CSEL XL, I, 93; PNF [1] II, 36.

[86] *Ibid.*, IV, 3: CSEL XL, I, 166; PNF [1] II, 66. Cf. the excellent studies of Heinrich Scholz, *Glaube und Unglaube in der Weltgeschichte im Kommentar zu Augustins De civitate Dei* (Leipzig, 1911), pp. 98-108, Edgar Salin, *Civitas Dei* (Tübingen, 1926), p. 190, and Otto Schilling, *Die Staats- und Soziallehre des hl. Augustinus* (Freiburg i. B., 1910), p. 111.

Dei may be enveloped in celestial haze, this, at least, is clear that the State on earth justifies its existence by serving the visible Church.[87]

We must not forget, however, that Augustine is the father of the liberals, as well as of the persecutors. He always objected to the death penalty. Rather would he see even those guilty of violence go scot-free than that their blood should be on the heads of the Catholics.[88]

Augustine also imposed limitations on the scope of heresy. Not every error is heresy, he held. Some questions are essential to the faith, others are immaterial, for example, as to the location of Paradise, how Methuselah could survive the deluge when he was not in the ark, whether the age of puberty was postponed for the patriarchs in proportion to their total longevity,[89] and even error on essential points does not constitute heresy unless it be associated with pride, curiosity, obstinacy, and a lack of love for God and for His Church.[90]

Of the passages which Castellio has taken from Augustine, only one comes from the early liberal period, that from the work *Against the Letter of Manichaeus Called Fundamental*. Later,

[87] Ep. XCIII, v, 19: CSEL XXXIV, 464; PNF [1] I, 389, in which Augustine blames his opponents for relying on Roman law against divine law, and calls upon kings to make laws for Christ. Compare the commendation of Constantine and Theodosius in "De civitate Dei," V, 25 and 26: CSEL XL, I, 262-66; PNF [1] II, 105-6. Troeltsch does not overlook such passages (*Augustin, die christliche Antike und das Mittelalter* [München und Berlin, 1915], p. 134, Historische Bibliotek, Bd. 36), but unduly minimizes the degree to which Augustine anticipates the Middle Ages. I am thoroughly in accord with Holl at this point (*op. cit.*, p. 92).

[88] Ep. CXXXIV, 4: CSEL XLIV, 87; Ep. C: CSEL XXXIV, 535-38; PNF [1] I, 411-12; Ep. CXXXIII, 1: CSEL XLIV, 81; PNF [1] I, 470; Ep. CXXXIX, 2: CSEL XLIV, 150; PNF [1] I, 488-89.

[89] "De peccato orig.," II, 23 (26 and 27): Migne, PL XLIV, 397-98; PNF [1] V, 245-46. Cf. Ep. LIV: CSEL XXXIV, 158-68; PNF [1] I, 300-2.

[90] Joseph de Guibert, "La Notion d'hérésie chez Saint Augustin," *Bulletin de littérature ecclésiastique publié par l'Institut catholique de Toulouse*, 3 sér. XXI, Nos. 1 and 2 (Jan.-Feb., 1920), 368-82; Joseph Mausbach, *Die Ethik des hl. Augustinus*, 2 vols. (Freiburg i. B., 1929), II, 330-41, "Häresie und Schisma als Abfall von der kirchlichen Einheit."

Augustine was not unwilling to inflict banishment upon his former coreligionists.[91] Of the other passages, those *Against Cresconius* and the letters to Marcellinus and Apringius recognize the legitimacy of coercion, but object to the death penalty. The passage from the tract *On Faith and Works* is really irrelevant, because here Augustine is discussing not the heretic, but the moral offender within the Church. The commentary on Matthew 13 is relevant, but is now commonly regarded as spurious.[92]

THE MIDDLE AGES

The Middle Ages had very little to add to the theory of persecution elaborated by Augustine. The introduction in the thirteenth century of the death penalty, to which he always objected, required a shift of emphasis. There were two ways in which the theory of Augustine was elaborated. The first involved a magnifying of the enormity of heresy, particularly in comparison with those offenses on which the death penalty was visited. Augustine had already declared that heresy, which destroys the soul, is worse than murder, which destroys only the body. Aquinas added the further illustration that the counterfeiting of divine truth is worse than the forging of money which is punishable by death.[93] Innocent III and Frederick II declared that heresy is worse than treason because it is more serious to offend the eternal than the temporal Majesty.[94] Here we have a feudalization of the conception of heresy.

[91] Thimme, *op. cit.*, pp. 170-71.

[92] For a discussion of this passage see my article, "The Parable of the Tares as the Proof Text for Religious Liberty to the End of the Sixteenth Century," *Church History*, I (June, 1932), 73.

[93] *Sanctae Aquinatis opera omnia*, 12 vols. (Rome, 1862-1906), VIII, 100. *Summa theologica*, II, ii, Quaest. XI, "De haeresi," art. 3.

[94] Innocent III, Reg. II, I: Migne, PL CCXIV, 539B (March 25, 1199); Frederick II, *Historia diplomatica Friderici Secundi*, ed. J. L. A. Huillard-Bréholles, IV, Pars 1 (Paris, 1854), p. 299 (Feb. 22, 1232), pp. 301-2 (March, 1232). These passages are also in *Mon. Germ. hist.*, Legum IV, II (Hanover, 1896), 195, 197. Compare the note in the excellent treatment of this whole subject by Ernest W. Nelson, "The Theory of Persecution," in *Persecution and Liberty: Essays in Honor of George Lincoln Burr*, pp. 3-20, esp. p. 11 n. 30.

The other line of justification was to shift love from the heretic to the society which he menaced. Aquinas said, "On the part of the Church there is mercy which looks to the conversion of the wanderer. Wherefore she condemns not at once, but after the first and second admonition, as the apostle directs: after that, if he is stubborn, the Church, no longer hoping for his conversion, looks to the salvation of others." [95]

ERASMUS

No one did more than Erasmus to break down the theory and practice of the medieval variety of intolerance, though the weapons which he forged did not attain their full effectiveness until wielded by men like Franck and Castellio, who were emancipated from the authority of the Church. Erasmus had his roots in the *Devotio moderna* and the Neoplatonism of the Italian Renaissance. Both aimed at a simplification of the organization and doctrine of the Church. The *Devotio* stressed inwardness, simplicity, humility, and love. The Italian school fostered historical criticism and took the pious heathen under the aegis of Christianity.[96] From these sources Erasmus marshaled arguments, partly religious, partly ethical and rational, in favor of religious liberty.

On the religious side he stressed inwardness and conceived religion as consisting "not merely in ceremonies and articles, but in the heart and the whole life." [97] Catholic and Protestant alike felt his lash because of their externality. With regard to Catholic relic worship he wrote, "If you revere mute and dead ashes and neglect Paul's living image, still speaking and as it were breathing in his letters, is not your religion preposterous?" [98] The crusades seemed to him merely an attempt to possess what the Turks possessed. Success in the enterprise would be more likely to degenerate Christians into Turks than to bring Turks to the fold of Christ. If we desire genuine success "let us first expel the worst sort of Turks

[95] *Loc. cit.*

[96] Paul Mestwerdt, *Die Anfänge des Erasmus* (Leipzig, 1917).

[97] *Opera omnia* (edited by Le Clerc, Ludg. Bat., 1703-6, referred to hereafter as *Opera*) V, 141C, "Paraclesis," 1516.

[98] *Opera* V, 31E, "Enchiridion," 1503.

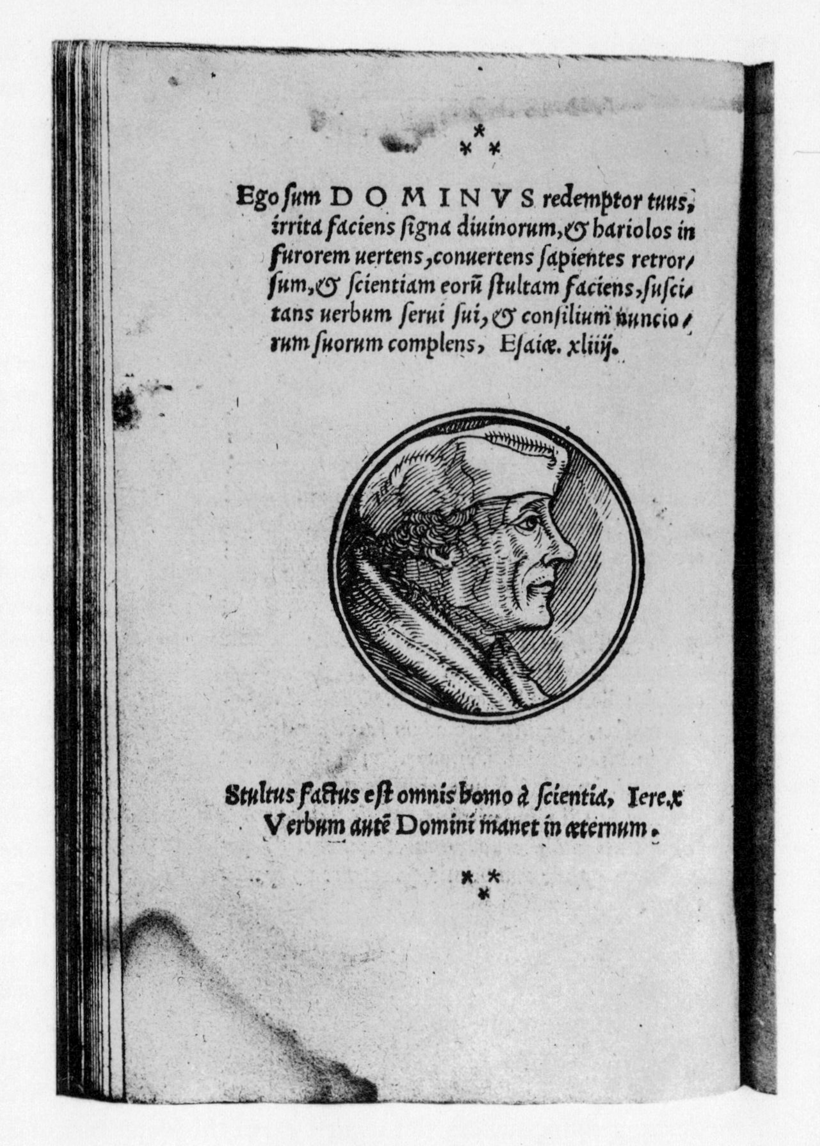

* * *

Ego ſum DOMINVS redemptor tuus,
irrita faciens ſigna diuinorum, & hariolos in
furorem uertens, conuertens ſapientes retror/
ſum, & ſcientiam eorũ ſtultam faciens, ſuſci/
tans uerbum ſerui ſui, & conſilium nuncio/
rum ſuorum complens, Eſaiæ. xliiij.

Stultus factus eſt omnis homo à ſcientia, Iere. x
Verbum autẽ Domini manet in æternum.

* * *

Erasmus of Rotterdam

from our hearts, avarice, ambition, and love of power." [99] Similar reproaches were cast at the Protestants. "They who are hot for any outrage think me timid. If my conscience approved, if I saw fruits of the Gospel they would not find me timid. What a magnificent progress of the Gospel it is indeed that images should be abolished from a community! Would that they would abolish the images from their hearts." [100]

From this point of view Erasmus defined heresy. "No heresy," he wrote, "seems to me more pernicious, no blasphemy more impious than for someone, like the Philistines, to fill up the wells of the Gospel . . . to turn the spiritual sense into the carnal, the celestial doctrine into the terrestrial, and to pervert and corrupt the sacred teaching of Christ in the teeth of all his precepts, his life, the doctrine of the apostles, the example of so many thousands of martyrs, and the interpretations of the early Fathers." [101] This outburst was occasioned by the attempt of many to find a justification for war in the words of Christ, "Let him sell his cloak and buy a sword." [102] Erasmus's point is partly that an isolated passage must be interpreted in accord with the sense of the whole, but partly that the spiritual is not to be turned into the carnal.

The heartfelt piety of Erasmus, like that of the *Devotio moderna,* was undogmatic. "What we are given to see, let us bow down and kiss. What is not given, but hidden, let us adore with simple faith and venerate from afar. Away with impious curiosity." [103] The dove of Christ is preferred to the owl of Minerva.[104] Scholastic propositions have a place as "theses to debate, not as articles of faith, especially since the schools do not agree with each other. . . . Even more intolerable is it to construct new

[99] *Opera,* V, 357C-E, "De bello Turcico" (1530).

[100] References to the letters of Erasmus are to the edition of P. S. Allen, *Opvs epistolarvm Des. Erasmi Roterodami,* 7 vols. (Oxford, 1906-28). The reference will be to the number of the letter, the volume, page, and sometimes the lines. The above quotation is from Ep. 1459, V, 482.80-85 (1524). Cf. *Opera,* X, 1578 C, "Ep. in Pseudoevangelicos" (1529).

[101] *Opera,* VI, 318F, "Ev. sec. Lucam" (1516).

[102] Luke 22: 19.

[103] *Opera,* V, 76E-77A, "Ratio Theol." (1519).

[104] Ep. 1526, V, 606.185-86 (Dec. 12, 1524).

dogmas every day and rear them to heaven as sacred and immovable towers of Babel. For these we fight more fiercely than for the dogmas of Christ. Some of these propositions are not essential to the integrity of the Christian religion and others open the door to the detriment of true piety." [105]

Erasmus is here formulating the method, to be used so extensively by Castellio and Acontius, of reducing to the lowest possible terms the points essential for salvation, the fundamentals. Erasmus does not venture to compile them, but says, "My advice would be to appoint a committee to draw up from the purest sources of the evangelists and apostles and from the most approved interpreters, a compendium of the entire philosophy of Christ, simple yet scholarly, brief but clear. That which has to do with faith can be disposed of in the very fewest articles." [106]

If Erasmus is too cautious to formulate the essentials, he does not hesitate to enumerate the nonessentials.[107] He ridicules the Catholic scholastics, Scotus, Occam, and Holcot,[108] and the Protestant scholastics, Oekolampadius and Luther, for wasting time on arid subtleties.[109] With regard to the Trinity, Erasmus writes, "I do not condemn investigation, but curious and contentious questions about this matter which angels adore rather than comprehend." What profit is there in discussing "whether the relation of origin is formally infinite?" [110] "God has deliberately hidden some things that we might adore Him in mystic silence . . . for example the distinction of the persons, the nature of the union of the human and divine in Christ, and the character of the unpardonable sin." [111] Erasmus complains of the constraint exercised against those

[105] *Opera*, V, 90B-C, "Ratio Theol." (1519). Cf. Ep. 985, III, 612.61-67 (June 1, 1519).
[106] Ep. 858, III, 365.139-44 (Aug. 14, 1518).
[107] *Opera*, VI, 928C-D, "Epist. Pauli ad Tim." I (1520).
[108] *Opera*, IV, 466, 468, "Stultitiae laus" (1511); *Opera*, V, 82-83, "Ratio Theol." (1519). Cf. Preserved Smith, *Erasmus* (New York, 1923), pp. 22-23.
[109] *Opera*, IX, 871E, "Ad censuras facultatis theologiae Parisiensis" (1532).
[110] *Opera*, IX, 1033C-E, "Adversus monachos quosdam Hispanos" (1528).
[111] *Opera*, IX, 1217A, "De libero arbitrio" (1524).

who say that monastic orders are not necessary to the Church, that it is better to pray to Christ than to the Virgin, who doubt whether confession was instituted by Christ, whether clerical celibacy is of divine ordination, and whether the Roman pontiff has authority over purgatory.[112]

Because religion is inward and simple, persecution is futile and inappropriate. Nowhere does Erasmus better set forth his whole view in this regard than in the preface to Hilary, from which the following passages are excerpted:

The ancients philosophized very little about divine things. . . . The curious subtlety of the Arians drove the orthodox to greater necessity. . . . Let the ancients be pardoned . . . but what excuse is there for us, who raise so many curious, not to say impious, questions about matters far removed from our nature? We define so many things which may be left in ignorance or in doubt without loss of salvation. Is it not possible to have fellowship with the Father, Son, and Holy Spirit without being able to explain philosophically the distinction between them and between the nativity of the Son and the procession of the Holy Ghost? If I believe the tradition that there are three of one nature, what is the use of labored disputation? If I do not believe, I shall not be persuaded by any human reasons. . . . You will not be damned if you do not know whether the Spirit proceeding from the Father and the Son has one or two beginnings, but you will not escape damnation, if you do not cultivate the fruits of the Spirit which are love, joy, peace, patience, kindness, goodness, long-suffering, mercy, faith, modesty, continence, and chastity. . . .[113] The sum of our religion is peace and unanimity, but these can scarcely stand unless we define as little as possible, and in many things leave each one free to follow his own judgment, because there is great obscurity in many matters, and man suffers from this almost congenital disease that he will not give in when once a controversy is started, and after he is warmed up he regards as absolutely true that which he began to sponsor quite casually. . . . Many problems are now reserved for an ecumenical council. It would be better to defer questions of this sort to the time when no longer in a glass darkly we see God face to face. . . .[114] Formerly, faith was in life rather than in the profession of creeds. Presently, necessity required that articles be drawn up, but

[112] *Opera,* IX, 1056A, 1057D, "Adversus monachos quosdam Hispanos" (1528).

[113] Gal. 5: 22, freely rendered.

[114] Cf. I Cor. 13.

only a few with apostolic sobriety. Then the depravity of the heretics exacted a more precise scrutiny of the divine books. . . . When faith came to be in writings rather than in hearts, then there were almost as many faiths as men. Articles increased and sincerity decreased. Contention grew hot and love grew cold. The doctrine of Christ, which at first knew no hairsplitting, came to depend on the aid of philosophy. This was the first stage in the fall of the Church. . . . The injection of the authority of the emperor into this affair did not greatly aid the sincerity of faith. . . . When faith is in the mouth rather than in the heart, when the solid knowledge of Sacred Scripture fails us, nevertheless by terrorization we drive men to believe what they do not believe, to love what they do not love, to know what they do not know. That which is forced cannot be sincere, and that which is not voluntary cannot please Christ.[115]

To Catholic and Protestant alike Erasmus pointed out the futility of persecution.[116]

The simple undogmatic piety which we find here exalted may seem to comport ill with the life of scholarship to which Erasmus dedicated himself. If he decried subtlety, he certainly did not glorify ignorance.[117] The discrepancy is met by a distinction between the masses and the experts. Erasmus's complaint against Luther was precisely that he dragged thorny problems from the schools to the street. "There are some questions, which, even if they be true and can be known, should not be divulged promiscuously. According to dialectic logic, it is possible to say that there are three gods, but to announce this before the untutored multitude would cause great offense." [118] Here Erasmus takes the position which Servetus found so objectionable in the late scholastics. This expertism explains why Erasmus could commence his tract *On Free Will* with a protest that the matter ought not to be discussed and

[115] Ep. 1334, V, 173-192: lines 142-45, 162-72, 207-11, 217-23, 231-34, 362-81. This preface is addressed as a letter to John Carondelet, Jan. 5, 1523.

[116] Ep. 1496, V, 550 (Sept. 6, 1524 to Melanchthon); Ep. 1526, V, 604.102-4; 606.167 (Dec. 12, 1524 to Duke George).

[117] *Opera*, IV, 471B, "Stultitiae laus" (1511); *Opera*, IX, 1219F, "De libero arbitrio" (1524).

[118] *Opera*, IX, 1217C, "De libero arbitrio" (1524); cf. *Opera*, V, 500D, "De amabili ecclesiae concordia" (1533).

then could launch into a technical discussion. He was an expert.

From the religious considerations we pass now to the rational and ethical. Closely associated with religious simplicity is a touch of rationalism. We are to leave knotty problems alone partly because they are detrimental to piety, but partly because they cannot be settled. The *sacra ignorantia* is a product in part of the *docta ignorantia*. Of course this affects the expert as much as the common man. Erasmus must excuse himself that as an expert he explores the insoluble on the ground that knowledge must be pursued before it can be despised.[119] The result of research is scholarly doubt. "I cannot be other than I am . . . ," writes Erasmus, "I cannot but hate dissension, I cannot but love peace and concord. I see how great is the obscurity in things human. . . . I do not dare to trust my own spirit in all things. Far be it from me to pronounce on the spirit of another. . . . Let them dance . . . among the prophets who are inspired by the Spirit of the Lord. This Spirit has not yet come upon me. When it does come I too, perhaps, may be said to be Saul among the prophets."[120] This explains in a measure why Erasmus was prepared neither to die nor to kill for a conjecture. He had the assurance neither of the martyr nor of the persecutor.[121]

On the other hand this very rationalism made Erasmus the more ready to take refuge in the authority of the Church. Skepticism is often the bulwark of absolutism. The simple faith of the *Devotio moderna* and of Erasmus is not far from the position of the late scholastics, who ridiculed the tenets of theology from the point of view of philosophy, only to fall back upon a supernatural logic and accept them again on the authority of the Church.[122] Erasmus was in search of certainty and could not find it in the infallibility of Scripture, or of the pope.[123] The inspired man might be in-

[119] *Opera*, X, 1709-10, "Antibarbarorum Lib.," I (1518). Cf. Mestwerdt, *op. cit.*, p. 265.

[120] Ep. 1342, V, 227.995-1012 (Feb. 1, 1523).

[121] Cf. Mestwerdt, *op. cit.*, 275.

[122] Cf. Mestwerdt, *op. cit.*, p. 110, and M. Van Rhijn, *Studiën over Luther's Rechtvaardigingsleer* (Amsterdam, 1921), pp. 155-56.

[123] *Opera*, V, 90F, "Ratio Theol." (1519).

fallible, but there is no infallible way of knowing that he is infallible. Erasmus could discover no unshakable basis of assurance in spite of his insistence that Christ would not suffer his people to err on the essentials for more than thirteen hundred years.[124] Who is to determine what are the essentials? Erasmus frankly admitted that weakness drove him to external authority. "Perhaps others may have more capacity and strength. I rest in nothing more readily than in the judgment of the Church. There is no end of reasons and arguments." [125] The authority of the Church is to be accepted and even that of her unworthy ministers *in the interests of public tranquillity*.[126] It is not a far cry from this position to the view that defection from the Church should be suppressed in the interests of good order, provided only that the suppression is not itself disturbing. Erasmus could praise the finesse with which Arcadius and Honorius "conserved public tranquillity without bloody battles, while gradually exterminating all the sects, first by rescinding the privileges of the pagan and heretical temples, then by confiscation, and finally by definitive measures." [127]

But Erasmus was prevented from going far in this direction by his love of mildness and mercy. His point is not simply that clemency saves trouble. Be reconciled with thine adversary *lest he deliver thee to the judge*.[128] On the contrary "we whose business it is to teach, prefer force *because it is easier*." [129] Rather the magistrate should seek to reclaim offenders and should be exceedingly slow to use the death penalty for any offense.[130] The ecclesiastic should seek

[124] *Opera*, IX, 1219B-20C, "De libero arbitrio" (1524). Cf. *Opera*, IX, 88B, "Apologia in dialogum Jac. Latomi" (1518).

[125] Ep. 1893, VII, 216.62-69 (Oct. 19, 1527). Cf. Johannes Lindeboom, *Erasmus* (Leiden, 1909), p. 92.

[126] *Opera*, V, 337A-B, "Enarr. in Ps.," XXII (1530).

[127] *Opera*, X, 1630E-F, "Ad fratres Germaniae Inferioris." Condensed.

[128] Matt. 5: 25. This point is very much overdone by Hermann Schlingensiepen, "Erasmus als Exeget auf Grund seiner Schriften zu Matthäus," ZKG XLVIII, NF XI, 1 (1929), 16-57. On this point, p. 39.

[129] Ep. 939, III, 531.116-17 (April 14, 1519).

[130] *Opera*, IV, 597, "Institutio principis Christiani" (1515). Cf. Adriana Wilhelmina de Iongh, *Erasmus' Denkbeelden over Staat en Regiering* (Amsterdam, 1927), pp. 114-21.

to cure the disease, not to kill the patient.[131] They who above all should exercise compassion seem only to thirst for human blood. This is the part of the executioner, not of the theologian.[132] Augustine besought clemency for the Donatists even though they were more brigands than heretics.[133] "I pray that Hoochstraten, Ecmontanus, and Beda will find God a more clement judge than they are." [134] Here is the root of the matter. Erasmus's mildness is grounded in his theology. God is merciful. He invites to repentance, rejoices over the lost sheep, puts the robe and the ring upon the prodigal. How shall we gain God's mercy? Not by sacrifice, but by the exercise of mercy.[135] His clemency extends even beyond the Christian fold. The natural man is not totally depraved, and those who have not heard of Christ are brought surreptitiously under the aegis of grace.[136] Even the Turks are semi-Christians.[137]

Erasmus's universalism rests in large measure upon an ethical basis. Deeds are exalted above creeds. The true theologian reveals himself not by syllogisms, but by his life.[138] Many a plea for fair treatment of Luther was based on the ground that none found fault with his conduct,[139] and, on the other hand, the Reformation was blamed because it did not produce a moral transformation.[140] Heresy and blasphemy are defined in the light of this ethical interest. "There is a certain heresy," Erasmus writes, "which, although it does not properly deserve the name, nevertheless causes

[131] *Opera*, V, 499C, "De amabili ecclesiae concordia" (1533); *Opera*, X, 1576A, 1583E-F, "Ep. in pseudoevangelicos" (1529).
[132] Ep. 1033, IV, 102.106-9 (Oct. 19, 1519).
[133] Ep. 1167, IV, 407.305-22 (Dec. 6, 1520).
[134] *Opera*, X, 1575F, "Ep. in pseudoevangelicos" (1529).
[135] *Opera*, V, 557-88, "De magnitudine misericordiarum Domini Concio" (1523).
[136] Cf. R. H. Murray, *Erasmus and Luther* (London, 1920), p. 33.
[137] *Opera*, V, 353E, "De bello Turcico" (1530).
[138] *Opera*, V, 140E, "Paraclesis" (1516). Cf. 113E, "Ratio Theol." (1519).
[139] Passages collected by Wallace Ferguson, "Erasmus and Toleration," in *Persecution and Liberty: Essays in Honor of George Lincoln Burr*, p. 175, n. 4.
[140] Ep. 1901, VII, 231 (Nov. 11, 1527); Ep. 1973, VII, 360 (March 19, 1528); *Opera*, X, 1578, "Ep. in pseudoevangelicos" (1529).

the greatest damage to the life of mortals and to the authority of the Church, namely when those who profess the philosophy of Christ and represent themselves as leaders of the Christian people, openly, by their whole lives . . . teach nothing but a more than theatrical ambition, insatiable avarice and passion, fury of wars. . . ." [141]

"What does it matter if there be no blasphemy of the tongue, if the whole life breathes blasphemy against God? . . . if the Beatitudes which bless the meek and the persecuted are called a lie? What blasphemy could be more detestable than this?" [142]

But Erasmus was by no means an unqualified advocate of liberty. The authority of the Church was always in reserve.[143] The criticism leveled at his reckless jibes caused him if not to retrench, at least to explain. One never quite knows whether he is retrenching. Erasmus would caressingly put a knot in the lion's tail and when the beast roared, draw off with an air of bewildered innocence. Nevertheless, there is a drift in emphasis toward order and authority.

The shift is noticeable in his interpretation of the historical growth of persecution, in his definition of heresy, and in his attitude toward the death penalty.

In interpreting the history of the Church and in particular the growth of persecution, Erasmus could pass deftly from pessimism to optimism. Often he complained that the Church had declined from a state of primitive purity,[144] and the rise of persecution was a mark of the decline.[145] Yet Erasmus found it possible to vindicate the Church by stressing the degeneration of society. Because men have grown worse, the Church has been compelled to accommodate her legislation to their condition. The apparent decline be-

[141] Ep. 1232, IV, 575 (Aug. 31, 1521).

[142] *Opera,* V, 560A-B, "De magnitudine misericordiarum Domini Concio" (1523).

[143] Ep. 1301, V, 92 (c. July 14, 1522); Ep. 1634, VI, 202.57-68 (Oct. 10, 1525).

[144] Ep. 858, III, 376, 366.164-65 (Aug. 14, 1518); Ep. 1526, V, 605 (Dec. 12, 1524).

[145] Ep. 1033, IV, 105.229-44 (Oct. 19, 1519); Ep. 1844, VII, 102.35-36 (July 6, 1527).

comes a real progress. After discussing indulgences, crusades, the temporal power, and the like, Erasmus comments, "I scarcely know whether the popes, if they did their utmost, could modify their laws, fashioned as they are in view of the common life of man, so as perfectly to correspond to the precepts of Christ, the foundation of all light and innocence. He legislated for heaven, the popes for weak men." [146] Even persecution can be fitted into this progression. Erasmus appends to a protest against constraint this qualification, "Not that I condemn the present severity which is *perhaps necessary*." [147] The fullest statement of this position is in a letter of the year 1529. Erasmus there says that the law of life is development. The mature man cannot be forced back into the cradle. A restoration of the conditions of the primitive Church would be undesirable. Even New Testament Christianity exhibited abuses. Paul complained of drunken love feasts and unseemly church services. In the age of persecution visits of both sexes by night to the tombs of the martyrs had untoward consequences. In the imperial period nightly processions ended in riots and episcopal elections in bloodshed. These and many similar abuses were rightly suppressed. On the other hand many excellent innovations were introduced, such as schools of theology. "Formerly no weapon was used against heretics save the sword of the Spirit, but when later the perversity of studies so frothed over that the world was involved in bloody tumult, the imperial power was forced to meet the peril with laws and arms. . . . If Paul were here today he would not disapprove of the state of the Church, I think, but would lament the vices of men. . . . These vices, however, are to be corrected without tumult, and we must take care lest the remedy be worse than the disease." [148]

There is something of a shift in Erasmus's definitions of heresy. In 1516 we found him of the opinion that the worst heresy is a rejection of the Spirit of Scripture. Yet early he stressed submission

[146] *Opera*, V, 89B, "Ratio Theol." (1519).
[147] *Opera*, V, 356C, "De bello Turcico" (1530).
[148] *Opera*, X, 1585-87, "Ep. in pseudoevangelicos" (1529).

to the authority both of Scripture and of the Church.[149] In the controversy with Luther in 1526 Erasmus declared that it is heretical to doubt what has been handed down by the unanimous consent of all the orthodox, and defined clearly by the Church as not to be disputed, but believed.[150] In 1521 and 1523 Erasmus defined heresy and blasphemy in terms of an evil life.[151] But he had pointed out long before that heresy is so dangerous precisely because all the evil actions of life arise from opinions.[152] In 1533 he could declare that the virtues of the heretics are vain outside of the Church.[153] "He who leaves the fellowship of the Church for heresy and schism is worse than he who lives impurely with saving doctrines." [154]

With regard to the penalty for heresy Erasmus was induced in the course of two controversies to repudiate an absolute rejection of capital punishment. The first controversy arose over his commentary on the parable of the tares.[155] This passage appears in Castellio's compilation under the name of Pellican, who had incorporated it bodily into his own work. Erasmus had been attacked for the liberalism of his interpretation by Noël Beda, the Spanish monks, and the Theological Faculty of the University of Paris, to each of whom he replied.[156] The excerpts introduced by Castellio under the name of Erasmus are from the replies to Beda and the Spanish monks. The reply to the Theological Faculty goes the farthest by way of retrenchment. Erasmus demands, "How could anyone infer from this passage [the commentary on Matthew thirteen] that I do not approve of killing heretics, when I

[149] *Opera*, V, 176E, 177A-B, "Enarratio Ps. beatus vir" (1515).

[150] *Opera*, X, 1259D, "Hyperaspistes" (1526).

[151] See notes 141 and 142, above.

[152] *Opera*, V, 177A, "Enarratio Ps. beatus vir" (1515).

[153] *Opera*, V, 485E, "De amabili ecclesiae concordia" (1533).

[154] *Ibid.*, 498B.

[155] *Opera*, VII, 80E, "Paraphrasis in Ev. Matthae," cap. XIII (1522).

[156] *Opera*, IX, 580-83, "Supputatio errorum in censuris Beddae Prop. xxxii" (1526); *Opera*, IX, 1054-60, "Adversus monachos quosdam Hispanos, Titulus IV, Contra sanctam haereticorum inquisitionem" (1528); *Opera*, IX, 905-6, "Ad censuras facultatis theologiae Parisiensis: Declaratio Erasmi lxxiv" (1532).

oppose the partisans of this position in published works?"[157]

Perhaps he had reference to what he had written in the other controversy with Geldenhauer (Noviomagus). This old friend had committed the offense of using as a preface to his own spirited plea for religious liberty several passages from Erasmus's notes on the imperial and papal laws against heresy, in which he pointed out that in the old days the offense was more serious and the penalty less severe.[158] Erasmus was incensed at the use to which Geldenhauer put his statements, and protested:[159]

> Was it fair . . . to quote me . . . as saying this [that the death penalty should not be inflicted on heretics] without putting in what I said by way of qualification? . . . I never teach that heretics are not subject to capital punishment. . . . I say merely that princes should not be severe. . . . He is not at once a heretic who lapses on an article of the faith. Unless there be perversity and obstinacy the fallen should be deprived of Christian charity, not killed. . . . I exhort [the leaders of the Church] to save rather than destroy. . . . Again there is heresy which is manifest blasphemy, and there is heresy . . . which makes for sedition. Shall we sheath the sword of the magistrate against this? To kill blasphemous and seditious heretics is necessary for the maintenance of the state.[160]

One wonders whether Erasmus might not have approved of the execution of Servetus on the score of blasphemous heresy. At any rate, he came to sanction the suppression of the Anabaptists. In a letter of uncertain, but late, date, he wrote, "The Anabaptists are by no means to be tolerated. For the apostles command us to obey the magistrates, and these men object to obeying Christian

[157] *Opera*, IX, 906C.

[158] The passage used by Geldenhauer was from the "Adversus monachos quosdam Hispanos, *Opera*, IX, 1057. See the *Bibliotheca Erasmiana* II, 146. The German of Geldenhauer and the Latin of Erasmus are reprinted by J. Prinsen, *Collectanea van Gerardus Geldenhauer Noviomagus* (Amsterdam, 1901), pp. 176-88. The Latin of Geldenhauer is reprinted by Paul Fredericq, *Corpus documentorum inquisitionis haereticae pravitatis Neerlandicae* V (Gent, 'S Gravenhage, 1902), No. 664, with an excellent discussion of the circumstances, pp. 292-97.

[159] *Opera*, X, 1574-87, "Ep. in pseudoevangelicos" (1529). Geldenhauer is masked under the name Vulturius Neocomus.

[160] *Opera*, X, 1575-76.

princes."[161] The penalty is not named, but the implication is that Erasmus condoned the imperial legislation which prescribed the death penalty. He was, to use a favorite figure of ancient divines, a bell calling others to church while he remained in the steeple.

[161] Cited by Preserved Smith, *Erasmus* (New York, 1923), p. 324, from the London edition of Erasmus's letters. The full reference is given by Wallace Ferguson, "Erasmus and Toleration," in *Persecution and Liberty*, p. 178, n. 15: *Epistolarum Des. Erasmi libri XXXI* (London, 1642), XXX, *Ep.* 77, col. 1963D.

Protestant Persecutors

LUTHER[1]

IN some respects Luther did more for religious liberty than did Erasmus and in some, less. The disruption of the unity of the medieval Church precipitated a situation in which toleration, however unpalatable, was the only alternative to mutual extermination. The decisive break with the authority of the Church provided room for the exercise of those weapons which Erasmus wielded in so cramped a fashion. At the same time Luther soon reërected the walls which he had demolished. A new institution, a new authority, and a new inquisition took the place of the old.

Luther's fundamental attitudes and his development show a striking similarity to those of Augustine. Both were dealing with the disintegration of a great institution. Augustine was called upon to explain the fall of the Roman State, and Luther was concerned to achieve the fall of the Roman Church. Over against these mighty societies the true Church appeared as a persecuted remnant.

[1] The evidence for unsupported statements in this section on Luther will be found in my article, "The Development and Consistency of Luther's Attitude to Religious Liberty," *Harvard Theological Review*, XXII, 2 (April, 1929), 107-49. I am listing below only that portion of the bibliography which deals specifically with the question.

Allen, J. W., "The Political Conceptions of Luther," in *Tudor Studies . . . presented to Albert Frederick Pollard* (London and New York, 1924), pp. 90-108.

Brieger, Theodor, "Die kirchliche Gewalt der Obrigkeit nach der Anschauung Luthers," *Zeitschrift für Theologie und Kirche*, II (Freiburg i. B., 1892), 513-34.

Burr, George L., "Anent the Middle Ages," *AHR* XVIII (1913), 710-26.

Evans, Austin P., *An Episode in the Struggle for Religious Freedom* (New York, 1924).

Faulkner, J. A., "Luther and Toleration," in *Papers of the American Society of Church History*, 2d series, IV (New York, 1914), 131-53.

Hermelink, Heinrich, *Der Toleranzgedanke im Reformationszeitalter* (Leipzig, 1908), pp. 37-70. SVRG, No. 98.

However, Augustine and Luther came to be interested in the suppression of a still smaller remnant, and then of necessity the ground shifted. This is not to imply, however, that Luther fabricated his views merely to meet a situation. His essential attitudes were matured in advance.

His picture of the Church as a remnant was rooted in his view of God who hides Himself from the wise and prudent and reveals His "power only in weakness, His wisdom as folly, His goodness as severity, His justice under the form of sin, and His mercy in the guise of anger." [2] The Word of God, by which He is made known, is that which goes counter to all the desires of the natural man.[3] Few are they who receive it and they are bound to be stones rejected by the builders.[4] In the main, history moves in terms of the Augustinian conflict of the *Civitas Dei* and the *Civitas terrena*. "Every Abel has his Cain and every Isaac his Ishmael, every Jacob his Esau and every Israel his Edom, every David his Saul, and every Christ his Judas. 'All that will live godly in Christ Jesus

---

Köhler, Walther, *Reformation und Ketzerprozess* (Tübingen, 1901). Sammlung gemeinverständlicher Vorträge und Schriften aus dem Gebiet der Theologie und Religionsgeschichte, No. 22.

Kühn, Johannes, *Toleranz und Offenbarung* (Leipzig, 1923).

Murray, Robert H., *Erasmus and Luther: Their Attitude to Toleration* (London and New York, 1920).

Paulus, Nikolaus, *Protestantismus und Toleranz im 16. Jahrhundert* (Freiburg i. B., 1911).

Poincenot, E., *Les Idées de Luther sur la répression de l'hérésie* (Thèse, Paris, 1901).

Völker, Karl, *Toleranz und Intoleranz im Zeitalter der Reformation* (Leipzig, 1912).

Wappler, Paul, *Inquisition und Ketzerprozesse in Zwickau zur Reformationszeit dargestellt im Zusammenhang mit der Entwicklung der Ansichten Luthers und Melanchthons über Glaubens- und Gewissensfreiheit* (Leipzig, 1908).

——— *Die Stellung Kursachsens und des Landgrafen Philipp von Hessen zur Täuferbewegung* (Münster i. W., 1910). Reformationsgeschichtliche Studien und Texte, Hefte 13/14.

[2] *Luther's Vorlesung über den Römerbrief 1515/1516*. Herausgegeben von Johannes Fricker, II [4] (Leipzig, 1930), 208. Anfänge reformatorischer Bibelauslegung, I.

[3] *Ibid.*, p. 249. [4] *Ibid.*, p. 87.

Martin Luther
as the German Hercules
Slaughtering the Scholastics

shall suffer persecution.' "[5] When Luther was himself subject to persecution he gave this teaching a turn which Augustine would not have admitted. "I am not terrified," wrote Luther, "because many of the great persecute and hate me. Rather, I am consoled and strengthened, since in all the Scriptures the persecutors and haters have commonly been wrong and the persecuted right. The majority always supports the lie and the minority the truth."[6]

At the same time Luther was deeply imbued with the conception of a Christian society in which Church, State, and school are alike concerned for man's welfare here and hereafter. The Church according to such a view is universal and Catholic and is not, or ought not to be, at war with the correlative agencies of the *Corpus Christianum*.[7] The duality in Luther's conception of the Church is not entirely expressed in the contrast of the Church invisible and the Church visible. There is also the polarity of the Church small and persecuted and the Church large and influential. So deeply was Luther affected by this view that he could call on the German nobility to reform the Church by virtue of their baptism into the Christian society,[8] and even when the government was hostile in 1523, Luther, while counseling civil disobedience and sharply demarking the spheres of Church and State,[9] did not push on to the Anabaptist extreme which denied the Christian character of the State. So far Luther never went, and when again the local state was friendly, he could easily forget the limits set to civil authority

[5] II Tim. 3: 12; WA III, 304.26-29: "Dictata super Psalterium, 1513-1516." A great deal of material on this point and some very interesting comments on Luther's treatment of Church history will be found in Erich Seeberg, *Luther's Theologie:* I, *Die Gottesanschauung* (Göttingen, 1929), pp. 133-41, and in Walther von Löwenich, "Luther's Theologia crucis," *Forschungen zur Geschichte und Lehre des Protestantismus,* 2te Reihe, II (München, 1929), 151-66.

[6] WA VII, 317, "Grund und Ursach aller Artikel Dr. Martin Luthers" (1521).

[7] For a review of the discussion as to the place of this conception in Luther's thinking see Kurt Matthes, *Das Corpus Christianum bei Luther im Lichte seiner Erforschung* (Berlin, 1929). Studien zur Geschichte der Wirtschaft und Geisteskultur, herausgegeben von Rudolf Häpke, V.

[8] WA VI, 408, "An den christlichen Adel" (1520).

[9] WA XI, 229-81, "Von weltlicher Obrigkeit."

under other circumstances and, without a qualm, could call upon princes for assistance in the reform of the Church.

Although these and other dualisms ran through Luther's thinking from the beginning to the end, nevertheless there is a distinctly traceable development from liberalism to persecution. Luther, while still technically an outlaw, soon became the head of a movement, and then the question arose as to what should be done to dissenters to the right and to the left.

Toward the Catholics in his early period Luther was on the whole moderate. In his soberer moments, at least, he objected to taking their lives. The magistrate might check abuses, the minister should undertake positive reform, the mob should say its prayers. Inflammatory outbursts are not to be taken too seriously. The words of Luther are as difficult to appraise as those of Erasmus. The one had his tongue in his cheek; the other, when attacked, would recoil, recast the offending statement and hurl it back in more provocative form. Take, for example, this blast of 1520. "If we punish thieves with the yoke, highwaymen with the sword, and heretics with fire, why do we not rather assault these monsters of perdition, these cardinals, these popes, and the whole swarm of the Roman Sodom, who corrupt without end the Church of God; why do we not rather assault them with all arms and wash our hands in their blood?" [10] In a soberer moment Luther confessed that he did not mean what his words imply. "Emser lies again when he says that I wish the laity might wash their hands in the blood of the priests. . . . I wrote, 'If we burn heretics why do we not rather attack the pope and his followers with the sword and wash our hands in their blood. . . . Since I do not approve of burning heretics nor of killing any Christian—this I well know does not accord with the Gospel—I have shown what they deserve if heretics deserve fire. There is no need to attack you with the sword.' " [11]

Toward the sectaries in his own movement Luther was un-

[10] WA VI, 347, "Epitoma responsionis ad Martinum Luther" (1520).

[11] WA VII, 645.26-646.3f. "Auf das überchristlich . . . Buch Bock Emsers Antwort" (1521).

willing to use any constraint. Over and over again he criticized papist persecution, implying that he would not indulge in the like. Among his finest utterances are those used by Castellio, the first from the tract on civil government of 1523, and the second from the comment on the parable of the tares of 1525.

This last year was the turning point. Two occurrences greatly affected Luther. The first was the accession of the stalwart reformer, John Frederick, as elector of Saxony in place of the hesitant Frederick the Wise. The second was the Peasants' War, conjoined with the finale of the career of Thomas Münzer. He did for Luther what the Donatists did for Augustine; in both cases religious radicalism was associated with social revolution in such fashion that constraint might well appear as nothing more than the preservation of the peace. Münzer was a weird figure, who combined mysticism and eschatology, the Inward Word and the Sword of Gideon. He decried outward ceremonies and books, and called upon the faithful to use the sword for the extermination of the tyrants who hindered the progress of the Gospel.[12] Luther was thoroughly shocked by this program. His very pacifism drove him to persecute. The sword he recognized as of divine ordination when wielded by the magistrate to protect the good and punish the bad, but the sword in the hands of the minister for the furtherance of the Gospel is simply monstrous. What shall we do with a man who preaches such a revolution of the saints? Let us hit him over the head.[13] This experience left Luther with a mental set against any part of Münzer's program. When such pacifists as Sebastian

[12] Münzer's works have only just become available in their entirety in *Thomas Müntzer: Leben und Schriften*, hrsg. von Otto H. Brandt (Jena, 1933). Quellen zur deutschen Kultur. The letters were brought out as *Thomas Müntzers Briefwechsel*, hrsg. von Heinrich Böhmer und Paul Kirn (Leipzig und Berlin, 1931). Aus den Schriften der sächsischen Kommission für Geschichte. There is a discriminating study by Annemarie Lohmann, *Zur geistigen Entwicklung Thomas Müntzers* (Leipzig und Berlin, 1931). Beiträge zur Kulturgeschichte des Mittelalters und der Renaissance, hrsg. von Walter Goetz, XLVII.

[13] WA XV, 212-13, "Ein Brief an die Fürsten zu Sachsen von dem aufrührischen Geist" (1524); WA XVIII, 367, "Eine schreckliche Geschichte und ein Gericht Gottes über Thomas Münzer" (1525).

Franck or Caspar Schwenckfeld talked of the Inward Word, Luther immediately saw shades of Thomas Münzer swallowing the Holy Ghost, feathers and all, and breathing forth manifestoes with tongues of fire.

The next few years saw a rapid development. By 1528 Luther was prepared to recognize banishment.[14] The next year the imperial diet at Speyer decreed the death penalty for Anabaptists. Luther did not object. In 1530 he was ready to punish blasphemous heretics. The penalty for blasphemy was, of course, death, and blasphemy he defined as a denial of an article of the Apostles' Creed.[15] A memorandum of 1531, approved by Luther, regarded a rejection of the ministerial office as blasphemy and the disruption of the Church as sedition against the ecclesiastical order, punishable like other sedition.[16] In his later years Luther belched brimstone on Catholics, sectaries, and Jews.

The liberal formulae of the early years were not abandoned, but were rendered innocuous by interpretation. Luther still said that conscience is not to be forced, but blasphemers have no conscience. He still said that faith is not to be constrained. A man may believe what he pleases provided he does not say what he believes. The parable of the tares was disposed of partly by identifying the tares with moral offenders rather than heretics, and partly by relegating the parable to the magisterial, rather than the ministerial, sphere. Such casuistry enabled Luther even in his later years to continue to upbraid the Papists and exonerate the Evangelicals of persecution. He did so in a sermon first published in 1535 and employed in the German version only of Castellio's work. The editors of the Weimar edition of Luther are dubious as to the year in which the sermon was preached, perhaps because of this very passage, but Luther said the like in 1541.[17]

[14] Enders und Kawerau, *Dr. Martin Luther's Briefwechsel* (Leipzig, 1884), VI, 299 (July 14, 1528).

[15] WA XXXI, 1, 207-9, "Der 82 Psalm ausgelegt" (1530), now available in English translation in *The Works of Martin Luther* (A. J. Holman Co. and the Castle Press, Philadelphia, Pa., 1931), IV, 309-10.

[16] *Philippi Melanthonis opera* (Halle, 1837), IV, 739-40). CR IV.

[17] WA LI, 497.25-29.

Most striking is the way in which Luther handled his former plea that the true Church is always a persecuted remnant. This conception recurs in the commentary of 1535-1545 on Genesis. The following passage from this work might well have served as a model for the peroration of Basil Montfort:

> The cross and condemnation are infallible signs of the true Church. "Precious in the sight of the Lord is the blood of his saints." [18] . . . All histories show that the true Church has always endured suffering at the hands of the false. There can be no doubt, therefore, today that the pope's Church is that of Cain, but we are the true Church. As Abel did not harm Cain so we not only do not harm, but rather endure vexation, condemnation, and death from the Church of the pope. . . . It is not only useful but exceeding joyous to have this most certain means of judging between the two Churches, between the purple harlot disguised as the true Church and the other despised, suffering, hungry, thirsty, and oppressed, as Christ recalled in Matthew 25 that he was hungry. Then follows the judgment between the full and the hungry, the sheep and the goats, between Cain and Abel in which God will declare that he approves the Church which is suffering and hungry and condemns the Church which is hypocritical and bloodthirsty.[19]

This picture was not unrealistic when applied to the papacy and the empire. However much the Lutheran Church might appear entrenched behind the princes of Saxony, they themselves, when set over against the pope and the emperor seemed but faithful shepherds of the little flock, and indeed even after Luther's death John Frederick and Philip of Hesse were led captive in the imperial train because of a too stout resistance to the Interim. But how did Luther fit the sectaries, whom he was suppressing, into this scheme of Cain and Abel? Why, they, too, were Cain persecuting Luther. How? By their odious accusation that he was worse than the Papists.[20] For sheer naïveté Luther was unsurpassed.

[18] Ps. 116:15.

[19] WA XLII, 188-89, condensed, "Vorlesungen über 1 Mose von 1535-1545."

[20] WA XL, I, 681, "In Epistolam S. Pauli ad Galatas comment." (Rörers notes of 1531 and 1535 are printed one above the other. The latter is the more complete.)

JOHN BRENZ AND DUKE CHRISTOPH OF WUERTTEMBERG

John Brenz, the reformer of Württemberg, figures prominently in our compilation. His tract against the persecution of the Anabaptists is incorporated in its entirety, and appeal is made to his authority in the dedication to his prince, Duke Christoph.

Brenz's activity in Württemberg falls into three periods, from 1522 to 1534, from 1534 to 1550, and from 1550 to 1570. The first corresponds to the period of Austrian domination; the second, to the administration of Duke Ulrich; the third extends to the death of Brenz and exceeds by only two years the rule of Duke Christoph.

During the first period we have to consider the mutual attitude of Catholic and Lutheran, and the stand of both toward the Anabaptists.

The attitude of the Catholic government to the Lutherans was, of course, one of hostility. An edict of November 26, 1522, complained of the progress of Lutheranism, which is described as disobedient alike to the pope and the emperor. "Wherefore this offensive, heretical, perversive teaching and preaching is prohibited under severe penalty in the duchy of Württemberg, and Lutheran books are neither to be sold nor read." In consequence of this mandate a printing press was suppressed and many Lutheran ministers exiled.[21] Yet the government was hesitant to resort to extreme measures. Many of the people were inclined to the new gospel and the local governments were favorable. Suppression might only provoke the restoration of the exiled Duke Ulrich.

This situation explains how Brenz could continue throughout this period in his pastorate at Hall. He began quietly and celebrated Mass until 1523, though with the explanation that he did not regard it as a sacrifice. Not until 1525 are we sure that it was abolished in his church.[22] Then he demanded that the government

[21] Julius Hartmann and Karl Jäger, *Johann Brenz,* 2 vols. (Hamburg, 1840-42), II, 2-3. Hereafter referred to as Hartmann and Jäger.

[22] Hartmann and Jäger, I, 43, 97.

suppress the Mass in the other churches of the city and throughout the countryside. This appeal to the State was based on the theory of the *Corpus Christianum,* dominant for the Church of the Middle Ages and still prominent in Luther. The Church, declared Brenz, can no more exist without the State than the Gospel without the law, and the State without the Church is but the discipline of the father without the love of the mother.[23] The association for Brenz was even more intimate than for either the Middle Ages or Luther. From the Protestant abrogation of the indelible character of the priesthood Brenz inferred that the ecclesiastic may exercise the office of the sword in case of need. Christ himself employed it when He drove out the money changers.[24] Brenz himself was not to be deterred by the fiction that the Church sheds no blood, from giving judgment as a theologian on cases involving civil penalties.[25]

The function of the State is to provide for the establishment of the true religion and for the suppression of the public profession of the false.[26] The State cannot compel belief, nor eliminate superstition, nor control conscience, but it can foster that which helps faith, prohibit that which hinders, and ward off the wrath of God by the suppression of abuses. In the Church Ordinance prepared for the city of Hall in 1526 Brenz declared that the Mass is a form of idolatry which God punishes by pestilence, war, and blindness of the understanding. Hence "the faithful Christian magistrate is bound not only by his office, but also by his soul's salvation to placate the wrath of God by the suppression of the blasphemous abuse of the Mass." If it be objected that the suppression will bring down the wrath of the Emperor, let it be remembered that the toleration of the Mass will bring down the wrath of God. Warrant for the eradication of the abomination may be found

[23] *Ibid.,* I, 319.
[24] *Ibid.,* I, 324-25.
[25] Walther Köhler, "Brentiana," *ARG* XI (1914), p. 274, § 23.
[26] Hartmann and Jäger, I, 322-23. R. Günther, "Zur kirchlichen u. theologischen Charakteristik des Johannes Brenz," BWKG, N. F. III (1899), 145-60.

in the examples of Jehu, Hezekiah, and Josiah.[27] But, Brenz declares elsewhere, the methods of Jehu are not to be imitated. The magistrate now "must undo the ungodly worship by Gospel means, with the proclamation of the Word of God and the establishment of a godly service," [28] and in the above document Brenz says that although the Mass ought to be suppressed "yet no one is to be driven by force from his faith, nor deprived by force of his living. The magistrates should remind the priests of the wrath of God and urge them to discontinue the Mass, but whether they heed or not they should be assured of their incomes for life. It is much more Christian to bind such people by kindliness to faith in the Word of God than by harshness to frighten them farther and farther away." [29] Brenz's thinking here is far from clear. He is attempting to combine an intimate union of Church and State with freedom for the individual conscience.

The council at Hall continued to have an eye to the wrath of Ferdinand and hesitated at the outright suppression of the Mass. Brenz then suggested that they purchase the right of patronage over the country churches. This was too expensive. Then let the council simply appoint evangelical ministers alongside of the Catholic.[30]

Against the Anabaptists the Austrian government proceeded with great severity. Michael Sattler, though of blameless life and moderate views, was burned at the stake at Rottenburg on the 21st of May, 1527, after his tongue had been cut out and his body lacerated with hot irons.[31] An imperial edict, promulgated at Speyer, on January 4, 1528, subjected the Anabaptists to the old law of Honorius and Theodosius the Younger, which inflicted the death penalty upon those who repeated the right of holy baptism.[32]

[27] Aemilius Ludwig Richter, *Die evangelischen Kirchenordnungen des sechszehnten Jahrhunderts*, I [2] (Leipzig, 1871), 40-41.

[28] *Anecdota Brentiana*, ed. Theod. Pressel (Tübingen, 1868), No. XI, p. 42 (June 1, 1529).

[29] Richter, *op. cit.*, I, 47-48.

[30] Hartmann and Jäger, I, 117-21.

[31] G. Bossert, "M. Sattler," in RE [3] XVII, 494.

[32] *Codex Theod.*, XVI, 6, 6; Bossert, *Quellen*, No. I, p. 1.

An Anabaptist martyrology enumerated fifty-five executions in Württemberg by 1531.[33]

Brenz shared the widespread indignation against this severity,[34] and by way of protest composed the tract which Castellio has utilized in its entirety. The manuscript was finished on July 7, 1528.[35] The first printed edition appeared on October 21, 1528.[36] The argument is that so commonly employed by the earlier Luther, that heresy, being spiritual, cannot be touched by the sword of the magistrate. The abrogation of civil rights Brenz allows only for those who refuse an oath of civil obligation. The long section on the law of Honorius and Theodosius II is directed against the use made of it in the imperial mandate of January 4, 1528. Brenz very properly infers that the severity of the old law must have been aimed at something more serious than religious error. Strange that he did not recognize the turbulence of the Circumcellions as provocative of this rigor.

The indignation of men like Brenz seems to have led to a modification of the policy of the Austrian government. Execution without examination was abandoned. Prisoners were instructed by theologians and arguments were based on Scripture.[37] This change of policy dates from October 1, 1528, so we cannot assume a direct influence of Brenz's tract unless it circulated in manuscript.[38]

The case of Augustin Bader illustrates the new procedure.

[33] Gustav Bossert, "Aus der nebenkirchlichen religiösen Bewegung der Reformationszeit in Württemberg, Wiedertäufer und Schwenckfelder," *BWKG*, N. F. XXXIII (1929), 1-41.

[34] Gustav Bossert, "Johann Brenz 'der Reformator Württembergs' und seine Toleranzideen." *BWKG* XV (1911), 150-61; XVI (1912), 25-47, in particular XV (1911), 155 ff.

[35] George L. Burr, "Anent the Middle Ages," *AHR* XVIII (1913), 723, n. 15.

[36] For editions and translations see Walther Köhler, *Bibliographia Brentiana* (Berlin, 1904). The numbers in heavy type represent editions of Castellio's work in which Brenz's tract is incorporated: editions, Nos. 29, **263**, 340, 644; translations, Latin, **261**, **262**, 415, **585**, 645, 730, French, **264**, Dutch, **595**, **670**.

[37] Gustav Bossert, "Aus der Zeit der Fremden Herrschaft," *Württembergische Jahrbücher für Statistik u. Landeskunde*, I (1911), 49-78.

[38] Cf. Gustav Bossert, *BWKG* XV (1911), 160.

Though more provocative, he was not treated so severely as Michael Sattler. Bader's case was largely political. He had predicted the overthrow of the government by a Turkish invasion, after which his infant son as Messiah should set up a new kingdom in which the Jews would be included. The scanty funds of a little communistic group were almost depleted to buy a crown and to plate an old sword with gold. The government feared that Bader might be an agent of Semitic malcontents or of the exiled Duke Ulrich, and took measures of military preparedness. Nevertheless Bader was granted many hearings, and was not burned at the stake, but was beheaded with his own gold-plated sword.[39]

The issue of religious liberty was raised anew. Some protested, as after the execution of Sattler, and used Brenz's arguments in favor of absolute religious liberty. Lazarus Spengler was puzzled. The treatment of Bader was more reasonable and the man more unreasonable than Sattler. Brenz was consulted on March 20, 1530.[40] He now applied to the Anabaptists the treatment which he had recommended four years earlier for the Catholics. Let the magistrate suppress their assemblies. The government has no authority over private belief, but may forbid the formation of a new church, just as it may prohibit the establishment of a new guild, or authorize or refuse to authorize the settlement of the Jews in a community. If it be objected that the apostles had no commission from the government, the answer is that they needed none, because of a direct commission from God certified by the power to work miracles. Again, if it be objected that these considerations would justify the suppression of the true faith by an unorthodox government, the answer is that such a government would be perfectly right from its own point of view. God must be feared even in a false faith.[41] Brenz had reached the principle, *cuius regio eius religio.*

Another problem remained, which was implicit in his earlier

[39] Gustav Bossert, "Augustin Bader von Augsburg, der Prophet und König, und seine Genossen nach der Prozessakten von 1530," *ARG* X (1912/13), 117-65, 209-41, 297-349; XI (1914), 19-64, 103-33.

[40] Gustav Bossert, *ARG* X (1912/13), 319; Hartmann and Jäger I, 293.

[41] Hartmann and Jäger, I, 293-98.

stand against the Catholics. How can suppression be reconciled with respect for conscience? Brenz began to wonder whether it is not an abuse of terms to apply conscience to the chiliastic chimaeras of a megalomaniac like Bader.[42] There can be no conscience without sense, no *Gewissen* without *Wissen*, no *conscientia* without *scientia*. Brenz is raising the fundamental issue as to whether superior intelligence may coerce the subnormal to their own good. The question comes up in connection with compulsory vaccination, compulsory education, and even parental discipline. What makes Brenz's tract so naïve is that he comes very close to saying that no one can have a conscience save a Lutheran. He is on equally unstable ground when he suggests that banishment is no constraint of conscience because a man can retain his convictions in exile. Might it not be said equally that the death penalty leaves intact the convictions of those who are cast in the heroic mold? Yet Brenz's point was to justify neither exile nor the death penalty, but merely compulsory religious education. And, he added, if obstinate fools will have none of it, let them go.[43]

Brenz's second period dates from the return of Duke Ulrich to his duchy in 1534. The whole situation was now changed. During his exile Ulrich had become a Protestant and refused flatly to clarify his relationship to his Austrian overlord by a repudiation of his faith. Ferdinand tacitly recognized his Protestantism, but compelled him to promise not to tolerate the Anabaptists.[44]

Ulrich's first task was the reconciliation of the Lutherans and Zwinglians, the former having gained a footing in the north, the latter in the south. Spheres of activity were practically agreed

[42] Bossert would place here Brenz's tract, "Ob eine Obrigkeit, wann sie falsche Lehr aussrottet, darumb uber die Gewissen herrsche" (Köhler, *Bibliographia Brentiana*, No. 730): *BWKG*, XVI (1912), 25-29. Nikolaus Paulus (*Protestantismus und Toleranz*, p. 121 n. 1) says that this tract must be placed later because Brenz had not yet advanced so far. Bossert seems to me to have rightly pointed out the relevancy of the document to the case of Bader. Paulus's whole treatment, by the way, is rather a compilation of sayings than a discussion of the total setting.

[43] The tract is printed in F. Bidembach, *Consiliorum theologicorum*, Decas III, No. IX (Frankfurt a. M., 1608), pp. 168-73.

[44] Bossert, *Quellen*, No. 57, p. 37.

upon. The Mass was gradually suppressed, the cloisters emptied, and the University of Tübingen given a Protestant complexion. There was no violence against the Catholics. They went unhindered to Mass in the neighboring localities and continued to hold civil posts.[45] But Brenz urged that they be compelled to listen to Protestant sermons.[46]

Toleration of the Anabaptists was definitely excluded by the treaty under which Ulrich held his principality. But what penalty should be inflicted upon them? Ulrich consulted the Faculties of Law and Theology in the University of Tübingen. The jurists recommended the death penalty, but the theologians were not willing to stain their hands with the blood of these ignorant but excellent people. Let the leaders be imprisoned on scanty fare. The ordinary members should not be banished lest they corrupt other lands, but should be placarded with the image of a wolf, serpent, or some other horrible beast. They should be denied membership in societies, attendance at weddings, etc.; and banishment might be inflicted upon those the low grade of whose intelligence would prevent them from converting anyone.[47]

Ulrich was guided by the spirit of the theologians more than by that of the jurists. The death penalty fell into abeyance. A distinction was drawn between the revolutionary Anabaptists and the peaceful. The latter were to be banished, and their goods were to be confiscated if they had no dependents. Those who returned from banishment might be punished corporally and capitally,[48] but this threat was never executed.

Ulrich had more to think about. After the failure of the Schmalkald war in 1546, Charles V undertook, even in opposition to the Pope, to force upon Germany a compromise between Protestantism and Catholicism, known as the Interim (1548), because it should

[45] Reinhold Schmid, *Reformationsgeschichte Württembergs* (Heilbronn, 1904), Chaps. V and VI. This is a good popular account.

[46] *Opera*, VI, 282, cited by Paulus, *op. cit.*, p. 118 n. 1.

[47] Bossert, *Quellen*, No. 75 (June 9, 1536), p. 50, and No. 80 (1536), pp. 53-57.

[48] *Ibid.*, No. 80, p. 60.

last only until the end of the Council of Trent. The compromise, though leaning in the direction of Catholicism, was no more acceptable to Catholics than to Protestants. Yet Ulrich was scarcely in a position to repudiate it so long as Charles V filled the land with Spanish troops and carried John Frederick of Saxony and Philip of Hesse as prisoners in his train. The Spanish soldiers even made Philip of Hesse kneel at Mass. Ulrich well knew that any indiscretion might cost him his duchy. Hence he adopted a policy of clandestine obstruction. He could not prevent the imprisonment of some of the ministers and the banishment of others. Brenz fled in the nick of time. From three to four hundred ministers were removed; but Ulrich encouraged them to stay in their communities if possible and exercise their functions in private. Others were supported in exile. Brenz was hid for a year and a half, as Luther had been at the Wartburg. Gradually many ministers were reinstated with the titles of teachers or catechists. The Interim, at the same time, was introduced in so far as it was possible to get any clergy to observe it. In the cloisters Catholicism pure and simple came back. Brenz could inform Melanchthon that there were now three religions side by side in the land.[49] They tolerated each other of necessity, but there was no tolerance.[50]

Brenz's third period dates from the death of Duke Ulrich in 1550. His son Christoph succeeded and continued the obstructionist policy. The Interim was buried on the meeting of the Council of Trent in 1552, the defeat of Charles, and the withdrawal of Spanish troops; but Christoph, like his father, was not given a free hand by the Austrian government. Only gradually could the Mass be abolished, and the cloisters cleared.[51]

The régime of Christoph was so thoroughly Lutheran that even Zwinglianism was associated in the mandates with Schwenck-

[49] February 2, 1549: CR VII, 290. On the date see Gustav Bossert, "Das Interim in Württemberg," *SVRG* XII, Nos. 46 and 47 (1895), 187.

[50] Cf. Nikolaus Paulus, *op. cit.*, p. 122 n. 2, and Ferdinand Buisson, *Sébastien Castellion*, II, 244.

[51] Gustav Bossert, "Das Interim in Württemberg," *SVRG* XII, Nos. 46 and 47 (1895), 1-204.

feldianism and Anabaptism.[52] Brenz urged that one cannot with a good conscience even listen to a Zwinglian sermon nor let oneself in for a discussion. Eve was lost when she allowed herself to be drawn into an argument with the serpent.[53] Christoph continued the policy of his father with regard to the Anabaptists. Torture, banishment, imprisonment, and branding were employed, but not capital punishment.[54]

Brenz, as superintendent, headed the organization for the prosecution of heretics.[55] He seems to have been ready for the rôle, since in 1557 he was willing, along with Melanchthon and others, to sign a memorandum, favoring the death penalty for the Anabaptists and specifically approving the execution of Servetus.[56] Whether he signed whole-heartedly may be doubted. In the copy of the memorandum preserved at Stuttgart the passages favoring the death penalty and the execution of Servetus are crossed out.[57] Did Brenz or Christoph do this? Of course Brenz did sign the complete memorandum at Worms, but on what grounds? The picture of Servetus, on which the group based its judgment, was furnished by Theodore Beza. Yet, whatever mitigating circumstances we may adduce, Brenz's signature marks a signal departure from his earlier liberalism. This document recognizes the eternal validity of the Mosaic legislation against blasphemy (Lev. 24: 16) as a part of the natural law, and denudes sedition of its ordinary connotation by the statement that "the erroneous opinion of the Anabaptists about civil government is certainly a great error *before God* and itself constitutes sedition." [58]

[52] For his illiberal attitude to Gribaldi, Curio, and Ochino consult Frederic C. Church, *The Italian Reformers, 1534-1564* (New York, 1932), pp. 234, 237, 238, 240, 284.

[53] *Anecdota Brentiana*, No. CCCV (June 19, 1568).

[54] Bossert, *Quellen*, Nachtrag No. 107, pp. 1022-47 (July 25, 1558).

[55] *Ibid.*, No. 154 (May 26, 1553).

[56] Paulus, *op. cit.*, pp. 73 n. 1, 122.

[57] Bossert, *Quellen*, No. 175, pp. 165.23, 166.34; cf. BWKG, N. F. XXXIII (1929), 24.

[58] Bossert, *Quellen*, pp. 164, 166. Italics mine. The entire memorandum occupies pp. 161-68.

CHRISTOPH HOFFMANN

Christoph Hoffmann was included in the collection probably because his commentary on Titus had been printed with the express approval of both Melanchthon and Luther.

Hoffmann took his baccalaureate degree at Wittenberg in 1521. He was preacher at Jena from 1536 to 1544, when he became court preacher to the elector. Our last notice of him is in 1549. He wrote the preface to Luther's "Exhortation to All Preachers," to pray that God scourge us with pestilence rather than with the Turk or the Papists.[59]

JAKOB SCHENCK (b. 1508)

Jakob Schenck was another of the fire eaters to be convicted out of his own mouth. His life was a succession of acrimonious controversies.[60]

The first outlet for his zeal came in connection with the attempt of Duke Heinrich of Torgau in Electoral Saxony to introduce the Reformation into his territory. The Duke wrote to his menacing Catholic brother, Duke George of Dresden, that since two religions could not exist peaceably side by side in the same place, the Reformation must be undertaken quickly and quietly. No one should be deprived of his goods, nor forced to believe against his conscience. The clergy who could not subscribe to the

[59] WA L, 482-87, "Eine Vermahnung an alle Pfarrherrn" (1539). On Hoffmann see: J. K. F. Knaake, "Bemerkungen zum Briefwechsel der Reformatoren: I, Melanchthon an Christoph Hoffmann den 2 Jan., 1540," *Theologische Studien und Kritiken*, LXX (1897), 167-70; Enders und Kawerau, *Luther's Briefwechsel*, XII, 240-41, No. 2763; WA L, 481 n.

[60] The only complete biography is that by Johann Karl Seidemann, *Dr. Jakob Schenk, der vermeintlicher Antinomer, Freibergs Reformator* (Leipzig, 1875). A number of documents are printed in the Appendix. Statements otherwise unsupported are based on this work. The following articles are valuable for special phases of Schenck's career:

Nikolaus Müller, "Jakob Schenck, kurf. Hofprediger in Berlin 1545 u. 6," *Jahrbuch für brandenburgische Kirchengeschichte* II/III, I (1906), 19-29.

Wilhelm Stieda, "Jakob Schenck und die Universität Leipzig," *ARG* XX, Nos. 77/78 (1923), 73-126.

Paul Vetter, articles in *Neues Archiv für sächsische Geschichte und Altertumskunde* (Dresden): "Schenck und die Prediger zu Leipzig 1541-3,"

new régime might leave.[61] In other words, *cuius regio eius religio*. Schenck was installed as superintendent in Freiberg, commissioned to do the work quickly and quietly. The first move bade fair to be neither quick nor quiet. When Duke Heinrich began to suppress nunneries, some noble relatives of the inmates reminded him that no good could come of driving out nuns to marry renegade monks, cobblers, and tailors to the disgrace of their families.[62] The Duke took his stand on the Word of God and Schenck prepared an evangelical confession to which the nuns should subscribe. He would not force them to give up the veil, leave the cloister, and take the sacrament in both kinds immediately, but would instruct them first. (Not so quickly after all.) They replied that they would stand by Christ and the Pope.[63]

Then Schenck's attention was called to a passage in the Saxon Visitation Articles of 1528, which provided that those who were weak in the faith and not sufficiently instructed might for a time be permitted to take the sacrament of the Lord's body and blood in one kind only.[64] Schenck wrote to the Elector that the articles should be reprinted with the omission of this concession,[65] and for support turned to some of the Wittenberg theologians. Melanchthon at length replied in favor of compromise.

XII (1891), 247-71. "Zu Jakob Schencks Ende," XXIII (1902), 145-47. "Lutherana II, 'Luthers Stellung im Streite Jakob Schencks mit Melanchthon und Jonas 1537,'" XXX, I (1909), 76-109. "Lutherana III, 'Luther und Schencks Abberufung aus Freiberg im Jahre 1538,'" XXXII, I (1911), 23-53.

"Visitationsartikel des Dr. Jakob Schenk von 1537," in Emil Sehling, *Die evangelischen Kirchenordnungen des XVI. Jahrhunderts*, I, 1 Abt. 1 Hälfte (Leipzig, 1902), 465-67.

There are frequent references to Schenck in *Luther's Briefwechsel*, ed. Enders und Kawerau, especially Nos. 2544, 2547, 2548, 2584, 2593, 2674a, 2767, 2809, 3371.

In Melanchthon's correspondence, see especially CR III, Nos. 1592, 1603, 1605, 1620.

[61] May 26, 1537; Seidemann, p. 19.

[62] Seidemann, Anhang § 7, p. 193.

[63] Seidemann, p. 22.

[64] Emil Sehling, *Evangelische Kirchenordnungen*, I, 1, 1, pp. 159-60.

[65] Seidemann, Beil. VI.

> Two years ago [he wrote] a young mother of five children came to me for counsel. She had been banished for having taken the communion in both kinds. Her husband was deeply distressed at the separation, but would not follow. . . . Should she leave him and the children? . . . I told her to go back to her husband and commune in one kind only. . . . Mercy is better than sacrifice. . . . I asked Luther what he would have advised, since women are plainly weak. He did not say. Many such have come to me because they know I am softer. . . . I counsel grown men to partake in both kinds and suffer persecution. . . . The case which you cite of prohibition by the government, I do not admit. . . .[66]

The controversy came to the ear of the Elector, who consulted Luther. He had deep misgivings over these counsels of concession. He hoped he would not have to part with Philip, but the truth of God must stand.[67] The Visitation Articles were revised in 1538 with Luther's approval, and the concession to the weak was omitted.[68]

The next controversy arose in connection with Schenck's attempt to secure recruits for the evangelical militia. He had sent two young men to Wittenberg for theological training, Georg Karg and Wernlen. The latter converted the former to Anabaptism. Schenck wrote to Karg:

> If you continue in this position I will not only hold you for an Anabaptist, a heretic and a devil, but I will take the proper action against you, and the more readily because of the trouble I have had to bring you up. If a brother, a father, or a son of mine should hold the view which you have put forth in the devil's name in the last few days, I should be the first to put him out. I testify by this letter and I swear by the Holy Trinity, the Holy Gospel, the sacrament of my Savior Jesus Christ, and by my soul's salvation that I will not countenance your devil's teaching,

[66] Melanchthon's letter is incorporated in Schenck's account to the Elector, Oct. 5, 1537, published by Vetter, *Neues Archiv für sächsische Geschichte*, XXX, 1/2 (1909), 106-7.

[67] Luther's opinion is quoted in the memorandum of Brück to the Elector. Vetter (*op. cit.*, pp. 103-4) gives the text and dates it Oct. 10, 1537. In Enders and Kawerau, XI, No. 2548, pp. 271-72, the date is given as Sept. 18 or 19. In CR III, No. 1620, pp. 427-28, the memorandum is dated around Oct. 12.

[68] Enders and Kawerau, VI, 170; WA XXVI, 186 and 214-16; Emil Sehling, *Evangelische Kirchenordnungen*, I, 40.

> but will oppose it to the day of my death with God's pure Word as proclaimed by my revered and learned father in Christ, Dr. Martin Luther, and I will denounce you before the ecclesiastical and civil authorities of Wittenberg and before the Elector of Saxony. . . . Send Wernlen to me. . . . Do not be ashamed to confess to me privately your heartfelt conversion. . . . I will not trust you lightly, but will take care that you do not cause offense to Christ, his Gospel, the churches at Wittenberg, the church at Freiberg and me. I would rather see you damned a thousand times than wink at such an offense. You are a member of Christ, but if you corrupt the body you must be cut off. . . . 23 November, 1537.[69]

Karg replied that he could not say yes or no without further investigation. "It is better to remain unwittingly for a time in error, if it be error, than to confess with the mouth what is not felt in the heart."

Schenck reported the affair to the Elector, John Frederick of Saxony, who caused Karg to be thrown into prison at Wittenberg (December 30, 1537), where he remained for a month and a half, until Luther was convinced of his orthodoxy. In spite of Schenck's energetic attempts to dissociate himself from his protégés, Luther still held him responsible for their vagaries.[70]

At the same time Schenck, like Agricola, was embroiled in the Antinomian controversy, and was accused of saying, "Moses be hanged." When a stone image of Moses in the church at Freiberg was discovered headless, Schenck was suspected of the decapitation.[71]

The situation became so unpleasant that Schenck left Freiberg to become court preacher to the Elector at Weimar (July 3, 1538). Friction with Wittenberg continued. In 1541 Schenck removed to Leipzig where his old patron, Duke Heinrich, had succeeded his Catholic brother, Duke George. Inasmuch as the Reformation had been introduced overnight, the theological faculty was naturally not cordial to the change and took offense at Schenck's declamatory zest, as well they might, if he declared, as he had done on a previous occasion, that "no words are strong enough to

[69] Seidemann, Beil. VIII, § 1. [70] Seidemann, pp. 27-32.
[71] Seidemann, pp. 34-36.

describe the abomination of the Mass. Murder, adultery, robbery, drunkenness, and gluttony are offenses against God, but none is so bad as this popish Mass."[72] Schenck's opponents on several counts at length brought him to prison for a short time. From the Leipzig period came the lectures on Titus from which Castellio has taken the extract. The liberal passage was perhaps more of a fling at the Papists than the expression of Schenck's habitual temper.[73]

After his release from prison Schenck went to Brandenburg (1543), where he was to become court preacher to Joachim II (April 19, 1545). As a last gesture of defiance against the Papists, Schenck preached on the resurrection at Christmas and on the birth of Christ at Easter. Joachim dismissed him after a year on grounds which suggest insanity. Since Schenck would not leave, Joachim caused him to be bodily deported to Saxony. When he died, we do not know.[74]

JOHANN AGRICOLA OF EISLEBEN (d. 1566)

Johann Agricola was said to be of Eisleben by a double right. There he was born, and there he exercised a ministry of nine years. At first he was an ardent disciple of Luther, and with him criticized Münzer's appeal to violence. The sole weapon of the Gospel, declared Agricola, is the sword of the Spirit. But soon differences arose which estranged Agricola from the Wittenberg circle. The first controversy was called rather infelicitously the "Antinomian." The debate centered about the place of repentance in the process of salvation. Luther contended that justification commences in terror of conscience because of the wrath of God visited upon those who transgress His law, whether expressed in the Old Testament or in the cross of Christ. This repentance constitutes a predisposition to grace. Agricola contended that the operation of grace is unconditioned and repentance follows the

[72] Vetter, in *Neues Archiv für sächsische Geschichte*, XXX (1909), 79, from the *Gutachten* of April 13, 1537.

[73] This period is covered by the articles of Vetter and Wilhelm Stieda.

[74] This period is covered by the articles of Vetter and Nikolaus Müller.

experience of God's mercy. Law has no place in the scheme, and the Old Testament law was a mistake. This indifference to the Old Testament might have had some significance for liberty, perhaps did, but was counter-balanced by the emphasis upon right belief as against good conduct. Agricola even went so far as to say that to defend clerical celibacy is worse than to live unchastely. The net result of the controversy was a residue of ill feeling toward the Wittenberg circle.[75]

Agricola was glad to accept the invitation of Joachim II, the elector of Brandenburg, to become the court preacher at Berlin. Then came the Interim. Agricola alone among the Protestant theologians was willing to take any cordial part in the drafting and promulgation of the document. The chief ground for his participation was the belief that the compromise would obligate the Catholics to recognize the essentials of Protestantism, but would bind the Protestants only to the nonessentials of Catholicism. The adiaphora might be left to the regulation of the government so long as the fundamentals were not imperiled. Agricola well stated the position in the following passage:

> Inasmuch as the Interim, thank God, includes the main points of the Christian teaching and religion, the Elector of Brandenburg does not know what better advice he can give than that everyone is obligated to obey the Emperor. . . . No one has reason to say that he is not at liberty to hold the true faith, since the essentials of the true religion are everywhere freely conceded. In ceremonies and outward practices everyone is bound to obey the government. . . . This serves public order and does not infringe upon liberty. One is not saved if one does these things, nor damned if one does not. Therefore the regulation of such matters belongs to the government.[76]

---

[75] Gustav Kawerau, *Johann Agricola von Eisleben* (Berlin, 1881).

——— "Briefe und Urkunden zur Geschichte des antinomistischen Streites," ZKG IV (1881), 299-324, 437-65.

C. E. Förstemann, *Neues Urkundenbuch zur Geschichte der evangelischen Kirchenreformation*, I (Hamburg, 1842), 291-356.

Werner, "Die erste antinomistische Streit," *Neue kirchliche Zeitschrift*, XV (1904), 801-24, 860-73.

[76] Spieker, "Beiträge zur Geschichte des augsburger Interims," *Zeitschrift für die historische Theologie*, XXI, Heft 1 (1851), 345-97, in particular pp. 363-64. Cf. Nikolaus Müller, "Zur Geschichte des Augsburgs Interims,"

Here we have a very interesting reversal of the rôle played by one of the slogans of religious liberty. Erasmus, Castellio, Acontius, and many others sought to reduce the essentials of salvation to the minimum in order to limit controversy and coercion. Leave the nonessentials, they urged, to the individual conscience. Speedily the argument was reversed to read: Concede the essentials to conscience. Commit the nonessentials to the State. This was the policy of Laud in the English revolution. Joachim II differed from Laud only in that he was not so "thorough." No actual constraint was employed, but the pressure was such that some ministers resigned. The opponents of the Interim protested in the name of liberty. One of them wrote:

> We should not only restrain our fists and abstain from murder, but also we ought not to kill or hurt our neighbor in our hearts, thoughts, and words, lest we suffer the judgment of God and hell fire. Wherefore, according to God's word and command all the murderous bloodthirsty Papists and Interimists will be cast into the pit of sulphur with the dreadful beast of the Apocalypse 19, because they destroy and kill Christians and members of Christ.[77]

As general superintendent in Brandenburg, Agricola would have to administer the church Ordinance of 1540, in which Joachim II announced himself as ordained of God to remove all "unchristian, devilish, subversive sects and teaching," as princes and kings in the Old Testament eradicated the abominations.[78] We have little evidence as to the spirit in which Agricola fulfilled his office, save that in recommending candidates for the ministry he reported them as free from "all fanatical opinions."[79]

Jahrbuch für brandenburgische Kirchengeschichte, V (1908), 51-171, in particular pp. 70-74 and 110-12; Gustav Kawerau, "Gutachten Joh. Agricolas für Christoph v. Carlowitz über die Annahme des augsburger Interims," *Neues Archiv für sächsische Geschichte*, I (1880), 266-80.

[77] Spieker, *op. cit.*, p. 392.

[78] Emil Sehling, *Evangelische Kirchenordnungen*, III, 39, 40, 42.

[79] Identical language is used in recommendations in the years 1550 and 1558. For 1550 see Friedländer, "Johann Agricola Eisleben in Berlin," *Märkische Forschungen, hrsg. von dem Vereine für Geschichte der Mark Brandenburg*, II (Berlin, 1843), 219-27; for 1558 see [Berend Kordes] *M. Johann Agricola's aus Eisleben Schriften* (Altona, 1817), p. 380. On this

URBANUS RHEGIUS (1489-1541)

To discover anything in the writings of Urbanus Rhegius suitable for inclusion in the *De haereticis* was a positive achievement. In his early days as a Lutheran at Augsburg in 1527 he conceived an ineradicable prejudice against the Anabaptists. Denck seemed to him abusive and evasive.[80] The party as a whole were lazy, irresponsible toward families, and unreliable toward the magistrate.[81] They established separate congregations and when forbidden to do so worked in secret, thus disturbing the public peace. For that reason they were subject to the sword of the magistrate.[82] Urbanus made no protest when cheeks were bored through and tongues cut out, when men and women were beaten, imprisoned, banished, and beheaded. When an Anabaptist woman of noble family desired to defend her position, Rhegius did sponsor her request to the council and in the debate refuted her arguments. Then she said to him, "There is a great difference between you and me, my dear Urbanus. You sit on a soft cushion beside the councillors and talk as from the tripod of Apollo, whereas I must dispute lying in chains on the ground." Urbanus retorted, "It serves you right, sister, for you were saved once by Christ from bondage to the devil, and now you have willingly given yourself again to his yoke and he has adorned you in this fashion as an example to others."[83]

In 1530, when the Protestant preachers were driven out of

---

period, cf. Georg Lösche, "Eine Agricola Urkunde," *ZKG* XLII (1923), 396-97; E. Thiele, "Denkwürdigkeiten aus dem Leben J. A.," *Theologische Studien und Kritiken*, LXXX, II (1907), 246-70.

[80] *D. Vrbani Regii, Dess weitberümpten Theologj/und trewen Lehrers/weiland Superintendenten im Fürstenthumb Lüneberg/Bücher und Schriften . . . widerumb zusammengedruckt* (Frankfurt, 1577), Pt. 4, Tract XIII, "Notwendige warnung wider den newen Taufforden" (1527), f. cxxvj and clij.

[81] *Ibid.*, Pt. 4, Tract XIV, "Zwen wunderseltzam Sendbrieff" (1528), f. cliiij, clxj, clxxxj verso.

[82] *Ibid.*, f. clvij.

[83] Gerhard Uhlhorn, *Urbanus Rhegius* (Elberfeld, 1861), p. 134. Leben und ausgewählte Schriften der Väter und Begründer der lutherischen Kirche, VII. The account is taken from the life of Rhegius by his son in the *Opera Latina*.

Augsburg, Rhegius entered the service of Ernst the Confessor, count of Braunschweig-Lüneburg in north Germany. The Count had already been active in suppressing Catholicism by civil authority. Rhegius, who soon became general superintendent, entered heartily into the task of intimidating nuns to accept the reform. They were forced to listen to Protestant sermons and in some cases their cloisters were demolished, but they were not actually banished and many of these noble women held out against all intimidation.[84]

Rhegius's defense of his course is set forth most fully in two tracts. The first is entitled, *Whether the magistrate may compel erring subjects against their will to hear the truth* (1535),[85] and the second, *Whether the magistrate may force Anabaptists and other heretics to the faith, and if they are obstinate in their heresy whether they may be punished with the sword because of their heresy* (1538).[86]

The arguments introduce nothing new. There is frequent appeal to Augustine. Heresy is regarded as worse than murder and

[84] Nikolaus Paulus, *op. cit.*, pp. 100-15. His account of the treatment of the nuns is based on Adolf Wrede, *Die Einführung der Reformation im Lüneburgischen durch Herzog Ernst den Bekenner* (Göttingen, 1887), which I have not seen. There is a briefer account by the same author, "Ernst der Bekenner, Herzog von Braunschweig und Lüneburg," *SVRG* VI, IV, No. 25 (Halle, 1888).

[85] "Frag/ob man die leute zum glauben zwingen kan? Ob ein Oberkeyt die jrrigen im glauben inn jhren Landen und gepieten/mag mit gewalt und straff vom jrrthumb dringen/das sie auch wider ihren willen müssen die warheyt hören." *D. Vrbani Regii . . . Bücher und Schriften* (Frankfurt, 1577), Pt. 1, Tract VI. "Enchiridion eines Christlichen Fürsten," f. lxxxiij-lxxxv. Reprinted in F. Bidembach, *Consiliorum theologicorum*, Decas III, Cons. X (Frankfurt, 1608). A Latin translation is given in the *Opera Vrbani Regii Latine edita. Cum eius Vita, ac Praefatione Ernesti Regii*, F[ilii] Impressa Noribergae in Officina Ioannis Montani & Ulrici Neuberi M. D. LXII. Pt. 2, Tract VIII, f. lxiij-lxxiij, "An homines ad fidem cogendi sunt? An magistratus errantes in fide, in suis detractionibus & regionibus, ui & supplicijs ab erroribus adigi possint, ad audiendam veritatem inuiti?" The work of which this is a part, *Christiani Principis & Magistratus Enchiridion*, is dated Cal. Feb. 1538. Copies of all of these works are available at Cornell.

[86] "Ein Bedencken der Lüneburgischen/Ob einer obrigkeit gezieme/die Widertauffer oder andere Ketzer/zum rechten Glauben zu dringen/und so

as involving sedition. Coercion is a work of mercy toward the culprit and toward society from which the rotten member must be cut off. The legislation of the Old Testament against blasphemy, idolatry, and false prophecy is still valid. The Sermon on the Mount is relegated either to private ethics or to an inward disposition.[87] Mildness toward the Anabaptists is described as "unseasonable mercy." [88]

Rhegius's attitude to the Catholics is sufficiently illustrated by his tract, *How to recognize and catch the false prophets* (1539),[89] the title-page of which is here reproduced. Urbanus calls the Catholics sectaries because they are divided into so many orders, and compares them to the ancient heretics, Marcion, Paul of Samosata, Arius, Pelagius, and Nestorius.

The passage used by Castellio from the *Loci communes* was rather indiscreet on the part of Urbanus, but probably meant no more than the passage cited from Jerome in which the saint says that God has hell fire in reserve for the heretics, but would prefer that they repent and be saved.

JOHN CALVIN[90]

Calvin brought Protestant persecution to a head. He began where Luther left off. Euphemisms disappeared. Calvin did not pretend that persecution is not constraint of conscience. He did not

---

sie in der ketzerey beharren/der ketzerey halben/mit dem Schwert zu richten," *D. Vrbani Regii . . . Bücher und Schriften* (Frankfurt, 1577), Pt. 4, Tract XVII, f. ccx-ccxv. Reprinted in Bidembach, *op. cit.*, Decas IV, Cons. II.

[87] Cf. *Opera Vrbani Regii Latine edita.* "Aliqvot concionum formulae," lxvj verso, and "Schlussrede D. Vrbani Rhegij/vom weltlichen gewalt/wider die auffrhürischen," § 8, Pt. 4, f. ccvij verso in *D. Vrbani Regii . . . Bücher und Schriften* (Frankfurt, 1577).

[88] "Bedencken der Lüneburgischen," etc., *Bücher und Schriften*, Pt. 4, f. ccxij verso. Bidembach, *op. cit.*, p. 451.

[89] *Wie man die falschen Propheten erkennen ia greiffen mag.* There are copies of the first edition at Yale and at Cornell. The work is reproduced in *D. Vrbani Regii . . . Bücher und Schriften* (Frankfurt, 1577), Pt. 4, Tract VIII, f. lxxxij verso—xcvj verso.

[90] For opposing accounts of Calvin's attitude to religious liberty consult: Nikolaus Paulus, *Protestantismus und Toleranz:* § 16, "Calvin im Dienste der

John Calvin

worry about any conscience save his own which compelled him to vindicate the divine majesty.[91] He did not pretend that heresy is punishable only when associated with blasphemy and sedition. Bullinger advised him to justify the execution of Servetus on the score of blasphemy,[92] and Musculus was of the same mind.[93] But Calvin called a spade a spade, and devoted a long section of his apology to demonstrating that Christian judges may punish heretics.[94] Nor does sedition play a more than incidental part in the Genevan heresy trials, save in the general sense that heresy was always regarded as subversive of the social and moral order. Gruet was indeed accused of conspiring against the State, but the primary charge against him was that the execrations which he disgorged against Christianity were enough to render the whole land accursed.[95] The only sedition which could be discovered in Bolsec's case was that he had "seditiously" disturbed the tranquillity of the Church,[96] and had *tumultuously* exhorted the people not to be deceived by the ministers.[97] The sentence against Michael Servetus was based on heresy. Calvin was wise enough to see that the denial of predestination and of the Trinity could scarcely be classed with the Anabaptist repudiation of the State.

On the other hand, not even Calvin persecuted merely error of opinion notwithstanding the statement of Lord Acton to the contrary.[98] Heresy was for him, as for the Middle Ages, a sin

---

päpstlichen Inquisition"; § 17, "Calvin als Verteidiger der Ketzerstrafen" (Catholic).

Émile Doumergue, *Jean Calvin* (Neuilly-sur-Seine, 1926), Vol. VI, Chap. xiii, "L'Intolérance et la tolérance de Calvin" (Calvinist).

There is no better biography of Calvin than the autobiography supplied by his letters. A vivid impression of his life's work is furnished by a reading of Rudolf Schwarz, *Johannes Calvins Lebenswerk in seinen Briefen*, 2 vols. (Tübingen, 1909).

[91] *Calvini opera*, XII, 338, Ep. 792.

[92] *Calvini opera*, XIV, 684, Ep. 1861.

[93] *Calvini opera*, XV, 47, Ep. 1916.

[94] *Calvini opera*, VIII, 461-81.

[95] *Calvini opera*, XIII, 569, Ep. 1370.

[96] *Calvini opera*, XIV, 252, Ep. 1590.

[97] *Calvini opera*, VIII, 206.

[98] *The History of Freedom* (London, 1922), p. 165.

against Christendom. The bond of civil society is religion, and religion is mediated by the Church,[99] by the visible Church outside of which there is no salvation.[100] However indefinable may be the exact relation of the invisible and the visible Church Calvin's emphasis was increasingly upon the visible.[101] He felt as keenly as Augustine the sin of schism and could not but regard heresy as an offense against Christian society.

This position may seem naïve if we picture Calvin as transferring to a French-speaking village the conceptions which were built up around the unified culture of the Middle Ages. We must not forget, however, that the disruption of Protestantism had not become definitive in his day. There was still hope for the unification of Calvinism, Lutheranism, and Anglicanism, and none worked harder than Calvin to effect it.[102] Nor were Poland and France as yet lost to the Reform.

Calvin's theory of the Church united the two varieties of intolerance which have appeared in Christianity, the one directed against doctrinal, the other against moral, offense. We have seen that those who think of the Church as an ark of salvation try to force in as many as possible, while those who regard the Church as a kingdom of the saints drive out the unworthy. Calvin did both. He may have unconsciously combined the Anabaptist and Lutheran positions.[103] But he was not aware of any incongruity since the vindication of the honor of God demands doctrinal and moral cleansing. The stress with Calvin, however, was upon the Church

[99] *Calvini opera*, XIX, 645, Ep. 3904.

[100] *Calvini opera*, II, 749 (Inst. IV, 1, 4, 1559); VI, 41 (Catechisme, 1542).

[101] Cf. Werdermann, *Calvin's Lehre von der Kirche in ihrer geschichtlichen Entwicklung*. Calvinstudien, Festschrift zum 400. Geburtstage Johann Calvins, unter Redaktion v. Lic. Dr. Bohatec, hrsg v. d. Ref. Gemeinde Elberfeld (Leipzig, 1909), pp. 246-338.

P. J. Kromsigt, "Het Kerkbegrip van Calvin," *Onder Eigen Vaandel*, II/3 (July, 1927), 212-31; II/4 (October, 1927), 286-304.

[102] Consult John T. McNeill, *Unitive Protestantism* (New York, 1930). Ernst Troeltsch, *Die Soziallehren der christlichen Kirchen und Gruppen* (Tübingen, 1923), p. 609.

[103] Cf. Troeltsch, *op. cit.*, pp. 621, 627-33.

as an agency of salvation. Greater rigor should be exercised against heresy than against impurity.[104]

The arguments used by Calvin in support of persecution are the familiar ones, except that everything is subordinated to the vindication of the honor of God. The cure of souls drops out. Calvin was too realistic to take cover under the subterfuges of the Inquisition. Or rather the cure of souls becomes the protection of those whom the heretic would lead to damnation. He is an enemy of the human race, a wolf who destroys the flock of Christ. His offense is worse than murder [105] and poisoning.[106] But these considerations are less important than the vindication of the divine majesty, and are introduced only because inseparable from it.[107] Calvin exalted the feudal conception of sin to the keystone of his system. Offenses are graded in accord with the rank of the person offended. God is supreme, and a sin against Him transcends all others.[108] To insult God is worse than to strangle an innocent man or to poison a guest.[109] Heresy is treason,[110] lese majesty,[111] sedition, yes, against God.[112] If the honor of an earthly prince should be avenged, how much more that of the King of Kings? [113] We may endure reviling of ourselves, but not of our Lord.[114]

But why cannot God look out for Himself? Calvin answered the question better than did Augustine. Certainly God has no need of human vindication, said Calvin, but He has honored us by placing us as lieutenants beside Him upon His throne or as sentinels at posts of danger. How intolerable that we should be faithless to such a trust.[115] Each must vindicate God in his own

[104] *Calvini opera*, I, 545-46 (editions of 1539-1554, Instit. VIII [IV], 14); *Calvini opera*, II, 756 (edition of 1559, Instit. IV, 1, 13).

[105] *Calvini opera*, XXVII, 244-45.

[106] *Calvini opera*, XLIV, 347 .

[107] *Calvini opera*, XXVII, 249.

[108] *Calvini opera*, XXIX, 337-38.

[109] *Calvini opera*, XLIV, 348.

[110] *Calvini opera*, XXVII, 245.

[111] See the excellent discussion of Calvin's views of *maiestas* by Gisbert Beyerhaus, "Studien zur Staatsanschauung Calvins," *Neue Studien zur Geschichte der Theologie und der Kirche*, VII (Berlin, 1910).

[112] *Calvini opera*, XXIV, 362.

[113] *Calvini opera*, XXVII, 244.

[114] *Calvini opera*, XXIX, 647; XV, 606, Ep. 2200.

[115] *Calvini opera*, VIII, 473-75; XIV, 313, Ep. 1619; LIII, 140-41.

way. The minister uses the word. Calvin thought of himself as God's watchdog.[116] The magistrate uses the sword. To that end he has been installed. Calvin was not hesitant with regard to the Christian character of the State. Luther was too deeply imbued with the Sermon on the Mount to feel altogether happy over a coercive society. For him the State is the result of man's sinful condition. Not so Calvin; the State is an immediately divine institution for the vindication of God's honor. The task of the ruler is to suppress not only murder, adultery, and the like, but also heresy, idolatry, blasphemy, and sacrilege.[117] Calvin continually exhorted princes to energetic action for the abolition of false religion.[118]

In contrast to Luther, Calvin did not dispose of the precepts of the Sermon on the Mount by relegating them to private ethics. He made a distinction, of course, between the rôle of the citizen and that of the magistrate, but the point was not that the one endures while the other resists, but that each resists with the weapons appropriate to his calling. Even the private man must not suffer his home to be polluted by sacrilege.[119] In the defense of God's honor everyone must do his uttermost in accord with his station.[120] The

[116] *Calvini opera*, VI, 503, 507.

[117] *Calvini opera*, XXIX, 532. See the excellent discussion by Hans Baron, *Calvins Staatsanschauung und das Konfessionelle Zeitalter* (Berlin, München, 1924). Beiheft No. 1, Historische Zeitschrift.

[118] Unless the reference is to a particular page, only the number of the letter is given in the *Calvini opera* X-XX.

To Sigismund of Poland, Epp. 1195, 2057, 2362. To Radziwil of Poland, Epp. 2113, 2370 (urging him to remain an unwearied soldier of Christ: *Calvini opera*, XV, 907), Ep. 3232. To Anthony of Navarre, Ep. 2774 (princes are more obligated than commoners: *Calvini opera*, XVI, 731). To Jeanne of Navarre, Ep. 3904. To the Duke of Somerset, Epp. 1053, 1085 (radicals and Catholics may be suppressed with the sword because they rise up not only against the king, but also against God who has instituted the king to protect both the royal and the divine majesty: *Calvini opera*, XIII, 81). To Edward VI, Epp. 1422, 1636. To John of Tarnow, Ep. 3133 (the minister must exhort, the magistrate must execute. Even if a revolution should ensue, the truth of God is worth more than a hundred worlds: *Calvini opera*, XVII, 673-74).

[119] *Calvini opera*, VIII, 470.

[120] *Calvini opera*, XXVII, 244, 246, 262, 344; XVI, 731, Ep. 2774. Cf. II, 1097-98 (Inst. IV, XX, 7), and Troeltsch, *op. cit.*, pp. 639-40, n. 332.

precepts on nonresistance are disposed of by Calvin in other ways. The first is to relegate them not to private ethics, but to an inward disposition. We may indeed go to law and even kill, provided we are not vindictive.[121] The second device is to interpret the New Testament in terms of the Old, the Sermon on the Mount by the imprecatory Psalms. This *tour de force* was facilitated by the typological exegesis which saw in the Old Testament characters types of Jesus and in the Psalms of David pronouncements of the preëxistent Christ. The gentle Savior who said, "Love your enemies" (Matt. 5: 44), was prefigured by David, who sang, "Do I not hate them, O Lord, that hate Thee?" (Ps. 139: 21).[122]

This resort to the Old Testament necessitates also a picture of God as ruthless and arbitrary. He is the God who through Moses [123] and Zechariah [124] commanded that the false prophet be slain, who moved Nebuchadnezzar to promulgate a decree that anyone who said aught amiss against the God of Shadrach, Meshach, and Abednego should be cut in pieces and his house made a dunghill,[125] who strengthened the aged Samuel that he might be able to hew Agag in pieces.[126] Even Calvin was sometimes aghast at the feats of the Almighty, but repressed every murmur and prostrated himself before the infinite wisdom of God's hidden judgments.[127]

In the service of such a God we must crush all considerations of humanity.[128] He does not feel them. God is not a father in the ordinary sense. What father would suffer his children to be eaten by lions and tigers or to be born morons? [129] The God who permits the inequalities of creation is bound by no law, not even by the law

[121] *Calvini opera*, II, 1107-10 (Inst. IV, XX, 17-21).

[122] *Calvini opera*, XX, 245, Ep. 4074. Calvin does not cite the texts, but the references are obvious.

[123] See the commentaries on Deut. XIII in *Calvini opera*, XXIV, 359-64, and XXVII, 250-74.

[124] *Calvini opera*, XLIV, 346-48.

[125] Dan. 3: 29, *Calvini opera*, XL, 646; cf. VIII, 466, 475.

[126] *Calvini opera*, XXX, 145.

[127] *Calvini opera*, XXX, 105, 107, 110, 145.

[128] *Calvini opera*, VIII, 476; XXIV, 360; XLIV, 346.

[129] *Calvini opera*, IX, 289. Cf. my article "Sebastian Castellio and the Toleration Controversy of the Sixteenth Century," in *Persecution and Liberty.*

of nature.[130] To be sure He is not absolutely arbitrary, as the Scholastics declare. He is just, and some day we shall understand His justice,[131] but for the present we can only sit like Job upon his dungheap and confess that God does well when He disposes of us according to His will.[132] Zeal for His glory must almost denude us of our nature and make us ready to repudiate the love of wife and child.[133] This was no idle talk. Calvin was not devoid of human feeling, he could be tender and moving; [134] but his ideal was Abraham sacrificing Isaac,[135] save that for Calvin all too often no ram was caught in the thicket.

The case would not have been so bad had Calvin been content to bow before the mysteries of life and cry simply, "O ineffable mystery," but with greater intensity than Augustine and Luther he exalted the anomalies into a system and projected the inequalities of birth into eternity. For him, as also for Augustine, this determinism strengthened persecution. When faced with the command in Deuteronomy to raze whole villages and kill even the children, Calvin could comment, "We may rest assured that God would suffer only those infants to be destroyed whom He had already damned and destined to eternal death." [136]

We may well wonder how Castellio could find anything in Calvin to include in this compilation. He had had no liberal period like Luther and Brenz. If Calvin ever wrote anything in favor of religious liberty it was a typographical error.[137] He urged the King of France to cease the constraint of the Protestants, not on the ground that heresy is not subject to the magistrate, but solely because the king was persecuting the truth.[138] The severity of the

[130] Cf. Beyerhaus, *op. cit.*, p. 72.

[131] *Calvini opera*, IX, 288. Cf. J. Bohatec, "Calvins Vorsehungslehre," *Calvinstudien* (Leipzig, 1909), pp. 398-404.

[132] *Calvini opera*, XXXV, 478.

[133] *Calvini opera*, VIII, 476.

[134] Cf. Epp. 1171 and 1173 on the death of his wife and the many letters of consolation and encouragement, e.g., Epp. 295 and 1977.

[135] *Calvini opera*, XXIII, 313-18.

[136] *Calvini opera*, XXIV, 363.

[137] Cf. Alexander Gordon, "Miguel Serveto-y-Revés," *Theological Review*, XV (1878), 305.

[138] Preface to the "Institutes" of 1536 in *Calvini opera*, I. Cf. XXXI, 23-24.

Papists, instead of deterring Calvin, rather stimulated him to emulation.[139]

The passages which Castellio has employed occur only in the earlier works, but the later excision was the removal merely of the irrelevant and the innocuous. The first citation from the dedication of the book of Acts to the King of Denmark [140] is no more than an exhortation not to make war without consulting God. The whole dedication fell out later because the king was not pleased to accept it. Calvin addressed the next edition to Radziwil of Poland with a significant warning against the anti-trinitarians.[141] The other passage is from the first edition of the *Institutes*, where Calvin protests against too great rigor in the use of excommunication and throws in an aside criticizing those who would coerce the Turks and the Jews to Christianity. This little irrelevancy it is which falls out in the later editions.[142]

On the other hand we must not suppose that Calvin was a bloodthirsty fanatic eager to destroy all who disagreed with him. He drew the line somewhere, and not merely at the Turks and the Jews. Calvin, like Augustine and Erasmus, distinguished the essentials from the nonessentials. The fundamentals are to believe that there is one God, that Christ is God and God's Son, that our salvation depends upon the graciousness of God, and similar articles.[143] Error can be condoned if it does not touch the points necessary for salvation.[144] The complaint against Servetus and Gribaldi was precisely that they overturned the primary heads of religion.[145] Although Calvin could not go so far as Melanchthon in regarding the practices suppressed by the Interim as nonessential,[146] nevertheless he looked upon many ceremonies and vestments as "tolerable ineptitudes." [147] His advice to the congregation at Frankfurt

[139] *Calvini opera*, XIV, 615; VIII, 465-66; XXIV, 357.
[140] Ep. 1607. [141] Ep. 3232.
[142] *Calvini opera*, I, 77, 552; II, 912.
[143] *Calvini opera*, I, 545; II, 756, Inst. IV, 1, 13(12).
[144] *Ibid*. Cf. *Calvini opera*, VIII, 477.
[145] *Calvini opera*, XIV, 615, Ep. 1793; XV, 644, Ep. 2220.
[146] *Calvini opera*, XIII, 594, Ep. 1381.
[147] *Calvini opera*, XV, 394, Ep. 2091.

and to John Knox, in the controversy over the form of the English prayer book, was that contention over such matters be dropped.[148]

Calvin also drew the line on the means which he was willing to employ. He would not countenance image smashing.[149] Although he could view the prolongation of torture through the maladdress of an executioner as an act of God, nevertheless he recommended the sword instead of the stake in the case of Servetus,[150] and did not wish the death penalty for Bolsec,[151] however much the victim and his friends suspected that he did.[152] The statement in the letter to the Duke of Somerset that the radicals and the Catholics might be suppressed by the sword does not necessarily mean that their heads should be cut off.[153] When it came to revolution on behalf of the Reform Calvin wrote to Coligny, "Better that we should all perish a hundred times than that the name and cause of Christianity and the Gospel should be subject to such a reproach."[154] These noble words should not be forgotten by the apologists who would extenuate the execution of Servetus on the ground that it was necessary for Calvin's success. Calvin knew that success is not the chief end of man.

Still it may be true that Calvin might have failed had he been less rigorous, not because the Genevan bibliocracy depended on the burning of a heretic, but because Calvin was an intellectual, easily seduced into endless discussions. Fate made him an administrator. As a man of action, in order to keep his grip upon himself, he had to wipe out these emissaries of Satan commissioned to waste his time.[155]

In the effort to understand Calvin we must bear in mind the circumstances. He lived in an atmosphere of war (an attack on

[148] To Frankfurt: *Calvini opera*, XV, 896, Ep. 2363; to Cox: *Calvini opera*, XV, 628-29, Ep. 2213; to Knox: *Calvini opera*, XVIII, 434-35, Ep. 3377. Cf. XV, 79, Ep. 1929.

[149] *Calvini opera*, XVIII, 580-81, Ep. 3461.

[150] *Calvini opera*, XIV, 590, Ep. 1772; 657, Ep. 1839.

[151] Ep. 1579.

[152] *Calvini opera*, VIII, 225-26.

[153] *Calvini opera*, XIII, 68, Ep. 1085.

[154] *Calvini opera*, XVIII, 426, Ep. 3374.

[155] *Calvini opera*, XI, 439, Ep. 421; XII, 281-82, Ep. 766.

Geneva was often imminent) [156] and he was a sick man. Let us hear him in his own defense against the remonstrances of Zurkinden, the magistrate of Bern, who carried the principles of his friend Castellio to the point of befriending persecuted Calvinists in Bernese territory. He had been sounding Calvin as to whether Castellio would be acceptable in Lausanne. Calvin replied: [157]

Although we seek the same goal we differ more than I should like in temperament and character.[158] I know what you think, and what you sometimes say, about me. I am not so fond of myself as not to dislike some of the shortcomings which you reprove. . . . But others I would not alter. We differ not only in temperament, but I deliberately pursue a different course. Mildness suits you and to it I also am not averse. If I seem to you too severe, believe me I have adopted the rôle only because I must. You do not consider how the Church is endangered by your latitude, which gives unrestricted license to evil doers, which confuses virtue and vice and makes no distinction between black and white. For example, take Castellio, whom you would like to see appointed at Lausanne, were it nor for your fear that there might be disturbance because of the "squabbles" which I had with him. This word does not so much hurt me as it violates the sacred name of God and vilifies all truth and religion. This good man would destroy the fundamentals of our salvation and is not ashamed to break into detestable blasphemies. He says that "the God of Calvin is a liar, a hypocrite, two-faced, the author of all evil, the enemy of justice, and worse than the devil." Have I not a right to complain that you treat me unkindly? I know that you are far from approving of the stinking detestable dung of this obscene dog. I should prefer that the earth swallow me up a hundred times than that I should not listen to what the Spirit of God dictates and prescribes for me by the mouth of the prophet in the words: "The reproaches of them that reproached Thee have fallen upon me" (Ps. 69:9). And now when I defend the faith which I cannot desert without treachery and perfidy, do you say that I "squabble"? Would that this rash word, of which I am ashamed as unworthy of a Christian, had never escaped you. If we have a spark of piety, such an indignity as that of Castellio should enflame us to the highest indignation. As for me I would rather rave than not be

[156] *Calvini opera*, XVII, 671, Ep. 3131.

[157] *Calvini opera*, XVII, 465-67, Ep. 3023.

[158] Zurkinden had first suggested that the difference was one of temperament. See *Calvini opera*, XVII, 235-37, Ep. 2908.

angry. You had better consider how you will answer before the Supreme Judge. . . .

I see what a bitter letter I have written, and I almost tore it into a hundred pieces, but it is not my way to conceal what presses on my heart, nor would you wish it. Otherwise I could not have written at all. I cannot lie and flatter. I have been made more irritable by a load of work, and I am afraid I have been inconsiderate enough to trouble you when you are nearly crushed with the weariness of cares and labors.

Protestant Liberals: Erasmians

THE intolerance of John Calvin by no means characterized all the Protestants. The inscription on the expiatory monument to Servetus is scarcely accurate in the statement that Calvin but shared the error of his times. Those in authority, to be sure, supported him. They could not well have been where they were had they objected to the alliance of Church and State. But many, including most of the Anabaptists, did object to the use of force in religion, whether exercised by the State or by a kingdom of the saints.

The liberals owed much to the influence of Erasmus. The first three whom I have classed as his followers were attached to him by personal friendship, maintained in spite of some interruptions even after they embraced the Reformation. Like him they were scholars laboring in the sanguine trust that a better knowledge of the Bible and of the Fathers would restore pure Christianity. The degree of their liberalism varied. I have arranged them in an ascending scale.

CASPAR HEDIO (1494-1552)[1]

Caspar Hedio while in his twenties came to know Erasmus at Basel (1518). Fourteen years later he was encouraged by a cordial

[1] Statements not otherwise supported are taken from Emil Himmelheber, "Caspar Hedio: ein Lebensbild aus der Reformationsgeschichte," in *Studien der evangelisch-protestantischen Geistlichen des Grossherzogthums Baden*, VII, I (Karlsruhe, 1881), 1-64. There is a bibliography of the works of Hedio by Joh. Adam, "Versuch einer Bibliographie Kaspar Hedios," *Zeitschrift f. die Geschichte des Oberrheins*, hrsg. v. der Badischen historischen Kommission, N. F., XXXI, I (Heidelberg, 1916), 424-29. The same journal has an article by Paul Kalkoff, "Hedio und Geldenhauer (Noviomagus) als Chronisten," N. F., XXXIII (Heidelberg, 1918), 348-62. Hedio's account of the Marburg Colloquy is printed by A. Erichson, "Strassburger Beiträge zur Geschichte des Marburger Religionsgesprächs. I. Hedio's Itinerarium," *ZKG* IV (1881), 416-36. Erichson gives a good brief biography in RE[3] VII, 515-

letter of congratulation from the prince of the humanists over the translations of sacred authors.[2]

While at Basel Hedio went over to the Reformation, which he served as a minister first in that city, next at Mainz, and then for the remainder of his life at Strassburg (1523-1552). His reputation for moderation was such that at his death Dryander could hold him up to Calvin as "one who pocketed many private vexations and inconveniences in order to preserve the tranquillity and union of the Church." [3]

Yet this same motive made him willing to join Bucer in the suppression of the Anabaptists. In 1533 Bucer reported that of all the Strassburg ministers the only two who drew the fire of the sectaries were himself and Hedio.[4] In that same year Hedio gave his consent to the articles of the Strassburg synod in which the declaration was made that "those who denied the right of the magistrate to punish a false and blasphemous worship of God are merely seeking an opportunity to indulge their own dissension and sedition." [5] The Strassburg Church Ordinance of 1534 ordered that if anyone should attempt to introduce strange teaching no citizen should listen to him, but should tell him to accept the decision of the town council.[6]

In a sermon preached in the cathedral at Strassburg on the 24th

---

17. There are a number of references in Johann Adam, *Evangelische Kirchengeschichte der Stadt Strassburg* (Strassburg, 1922), pp. 54, 128, 195, 246, 248, 276. Hedio appears not infrequently in the correspondence of Erasmus, Zwingli, Luther, and Calvin.

[2] March 2, 1532, manuscript: Thesaurus Baumianus (Strassburg), V, 36.

[3] *Calvini opera,* XIV, 402-4, Ep. 1670 (Oct. 30, 1552). Hedio died Oct. 17.

[4] Himmelheber (p. 33) quoting Bucer to Myconius, Nov. 28, 1533.

[5] Article 15, printed by Timotheus Wilhelm Röhrich, *Geschichte der Reformation in Elsass und besonders Strassburg,* 2 vols. (Strassburg, 1830 and 1832), II, 267.

[6] Aemilius Ludwig Richter, *Die evangelischen Kirchenordnungen des sechszehnten Jahrhunderts,* 2nd ed., 2 vols. (Leipzig, 1871), I, 231-39, No. XLVII, "Strassburger Kirchenordnung," 1534, p. 233. Hedio had a share in the Ordinance prepared for Cologne in 1543 (Richter, *op. cit.,* II, 30-54, No. LXXXI). Unfortunately Richter has omitted all save the title of the section against the Anabaptists (p. 35).

Caspar Hedio

of January, 1534, Hedio justified the maintenance of the unity of the faith by the magistrate. The State, he said, which has no care for religion is (in the language of Augustine) but piracy on a large scale. They are enemies of the cross of Christ who would allow every man to do as he pleases, who recommend only gentleness and friendliness in preaching and call zeal and earnestness the erection of a new papacy. Satan is the author of the poisonous plea that the magistrate should not concern himself with religion. This is as if someone should poison the only spring in a town, and worse than that, to the extent that the soul is nobler than the body, the eternal than the temporal.[7] On the other hand Hedio nowhere suggests any penalty in excess of banishment.

The passage used in the *De haereticis* is taken from a book of sermon outlines published by Hedio in 1537,[8] after the attitude of intolerance to the Anabaptists was fully formed. The protest against those who preferred to kill Jews, Turks, and infidels rather than to take them alive was evidently not meant to interfere with Protestant constraint. On the other hand it is only fair to add that Hedio did prefer to take men alive. His friendliness toward Engelbrecht made Bucer uneasy,[9] and Caspar Schwencfeld turned to Hedio to appease Bucer's severity.[10]

CONRAD PELLICAN (1478-1556)

Pellican like Erasmus was a scholar inclined to moderation. From Erasmus's *Paraphrases* he borrowed for his own commentary

[7] *Radts Predig. Wie die Oberkeit für sich selbs/und die Underthonen für jre Oberkeiten/in disser geuerlichen sorglichen zeit zů bitten haben. Beschehen in beysein eins Ersamen Radts/vnd der Burgerschafft Strassburg.* M. D. XXXIIII. Den XIIIJ. tag Jenners. Durch Casparn Hedion Doctor im Münster daselbst. A—Diiij. See especially Biv verso to Cij. This is number 11 in Adam's bibliography. I have a photostat of the copy in the Preussische Staatsbibliothek at Berlin.

[8] Adam, No. 18.

[9] Traugott Schiess, *Briefwechsel der Brüder Ambrosius u. Thomas Blaurer*, I (Freiburg i. B. 1908), 466, Ep. 396 (Feb. 3, 1534). This letter is incorrectly referred by Himmelheber (p. 34) to Hedio's dealings with Melchior Hoffmann.

[10] *Corpus Schwenckfeldianorum*, Vol. IV (Leipzig, 1914), 813.

not only the passage on the parable of the tares, which is reproduced in our compilation, but also the comment on the desire of the disciples to bring down fire from heaven.[11] "The spirit of the Gospel," Erasmus had written, "is more merciful [than that of Elijah]. There will some day be a time of vengeance, but in the meantime 'the Son of Man is come not to destroy men's lives, but to save them.' [12] Those who now reject him may receive him later on. They are to be saved, therefore, in order that they may have an opportunity to repent." [13] In the case of Ananias, the point is made that Peter gave him a chance to confess his fault. When he refused to avail himself of the opportunity, and thereby sinned against the Holy Spirit, God killed him.[14] Pellican's exposition of Deuteronomy is independent. Here he sets forth the conditions on which the false prophet may be stoned with such explicitness as to render the entire chapter irrelevant in contemporary controversies.[15]

Circumstances made Pellican a Zwinglian, but he was friendly to Catholics, Turks, and Lutherans. To the abbot of St. Gall he expressed a hope that the monasteries would devote themselves to the study of the Scriptures and to purity of life,[16] and to the bishop of Strassburg he sent a copy of his translation of the *Paraphrases of Erasmus* with the wish that the godly bishop might be preserved by the Lord Jesus for the renewal of his kingdom.[17] If the pope was Antichrist for Pellican it was in part because he had

[11] Luke 9: 55. [12] Luke 9: 56 in some manuscripts.

[13] Erasmus, *Opera*, VII, 373: Pellican, *In qvatvor evangelistas, Matthaeum, Marcum, Lucam & Ioannem, item in Acta Apostolorum commentarij Conradi Pellicani sacrae lingvae in schola Tigurina professoris.* Tigvri excudebat Christophorus Froschoverus anno M. D. LXXXII. There is a copy in the Yale library bound with and after *In libros, qvos vocant Apocryphos, vel potivs ecclesiasticos.*

[14] Erasmus, *Opera*, VII, 685; Pellican, *op. cit.*, p. 291 verso § B.

[15] *In Pentatevchvm sive qvinqve libros Mosis, nempe Genesim, Exodvm . . . Conradi Pellicani,* Tigvri, 1582. In the copy at Yale this is bound with *In libros historicos*, etc., 1582.

[16] *Das Chronikon des Konrad Pellikan zur vierten Säkularfeier der Universität Tübingen,* durch Bernhard Riggenbach (Basel, 1877), p. xxv.

[17] *Ibid.*, p. 154.

stirred up kingdoms against the Turk for the increase of his own power.[18] It would be better to learn Turkish "that by the words of doctrine we may soften them toward Catholic truth, make them less cruel and less justly incensed because of our vanities." [19] As for the Lutherans, Pellican entertained no illusions regarding the possibility of an understanding,[20] but nevertheless urged that "love should not be forgotten because of an opinion about the love feast." [21]

Such generous dispositions toward other religions and groups would, of course, be perfectly consonant with severity toward Protestant sectaries. I can find little to indicate Pellican's position on this score. In the *Chronicon* he speaks in a friendly way of Ludwig Hätzer, Sebastian Franck, and Lelio Sozini, but in innocuous connections.[22] One passage records that many pernicious sects have arisen in the Netherlands. Their names are outlandishly misspelled. Some of them, says Pellican, fly in the air and come down again, but whether they should be punished either for the ascent or the descent he does not say.[23] But probably he would no more have objected to their suppression than did Erasmus. When Balthazar Hübmaier lay in prison at Zürich for his Anabaptism, Pellican wrote to Zwingli, "The judgment of God on Dr. Balthazar terrifies me. I am sorry that he has become a Satan to the Gospel. May a thousand others from among the Papists come and take his place." [24]

COELIUS SECUNDUS CURIO (1503-1569)

Curio as we have seen, was one of those credited with a share in the compilation of the *De haereticis*. A brief excerpt from his pen is also included in the work. Probably no better example was

[18] *Ibid.*, p. 160. [19] *Ibid.*, pp. 135-36.

[20] Cf. Bucer's disgust. Traugott Schiess, *Briefwechsel der Brüder Ambrosius und Thomas Blaurer*, II (Freiburg i. B., 1910), Brief 1151, p. 331.

[21] *Ibid.*, I (1908), Brief 486, p. 592—Konrad Pellican to Ambrosius Blaurer (Zürich), October 27, 1534.

[22] *Chronicon*, pp. 108, 168, 177. [23] *Ibid.*, p. 170.

[24] *Zwinglis sämtliche Werke*, *CR* VIII, No. 437, p. 495—Pellican to Zwingli, Basel, beginning 1526.

available in 1554, but this passage is as ambiguous as Erasmus in his most elusive moods. The Anabaptists, said Curio, should be punished only for sedition, not for heresy. But what is sedition? Does heresy itself constitute sedition? Is mere denial of the Christian character of the State sedition? Where Church and State are one, is ecclesiastical revolt to be called civil sedition?

Later on Curio was to give a much clearer account of himself. In the same year as the *De haereticis* appeared a work entitled, *On the Wideness of the Blessed Kingdom of God.*[25] The title alone recalls the tract of Erasmus on the *Immense Mercy of God.* In Curio's booklet we have both an account of his general theological position and a specific statement of his attitude with regard to the jurisdiction of the State in matters of religion.

The general point of view is that of Erasmus. Like him, Curio declared Scripture to be obscure (p. 6).[26] Like him, he stressed God's mercy and man's worth. "What good, great, or splendid deed," inquired Curio, "was ever conceived or executed by one constantly in doubt as to his salvation" (p. 11)? The moral is not that man should not worry, but that God has removed all occasion for worry. He saves not only by overt faith in Christ, but also by the natural law implanted in the heart of man. Here Curio was in

[25] *Coelii Secundi Curionis de amplitudine Beati Regni Dei dialogi sive libri duo. Ad Sigismundum Augustum Poloniae regem potentissimum et clementissimum.* Basel, 1554. Copy at Cornell. Gouda, 1614. Copy at Union Theological Seminary. My references are to this edition. The page notation is about ten lower than in the first edition. This work was a continuation of the theme of another which Curio's son translated, namely, the *De amplitudi/Ne Misericordiae/Dei absolutissima Oratio, à Mar-/silio Andreasio Mantuano Italico/sermone primum conscri-/pta, nunc in latinum/conuersa,/Caelio Horatio C V/rione C. S. F. Interprete./Item, Sermones tres D. Bernardini Oc-/chini, de Officio Christiani principis,/eodem interprete./Item, Sacrae Declamationes quinq./Ad Sereniss & clementiss. Angliae Re-/gem Edvardum VI./Proverb. 1. Domini metus, caput est sapientiae./Basileae.* The following further description is given in *Museum Helveticum*, XXV (Zürich, 1752), p. 557, "ex Off. Joh. Oporini 8 M. Majo. Basileae 1550. Ad finem adjicitur explicatio Psalmorum 93 & 130 Johanne Witlingio authore." Note the pseudonym for Brenz. Compare Walther Köhler, *Bibliographia Brentiana*, No. 163. There is a copy of the book at Harvard.

[26] Since all of the references are to this one tract the page numbers will be given in parentheses.

accord with the Alexandrian tradition of early Christianity,[27] and the Erasmian in his own day. But he goes beyond Erasmus in his optimism. Curio was of the opinion that all the nations of the earth would speedily embrace the Protestant Reformation. Switzerland, Germany, Denmark, Poland, and other northern countries had already been gained. The King of Kings ruled for a time over England and would do so again. Russia would come in. France and Italy were on the point and Spain would follow. The Jews would be easier to win when they saw Christians no longer worshiping idols and a mystical crust of bread (pp. 164-65). The Marrani and the Mohammedans would also be gathered into Christ's fold (p. 50). As for the Tartars and the Americans (p. 53), God would employ an angel for their conversion or save them by the knowledge of Himself implanted in all men (p. 150). Anyone with such sanguine hopes could afford to dispense with coercion in religion. Any extreme optimism whether based on religious eschatology or the hope of human progress can rest content with non-violence.

At the same time Curio by no means abandoned the view that the magistrate should foster the faith.

> The king is under obligation to provide not only that the citizens enjoy civil justice, but also that they be educated in the evangelical doctrine of Christ [i.e., Protestantism]. I do not mean to imply that men are to be compelled to religion by force, but all are to be acquainted with genuine Christian doctrine. Preachers should have free opportunity of teaching and of disputing with adversaries in all moderation so that they alone will come to Christ who are willing, instructed, and persuaded. The unwilling are to be left alone, provided they are quiet.

Just what does that mean? Provided they do not disturb the peace? Or provided they keep their conviction to themselves? Many in Curio's day would have said that.[28] Curio continues, "He who lacks devotion and faith is useless to God, since these are impossible

[27] He cited Clement of Alexandria and Origen, p. 148.

[28] Cf. Heinrich Hoffmann, "Reformation und Gewissensfreiheit," *Aus der Welt der Religion.* Religionswissenschaftliche Reihe. Heft 18 (Giessen, 1932), p. 18, n. 81.

in one who is coerced and unwilling, as Lactantius says."[29] "But you [addressing Sigismund II of Poland] may abolish public superstition and false rites. You may abrogate human decrees and mitigate offenses with Christian moderation. David did this and Asa, also Hezekiah and Josiah, the kings of Israel, as well as the Emperors Constantine V, Constantine VI, Leo III. . . . If you imitate their examples in abolishing superstition and instituting the true religion you will be pleasing to Jesus Christ, the Son of God, the eternal King by whose grace you rule" (pp. 4b-5). Concretely this meant that the kings of the earth as agents of the heavenly King might drive out the Beast and Harlot and all her wares (p. 55). In other words the Catholic Church should be suppressed by the State.

This course did not seem to Curio at all inconsistent with his contention that religion is not to be forced. Here is another example of his insistence on that point. "The Gospel of our Lord Jesus Christ," he said, "is not to be propagated by force of arms, but by preaching, by the force and evidence of the Spirit, by good conduct, patience, charity, moderation, justice, temperance and constancy, goodness, faith, and mildness, by which the power of the Holy Spirit will come forth and show itself. This is the way in which the Lord and His disciples advanced the Gospel and instilled divine truth into human hearts" (p. 162).

OTTO BRUNFELS (1488-1534)

Brunfels, too, was an Erasmian, in spite of a temporary breach with his idol. Before the rift he made a bid for friendship and after the estrangement a gesture of reconciliation which was accepted.[30] The controversy was partly personal, partly because of a principle. Ulrich von Hutten, the benefactor of Brunfels, had charged

[29] *Inst.* V, 20. This is one of the passages used in the *De haereticis.* See p. 198, below.

[30] *Briefwechsel des Beatus Rhenanus,* hrsg. von Adalbert Horawitz und Karl Hartfelder (Leipzig, 1886), Epp. 145 and 176. *Opvs epistolarvm Des. Erasmi Roterodami,* ed. P. S. Allen, VI (Oxford, 1926), Ep. 1614. Cf. V (Oxford, 1924), Epp. 1405 and 1406. An excellent biographical and bibliographical notice is prefixed to Ep. 1405.

Otto Brunfels

Erasmus with cowardly desertion of the Reform through a meretricious neutrality.[31] Erasmus retorted that he would be willing to die for Christ, but not for the paradoxes of Luther, whose violence ill accorded with the spirit of the Gospel. The points debated by the Reformers he did not regard as articles of faith, but as themes for scholastic discussion. Here we have again the distinction between the fundamentals and the nonessentials. Among the latter, Erasmus would class free will, salvation by faith, the sacrifice of the Mass, and good works.[32] By the time the reply of Erasmus appeared, Hutten was dead. Brunfels came to the defense, characterizing Luther's violence as backbone,[33] and the dominion of the Roman pontiff as of the devil.[34]

But Brunfels was equally able to remonstrate with Luther in the spirit of Erasmus and here again on behalf of a friend, this time Carlstadt. To Luther, Brunfels wrote:

> The dissension between you and Carlstadt pains me grievously, for I am devoted to you both. But I do not so love you that I cannot sincerely embrace Carlstadt. Although I see some scoffers ridiculing him because their missiles have fallen short, I have learned to despise no man in whom is the Spirit of God. . . . We are the more to blame because we cleave to men, that is, to Carlstadt and you. If we looked to Scripture and desired to be taught of the Father He would certainly give a good spirit to those who ask Him. But now that we contend for men, there is danger lest we eat each other up. I say this because I wish that greater modesty were exercised on both sides.[35]

At the time of these controversies with Erasmus and Luther, Brunfels was teaching school at Strassburg and producing works on medicine, botany, and theology.[36] He associated himself with

[31] Hutten's *Expostulatio* (1523) is printed in Eduard Boecking, *Ulrich von Hutten: Schriften,* II (Leipzig, 1859), document cccx.

[32] *Ibid.,* II, document cccxxxiii, especially pp. 292 and 309.

[33] *Ibid.,* document cccxxxiiii, p. 333.

[34] *Ibid.,* p. 338. Cf. Karl Hartfelder, "Otto Brunfels als Verteidiger Huttens." *Zeitschrift für die Geschichte des Oberrheins,* N. F., VIII (Karlsruhe, 1893), 565-78.

[35] Enders and Kawerau, *Dr. Martin Luther's Briefwechsel,* V (*Calw & Stuttgart,* 1893), 161-62, Ep. 915, early May, 1525.

[36] For a bibliography, see F. W. E. Roth, "Die Schriften des Otto Brun-

the radicals Sapidus, Engelbrecht, and Schultheiss.[37] The latter sponsored the cause of Servetus in Strassburg,[38] and composed a tract in favor of religious liberty in which he declared:

> We should leave the spirits free and not despise what God has revealed through them. Each man should be free to teach and then there would be no division. But the preachers wish to erect a new papacy. They are vexed if one says anything against them, even though it be a revelation from God. He who contradicts must be a radical and a fanatic. . . . They call in the magistrate to protect what they have written. He who does not believe it must leave the country.[39]

After the synod of 1533 the hand of the authorities came down heavily upon this group. Sapidus made his peace. Engelbrecht was deposed on grounds of immorality, and went over to Rome. Schultheiss was removed because of his "contempt for the government."[40] Brunfels could congratulate himself that in the fall of 1533 he had been called as city physician to Bern.[41] Bucer was relieved.[42]

fels," *Jahrbuch für Geschichte, Sprache und Litteratur Elsass-Lothringens*, hrsg. von dem Historisch-Litterarischen Zweigverein des Vogesen-Clubs, XVI (Strassburg, 1900), 257-88. For a biography, see F. W. E. Roth, "Otto Brunfels nach seinem Leben und litterarischen Wirken geschildert," *Zeitschrift für die Geschichte des Oberrheins*, hrsg. von der Badischen historischen Kommission. N. F. IX (Karlsruhe, 1894), 284-320; Ludwig Keller, "Otto Brunfels. Ein Gottesgelehrter, Arzt und Naturforscher des 16. Jahrhunderts," *Monatshefte der Comenius-Gesellschaft*, VIII, Heft 19 (Berlin, Nov.-Dec., 1899), 267-79. On his scientific work, consult F. A. Flüchiger, "Otto Brunfels, Fragment zur Geschichte der Botanik und Pharmacie." *Archiv der Pharmacie*, Dritte Reihe, XII, der ganzen Folge CCXII (1878), 493-514.

[37] Johann Adam, *Evangelische Kirchengeschichte der Stadt Strassburg* (Strassburg, 1922), pp. 204-9. For a sketch of Brunfels see *Ibid.*, p. 93. Timotheus Wilhelm Röhrich, *Geschichte der Reformation in Elsass und besonders Strassburg*, I (Strassburg, 1830), 325-49, and his article, "Zur Geschichte der strassburgischen Wiedertäufer," *Zeitschrift für die historische Theologie*, XXX (Gotha, 1860), 1-121, in particular pp. 6-7.

[38] Traugott Schiess, *Briefwechsel der Brüder Ambrosius und Thomas Blaurer*, hrsg. von der Badischen historischen Kommission, I (Freiburg i. B., 1908), 306, n. 2.

[39] T. W. Röhrich, *Geschichte der Reformation in Elsass*, I, 88.

[40] Adam, *op. cit.*, p. 204.

[41] Röhrich, *op. cit.*, pp. 96-114.

[42] Traugott Schiess, *op. cit.*, I, No. 368.

Brunsfels's works cover a wide range in the fields of science and religion. We are concerned only with those which deal with religious liberty. A tract on the *Offense of the Gospel* (1523) asserted that the minority alone espouses the truth, and the majority always cries heresy.[43]

The passage used by Castellio is taken from the *Pandects*, a collection of passages in support of various propositions. The first edition appeared in 1527, and was followed by many others.

There are some passages of even greater significance in Brunfels's *Annotations on the Gospels and Acts*.[44] Here are two of the comments:

On John 8:40: "But now ye seek to kill me." So we may reply to those who proclaim themselves the mighty, princes and pontiffs. "If you are so holy, so true, such protectors of the faith and the truth, you ought not to kill those who tell you the truth." Let these pontiffs of ours, these sons of Abraham, tell us where Abraham or the Scriptures teach that rebels against the faith should be killed. It is the work of the devil to compel men to the faith by fire or the sword.

On Acts 3:17: "I wot that through ignorance ye did it." "Had they known it they would not have crucified the Lord of glory." [45] This is a remonstrance against those who contend that heretics and opponents of the Gospel should be killed. Let them say where there is an example of such tyranny in the Scripture, or where any plain testimony of Scripture. If Peter had wished to kill not only unbelievers, but even the murderous Jews he would not have declared so magnanimously, "Brethren, I wot that through ignorance ye did it." All who resist truth, sin through ignorance, for if they knew, they would not persecute. This is why the apostle says, "The servant of the Lord must not strive . . ." [46]

Let no one, therefore, be despised, be he a schismatic or a heretic. We have an example in Paul, who was a blasphemer and a persecutor of the Church, but nevertheless he obtained mercy and became an apostle of the Church and a teacher of the gentiles in the truth. We have an

[43] This tract is analyzed in the *Corpus Schwenckfeldianorum* I (Leipzig, 1907), 582-83.

[44] I am indebted to Professor George L. Burr for his transcript of these portions from the *Annotationes Othonis Brvnfelsii . . . in quatuor Evangelia & Acta Apostolorum* . . . Argentorati . . . M.D. XXXV (Roth, *op. cit.*, p. 284).

[45] I Cor. 2:18.

[46] Quotation in full, II Tim. 2:24-26.

example again in Christ who tolerated the Pharisees, and commanded his followers to beware of their doctrine, but not to kill them.[47] Some of the parables are also relevant—such as those of the tares and the wheat, and the good and bad fishes—by which Christ shows that unbelievers should be tolerated. I cannot see what other meaning the words of Stephen and Christ can bear. Christ said, "Father, forgive them, for they know not what they do." [48] Stephen said, "Lay not this sin to their charge,[49] because they know not what they do." Nevertheless I do not object if anyone feels that the magistrates, who have the sword as ministers of justice, should punish manifest blasphemers. . . .

What an Erasmian conclusion! Was it meant to nullify all that had gone before, or was it merely a sop for critics?

[47] Many of the texts used in the *Pandects* are here omitted.

[48] Luke 23: 34.

[49] Acts 7: 60. The last clause is mistakenly carried over from the words of Christ.

Protestant Liberals: Independents

WILLIAM COUNT OF HESSE (1532-92)

WILLIAM, count of Hesse, was the son-in-law of Christoph of Württemberg and the son of Philip of Hesse. The dedication of the French translation to William as to a reigning prince in 1554 may occasion surprise, since he did not succeed his father until 1567 when the territory was divided among the four sons and William received Hesse Cassel. The explanation is probably that the major responsibility for the administration of the whole of Hesse fell to him during the five years of his father's captivity, from 1547 to 1552. During the lifetime of his father he is referred to simply as Landgraf Wilhelm.[1]

Both father and son maintained a stalwart liberality toward the Anabaptists, as things then went. Philip of Hesse was under constant pressure from the Saxon princes to exact the death penalty in sections where their authority overlapped, but could never be induced to exceed banishment and imprisonment. In 1545 he wrote to the princes of Saxony that the Anabaptists were not all of one kind, and that their steadfastness in martyrdom served to win converts. Then, after citing the parable of the tares (Matt. 13: 24-30), the rebuke to the disciples who wished to call down fire from heaven (Luke 9: 52-56), and the verses on the sword in Romans (13: 1-5), he continued: "These passages stand in the way so that we cannot feel easy of conscience that a man who errs in faith should be so sharply dealt with, since over night a man may be instructed and turn from his error. If we should condemn

[1] Wigand Lauze, "Leben und Thaten des durchleuchtigsten Fursten und Herren Philippi Magnanimi Landgraffen zu Hessen," *Zeitschrift des Vereins für hessische Geschichte und Landeskunde*, 2tes Suppl., 2 Bd. (Kassel, 1841-47), II, 317, 339, 343, 423. Christoph von Rommel, *Philipp der Grossmüthige Landgraf von Hessen*, 3 vols. (Giessen, 1830), I, 547.

such a one so summarily to death we fear greatly that we should not be innocent of his blood." [2] Again, in a memorandum of 1559 Philip recommended the sword for revolutionists, but unwearying love and patience toward those who merely err in the faith. To put to death men of this sort cannot be justified by means of the Gospel or the Fathers. His attitude to Schwenckfeld, whom he had met, was liberal, though he made no objection to the execution of Servetus about whom he had only the testimony of opponents.[3] Finally in the will of 1562 Philip declared, "We have never put a man to death for incorrect belief, and we urge our sons not to do so, for it is contrary to the Gospel and Augustine and Chrysostom and other teachers as well as the *Tripartita historia*." [4] We recall that there are several citations from these works in the *De haereticis*, in the section by Basil Montfort.

The son William followed the paternal example. During the period of his father's captivity he would inflict no penalty upon Theobald Thamer other than to remove him from his ministerial post with a compensation of fifty gulden pending the return of Philip.[5] During William's own administration the question was raised whether the children of Anabaptists should be forcibly baptized (September 2, 1569). He declared that they should no more receive this treatment than should the children of the Jews and the Turks. "The magistrate must often limit his authority to avoid a worse evil and for the sake of Christian love. That we give com-

[2] Paul Wappler, *Die Stellung Kursachsens und des Landgrafen Philipp von Hessen zur Täuferbewegung* (Münster i. W., 1910), Anhang 1, Nr. 89 (19 Aug. 1545), pp. 232-34. Reformationsgeschichtliche Studien u. Texte, Heft 13 u. 14.

[3] *Melanthonis opera, CR* IX, No. 6704, "Landgraffen Philipps zu Hessen Bedenken auf der Fürsten zu Sachsen confutationes," 1559, die 7 Martii, pp. 752-63.

[4] Johann Christian Lünig, *Des Teutschen Reichs-Archivs*, IX (Leipzig, 1712), p. 778, right col. The passage is cited without the date by Christoph von Rommel, *op. cit.*, II, 341, and from him by Wappler, *op. cit.*, p. 117.

[5] Karl Wilh. Herm. Hochhuth, *Mittheilungen aus der protestantischen Secten-Geschichte in der hessischen Kirche*, I Theil, 3 Abt. "Theobald Thamer u. Landgraf Philipp," *Zeitschrift für die historische Theologie*, XXXI (1861), pp. 165-277, especially pp. 201 and 219.

fort to the Papist rulers when we banish these poor deluded folk and forcibly baptize their children ought to give us serious pause." [6] Protestant minorities oppressed by the Counter-Reformation and Philippists (followers of Philip Melanchthon) belabored by the ultra-orthodox Lutherans elicited his warm sympathy.[7]

SEBASTIAN FRANCK (1499-1542 OR 1543)

Sebastian Franck is one of the most important figures in the *De haereticis*. From him Castellio borrowed citations, references, and ideas. Franck had already gathered in large part the materials used by Castellio from Brenz, Erasmus, Chrysostom, Jerome, Augustine, and Luther. Probably no one, except Erasmus, exerted so marked an influence on Castellio's point of view.

Franck was a disillusioned reformer. Originally a Catholic priest, he became a Lutheran minister; [8] but he was soon alienated because justification by faith did not issue in improvement of life.[9] Like the Anabaptists Franck for a time hoped that the Church might be purified by a rigorous exercise of the ban,[10] but Anabaptism ran into extravagances [11] and Puritanism—"a new monkery," Franck called it.[12] He was disillusioned with regard to all sects and people, himself included.[13] Antichrist, he decided, is everywhere.[14] In 1528 he resigned his ministry and supported himself thereafter by manual labor and extensive publication of varied character, including history, translations, popular handbooks, and

[6] Karl Wilh. Herm. Hochhuth, *Mittheilungen aus der protestantischen Secten-Geschichte in der hessischen Kirche*, I Theil, 2 Abt. "Die Wiedertäufer unter den Söhnen Landgraf Philipps." *Zeitschrift für die historische Theologie*, XXIX (1859), 210-34. The passage translated above is on p. 226. The article is completed in XXX (1860), 258-84. Compare the first article of the series, *Landgraf Philipp u. die Wiedertäufer*, XXVIII (1858), 538-644; XXIX (1859), 167-209.

[7] RE [3] IV, 443-50; VIII, 456; X, 737; XV, 417; XX, 494-95.

[8] For biographical details see Alfred Hegler, RE [3] VI, 142-50.

[9] GB, 396b. The abbreviations for Franck's works are explained in the Appendix.

[10] Paul Joachimsen, "Zur inneren Entwicklung Sebastian Francks," *Blätter f. deutsche Philosophie*, II (Berlin 1928/29), 1-28. On this point, p. 4.

[11] GB, f. 452b.

[12] *Ibid.*, f. 448b.

[13] ME, Bl. 3, reprint p. 13.

[14] GB, f. 255.

works of theology. His radical views rendered his tenure in any place insecure. After two years he was banished from Strassburg and after five, from Ulm. His last days were spent in Basel where he died in his early forties.

Tolerance was primary, not derivative in Franck's system.[15] He was a pacifist like Erasmus.[16] War for Franck is an abomination, a crusade an anomoly,[17] and persecution a crime. The acrimony of the controversy over the Lord's Supper [18] and the execution of more than two thousand Anabaptists [19] revolted him. This was simply wrong. Any theology which supported such procedure must need revision. Franck does not tell us in so many words that the sight of persecution caused him to reëxamine his entire outlook, and doubtless, in any case, so eclectic and independent a spirit would have recast what he derived from others. From Luther he took justification by faith, the method of paradox, and the interpretation of history in terms of the cross; from Erasmus, pacifism; from Denck, the Inward Word; from Erasmus and Zwingli, hospitality to the heathen of classical antiquity. Yet it is striking that the many discrepant elements which Franck gleaned from contemporaries and from the waning Middle Ages [20] were all made to point the moral of religious liberty. Pessimism and optimism, determinism and indeterminism alike served.

Take his pessimism. History for Franck is an eternal Golgotha of the spirit. He went beyond Luther in intensifying the Augustinian conflict of the two societies by interpreting it in terms of the mystic antipodes of spirit and flesh, God and the world, the

[15] Compare Alfred Hegler, *Geist und Schrift bei Sebastian Franck* (Freiburg i. Br., 1892), p. 97.

[16] Witness the *Kriegbüchlein des Friedens.* For passages against war in Franck's other works see Hegler, *op. cit.*, pp. 180-81.

[17] GB, f. 189b. [18] *Ibid.*, f. 441b. [19] *Ibid.*, f. 444b.

[20] See the excellent work of Rudolf Stadelmann, "Vom Geist des ausgehenden Mittelalters: Studien zur Geschichte der Weltanschauung von Nicolaus Cusanus bis Sebastian Franck," *Deutsche Vierteljahrsschrift f. Literaturwissenschaft und Geistesgeschichte*, XV (Halle, 1929). Stadelmann traces the influence on Franck of Cusa, Tauler, the *Theologia Germanica*, the *Devotio moderna*, Italian Neoplatonism, Paracelsus, and Agrippa of Nettesheim.

old Adam and the new, the spirit and the letter. "As the Lamb was slain from the foundation of the world so to the end will it be slaughtered." [21] The cross is always recurring. Wherever Christ is found there also is Caiaphas.[22] The present age is as much responsible for the blood of Christ as the generation which actually put him to death.[23] The true Church is always small and always persecuted.

Who considered the captive Israelites in Egypt as the people of God? Who regarded the despised shepherds as His prophets? Who esteemed Christ, the apostles, and the little congregations of the early Church, composed as they were not of princes, priests, and scribes, but of poor simple folk and fishermen, who esteemed them as the people of God? Nobody, but all the world took them for heretics, and could have no peace until it had filled up the measure of its fathers and cleansed itself in the blood of the heretics in the name, but against the will, of God. The Jews had a command to kill false prophets, but always applied it to the true. So will it ever be with the corrupt world to the end. Christs must be Antichrists, and Antichrists must be Christs. But God reverses everything. Those whom the world curses, persecutes, and executes as Antichrists and heretics, these He recognizes as Christians. He blesses those whom the world curses and curses those whom the world canonizes.[24]

"The characteristic trait of heretics is that they regard all others, and especially Christians, as heretics and denounce and persecute and put them to death." [25]

Franck's pessimism interprets history not only as a poised conflict with the world ever in the ascendent, but also as a progressive deterioration, and this theory also serves the interests of liberty. Church history in the sixteenth century was commonly interpreted as a process of degeneration, though there was great diversity of opinion as to when and how the fall occurred.[26] Franck found it in

[21] GB, f. 335. Translated below, p. 184.
[22] Par., Nos. 15-17, pp. 34-41, and Nos. 234-35, pp. 273-77.
[23] GA, f. 100 a and b.
[24] Par., Nos. 15-17, pp. 38-39, condensed.
[25] WB, 44b-45.
[26] Erich Seeberg, *Gottfried Arnold* (Meerane i. Sa., 1923), Chap. V, § 1: "Verfalls u. Traditionsidee im Mittelalter u. in der alten Kirche." Stadelmann, *op. cit.*, Chap. V, § 1: "Typen der Verfallsauffassung."

the externalization of the Church and in the rise of religious persecution. The degeneration began directly after the days of the apostles,[27] and reached a peak under Pope Pelagius I, who turned over to the civil arm heretics and apostates for their refusal to accept the Roman, which he called the Christian, faith.[28] The corruption was already so great at the time of the conversion of the Franks that their acceptance of Christianity perverted their morals.[29] Franck sympathized with the resistance of the heathen Saxons to Charlemagne's attempts to convert them by force of arms to the Roman faith,[30] and believed that in the century of the Reformation the rabid intolerance of Christian against Christian was greater than that of the Romans against the Christians. Gallio, Festus, Felix, and even Pilate exercised comparative moderation. "Our age fulfills the prediction of Paul (II Tim. 4: 3), 'For the time will come when they will not endure sound doctrine.' As the Jews were zealous for the letter rather than the sense of the law so today men are zealous for the letter of the Gospel against the mind of Christ." [31] The climax is reached in Protestantism which allows less freedom to rebuke the offenses of princes than does the Church of Rome.[32]

Geographical pessimism is added to the historical, perhaps in part as a homiletical device. Franck exalted any culture other than his own. The Turks especially served his purpose, and one of the marks of their superiority was the refusal to force anyone to the faith.[33] Franck is candid enough to record that the Turks persecute their own heretics. Here his tactics change and he uses this example to

[27] Letter to Campanus printed by John George Schelhorn, *Amoenitates literariae,* XI (Frankfurt u. Leipzig, 1729), 59-61, where the letter is wrongly dated 1541 instead of 1531. See Karl Rembert, *Die "Wiedertäufer" im Herzogtum Jülich* (Berlin, 1899), p. 212, n. 2.

[28] GB, f. 461; cf. 283b, and see p. 195, n. 62, below.

[29] Stadelmann, *op. cit.,* p. 181, n. 2, citing from Franck's translation of Trithemius.

[30] Germ. Chr., f. 72b, cf. f. 80. See Arnold Reimann, *Sebastian Franck als Geschichtsphilosoph* (Berlin, 1921), pp. 68-70. Comenius-Schriften zur Geistesgeschichte. Beihefte der Zeitschrift der Comenius-Gesellschaft Geisteskultur und Volksbildung, I.

[31] GB, f. 132 a-b. [32] WB, Vorrede, f. 3b. [33] WB, f. 105a, 120b.

point out that persecution can do no more than drive heresy into hiding.[34]

Along with this pessimism as to his own time and land, Franck has an equally profound optimism. Man is by nature good. The fall of Adam corrupted merely man's characteristics, not his substance.[35] In spite of all revulsion against the vulgar rabble, Franck saw an element of the divine in all men, even in those who have no direct experience of Christ. "So far as human language can describe it, the Word of God is nothing other than an emanation, essence, outpouring, image, picture, and appearance of God in all creatures, but especially in all surrendered hearts . . . illumining and teaching men from the beginning, Adam, Abel, Noah, Lot, Abraham, Job, Trismegistus, Mercury, Plotinus, Cornelius, and all the godly heathen." [36] Even when emphasizing the necessity of the repetition of the cross in the experience of the Christian, Franck could draw illustrations from the sacrificial deaths of Socrates and Regulus.[37] This universal theism enabled him to find fellows everywhere.

> Wherefore my heart is alien to none. I have my brothers among the Turks, Papists, Jews, and all peoples. Not that they are Turks, Jews, Papists, and Sectaries or will remain so; in the evening they will be called into the vineyard and given the same wage as we. From the East and from the West children of Abraham will be raised up out of the stones and will sit down with him at God's table.[38]

Free will and determinism are similarly handmaids of liberty. Indeterminism is relevant because it shows that God Himself is averse to constraint. He will not force a man against his will, but seeks to win by persuasion and attraction.[39] "Where the Spirit of God is, there is freedom—no constraint, tyranny, partisanship, or

[34] WB, f. 113a.

[35] BW, f. 104b, cited by H. W. Erbkam, *Geschichte der protestantischen Sekten im Zeitalter der Reformation* (Hamburg und Gotha, 1848), p. 331; GA, f. 95; Edw. Tausch, *Sebastian Franck von Donauwörth und seine Lehre* (Halle, 1893), Chap. V.

[36] BW, f. 164-66b, cited by Erbkam, *op. cit.*, p. 328-29.

[37] GA, f. 267.

[38] VB, f. 429.

[39] Cf. Hegler, *Geist u. Schrift*, pp. 138-46. Tausch, *op. cit.*, Chap. VIII.

compulsion, that He should drag anyone to heaven by the hair or push anyone into hell and deprive him of the grace which is extended to all men. Man alone deprives himself of it."[40] "God is not moved by his enemies to slay them, for He is immovable, a firm mountain of goodness and love. If we renounce Him he lets us go unconsoled until we are wrecked upon Him. Then we say that He has slain us, whereas we have rushed to our own death. The immovable God overcomes us with patience. No, He does not overcome us, but we run upon Him to our destruction and are overcome of ourselves."[41]

But although Franck allows freedom to the individual—or does he?—in spite of all freedom God's will comes to pass, and without Him we cannot raise a finger.[42] Not infrequently one suspects that Franck maintains the fiction of freedom merely to save God from the exercise of constraint. At any rate the course of history is not free. Degeneration is the law. "They have a foolish zeal who think they can make this devil's pigsty and perverted Babylon into a paradise and bring everything into order. It cannot be done. The devil's kingdom must remain to the end, confused and dark, full of lies, disorder and injustice. . . . We try to improve things, but in vain. Experience has taught me this and has cooled my unseasonable zeal." The moral is to leave things alone. "Cast not your pearls."[43]

Another determinism applies to the intellect and moral conviction. Although God does not force men to the faith, yet "God's Word grips and holds the heart so mightily that though a man would oppose his heart he must nevertheless conclude and say, 'It is so and must be so and not otherwise.' "[44] Hence the futility of forced conversions.[45]

Such discrepancies were too glaring to escape Franck's attention. He worked out a theory of knowledge to meet them, and this in

[40] Par., Nos. 264-68, p. 335.
[41] Par., Nos. 12-13, p. 29.
[42] Par., Nos. 264-68, p. 325.
[43] WB, f. 158 a-b.
[44] BW, f. 150, cited by Hegler, *Geist und Schrift*, p. 98, who refers to this tract as "Enc."
[45] WB, f. 113b-114a.

turn served as a basis for religious liberty. Truth, according to Franck, can be expressed only in the form of a paradox. God is angry, and He is passionless. He is never so near as when he is far. The Christian hates all men and loves all men. He who breaks the law keeps the law, and so on.[46] Franck had learned his method in part from Luther who was fond of saying that God is both hidden and revealed; the Christian is of all men the most bound and the most free, and so on. But Franck's paradoxes were more far-reaching. Luther could find clarity in Scripture, even though God is obscure. Erasmus could find clarity in God, even though Scripture is obscure. Franck saw paradox everywhere. The difficulty may be resolved by assuming a difference in perspective. Some propositions are both true and false, depending on the angle from which they are viewed whether it be human or divine. Yet the paradox remains, for the perspective itself is true for man, but false for God.[47] The moral is that when any man is unduly devoted to the letter of a particular passage of Scripture he is to be detached by a contradictory passage. Christ did not allegorize when the devil quoted to him the 91st Psalm, but confronted Scripture with Scripture.[48]

These discrepant elements, as well as the attempt at synthesis, all served for Franck the cause of liberty. There was no inherent reason for this. Determinism and pessimism are associated with persecution in the cases of Augustine, Luther, and Calvin; indeterminism and optimism in the case of the Catholic Church. The theology of dialectic is professed by one of the most intolerant of modern schools. They might learn from Franck that the light that lighteth every man that cometh into the world is not only false, but also true. For Franck tolerance was primary.

For that reason he could not content himself with these inci-

[46] The *Paradoxa* and *Das verbütschiert mit siben Sigeln verschlossen Bůch* are collections of antitheses of this sort.

[47] Compare two articles in the *Blätter für deutsche Philosophie*, II (Berlin, 1928/29): Gerhard Lehmann, "Realdialektick und Subjectivitätsprinzip in Francks Religionsphilosophie," pp. 29-40; A. v. Grolman, "Das Wissen und das Verhältnismässige in der Paradoxie des Seins," pp. 57-72.

[48] VB, f. 400 a-b.

dental confirmations of his position, but worked out a positive theory of religious liberty by an attack upon the prevailing conceptions of heresy and of the Church.[49] For his own attitude two presuppositions were determinative. The first was a rejection of the authority of Rome. The weapons of the humanists and reformers became more effective in the hands of one who stood squarely on the ground broken by Luther. The second principle was an adherence to the religion of the Spirit. By this standard everything must be measured. Franck's consistency in this regard carried him to the end of the road forsaken by Luther.

In the light of this criterion heresy becomes simply an "obstinate rejection of the sense of Scripture demanded by the Spirit which wrote the Scripture." [50] "Heretics are those who separate from the congregation of God and sever the bonds of love on account of externals which have no significance save as symbols of love." [51] How can heresy be a rejection of an article of the faith when the only faith that matters is "a living faith active through love, which crucifies the flesh and is at enmity with the world, which looks only to God, renounces all and fulfills all law, yea, that of the Holy Spirit"? [52] Or how can heresy be a rejection of some statement of the Scripture so long as the Bible is a book sealed with seven seals which no man can open, unless he have the key of David, which is the illumination of the Spirit through the way of the cross? [53]

Since this witness of the Spirit is the one essential, the points around which the controversies of the day raged were to Franck irrelevant. This was his formulation of the problem of the fundamentals. Cusa, Erasmus, Castellio, and Acontius endeavored to reduce to a minimum the number of beliefs essential to salvation, that the sphere of controversy might be restricted. Franck was not interested in the number. The whole attempt to formulate a theology in articles was for him an idle performance. He was an

[49] Cf. Lotte Blaschke, "Der Toleranzgedanke bei Sebastian Franck," *Blätter für deutsche Philosophie*, II (Berlin, 1928/29), 40-56.

[50] GB, f. 453b. [51] *Ibid.*, f. 453. [52] WB, f. 123b.

[53] VB, Vorrede and f. 412b; cf. f. 401 a-b.

extreme disciple of the *ignorantia sacra,* and gained great comfort from the lament of Erasmus that "when faith came to be in writings rather than in hearts, then there were almost as many faiths as men." [54] "The theology of the world is nothing but an idle quibble about Moses' grave . . . about ceremonies and elements, whether leavened bread may be consecrated, whether Mary was conceived in sin, whether she may be called the Mother of God, questions which are *not necessary for salvation, but are rather detrimental.*" [55] God help us, what debates there are as to the four and a half weeks in Daniel, the genealogy of Christ, as to the necessity of dying first in order to be present at the last judgment, as to the distinction of the persons in the Trinity and of the natures in Christ." [56] "The cross alone is the Christian's theology." [57] "Yet today Christians drag Christians before the judgment seat, if a man but opens his mouth to doubt a single article of the Church, yes, over a mere dove-dropping." [58]

If all the points which divide the sects and religions are really unessential, it must, of course, be because God regards them so. Franck's theory of tolerance is rooted in his view of God, who is nonpartisan. He elected Israel as a chosen people merely to aid the rest. "Today the impartial God loves all men alike, cordially, without regard to person, name, or people, the heathen as the Jew. . . . Every sect swears a thousand oaths, like the Jews, that the God of all peoples belongs to it alone." [59] "God and love without favoritism love all alike. . . . Love is such a fool that it cannot but love all, the same, especially that which is lost." [60] "The Turk and the heathen are made in the image of God as much as the

[54] Ep. 1334, V, 176.142 ff. Franck's statement is in Alfred Hegler, *Beiträge zur Geschichte der Mystik in der Reformationszeit* (Berlin, 1906), p. 175. Edited by Walther Köhler in ARG, Ergänzungsband I; referred to hereafter as *Beiträge.*

[55] Par., Nos. 200-203, p. 248. I have inverted the order. Italics mine.

[56] BW, f. 114b, cited by A. Koyré, "Sébastien Franck," *Revue d'histoire et de philosophie religieuse,* XI, No. 4-5 (Juillet-Octobre, 1931), 353-85. This passage is on page 355, n. 9. The form of his reference is *Morie enkomion* 114b.

[57] GA, f. 245b.

[58] GB, f. 132b.

[59] Par., No. 82, pp. 104-5.

[60] *Ibid.,* Nos. 227-29, pp. 267-68.

German, and the nonpartisan God has written His law and word in their hearts."[61] Franck is but imitating God when he says, "I am by God's grace not so sectarian as not to hold every man as a brother, as my own flesh and blood, provided he holds me for one and does not separate from me."[62]

The religion of the Spirit is the primary element in Franck's system which undermines the current conception of heresy. But the religion of the Spirit by itself would not have been sufficient to overcome intolerance. Some of the Anabaptists were so sure of their revelations that they could demand an unqualified submission to their authority. Franck was prevented from such dogmatism by a touch of the rational and the ethical. These elements are but slight in his system. His appropriation of Agrippa of Nettesheim's attack on the "Vanity of All Human Disciplines" applies only to the natural man,[63] and although the spirits must be proved, the test is itself spiritual. To the objection that the Spirit will lead men in diverse directions Franck replied that each must interpret according to the Spirit, and afterwards we must prove the spirits "whether they are of God and whether they *bear witness to and agree with our heart*."[64] Yet in one passage Franck voices a genuine doubt as to the ability of even the twice-born man to attain perfect certainty. "We know in part. Socrates was right, that we know only that we do not know. We may be heretics quite as much as our opponents."[65] The ethical emphasis comes to the fore when Franck remarks, "Every man is dear to me who pants after God and lives uprightly. I do not ask what he believes, but how he lives."[66]

The religion of the Spirit is fatal alike to heresy defined in terms of dogma and to the Church as a cultural institution allied with the State and coterminous with the community. "It does not seem to me good," wrote Franck, "to establish the peace of the Church, like that of the world, with the sword as Charlemagne

[61] WB, Vorrede, f. iij; cf. GA, f. 96a. [62] Par., Vorrede, p. 9.
[63] ME, f. 36, reprint p. 82; Hegler, *Beiträge*, p. 167; GA, f. 81a.
[64] VB, f. 415b, italics mine. [65] GB, Vorrede, f. aiij.
[66] Hegler, *Beiträge*, p. 194.

did the papacy, to force men into one fold of the faith by necessity, since faith is a gift of the heart, conscience, and spirit. It is not every man's affair. Force can no more touch it than conquer the wind." [67]

The religion of the Spirit, however, is compatible with a community of the saints which may be very intolerant in attitude. Franck was not altogether hostile to the formation of such a group. Now and again in his writings he suggests that the Church be kept pure by the ban.[68] But he was prevented from going far in this direction by his universalism. Even the kingdom of the saints needs some dogmatic basis, but Franck universalized the Christian drama of redemption. The incarnation, the atonement, the crucifixion, are not isolated facts of history, but continually recurring experiences vouchsafed also to those outside the professedly Christian fold.[69] To bring together those who have had this experience into any sort of organization would be exceedingly difficult. At times Franck entertained the thought of a spiritual Church, to be assembled from the ends of the earth.[70] Though, again, he declared that he looked for no new Church to be established by the Spirit, because the Church is not bound to time and place, "but is a spiritual, invisible body of all the members of Christ, born of God in one mind, spirit, and faith, not in one city or place outwardly assembled . . . a community in which we believe and do not see save with the eye of insight and of the inner man." [71] Franck's individualism stood in the way of the formation of any Church. He lamented the dependence of those who feel that they cannot have a true faith without a large following. Let them remember Daniel in Babylon and Naaman in Syria.[72]

One may wonder why Franck did not become a hermit. Had he been a Catholic he probably would have done so, but he was restrained from this course by acceptance of Luther's repudiation

[67] Hegler, *Beiträge*, p. 171.

[68] See p. 93, n. 10, above.

[69] GA, f. 41; Par., Nos. 83-85, pp. 108, 112. Cf. Hegler, *Geist und Schrift*, pp. 143, 194-223.

[70] *Chronica und Beschreibung der Türkey* (Nürnberg, 1530), f. Kiij b, cited by Hegler, *Geist und Schrift*, pp. 49-50.

[71] Par., Vorrede, p. 9.

[72] GB, Vorrede, f. aij b.

of monasticism.[73] Franck's only recourse was to make a cloister of his own heart.[74]

SEBASTIAN CASTELLIO

Sebastian Castellio's theory of religious liberty need not detain us long in spite of its importance, partly because he speaks for himself at length in the present work and partly because he is dealt with elsewhere.[75] Suffice it here to emphasize his indebtedness to Erasmus and to Sebastian Franck, and to comment briefly on the tract *Concerning Doubt and Belief, Ignorance and Knowledge.*

With Erasmus Castellio took an optimistic view of man's capacity and God's judgments. The simple, undogmatic piety of the *Devotio moderna* appealed to them both. Devotion to Biblical criticism they have in common, though Castellio was ready to draw more radical inferences. The authority of the Church lay no longer in reserve, and Castellio was prepared to relinquish even the authority of Scripture if compelled by the facts.

With Sebastian Franck and Luther, too, Castellio saw the persecution of the minority as the law of history. More especially from Franck he drew his picture of religion as an affair of the spirit which eludes the sword of the magistrate.

The tract *Concerning Doubt and Belief, Ignorance and Knowledge* calls for a word of introduction. The sceptical utterances of the *De haereticis*[76] were declared by Beza to be diametrically opposed to the Christian religion. "If such a view were accepted Christianity would perish from its very foundations. On what basis can the Church rest if the firmness of the Word of God be removed by someone who would make it too obscure for the settlement of religious controversies?"[77]

[73] Par., Nos. 227-29, pp. 269-70. [74] GB, f. 465 a-b.

[75] Roland H. Bainton, "Sebastian Castellio and the Toleration Controversy of the Sixteenth Century," in *Persecution and Liberty*, pp. 183-209. I am contributing a chapter on the tract *De arte dubitandi et sciendi* to a forthcoming Festschrift.

[76] See pp. 215, 218, 229-30, below.

[77] *De Haereticis a ciuili Magistratu puniendis Libellus*, p. 66. See below, p. 107, n. 1.

There was enough truth in such a criticism to rankle. Castellio found himself faced with the problem of demolishing the grounds of Calvin's terrific assurance without disintegrating all religious knowledge in the process. The initial attack was directed against Calvin's equation of faith and knowledge. In the *Institutes* Calvin declares that faith is certitude, though not apprehension, and may be equated with knowledge. He uses four Latin words which are difficult to differientiate in English, *agnitio, cognitio, notitia,* and *scientia.*[78] The next point of attack was Calvin's picture of the vitiation of the human intellect by the fall of Adam.[79]

Castellio's own system of religious knowledge posits three sources, sense experience, reason, and revelation. He is on Stoic ground at this point and drew probably from Cicero. The defense of the validity of sense experience [80] might well have been taken from Cicero's reply to the Academics,[81] and the praise of reason [82] combines the early Patristic use of the logos doctrine [83] with Ciceronian strains.[84] The assertion of Castellio that reason "worked upon the Sabbath" [85] is probably a rebuttal of Calvin's statement that reason balks at the creation of the world in six days until it learns to submit to faith and enjoy a Sabbath rest.[86]

Castellio unfortunately nowhere defines reason, but his meaning can be inferred from his practice. One characteristic of reason is that it is universal. It is that to which all men everywhere assent. Hence the employment [87] of Cicero's inference of the existence of God from universal consent.[88] Reason, again, is that which is in accord with nature, a favorite conception of the Stoics and

[78] *Calvini opera,* II, 399-410, *Instit.,* III, ii, 2-14. For the place of Calvin's religious epistemology in the history of Christian thought consult Karl Heim, *Das Gewissheitsproblem in der systematischen Theologie bis zu Schleiermacher.* Leipzig, 1911.

[79] *Calvini opera,* II, 186-209, *Instit.* II, ii.

[80] Pages 298-99, below.

[81] *Lucullus,* 7.

[82] Page 297, below.

[83] Justin Martyr, "Apology I," xlvi, 1-4: Migne, PG VI, 397; ANF I, 178; "Apology II," xiii: PG VI, 465; ANF I, 192-93.

[84] *De legibus* II, iv, 9-10; *De finibus* II, xii, 37; *De natura deorum* II, xiii.

[85] Page 297, below.

[86] *Calvini opera,* II, 118, *Instit.,* I, xiv, 2.

[87] Page 302, below.

[88] *De natura deorum* I, 16.

their disciple, Cicero.[89] Nature for Castellio, be it observed, is the state of innocence enjoyed by Adam before the fall,[90] and not the condition of the *bon sauvage* of the eighteenth century Enlightenment.

A further characteristic of reason is a certain anti-intellectualism, if you please. The reasonable involves no intricate processes of thought and lies within the compass of the publicans, the sinners, and the penitent thief.[91] Here Castellio is the heir of the *docta ignorantia* and the *sacra ignorantia* of the fifteenth century.[92] Finally, reason involves Biblical criticism. Here it is that Castellio comes most intimately to grips with Calvin and here it is that he is most successful in undermining that assurance which could banish a Bolsec for a denial of predestination and burn a Servetus for a misinterpretation of the Trinity.

[89] *De legibus* I, xxi, 56; *Tusc.*, IV, xxi, 47.
[90] Page 301, below. [91] Pages 303-304, below.
[92] Consult Rudolf Stadelmann, *Vom Geist des ausgehenden Mittelalters.* Halle, 1929.

The Influence of the De haereticis

THE first response to the *De haereticis* was a vigorous refutation from the pen of Theodore Beza. Calvin had already published a defense of the execution of Servetus. Now his colleague at Lausanne took up the cudgels.[1] Beza had not the slightest difficulty in showing that the excerpts in the *De haereticis* were not representative of the opinions of Luther, Brenz, and Rhegius,[2] and that Erasmus was protesting merely against Papist cruelty.[3] Beza also found it easy to show that the authors of this "hodgepodge" had not thought through the implications of their statements for a theory of Church and State. If we are to imitate the clemency of Christ to the letter, what becomes of the State? Could the magistrate hang a thief? [4] If conscience is absolutely inviolable, what is the State to do with a conscientious objector to military service? [5] Or with a conscientious homicide who commits human sacrifice in response to a divine revelation? Readiness to die for an opinion does not prove that it is correct. The Jews will die for a false Messiah, the Mohammedans for Mohammed, the Papists for transubstantiation, and the Anabaptists for community of wives and goods.[6] Is the magistrate to interfere with none of them because they are equally conscientious? With regard to the Church, these sceptics must realize that their program would mean a complete disintegration. Schwenckfelders, Servetians, Osiandrians, and others, would initiate their own denominations which in turn would develop dissenters *ad infinitum*. The Church in her distress cannot expect to be succored by an angel, but must turn for assistance to

[1] *De Haereticis a ciuili Magistratu puniendis Libellus, aduersus Martini Bellii farraginem, & nouorum Academicorum sectam, Theodoro Beza Vezelio auctore.* Oliua Roberti Stephani. M. D. LIIII.

[2] Pages 201-2 and 32-34. [3] Pages 34-35.

[4] Page 102. [5] Page 95. [6] Page 72.

the magistrate.[7] The parable of the tares, said Beza, is a counsel of hope, and not a law for ecclesiastical or civil discipline. By this excellent piece of exegesis the decks were cleared for persecution.[8]

But Beza entirely missed the force of Castellio's definition of heresy and repeated again the old definitions and distinctions of heresy, infidelity, error, schism, and the like. The plea that we do not know enough to settle the controverted points touched Beza to invective rather than argument. The attempt of Castellio to reduce the number of the fundamentals elicited the following blast:[9]

> There is one way that leads to God, namely, Christ; and one way that leads to Christ, namely, faith; and this faith includes all those dogmas which you reject as unnecessary. O Lord, do Thou drive far from Thy flock all those pests and whited wolves who deny Thee and say that Thy state and office are not necessary. . . . Bellius says that the publicans and sinners were saved without this condition. O unheard-of impudence! Saved by Him on whom they had not called? Did they call on Him in whom they did not believe? Did they believe in Him whom they had not known? . . . You do not want to know where Christ is, what he is doing, and how he is seated at the right hand of God the Father. In vain, then, it is written that we have a high priest who will enter the heavens above every principality and power, virtue and dominion, and every name that is named. . . . You number the Trinity among the matters which need not be known and if known make a man no better. What can we call you but new devils who would drive God from the throne? . . . O Athanasius, you who stood against the world, you who gave your creed with such wonderful brevity, I ask you, cannot we prove from Scripture that Christ is one with the Father and that three hypostases may be distinguished in one essence? . . . This, you say, makes a man no better. O blasphemy! O sacrilege! . . . We should have to cut out the prologue of John. . . . We should have to give up the beginning of Romans. If these are gone, where is our faith and consolation? . . . If Christ is not true God, coeternal and consubstantial with the Father, how is He our Savior? How is He our sanctifier? How is He victor over sin, death, and the devil? Unless He is true man, save for sin, how is He our mediator?

Beza was especially incensed by the comparison of Calvin's Christ to a Moloch ready to burn those who in the midst of the flames call upon His name. "Would you say that God was a Moloch

[7] Pages 187-88. [8] Pages 140-155. [9] Pages 48-53.

for swallowing up Dathan and Abiron? God is not a Moloch but a vindicator of His majesty." [10] And as for calling upon Christ in the midst of the flames,

Servetus on the point of death was exhorted with tears to confess that Christ is the eternal Son of God, but he would say only that Christ is the Son of the eternal God. And when the inadequacy of this statement was pointed out to him he preferred to be silent rather than give due honor to the Son of God. Do you consider this calling upon the name of Christ? Never. . . . Your accusation does not touch us.[11]

But in spite of Beza's protest, perhaps in part because of it, the influence of the *De haereticis* began speedily to ramify. In the year after the publication of both books, that is, in 1555, a Calvinist minister in Montbéliard, an appanage of Württemberg, complained to the count of a very cold reception at the hands of the Bellianists. One of the worst offenders was Jacques Gète, who was singing the praises and circulating the books of Bellius. "They complain that I am a troubler of Israel, but it is not I who trouble Israel, but those who are clad in the white robe of Bellius." [12] Pierre Toussain, the leading reformer of the district, took the side of Gète and thereby suffered a rupture of his old friendship with Farel and Calvin. The former complained that Toussain would prefer to have his ministers "Academics" (this was the term which Beza had applied to Bellius) than Christians.[13] In an ecclesiastical synod Toussain declined to condemn the work of Bellius and was commended by Count George on the ground that ministers have something more to do than to condemn books.[14]

Calvin took fright when he discovered in the same year that the *De haereticis* had been carried to Poitiers in France by a disciple of Castellio, a certain De la Vau. To the reformed congregation at Poitiers, Calvin wrote:

[10] Page 105. [11] Page 99, condensed.

[12] *Calvini opera,* XV, 460-64, Ep. 2128 (March 1, 1555).

[13] *Calvini opera,* XV, 509, Ep. 2153 (March 21, 1555).

[14] John Viénot, *Histoire de la réforme dans le pays de Montbéliard depuis les origines jusqu'à la mort de P. Toussain 1524-1573,* 2 vols. (Montbéliard, 1900), I, 204; cf., pp. 195-208.

> The three [Castellio, Curio, and Borrhaus to whom De la Vau appeals] agree like cats and dogs, but they have conspired on one point, namely, that heretics should not be punished. This they have done in order to gain opportunity to disgorge whatever they like. . . . For that reason they have published this fine book on not burning heretics. The names of places and persons are falsified because the book is a hodgepodge of insufferable blasphemies. They say that if Jesus Christ wished to punish those who blaspheme him he would be another Moloch, that controversies should not be interfered with, because nothing can be settled since Scripture is a nose of wax, so much so, in fact, that the beliefs of all Christians in the Trinity, predestination, and free justification are nonessentials to be debated at pleasure.[15]

The debate of Beza and Bellius repeated itself in the Grisons in 1570 between Egli and Gantner. The latter defended the view that the magistrate should suppress only those Anabaptists who actually disturb the peace, and for support cited the opinions of Augustine, Jerome, Tertullian, Brenz, Erasmus, and Sebastian Franck.[16] This material was taken from the *De haereticis*, for Bullinger, in supplying Egli with Beza's refutation, remarked that the use of "Wittlingius" for "Brenz" and the other pseudonyms of Montfort betrayed a lack of confidence in the cogency of the argument.[17] The case came before the civil authorities, but Gantner could not be dislodged. Egli complained that "There is no magistrate with enough piety toward God to treat these patrons of heretics in the proper fashion." [18] In 1574 he reported: "Gantner's teaching that no one should be compelled to faith has taken root. The magistrate punishes no one." [19]

[15] *Calvini opera*, XV, 441, Ep. 2118 (Feb. 20, 1555). Cf. Ferdinand Buisson, *Sébastien Castellion*, II, 248 f., and Charles Bost, "Sébastien Castellion et l'opposition protestante contre Calvin," *Revue de theologie et de philosophie*, N. S., No. 10 (Lausanne, Juillet, 1914), pp. 301-21.

[16] Traugott Schiess, *Bullingers Korrespondenz mit den Graubündnern*, 3 vols. (Basel, 1904-6), III, 222, 228, 252. Quellen zur schweizer Geschichte XXIII-XXV.

[17] Walther Köhler, *Bibliographia Brentiana* (Berlin, 1904), No. 926. The reference to Montfort is omitted in the summary of Schiess, *op. cit.*, p. 227. Cf. *ibid.*, p. 240.

[18] *Ibid.*, p. 429.

[19] *Ibid.*, p. 500. References to this affair run through nearly three hundred

In the meantime the controversy was being carried on by the Italian exiles and bore fruit in the book of Minus Celsus, *Whether Heretics Should Be Subject to Capital Punishment*.[20] The work was a more extensive compilation than the *De haereticis*, from which many sections were incorporated bodily. Evidently the works of Sebastian Franck were not directly consulted, since he appears under the pseudonym "Augustinus Eleutherius." [21] Minus Celsus must have used the *Traité des hérétiques*, the only version which has the full quota of excerpts from Hedio, Agricola, Schenck, and Hoffmann.[22]

In Germany we find the *De haereticis* employed in 1557 by the intrepid Katherine Zell, widow of the minister Matthew Zell, in her remonstrance to one of the pastors who wished to persecute Zwinglians, Schwenckfeldians, and Anabaptists.

---

pages of Bullinger's correspondence. See the Index. An account of the controversy is given in Buisson, *op. cit.*, II, pp. 298-305. The letters were available only in manuscript when he wrote.

[20] The work bore the title, *In haereticis coercendis quatenus progredi liceat Mini Celsi Senensis disputatio. Ubi nominatim eos ultimo supplicio affici non debere aperte demonstratur*. Christlingae, anno MDLXXVII.

The copy described by M. Bernus in Buisson, *op. cit.*, II, 310, n. 2, is now at Cornell. The library at Zürich has another copy which has two more pages. Cornell has also an edition of 1584 of which George L. Burr writes me: "The so-called edition of 1584 is not a new impression, but only a device (then a very common one) to work off the old stock. Of its 283 leaves, all but the first eight and those following fol. 223 were printed for the original edition, the broken type being the same in both and the 'errata' identical. In other words, in the so-called edition of 1584, one has entire the original edition of 1577 except that the title-page is changed and that, for the *praefatio ad lectorem* of Fischart (for the 'I. F. D. M. D.' who writes it can, of course, be no other than he) is substituted an *epistola dedicatoria* from one 'Valens Titius Ligius' to one 'Christophorus Cnipius Saxo.' But the latter is a transparent fraud; for it is only a working over of Fischart's preface, much of which is retained intact, and its pretense that the type has been reset, and the letters of Beza and Dudith newly added, is clearly false. The 1584 copy is complete, containing at the end the letters of Beza and Dudith, a list of sources and of texts, and a useful index, while our copy of the original edition of 1577 lacks at the end all after fol. 229, i.e., all after the close of Mino Celso's treatise."

[21] P. 128b.

[22] *Ibid.*, pp. 117b-18b. The German translation *Von Ketzeren* has Hedio and Agricola, though not Schenck and Hoffmann.

You hound the magistrate [she charged] against the poor Anabaptists as against a boar or a hare. Yet these folk agree with us on the main point of the redemption of Christ on which we separated from the papacy. Because of divergence on other points should they be persecuted and Christ in them, whom they confess with zeal in the midst of imprisonment, fire, and water? You are the cause of their separation from us on the ground of our life and doctrine. Let the magistrate punish the evildoer, but not constrain faith, which belongs to the heart and conscience and not to the outward man. Read all the old authorities, and those who have recently restored the Gospel among us, our dear Luther, and Brenz who still lives. . . . Read the book of that good man, Martin Bellius, addressed to Duke Christoph of Württemberg, when poor Servetus was burned at Geneva. . . . The good Samaritan did not ask the man who fell among thieves to what denomination he belonged, but put him on his beast.[23]

In Scotland, in 1560, John Knox felt constrained to reply to an Anabaptist whom he described as a disciple of Castellio. This anonymous champion of liberty declared that the blood of Servetus cried for vengeance. The persecutors have disclosed their motive as malice rather than "humane infirmitie" in that

they have, for a perpetuall memorie of their crueltie sett furth bookes, affirming it to be lawfull to persecute and put to death such as dissent from them in controversies of religion, whome they cal blasphemers of God. Notwithstanding they, afore they came to autoritie, they were of an other judgment, and did bothe say and write, that no man ought to be persecuted for his conscience saik; but now they are not onely become persecutors, but also they have given, as far as lieth in them, the sword into the hands of bloodie tyrantes. Be these, I pray you, the shepe whom Christ sent furth in the middest of wolves? can the shepe persecute the wolf? doth Abel kill Cayn? doeth David (thogh he might) kill Saul? Shortly, doeth he which is born of the Spirit kill him which is born after the fleshe? Mark how ye be fallen into most abhominable tyranny, and yet ye see it not.

All of this sounds very much like the *De haereticis* and we are not surprised to hear Knox answer, "Trew it is, that bookes are

[23] Katherine Zell to Ludwig Rabus (March 24, 1557), in Johann Conrad Füssli, *Beyträge zur Erläuterung der Kirchen-Reformations-Geschichten des Schweitzerlandes* (Zürich, 1753), V, Br. IV, pp. 237-77, especially 273-76.

written bothe by you and by us. For your Master Bellius affirmeth, That lawfull it is not to the Civil magistrat to use the sworde against heretikes. To whom that godlie learned man, Theodorus Beza, hath answered." [24]

In England our authors were brought into a controversy, precipitated in 1560 by the command of Elizabeth that all the Anabaptists leave the realm within twenty days. The pastor of the Dutch refugee congregation, Adriaan van Haemstede, protested on the ground that the Anabaptist doctrine of the flesh of Christ touched only the nonessentials, and not the fundamentals, of the Christian religion.[25] The pastor of the French refugee congregation at London, Des Gallars, attacked him as a disciple of Franck, Castellio, and Curio.[26] A definite employment of the *De haereticis*, however, I fear cannot be based on the evidence cited by Van Schelven. He calls attention to the fact that Haemstede's party was accused of raising the question whether "the color of the robe was red or white." [27] The point, however, was not that of Bellius as to the importance of wearing the white robe of Christ, but

[24] *An Answer to a great nomber of blasphemous cauillations written by an Anabaptist and aduersarie to Gods eternal Predestination and confvted by Iohn Knox, minister of Gods worde in Scotland.* Crespin M. D. LX and London, 1591. Reprinted in *The Works of John Knox*, ed. David Laing, V (Edinburgh, 1856), the above passages on pp. 207, 208, 229.

[25] The controversy is discussed by F. de Schickler, *Les Églises de refuge en Angleterre*, 3 vols. (Paris, 1892), I, 117-21, and by A. A. Van Schelven, *De Nederduitsche Vluchtelingenkerken der XVIe Eeuw in Engeland en Duitschland* (The Hague, 1909), pp. 144-52. The documents are in *Ecclesiae Londino-Batavae archivvm*, II. *Epistulae et tractatvs cvm reformationis tvm ecclesiae Londino-Batavae historiam illvstrantes* (1544-1622), ed. Joannes Henricvs Hessels (Cambridge, 1889), especially numbers 46, 47, 49, 53, 54, 66 and 73. There are further documents in A. A. Van Schelven, *Kerkeraads-Protocollen der Nederduitsche Vluchtelingen-Kerk te Londen 1560-1563* (Amsterdam, 1921). Werken uitgegeven door het Historisch Genootschap, III Ser., No. 43. The case occupies most of the documents for 1560-61.

[26] *Calvini opera*, XVIII, 367, Ep. 3341 (Feb. 14, 1561). Cf. pp. 174-75, Ep. 3241 (Sept. 6, 1560).

[27] "De Opkomst van de Idee der politieke Tolerantie in de 16e eeuwsche Nederlanden," *Tijdschrift voor Geschiedenis*, XLVI, 4 (1931), Pt. 2, p. 337, n. 2, citing his work listed above, *Kerkeraads-Protocollen*, p. 454, with which compare pp. 31, 452.

rather that the controversy with the Anabaptists about the nature of the flesh of Christ is as trivial as a discussion of the color of the wedding garment.[28] Bellius expresses the same thought by a comparison with the controversy over the hour of baptism or the image on the gold coin, but neither thought nor language demonstrates a literary relationship.

Dependence is more probable in the case of one who broke a lance for Haemstede, the Italian Jacob Acontius. To Archbishop Grindal he pointed out that no article of faith had been called into question. The only doubt was whether a belief in the incarnation is necessary for salvation. Was not Zwingli himself willing to admit Socrates and others to salvation, although ignorant on this point? [29] Here we have the question which Curio had brought into such prominence. Acontius had been in Basel and almost certainly knew both Curio and Castellio. Here it was that, in 1565, he brought out his famous plea for religious liberty entitled, *On the Wiles of Satan.*[30] In this case it is impossible to establish a direct literary dependence, but the work of Acontius certainly moves in the same circle of ideas.

The influence of our book, however, was not marked in the England of this period. Jordan asserts that the work had little effect until after the appearance of the Dutch translation in 1610,[31] but unfortunately he cites no specific instances after that date. I am able to supply but one. In Potter's *Charity Maintained by Catholics* (chap. iii, § 19), which is incorporated for purposes of

[28] This appears more clearly in *Ecclesiae Londino-Batavae archivvm*, II, 203, Quinto: "non referre cuius sit coloris vestis Regia et litigantes de carne Christj, militibus de tunica Christi alea ludentibus comparando, ceterisque huiusmodi."

[29] *Ecclesiae Londino-Batavae archivvm*, II, No. 73, and again in *Jacobi Acontii Satanae stratagematum libri octo* . . . curavit Gualtherus Koehler (Monaci, 1927), pp. 235-42, especially p. 242.

[30] *Jacobi Acontii Satanae stratagematum libri octo* . . . curavit Gualtherus Koehler (Monaci, 1927). There is a summary of the content in W. K. Jordan, *The Development of Religious Toleration in England from the Beginning of the English Reformation to the Death of Queen Elisabeth* (Cambridge, Mass., 1932), pp. 315-65.

[31] *Op. cit.*, p. 159. What is the authority for this date? Buisson, *op. cit.*, II, 363, says *vers 1620.*

commentary in William Chillingworth's *Religion of Protestants* (Oxford, 1638, p. 126) appears this statement, "Some, as *Castalio*, and the whole Sect of the Academicall Protestants, hold, that doctrines about the Supper, Baptisme, the state and office of Christ, how He is one with His Father, the Trinity, Predestination and divers other such questions, are not necessary to Salvation."

The greatest influence of our book was to be exerted in Holland. In 1566, Beza wrote to a pastor in the Low Countries saying, "I tell you, moreover, that in this pamphlet against the placards there are some things poorly digested and taken word for word from Castellio." [32] Van Schelven has been unable to identify the pamphlet in question and cannot, therefore, determine from which work of Castellio the citations were taken. In any case, he thinks that Beza was mistaken in classifying the movement for religious liberty in the Netherlands as Castellionist prior to 1578. The Dutch literature, he contends, is affected rather by the political considerations of the French *Politiques* than by the religious latitudinarianism of Castellio. Such a generalization is too sweeping. The arguments for toleration, which Van Schelven lists as characteristic of the French and Dutch pamphlets, as a matter of fact are very common in Castellio, as, for example, that faith is a gift of God and cannot be constrained, that God takes no delight in forced confession, that diversity of religion will not endanger the State, that we should take the advice of Gamaliel, and learn from the examples of the early Roman emperors and the Turks.[33]

After 1578 the influence of Castellionism in the Netherlands is certainly marked. The following year Dirck Volckertszoon Coornhert commenced his protest against constraint of conscience. He was thoroughly steeped in the works of Castellio, some of

[32] H. de Vries de Heekelingen, *Genève pepinière du Calvinisme hollandais*, 2 vols. (Fribourg, Suisse, 1918 and The Hague, 1924), II, 161, No. LXIII (Aug. 19, 1566).

[33] A. A. Van Schelven, "De Opkomst van de Idee der politieke Tolerantie in de 16e eeuwsche Nederlanden," *Tijdschrift voor Geschiedenis*, XLVI, 3 and 4 (1931), 235-48, 337-88, especially 354-59.

which he translated.[34] His *Proces Van't Ketter-dooden of 1589* [35] employs the Castellionist arguments that it is impossible to tell who is a heretic, that false teaching does not mean a bad life, that the heretic dies for his conviction, and that the logical outcome of Beza's policy is the extermination of all. Some of the materials of the *De haereticis* appear, but that they have been borrowed directly cannot be established. Professor Burr informs me that the Dutch Mennonite, Pieter Janszoon Twisck, in his *Religions Vryheyt* of 1609 makes lengthy use of *Martinus Bellius, Castalio,* and *Basilius Montfoort.*

Our work played a rôle in high political circles when an attempt was made at Cologne in 1579 to pacify the dissensions of the Netherlands by means of a conference. The representatives of the Low Countries chose as their spokesman Aggäus Albada, a Schwenckfelder, though nominally Catholic. He pled for religious liberty, and in the account (which he later published) of the proceedings adorned the margins with references to contemporary literature. Among other authors he cited *Joannes Witlingius, Georgius Kleinbergius,* and *Aretius Catharus.*[36] We recognize at once the pseudonyms of our compilation.

The *De haereticis* was twice translated into Dutch, once about 1620 and again in 1663.[37]

Its influence extended to a distinguished advocate of liberty in the Netherlands, the Huguenot refugee Pierre Bayle, who in his

[34] Buisson, *op. cit.*, II, 374, 377.

[35] Wercken II (Amsterdam, 1630). There is a copy at Cornell.

[36] Max Lossen, "Aggäus Albada und der kölner Pacificationscongress im Jahre 1579." *Hist. Taschenbuch*, V. Folge, VI. Jhrg. (1876), 275-362.

[37] Buisson, *op. cit.*, II, 363 f., and Walther Köhler, *Bibliographia Brentiana* (Berlin, 1904), Nos. 670 and 595. See Buisson for translations of other works of Castellio into Dutch. The interesting fact has been brought to light that the *Conseil à la France désolée* was not only translated into Dutch, but was worked over as *Vermaninghe ende Raet voor de Nederlanden* (1578). See Albert Elkan, "Ueber die Entstehung der niederländischen Religionsfriedens von 1578 und Mornays Wirksamkeit in den Niederlanden." *Mitteilungen des Instituts für österreichische Geschichtsforschung*, XXVII (Vienna, 1906), 460-80.

The influence of Castellio's thought in the Netherlands is discussed by Etienne Giran, *Sébastien Castellion* (Haarlem, 1914).

commentary on the text, "Compel them to come in," says that Castellio treated of tolerance under the pseudonym Martinus Bellius, but did not make the case as strong as it had subsequently become. Had he done so Beza would not have been able to reply.[38]

[38] *Oeuvres diverses de Mr. Pierre Bayle,* II (The Hague, 1727), 497. *Commentaire philosophique sur les parolles de Jesus Christ Contrain-les d'entrer.* Cantorbéry (Amsterdam), 1686.

Concerning Heretics

Whether they are to be persecuted and
How they are to be treated
A collection of the opinions of learned men
Both ancient and modern.

**A most timely book in view of the present turbulence
And highly instructive to all
And especially to princes and magistrates
To show them their duty in a matter
So controversial and dangerous**

"He that was born after the flesh persecuted him that was born after the Spirit." Gal. 4 (29).

Dedication by Martin Bellius to Duke Christoph of Württemberg

Martin Bellius to Duke Christoph of Württemberg, Greeting.

Most Illustrious Prince, suppose you had told your subjects that you would come to them at some uncertain time and had commanded them to make ready to go forth clad in white garments to meet you whenever you might appear. What would you do if, on your return, you discovered that they had taken no thought for the white robes but instead were disputing among themselves concerning your person? Some were saying that you were in France, others that you were in Spain; some that you would come on a horse, others in a chariot; some were asserting that you would appear with a great equipage, others that you would be unattended. Would this please you?

Suppose further that the controversy was being conducted not merely by words but by blows and swords, and that one group wounded and killed the others who did not agree with them. "He will come on a horse," one would say.

"No, in a chariot," another would retort.

"You lie."

"You're the liar. Take that." He punches him.

"And take that in the belly." The other stabs.

Would you, O Prince, commend such citizens? Suppose, however, that some did their duty and followed your command to prepare the white robes, but the others oppressed them on that account and put them to death. Would you not rigorously destroy such scoundrels?

But what if these homicides claimed to have done all this in your name and in accord with your command, even though you had previously expressly forbidden it? Would you not consider that such outrageous conduct deserved to be punished without mercy? Now I beg you, most Illustrious Prince, to be kind enough to hear why I say these things.

Christ is the Prince of this world who on His departure from the earth foretold to men that He would return some day at an uncertain hour, and He commanded them to prepare white robes for His coming, that is to say, that they should live together in a Christian manner, amicably, without controversy and contention, loving one another. But consider now, I beg you, how well we discharge our duty.

How many are there who show the slightest concern to prepare the white robe? Who is there who bends every effort to live in this world in a saintly, just, and religious manner in the expectation of the coming of the Lord? For nothing is there so little concern. The true fear of God and charity are fallen and grown cold. Our life is spent in contention and in every manner of sin. We dispute, not as to the way by which we may come to Christ, which is to correct our lives, but rather as to the state and office of Christ, where He now is and what He is doing, how He is seated at the right hand of the Father, and how He is one with the Father; likewise with regard to the Trinity, predestination, free will; so, also, of God, the angels, the state of souls after this life and other like things, which do not need to be known for salvation by faith (for the publicans and sinners were saved without this knowledge), nor indeed can they be known before the heart is pure (for to see these things is to see God Himself, who cannot be seen save by the pure in heart, as the text says, "Blessed are the pure in heart for they shall see God)." [1] Nor if these are known do they make a man better, as Paul says, "Though I understand all mysteries and have not love it profiteth me nothing." [2] This perverse curiosity engenders worse evils. Men are puffed up with knowledge or with a false opinion of knowledge and look down upon others. Pride is followed by cruelty and persecution so that now scarcely anyone is able to endure another who differs at all from him. Although opinions are almost as numerous as men, nevertheless there is hardly any sect which does not condemn all others and

[1] Matt. 5: 8. [2] I Cor. 13, verses 2 and 3 combined.

desire to reign alone. Hence arise banishments, chains, imprisonments, stakes, and gallows and this miserable rage to visit daily penalties upon those who differ from the mighty about matters hitherto unknown, for so many centuries disputed, and not yet cleared up.

If, however, there is someone who strives to prepare the white robe, that is, to live justly and innocently, then all others with one accord cry out against him if he differ from them in anything, and they confidently pronounce him a heretic on the ground that he seeks to be justified by works. Horrible crimes of which he never dreamed are attributed to him and the common people are prejudiced by slander until they consider it a crime merely to hear him speak. Hence arises such cruel rage that some are so incensed by calumny as to be infuriated when the victim is first strangled instead of being burned alive at a slow fire.

This is cruel enough, but a more capital offense is added when this conduct is justified under the robe of Christ and is defended as being in accord with his will, when Satan could not devise anything more repugnant to the nature and will of Christ! Yet these very people, who are so furious against the heretics, as they call them, are so far from hating moral offenders that no scruple is felt against living in luxury with the avaricious, currying flatterers, abetting the envious and calumniators, making merry with drunkards, gluttons, and adulterers, banqueting daily with the scurrilous, impostors, and those who are hated of God. Who then can doubt that they hate not vices but virtues? To hate the good is the same as to love the evil. If, then, the bad are dear to a man there is no doubt but that the good are hateful to him.

I ask you, then, most Illustrious Prince, what do you think Christ will do when he comes? Will he commend such things? Will he approve of them?

Consider this case for a moment, I beg you. Suppose that accusation were brought in your city of Tübingen against a man who spoke of you in this fashion: "I believe that Christoph is my prince, and I wish to obey him in all things, but I do not believe what you say, that he will come in a chariot. I think he will come on horseback. Neither do I agree with you that he will be clothed in red. I think he will wear white, and as for his command that we bathe in this river, I think we should do so in the afternoon, you think it should be done in the morning. If I thought that he wished me to bathe in the morning I would do it, but I am afraid of offending him, and I wish to follow my conscience."

Now I ask you, Prince, would you condemn such a citizen? I do not think so. If you were present you would rather commend the simplicity and obedience of such a man than condemn his ignorance, and if others put him to death you would certainly punish them.

Now take this case in the same way. There is a citizen of Christ who speaks of him in this manner: "I believe in God the Father and in Jesus Christ His Son, and wish to live according to their commandments, which are contained in Holy Scripture, but as for his command that we take his body and blood, I think this should be in both kinds,[3] and with regard to the command that we be baptized, this I think should be done on the eighth day from the birth of the child after the manner of circumcision." Do you think that such a man should be put to death for this? I do not think so.

And if he says this: "I believe that a man ought not to be baptized until he is first able to give a reason for the faith that is in him.[4] If I thought otherwise, I would act otherwise, for it would be no more difficult for me to baptize an infant than an adolescent. But I dare not violate my conscience lest I offend Christ who has forbidden by his servant Paul that I do anything about which I am in doubt[5] whether it is good or bad. I must be saved by my own faith and not by that of another." I ask you whether Christ, who is the judge of all, were he present, would command that such a man be put to death? I do not think so, especially when you look at the life and nature of Christ, who certainly never commanded nor did anything of the sort, but rather the absolute contrary. And if Christ did not so act, neither should they who

[3] The passage, "but . . . both kinds," occurs in the Latin version only.

[4] I Peter 3: 15.

[5] Rom. 14: 23.

have their authority from him, lest they be reproached, and rightly reproached, with the common proverb, "You are a servant of the devil because you have done more than you were told," [6] or rather you have done the opposite of what you were told. If God so severely punished Saul for not having killed him whom God had commanded to kill,[7] how much more severely will he now punish those who kill them whom God has forbidden to kill? especially in view of the fact that God now is much more inclined to mercy than to wrath.

What I have said with regard to baptism applies equally to the other articles of religion which are in dispute, where someone believes in God and in Christ His Son, and serves Him according to conscience, but errs somewhat in ignorance, or to us seems to err. When I consider the life and teaching of Christ who, though innocent Himself, yet always pardoned the guilty and told us to pardon until seventy times seven,[8] I do not see how we can retain the name of Christian if we do not imitate His clemency and mercy. Even if we were innocent we ought to follow Him. How much more when we are covered with so many sins? When I examine my own life I see so many and such great sins that I do not think I could even obtain pardon from my Savior if I were thus ready to condemn others. Let each one examine himself, sound and search his conscience, and weigh his thoughts, words, and deeds. Then will he see himself as one who is not in a position to remove the mote from the eye of his brother before he has taken the beam from his own.[9] In view of the many sins which are laid to us all, the best course would be for each to look to himself, to exercise care for the correction of his life and not for the condemnation of others. This license of judgment which reigns everywhere today, and fills all with blood, constrains me, most Clement Prince, to do my best to staunch the blood,

[6] Karl F. W. Wander, *Deutsches Sprichwörter-Lexikon*, 5 vols. (Leipzig, 1867-80), under the heading, "Viel," 88, "Zu viel ist Satans Spiel." Under the heading, "Lützel," 2, "Zu lützel und zu viel ist des Teufels Spiel." Cf. "Lützel," 3.

[7] I Sam. 15. [8] Matt. 18: 22. [9] Matt. 7: 3; Luke 6: 41.

especially that blood which is so wrongfully shed,—I mean the blood of those who are called heretics, which name has become today so infamous, detestable, and horrible that there is no quicker way to dispose of an enemy than to accuse him of heresy. The mere word stimulates such horror that when it is pronounced men shut their ears to the victim's defense, and furiously persecute not merely the man himself, but also all those who dare to open their mouths on his behalf; by which rage it has come to pass that many have been destroyed before their cause was really understood.

Now I say this not because I favor heretics. I hate heretics. But I speak because I see here two great dangers. And the first is that he be held for a heretic, who is not a heretic. This happened in former times, for Christ and his disciples were put to death as heretics, and there is grave reason to fear a recurrence in our century, which is not better, but rather worse. The danger is greater because Christ said, "Think not that I am come to send peace on earth; I came not to send peace, but a sword. For I am come to set a man at variance against his father, and the daughter against her mother,"[10] etc. You see how easy it is for calumniators to say of a Christian, "This man is seditious. He sets a son at variance against his father and disturbs the public peace." Great care must be exercised to distinguish those who are really seditious from Christians. Outwardly they do the same thing and are adjudged guilty of the same crime by those who do not understand. Christ was crucified among thieves.

The other danger is that he who is really a heretic be punished more severely or in a manner other than that required by Christian discipline. For these reasons I have collected in this book the opinions of many who have written on this matter, in order that a consideration of their arguments may lead to less offense for the future. I have given first place to the opinions of contemporaries, partly because they cite the ancients, so that in the moderns you have both the old and the new, and partly because contemporaries write more fully and accurately and with an eye

[10] Matt. 10: 34-35; cf. Luke 12: 51-53.

to our own time. They have learned something from these very persecutions. The ancients wrote principally against the pagans by whom they were persecuted so long as they followed Christ and the apostles, who never persecuted anyone, but rather were persecuted by all. But when sins increased and the Gentiles ceased to persecute, then Christians rose up against Christians, especially if they saw anyone a trifle too stiff in his defense of the truth. If his conduct were irreproachable they would cavil at his doctrine of which the common man could not judge so easily as of conduct. So it has come about that all the saints have suffered persecution, although not all who have suffered persecution are saints. This you will discover, that persecution has always accompanied genuine religion, and when true religion has ceased, then persecution has also ceased. The ancient Church was persecuted so long as she retained true godliness, but later on, when all had entered the service of the devil and no one resisted him, then the Church was freed from persecution. If in our age none were genuinely religious there would be no persecution, for why should Satan persecute his servants? But as soon as the godly arise there appear also those who shall vex them. This vexation has sharpened their wits and has enabled them to write many things well and pointedly concerning persecution.

If, however, any of those whom I have cited have elsewhere or afterwards written or acted in a different sense or shall so write or act, let us, nevertheless, adhere to their first opinion, because it was written in a time of tribulation when men are the more accustomed to write the truth, and because it is especially consonant with the meekness and mercy of Christ. If anyone should preach another gospel, be he St. Paul or an angel from heaven, let him be anathema; [11] for often it happens that when men first embrace the Gospel they think and judge well of religion so long as they are poor and afflicted, especially because poverty and affliction are peculiarly capable of the truth of Christ, who was himself poor and afflicted. But these same men, when elevated to riches and power, degenerate, and those who before defended Christ, now

[11] Gal. 1: 8.

defend Mars and convert true religion into force and violence. Wherefore, in such matters none may be more surely trusted than those who are afflicted and have not where to lay their heads.[12] I was moved by many reasons, Prince Christopher, to send you the opinions of many, though not of all, such authors. First, because I hear that you have always favored the Gospel and persevered therein even in the midst of calamities and afflictions. Witness the confession which you alone of all the princes of Germany sent to the last meeting of the Council of Trent,[13] by which you made it plain that you did not flee the light, but wished to make known to all the world your faith and religion. A further reason was that in your exalted position of authority it is highly expedient that you be well versed in this matter in order that you may rule your people justly and well. I hope, too, that you may be able to persuade neighboring princes to do the like, and especially the king of France, if by any means it be possible to restore tranquillity to this Christian state which has been so long and so miserably distraught, that the people may be summoned to correct their lives, if perchance God may turn away His wrath which He has conceived against the race of men and may enlighten us by the light of His countenance.

Finally, I have dedicated this book to you because the opinion of your doctor John Brenz [14] is included among the others. Immediately after the publication of this work, as I hear, the cruelty of persecution was diminished and not so many were put to death thereafter. Such was the force of the opinion of one man of sound judgment even in times so corrupt.

[12] Luke 9: 58.

[13] The confession was composed by Brenz and was submitted to the council on January 24, 1552. For editions of the confession see Walther Köhler, *Bibliographia Brentiana*, Nos. 219-28, 239-40, 241, 309, 356, 357, 669. For the acts relating to the fortunes of the embassies sent by Christoph to the council see Nos. 242-46. For Brenz's memoranda in this connection see No. 730, p. 345, which lists the works of Brenz printed in Felix Bidembach, *Consiliorum theologicorum*, Decas VII (Franckfurt am Meyn, 1611). On the circumstances see RE [3] IV, 57.45 f., and Julius Hartmann, *Johann Brenz*, II (Hamburg, 1842), Chap. XXII and especially p. 206.

[14] *Witlingius* in the second Latin version.

Keep on, Brenz,[15] and advance in this Christian clemency in which you have commenced. You have already staunched much blood by your little book. You could have done nothing more pleasing to Christ nor more displeasing to Satan. Would that others had done as you and had sought like you not to shed blood, but to stem the flow. Then we should not have seen so many fires, so many swords dripping with the blood of the innocent, and we should not now be eating fish fattened on the blood of those for whom Christ gave his own. O Princes, open your eyes and make not so cheap the blood of men that you shed it thus lightly, especially for the sake of religion. If anyone judge without mercy, with that same measure shall it be meted to him again.[16]

Furthermore, inasmuch as the following opinions discuss only the treatment and not the definition of a heretic, and the point is of prime importance, I shall briefly explain, in accord with the Word of God, who is a heretic, in order that we may the better understand how such an one is to be treated, for I do not consider that all those are heretics who are so called. The term heretic in the days of St. Paul was not so obnoxious that the heretics were considered worse than the avaricious or hypocrites, or the scurrilous or flatterers. Today no one is put to death for avarice, hypocrisy, scurrility, or flattery, of which it is often easy to judge, but for heresy, of which it is not so simple to judge, so many are executed. After a careful investigation into the meaning of the term heretic, I can discover no more than this, that we regard those as heretics with whom we disagree. This is evident from the fact that today there is scarcely one of our innumerable sects which does not look upon the rest as heretics, so that if you are orthodox in one city or region, you are held for a heretic in the next. If you would live today, you must have as many faiths and religions as there are cities and sects. Just as he who travels from country to country must change his money from day to day, since the coin which is accepted in one place is rejected in another, unless indeed the money be gold, which is valid everywhere regardless of the imprint.

[15] *Witlingius* in the second Latin version.

[16] Matt. 7: 2, loosely.

Likewise in religion let us use the gold coin which is everywhere acceptable no matter what the image. Now, to believe in God the Father Almighty, the Son, and Holy Spirit, and to approve of the commandments of true religion as set forth in Holy Scripture, this is the gold coin, which is better certified and approved than gold itself. But until now this money has had many different imprints and images according as men disagreed with one another with regard to the Lord's Supper, baptism, and the like. Let us bear with one another and not readily condemn the faith of someone else, a faith which is based on Jesus Christ. And now to come to the point, let us not make the opinion of the common man the test of heresy, but rather the Word of God, and let us thus see who is a heretic.

The name "heretic" is found only once in the Scriptures, in the Epistle of Paul to Titus, the third chapter, "A man that is an heretic after the first and second admonition reject; knowing that he that is such is subverted, and sinneth, being condemned of himself." [17] If we compare this passage with the command of Christ in Matthew eighteen we shall understand who is a heretic: "Moreover if thy brother shall trespass against thee, go and tell him his fault between thee and him alone: if he shall hear thee, thou hast gained thy brother. But if he will not hear thee, then take with thee one or two more, that in the mouth of two or three witnesses every word may be established. And if he shall neglect to hear them, tell it unto the Church: but if he neglect to hear the Church, let him be unto thee as an heathen man and a publican." [18] From this passage it is evident that the heretic is an obstinate man who does not obey after due admonition, since the man whom Paul calls a heretic, Christ describes with the words, "if he will neither hear thee nor the others," and again, "Shake off the dust of your feet." [19] The words of Paul that he "sinneth being condemned of himself" [20] are equivalent to those which Christ adds directly to the above passage,

[17] Titus 3: 10, 11. The American Revised Version reads, "A factious man after the first and second admonition refuse," etc.

[18] Matt. 18: 15-17.

[19] Matt. 10: 14; Mark 6: 11; Luke 9: 5; 10: 11. [20] Tit. 3: 10.

"Verily I say unto you, Whatsoever ye shall bind on earth shall be bound in heaven: and whatsoever ye shall loose on earth shall be loosed in heaven,"[21] that is to say, All those whom you hold as heathen and publicans the Lord also will hold as heathen.

Moreover, there are two kinds of heretics or obstinate persons: the first are obstinate or stubborn as to conduct, such as the avaricious, scurrilous, voluptuous, drunkards, persecutors, and the like, who being admonished, do not correct their lives. Such are the Jews, Scribes, and Pharisees; wherefore the Savior avoided them when He said, "Your house is left unto you desolate."[22] Such also were those of Jesus' own country among whom He could do no mighty work because of the hardness of their hearts.[23] The second are those who are obstinate in spiritual matters and in doctrine, to whom the term properly belongs, for the word heresy is Greek and means a sect or opinion. Wherefore those who adhere to some vicious sect or opinion are called heretics. Of this sort was Hananiah, the false prophet whom Jeremiah avoided when he could not recall him from his error. Jeremiah predicted to him his death in accord with the command of the Lord, not of the magistrate. This Hananiah was a pernicious heretic, who withdrew the people from their obedience. From this example alone we may readily see how heretics of this sort are to be treated.

But to judge of doctrine is not so simple as to judge of conduct. In the matter of conduct, if you ask a Jew, Turk, Christian, or anyone else, what he thinks of a brigand or a traitor, all will reply with one accord that brigands and traitors are evil and should be put to death. Why do all agree in this? Because the matter is obvious. For that reason no controversies are raised and no books are written to prove that brigands, etc., should be put to death. This knowledge is engraved and written in the hearts of all men from the foundation of the world. This was what St. Paul meant that the Gentiles have the law written in their hearts,[24] for infidels themselves may judge of these matters.

Now let us take up religion and we shall find that it is not so

[21] Matt. 18: 18.
[22] Matt. 23: 38; cf. Luke 13: 35.
[23] Mark 6: 5; Matt. 13: 58.
[24] Rom. 2: 15.

evident and manifest. The heathen were formerly of the opinion that there are many gods. Christ, by his coming, removed this error, so that now neither the Turks nor any other nations entertain a doubt whether there is but one god. On this point all agree with the Christians. If anyone denies the Lord God, this one is an infidel and atheist and is deservedly to be abhorred in the eyes of all. The Turks go further and believe in that God of whom Moses wrote. In this they agree with the Jews and with the Christians without any controversy. The faith of the three peoples is common up to this point. But the Turks share with the Christians a higher regard for Christ than that of the Jews. The Christians go beyond all others in that they regard Jesus Christ as the Son of God, the Savior and Judge of the world. And this belief is common to all Christians. And just as the Turks disagree with the Christians as to the person of Christ, and the Jews with both the Turks and the Christians, and the one condemns the other and holds him for a heretic, so Christians disagree with Christians on many points with regard to the teaching of Christ, and condemn one another and hold each other for heretics. Great controversies and debates occur as to baptism, the Lord's Supper, the invocation of the saints, justification, free will, and other obscure questions, so that Catholics, Lutherans, Zwinglians, Anabaptists, monks, and others condemn and persecute one another more cruelly than the Turks do the Christians. These dissensions arise solely from ignorance of the truth, for if these matters were so obvious and evident as that there is but one God, all Christians would agree among themselves on these points as readily as all nations confess that God is one.

What, then, is to be done in such great contentions? We should follow the counsel of Paul, "Let not him that eateth despise him that eateth not. . . . To his own master he standeth or falleth." [25] Let not the Jews or Turks condemn the Christians, nor let the Christians condemn the Jews or Turks, but rather teach and win them by true religion and justice, and let us, who are Christians,

[25] Rom. 14: 3-4.

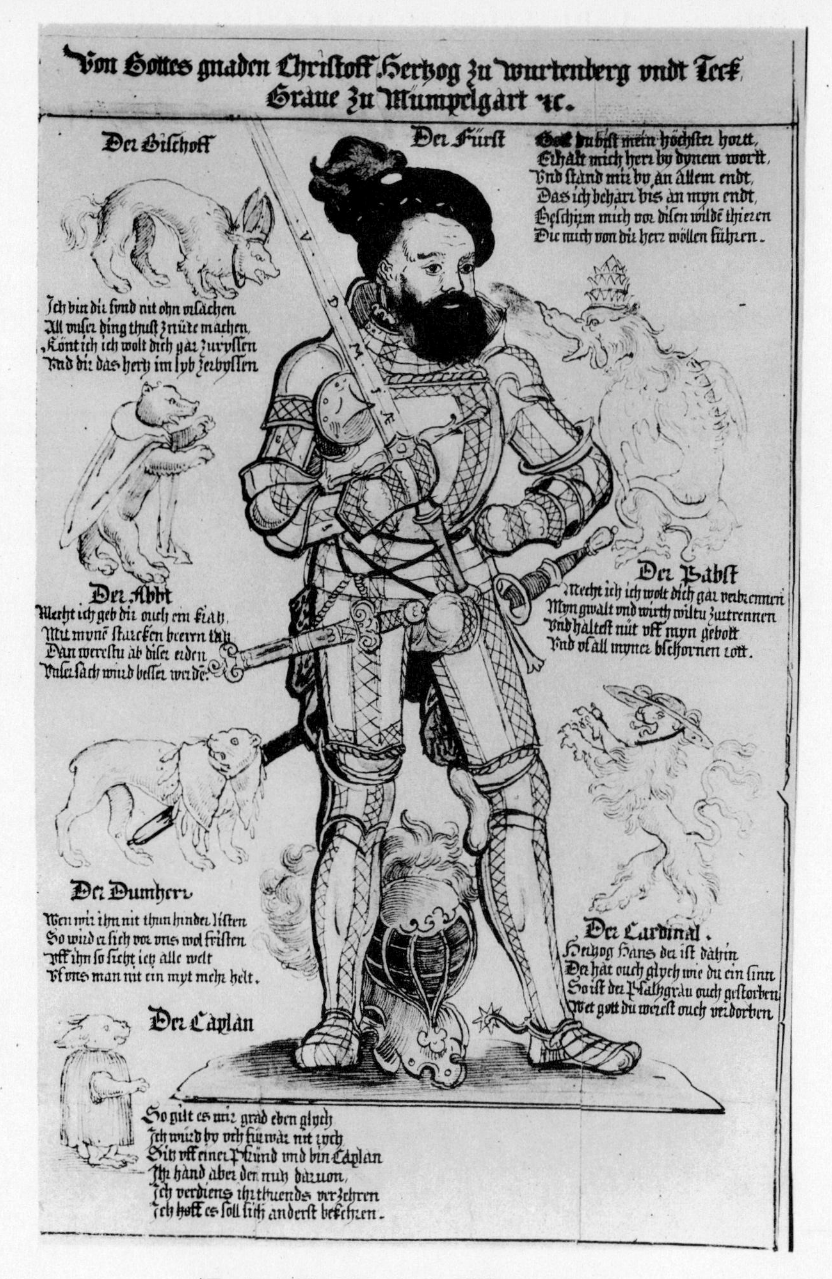

Duke Christoph of Württemberg

not condemn one another, but, if we are wiser than they, let us also be better and more merciful. This is certain that the better a man knows the truth, the less is he inclined to condemn, as appears in the case of Christ and the apostles. But he who lightly condemns others shows thereby that he knows nothing precisely, because he cannot bear others, for to know is to know how to put into practice. He who does not know how to act mercifully and kindly does not know the nature of mercy and kindness, just as he who cannot blush does not know the nature of shame.

If we were to conduct ourselves in this fashion we should be able to dwell together in concord. Even though in some matters we disagreed, yet should we consent together and forbear one another in love, which is the bond of peace, until we arrive at the unity of the faith.[26] But now, when we strive with hate and persecutions we go from bad to worse. Nor are we mindful of our office, since we are wholly taken up with condemnation, and the Gospel because of us is made a reproach unto the heathen,[27] for when they see us attacking one another with the fury of beasts, and the weak oppressed by the strong, these heathen feel horror and detestation for the Gospel, as if it made men such, and they abominate even Christ himself, as if he commanded men to do such things. We rather degenerate into Turks and Jews than convert them into Christians. Who would wish to be a Christian, when he saw that those who confessed the name of Christ were destroyed by Christians themselves with fire, water, and the sword without mercy and more cruelly treated than brigands and murderers? Who would not think Christ a Moloch,[28] or some such god, if he wished that men should be immolated to him and burned alive? Who would wish to serve Christ on condition that a difference of opinion on a controversial point with those in au-

[26] Free use of Eph. 4: 2-3. [27] Ezek. 22: 4.

[28] The King James version has the spelling Moloch in Amos 5: 26 and Acts 7: 43 and Molech in Lev. 18: 21 and other passages. In Castellio's Bible Moloch is used throughout. On the practice of child sacrifice to Moloch see Hasting's *Dictionary of the Bible, sub voce.*

thority would be punished by burning alive at the command of Christ himself more cruelly than in the bull of Phalaris,[29] even though from the midst of the flames he should call with a loud voice upon Christ, and should cry out that he believed in Him? Imagine Christ, the judge of all, present. Imagine Him pronouncing the sentence and applying the torch. Who would not hold Christ for a Satan? What more could Satan do than burn those who call upon the name of Christ?

O Creator and King of the world, dost Thou see these things? Art Thou become so changed, so cruel, so contrary to Thyself? When Thou wast on earth none was more mild, more clement, more patient of injury. As a sheep before the shearer Thou wast dumb.[30] When scourged, spat upon, mocked, crowned with thorns, and crucified shamefully among thieves, Thou didst pray for them who did Thee this wrong.[31] Art Thou now so changed? I beg Thee in the name of Thy Father, dost Thou now command that those who do not understand Thy precepts as the mighty demand, be drowned in water, cut with lashes to the entrails, sprinkled with salt, dismembered by the sword, burned at a slow fire, and otherwise tortured in every manner and as long as possible? Dost Thou, O Christ, command and approve of these things? Are they Thy vicars who make these sacrifices? Art Thou present when they summon Thee and dost Thou eat human flesh? If Thou, Christ, dost these things or if Thou commandest that they be done, what hast Thou left for the devil? Dost Thou the very same things as Satan? O blasphemies and shameful audacity of men, who dare to attribute to Christ that which they do by the command and at the

[29] Phalaris was a tyrant of classical antiquity for whom was constructed a bronze bull in which a man could be burned. The cries of the victim would seem to issue from the nostrils of the bull. Erasmus has an account of it in "Adagiorum," Chil. I, Cent. X, 86, *Opera,* II, 392 D-F. References in classical authors are collected in A. Otto, *Die Sprichwörter und sprichwörtlichen Redensarten der Römer* (Leipzig, 1890), p. 277. There is a reference in the translation of Diodorus Siculus, to which Castellio contributed several chapters (*Diodori Sicvli bibliothecae historicae,* Basel, 1578, Lib. XX, p. 686), but the salient fragment was not included in this translation. It is to be found in modern editions, Lib. IX, Cap. 19.

[30] Isa. 53: 7.

[31] Luke 23: 34.

instigation of Satan! But I will restrain myself. I think, Prince, you already sufficiently understand how far such deeds are contrary to the teaching and practice of Christ. Let us, then, now hear the opinions of others. You will find them speaking, however, as if it were already clear who are the true heretics.

Dedication of the French Version to William of Hesse

To the Most Illustrious Prince, Count William of Hesse.

Noble and exalted Prince, for three reasons I have been moved to dedicate to you this present work which I have translated from Latin into French. The first is that I understand you like to read French, and the second is that, while practicing the language, you may be increasingly instructed as to your exalted office, of which King David admonishes you saying, "Be wise now therefore, O ye kings: be instructed, ye judges of the earth. Serve the Lord with fear, and rejoice with trembling." [1] If you do this, you will take care, along with all good princes, not to credit lightly the tales of the envious in whatever station they be, who often accuse an upright and God-fearing man. If they find nothing amiss in his life or conversation they seek an occasion against him touching the law of his God and call him a heretic, as we read that this was done to Daniel by the counsellors of Darius, king of the Chaldaeans. They were angry with Daniel because he had authority over them and because "a more excellent spirit was in him," and they "sought to find occasion against him concerning the kingdom: but they could find none occasion nor fault, forasmuch as he was faithful." Then they contrived an accusation "concerning the law of his God." Would that good kings and princes would diligently consider this account which, like the rest of Scripture, has been given for their instruction.[2] Let them beware of believing those who would impel them to kill and burn anyone for faith and religion, which above all else should be free, since it resides not in the body but in the heart, which cannot be reached by the sword of kings and princes. Let rulers content themselves to prevent the

[1] Ps. 2: 10-11.

[2] II Tim. 3: 16.

bad from injuring the good either in their property or their persons, as St. Paul teaches in Romans 13.

Sins of the heart, such as infidelity, heresy, envy, hate, etc., are to be punished by the sword of the Spirit which is the Word of God. If anyone disturbs the commonwealth by an assault under color of religion, the magistrate may punish such an one not on the score of religion, but because he has done damage to bodies and goods, like any other criminal. If anyone conducts himself amiss in the Church, both in his life and in his doctrine, the Church should use the spiritual sword, which is excommunication, if he will not be admonished. Then, if after excommunication, he perseveres in his evil design to the point of disturbing the peace, the Christian magistrate may see to it that he no longer trouble the Church with his heresies and blasphemies which are plainly contrary to the Word of God. Of such a character is the teaching of those who deny the creation of the world, the immortality of souls and the resurrection, as well as of those who repudiate the office of the magistrate in order that they may the better disturb the state to their hearts' content without reproof. These men thrive on disturbance, to which the Spirit of God is utterly alien. If they continue to disobey princes and magistrates, they may be punished, but not with the death penalty, as St. Augustine teaches, especially in the case of those who admit one true God, the source of all good, but err obstinately in the understanding of some passages of Scripture. The good magistrate will content himself with punishing them by a fine or some similar penalty. Then, if they continue, he may banish them from the land. This is the extreme penalty. If they come back they may be imprisoned if they do not amend. This, Prince, is the way in which emperors and magistrates punished the heretics in the early Church, as you may read in the present book, which is both useful and necessary in these last days in which not only those who have never properly known the truth, but even those who glory in it, nevertheless thirst for the blood of any who contradict them and try to stop bloodshed for the sake of religion. Hereby the persecutors show how far they are from the clemency of Christ and His apostles, from the mercy of the doctors of the primitive Church who begged the princes and magistrates not to kill and burn the heretics, as you may read in this book. Follow St. Augustine, Chrysostom, and Jerome and the other doctors so long as they follow Scripture, as Augustine himself advises us to do,[3] and, on the contrary, avoid those who urge that we kill and burn any for the faith. Certainly they are of the nature of the devil and of Antichrist, who desire the death of poor souls, whereas true Christians desire that sinners and adversaries of the truth turn and live. Beware of false doctors and the writings of those who cannot suffer the assertion that heretics should not be killed lest their souls be destroyed. These doctors make simple people believe that those who object to coercion do so in order the more readily to disseminate their poison. But the same may be said of these doctors. That is just what they have done. May the Lord cause them to recognize their blindness and ill will.

But here we must be careful not to brand as seditious those who reprove the false doctors and teachers for their evil life and teaching. It is certain that the prophets and the apostles and even our Savior Jesus Christ were held as seditious blasphemers and heretics. The charge was brought against them that they wished to destroy the law of Moses which was ordained of God and declared to be eternal. But Christ and the apostles came not to destroy, but to fulfill,[4] and to show for what purpose the ceremonies were instituted. Yet the people would not hear, especially when reproved for their faults, and sought to remove the critics from the earth, just as men do today when fraternally admonished.

The third reason is that you may avoid the great and terrible wrath of God which shall come upon those who shed blood for religion, and that rather all manner of good may come to you and to your subjects. If because of bloodshed the Savior destroyed Jerusalem which was so dear to him, as you may read in the Lam-

[3] "Liber de gratia Christi," Cap. XLIII(47): Migne, PL XLIV, 381. When Pelagius appealed to Ambrose, Augustine answered that no matter how great the virtues of Ambrose his authority did not equal that of Scripture.

[4] Matt. 5: 17.

entations of Jeremiah: "For the sins of her prophets and the iniquities of her priests, that have shed the blood of the just in the midst of her" [5] she was destroyed, what will be done to those who, under the guise of heresy and false prophecy, kill those who contradict them? It were better to let a hundred, or even a thousand, heretics live than to kill one upright man under the color of heresy. We know well that all the prophets, apostles, and martyrs, and even our Savior Jesus Christ, were put to death as false prophets, blasphemers, and heretics. This ought to fill us with fear and trembling when it comes to persecuting a man for his faith and his religion, which consists not in some ceremony or indifferent matter, not in some dubious or ambiguous doctrine (for he who persecutes may quite as well be mistaken as the one who is persecuted), as to the manner of receiving the body and blood of Christ in the Lord's Supper, whether it should be given to infants since they are baptized, or whether it is better to wait until they be grown and understand, etc. Religion does not consist in some point which transcends human understanding and concerning which we have no indisputable passages of Scripture, as, for example, in the understanding of the three persons, the Father, Son, and Holy Spirit. It is enough for us to believe that there is one substance in three persons without bothering ourselves unduly as to how one is related to the other. We need not worry whether the body of Christ is in heaven, whether God has created some to be damned and others to be saved, how Christ descended into hell, and the like. On these points each may be left to his own opinion and to the revelation of the Savior. It is sufficient to accept the fundamental points of true religion which consists in believing that God is the source of all good, that man is condemned because of the disobedience of the first man and saved by the obedience of the second, who is Jesus Christ our Savior, provided a man, moved by the true fear of God, repent of his former evil life and resolve firmly not to return to it again, and that he apply especially to himself with a firm faith the death and resurrection

[5] Lam. 4: 13.

of Jesus Christ who was born, suffered, died, and rose for us, that we might be planted in him as the apostle shows us when he says, "For if we have been planted together in the likeness of his death, we shall be also in the likeness of his resurrection." [6] He died for us, to reconcile us to his Father, to justify all those who believe truly in Him and die also to the world and to their desires. Therefore it is said that "Christ is raised up from the dead that we also should walk in newness of life." [7] This is the cause of His death and resurrection. In a word, we are the servants of Him whom we obey.[8] If of sin then are we of all men the most miserable,[9] even though we believe the twelve articles of the faith,[10] and agree with the whole Church in doctrine and ceremonies, and attend church diligently.

Illustrious Prince, would you not consider one of your officers craven if he left your service for some good-for-nothing? To be sure. How much more craven is he who leaves the service of the King of Kings, of the Prince of Princes to serve the devil, that is, himself, his flesh, his desires, his ambition, and his appetite for honor and riches? There is no comparison. Indeed, if we consider a moment the grandeur and the power of God and the littleness and feebleness of man, however great he may be in this world, we should never leave the service of such an exalted prince, which consists in keeping His command to let the tares grow together with the wheat.[11] We should never leave Him to serve such a poor knave as the devil, the father of lies and a murderer from the beginning,[12] of whom our God, by His dear Son Jesus Christ, our Savior, tells us to beware. Amen, Amen.

"Let us, therefore, as many as be perfect, be thus minded: and if in anything ye be otherwise minded, God shall reveal even this unto you. Nevertheless, whereto we have already attained, let us walk by the some rule, let us mind the same thing." Philip. 3.

[6] Rom. 6: 5.
[7] Rom. 6: 4, condensed.
[8] Rom. 6: 16.
[9] I Cor. 15: 19.
[10] The reference is to the Apostles' Creed which was divided into twelve articles, one for each of the apostles.
[11] Matt. 13: 30.
[12] John 8: 44.

Excerpts

MARTIN LUTHER (ARETIUS CATHARUS)[1]

On Civil Government, the Second Part, "On the Scope of the Magistrate's Authority." [2]

WE come now to the main portion of this discussion. Having learned that there must be civil government on earth and how it may be exercised in a Christian and helpful manner, we must now consider the question of its jurisdiction, lest it encroach upon the domain of God. This point is very important, for grievous disaster may result either from an undue extension or from an undue restriction. In the one case the government punishes too little, in the other too much. Though it is better to err on the side of leniency, since it is altogether preferable to spare the guilty than to kill the innocent [according to the law "Absentem," "de poenis"].[3] The world has rascals in abundance, but the good are scarce.

First of all we must observe that the children of Adam fall into two groups, the one in the kingdom of God under Christ, the other in the kingdom of the world under the magistrate, as we have said above. These two groups have two sets of laws, for every kingdom must have laws, since without laws no kingdom can stand as daily experience reveals. Civil government has laws which extend only to bodies and goods on earth. God, who alone has juris-

[1] In the second Latin version.

[2] "Von weltlicher Obrigkeit, wie weit man ihr Gehorsam schuldig sei," 1523. WA XI, 261-71. *The Works of Martin Luther*, published by the A. J. Holman Co. and the Castle Press, III (Philadelphia, 1930), 250-62.

[3] In the French version only. Attention is here directed to the explanation of symbols on p. xiii, above. *Corpus iuris ciuilis*, Digesta XLVIIJ, 19 "De poenis," 5 "Absentem in criminibus damnari non debere . . . satius enim esse impunitum relinqui facinus nocentis quam innocentem damnari." Ed. Mommsen and Krueger, I Digesta (Berlin, 1922), p. 864.

diction and authority over the soul will not suffer it to be subject to mundane laws.[4] When civil government undertakes to legislate for souls, then it encroaches upon the province of God and merely perverts and corrupts souls. I wish to make this clear as day that our [5] bishops and princes may see what fools, not to say scoundrels,[6] they are when they seek to coerce men by laws and commandments to believe this or that.

If a man imposes laws, according to his fancy, upon the souls of men, this certainly is not in accord with the Word of God,[7] and must of necessity displease God, who desires that our faith be built solely upon His Word, as He says in the sixteenth chapter of Matthew,[8] "On this rock I will build my Church," and John, the tenth chapter,[9] "My sheep hear my voice and know me. A stranger they will not follow, but will flee from him." Hence it follows that the civil ruler forces souls to eternal death by such an iniquitous law, for he compels men to believe that that is pleasing and acceptable to God, which is most certainly displeasing and unacceptable because unconfirmed by the testimony of the divine Word. He who believes that to be true and certain, which is false and uncertain, prefers error to truth and embraces injustice for justice.[10]

Wherefore they ought to be sent to the asylum who command that men believe the Church, the Fathers, and the councils even though unsupported by the Word of God. The devil's ministers do that, not the Church, for the Church commands nothing without a sure word of God, as St. Peter says [in the fourth chapter]: [11] "If any man speak let him speak as the oracles of God." But they will succeed in proving that their counsels [12] are the Word of God

[4] Luther says merely that God neither can nor will allow anyone to rule over the soul save Himself alone.

[5] Castellio omits *Junkers*.

[6] The French version omits "not . . . scoundrels."

[7] Castellio has condensed Luther.

[8] Matt. 16: 18.

[9] John 10: 27, 5.

[10] Castellio's rendering is free.

[11] I Peter 4: 11; "in . . . chapter" added in the French version.

[12] Luther is not talking about the counsels of the persecutors, but about the decrees of councils.

[when crows are white],[13] [when Nibas crows, as the proverb has it.] [14]

Even greater is the folly when the objection is made that kings, princes, and the multitude believe thus. Away with the multitude. We were not baptized into kings, princes, and the multitude, but into Christ and God himself. We are called Christians from Christ and are not named after these. No one ought or can command the soul unless he is able to show it the way to heaven, but no man can do that, only God. Wherefore in matters which affect the soul nothing is to be taught or received except the pure [and eternal] Word of God.

Yet, consummate fools though they be, they must confess that they have no authority over souls. No man can kill the soul or make it alive, lead it to heaven or to hell. Christ makes this plain in the tenth chapter of Matthew; [15] "Fear not them which kill the body, but are not able to kill the soul: but rather fear him which is able to destroy both soul and body in hell." These words show clearly enough that the soul is exempt from the hand of man [and the secular magistrate] and is subject only to the authority of God. Now tell me, how much sense has he who lays commands on a region over which he has no jurisdiction? Who would not think such an one more foolish than Melitide (Tribolet) [16] who commanded the moon to shine according to his fancy? Suppose that

[13] In the French version only. Cf. Erasmus, "Adagiorum," Chil. IV, Cent. VII, 35, "Corvus albus," *Opera,* II, 1105D.

[14] In the Latin version only. Erasmus explains in the *Adages* that according to Pliny Nibas was a town in Thessaly where cocks were never known to crow. "Adagiorum," Chil. III, Cent. III, 47, *Opera,* II, 792E.

[15] Matt. 10:28.

[16] The Latin version has "Melitide," the French "Tribolet"; Luther has neither. Melitide was a fool in classical antiquity of whom it was told that he could not count beyond the fingers of one hand and did not know from which of his parents he was born. Castellio may have taken the reference from Erasmus, "Adagiorum," Chil. IV, Cent. IV, 69, "Stultior Melitide," *Opera,* II, 1040E-41A. Cf. A. Otto, *Sprichwörter*, p. 218, and Pauly-Wissowa, *Real-encyclopädie der classischen Alterthumswissenschaft,* XXIX (Stuttgart, 1931), 549. Triboulet was an imbecile at the court of Louis XII. Of Triboulet it was told that he sold his horse to buy some hay, and sold the hay for a curry-comb. He appears as a simpleton in Rabelais's *Pantagruel,* Bk. III, Chaps. 45,

Geneva should legislate for Venice,[17] or *vice versa,* would they not need a dose of hellebore to cure their insanity? [18] Nevertheless our kings [19] and princes suffer themselves to be led by the blind guides, the pope, bishops, and sophists, to the point of enjoining their wishes upon the belief of subjects regardless of the Word of God, and yet our rulers desire to be known as Christian princes.

No authority whatever has the right to act except in so far as it is able to see, know, judge, pass sentence, add or alter, for nothing should be more certain than judgment, to which everything should be clear, investigated, and weighed; [20] but the secrets of the heart and soul are manifest to God alone, who, in the tenth chapter of Acts [21] is described as "one who knows hearts," and in many passages of the prophets.[22] Hence it is both futile and presumptuous to command or to try to compel anyone to believe this or that. Force achieves nothing. Another way must be adopted. I am astounded at the big fools, for they all confess, "De occultis non judicat ecclesia," [23] the Church does not judge of secret matters. Nevertheless they venture to judge and regulate something so secret and divine [24] as faith.

Now everyone is in danger for himself regarding his belief and must see for himself that he believes correctly. As nobody can go

---

46. In later legend he becomes capable of clever repartee. See A. Joly, *La Vraye Histoire de Tribovlet* (Lyons, 1869).

[17] Luther has Wittenberg and Leipzig.

[18] Castellio here omits a turn which Luther borrows from the humanists. See WA XI, 263.20 f. and the note on p. 482.

[19] Luther has "our Emperor," referring to Charles V.

[20] Luther's German is much simpler: For what kind of a judge were he who should blindly decide matters which he had neither seen nor heard?

[21] Acts 1:24 and 15:8. Castellio has not corrected Luther's reference, but in the Latin has introduced the Greek word from Acts 15:8.

[22] Luther quotes Ps. 7:10 and Jer. 17:9.

[23] Quaestio XI, Art. II, Commentaria Cardinalis Caietani, "Ecclesia non iudicat occulta," in *Sancti Thomae Aquinatis opera omnia,* 12 vols. (Rome, 1882-1906), VIII, 100. Compare the passages collected by Cardinal Gasparri in *Codex iuris canonici* (Rome, 1919), p. 682, n. 1, especially Dist. XXXII, c. xi (Friedberg, I, 120) and Causa XI, Quaestio III, c. 22 (Friedberg, I, 650).

[24] Instead of "divine" Luther has "spiritual and hidden."

to heaven or hell for you, so nobody can believe or not believe for you; and as nobody can open or close heaven or hell for you, so nobody can drive you to faith or to unbelief.[25] Since, then, belief or unbelief pertains to the conscience of each, civil authority, which is not lessened thereby, should be content to attend to its own affairs. Every man should be allowed to believe as he will and can, and no one should be constrained. Nothing should be so free as faith and religion to which no one can be driven.[26] Since this is a divine work in [the Holy] Spirit, human force is of no avail. Hence the common saying which Augustine also uses, "no one can or ought to be constrained to believe." [27]

These poor blind folk do not see how futile and impossible are their attempts. However much they command and rave, they cannot force men to follow save with the mouth and the hand. The heart they cannot compel, though they burst themselves in the attempt. True is the proverb, "Thoughts are tax free." [28] Why, then, do they try to make men believe with the heart, when obviously it cannot be done? Why do they compel weak consciences to lie, to deny [Christ], to say what they do not believe in their hearts, to burden themselves with the sins of others? All of the lies and confessions of weak consciences shall recoil on the heads of those who compel them. It were much simpler to let subjects err than to drive them into lies and false confessions.

Would you know why God suffers the civil rulers to act so atrociously? I will tell you. "God gave them over to a reprobate mind" [29] that He might make an end of them as also of the spiritual lords, who ought to perform their office and preach the pure Word of God, but leaving this they have become civil lords ruling with laws which apply only to the body. How completely the rôles are reversed! Whereas bishops ought to feed souls with the Word of God, instead, they rule castles, cities, lands, and people with external domination and plague souls with unspeakable atroci-

[25] Luther has throughout "me" instead of "you."

[26] Luther: "for faith is a free work to which no one can be forced."

[27] *Contra litteras Petiliani*, II, 83 (184): CSEL LII, 112.25-26; PNF [1] IV, 572.

[28] See the note in WA XI, 264, n. 1. [29] Rom. 1: 28.

ties. Likewise, the civil authorities ought to govern their subjects with even-handed justice; [30] on the contrary they do nothing but fleece and flay, impose tax upon tax and tribute upon tribute, and entrust public affairs to the wolves, until not a vestige remains of justice, truth, and faith. Little wonder that our society is decadent, since it is disturbed by those who should establish tranquillity.[31] Princes, leaving their natural function, wish to legislate for hearts and consciences, bishops assume the administration of worldly affairs. Sacred and secular are confused and each is contaminated by the sins of the other, until the civil government, laden with the hate of God and men, goes under, along with bishops, priests and monks, one scoundrel with another. Then they blame the Gospel, and rather than praise God [32] they curse and blaspheme. Thus they suffer only what they have richly deserved.[33] This is the counsel of God on the mighty of the world. But they will never have faith lest the wrath of God should be turned away by their repentance.

Someone may object, Does not Paul say in the thirteenth chapter of Romans, "Let every soul be subject unto the higher powers"? [34] And Peter says, "Submit yourselves to every ordinance of man." [35] Precisely! These passages are on my side. St. Paul was talking about civil government. You have just heard that no one has authority over souls except God. Hence Paul cannot be talking about an obedience where there is no jurisdiction. We readily see, therefore, that he is not talking about faith, lest it be made subject to the commands of civil government. But he is talking about external goods, which the magistrate may regulate on earth. That this is the meaning, his words abundantly show where he prescribes the limits of authority and obedience,[36] "Render, therefore, to all their dues: tribute to whom tribute is due; custom to whom custom; fear to whom fear; honor to whom honor." [37] You

[30] Castellio here has almost obliterated Luther's contrast between inward and outward.

[31] Luther's point is merely that civil government is at as low an ebb as the spiritual.

[32] Luther: "instead of making confession."

[33] Castellio omits Luther's illustration from the fall of Rome.

[34] Rom. 13: 1. [35] I Pet. 2: 13. [36] Rom. 13: 7. [37] Cf. index, Rom. 13.

see that civil obedience and authority apply only externally to tribute, custom, honor, and fear. Again especially where he says, "Rulers are not a terror to good works, but to the evil,"[38] he assigns limits to the magistrate, that he should punish crimes and not coerce faith and the Word of God. Likewise St. Peter, when he says, "ordinance of man."[39] An ordinance of man does not reach to heaven, nor can it touch the soul, but remains on earth and cares for earthly things where men are able to see, judge, pass sentence, punish, and save.

Christ also made this distinction neatly, when he said in the twenty-second chapter of Matthew,[40] "Render therefore unto Caesar the things that are Caesar's and unto God the things that are God's." If the hand of Caesar reaches unto the kingdom and authority of God, there would be no difference, and why then should a distinction be made? For, as we have said, the soul is not subject to the authority of Caesar. He can neither teach nor guide it, kill nor make alive, bind nor loose, judge nor absolve, retain nor remit, all of which he would be able to do, if his authority extended to souls. And all of this he may do with regard to bodies, goods, and honor, because these are subject to his jurisdiction.

And David, too, long ago clearly and briefly stated this truth in the one hundred and thirteenth Psalm:[41] "The heaven, even the heavens, are the Lord's: but the earth hath he given to the children of men." That is to say, man has authority from God with regard to that which is on earth and pertains to earthly rule, but God alone is Lord of heaven and the celestial kingdom. And did not Moses mean the same thing, when he said, "Let us make man, and let him have dominion over the fish of the sea, and over the fowl of the air, and over the cattle, and over all the earth, and over every creeping thing that creepeth upon the earth"?[42] And the sum of the whole matter is contained in this, "We ought to obey God rather than men,"[43] as St. Peter says in the fourth chapter of Acts, where he assigns limits to the secular magistrate, for if we ought to do everything which the civil government com-

[38] Rom. 13: 3.
[39] I Pet. 2: 13.
[40] Matt. 22: 21.
[41] Ps. 115: 16.
[42] Gen. 1: 26.
[43] Acts 5: 29.

mands, what point would there be in saying, "We ought to obey God rather than men"?

If, then, a prince or civil ruler tells you to believe this or that, or to go counter to Holy Scripture,[44] then you must say, "Lucifer may not sit by the side of God. I owe you obedience, noble prince, in that which affects body and goods. Command me to the extent of your authority on earth and I will promptly obey, but if you command me to believe according to the judgment of others or to give up my books, I will not obey, for in this you play the tyrant and exceed the bounds of your jurisdiction commanding that which lies neither in your authority nor power." If, then, the magistrate, like a plunderer, despoils you of your goods on account of such disobedience, blessed are you. Praise God, who has deemed you worthy to suffer for His obedience. Let the fool rage; he will find his judge. I tell you if you do not withstand him, but instead consent to let him rob you of faith and books, you have denied God.

I will give you an example; the tyrants have somewhere[45] promulgated an edict that whoever has a New Testament should give it up to the magistrates and their delegates. In this case the duty of the subject is to refuse to give up one page or syllable, lest he lose his eternal salvation. He who obeys, betrays Christ to Herod, for these Herods wish to kill Christ. One should suffer, however, invasion of premises and seizure of books and goods at the behest of tyrants. Violence is not to be resisted, but endured, yet not without protest [before God], since these tyrants act like princes of the world to which they belong. Now the world is the enemy of God. If, then, the tyrants would receive honor, they must do what the world approves and what God disapproves. Thus they remain princes of the world. Marvel not if they fume and rage against the Gospel. They must be true to their name and title.

Truly from the beginning of the world a wise prince is a rare bird, and a just and good prince still more rare. Much more numerous have been the [Midases, Caligulas, and Neros]. Many

[44] Luther: "Tells you to hold with the pope, to believe this or that or commands you to give up certain books."

[45] Luther: "In Meissen, Bavaria, and the Mark."

of them are God's torturers and hangmen whom the Almighty uses in His wrath to punish the bad and maintain the civil peace.

Wherefore, since it is necessary to have rich, noble, and powerful hangmen, God is pleased that we should call the agents of His wrath by imposing titles, as "clement and gracious Lords," that we bow down before them and obey them in all humility,[46] so long as they keep within bounds and do not become butchers and gladiators. But when God does grant a good Christian prince, prudent and God-fearing, that is a great and most precious sign of God's love toward His people. Usually the princes fulfill the saying of Isaiah in the third chapter:[47] "I will give children to be their princes, and babes shall rule over them." Or of Hosea, thirteen:[48] "I gave thee a king in mine anger and took him away in my wrath." The world is too bad and perverse to deserve good and prudent princes. Serpents must rule over frogs.[49]

Again, you may object that civil government compels no one to faith or religion, but merely provides that men shall not be seduced by false doctrine. How otherwise are heretics to be avoided? I answer: that this care appertains to the office not of the prince, but of the bishop, for heretics cannot be avoided by any outward force. Some other means must be employed than the severity of the sword. God's Word is the sole recourse, and if this does not avail worldly constraint is vain, though the earth be inundated with blood. Heresy is a spiritual thing which can be cut with no iron, burned with no fire, and drowned with no water. Only with the Word of God can it be cut, burned, and drowned, as Paul says in II Corinthians 10,[50] "The weapons of our warfare are not carnal, but mighty through God to the pulling down of strongholds, casting down imaginations and every high thing that exalteth itself against the knowledge of God, bringing into captivity every thought to the obedience of Christ."

[46] Castellio has obscured Luther's point that because God is a great god He must have rich and powerful hangmen, etc.

[47] Isa. 3:4. [48] Hos. 13:11.

[49] Castellio has missed the allusion to Aesop's *Fables*. Luther has, "Frogs must have storks." See WA XI, 268, n. 2.

[50] II Cor. 10:4-5.

Moreover, faith and heresy are never so entrenched as when they are opposed by sheer violence apart from the Word of God, for everyone can see that such violence lacks a just cause, since it proceeds without the Word of God, and can defend itself only by pure force like a brute beast. Even in civil affairs force has no place unless injustice has already been convicted by justice. How much more is it impossible to proceed in these exalted and arduous [51] cases by sheer violence without justice and the Word of God? See what wise lords these are who wish to drive out heresy, but succeed only in fortifying their enemies and making themselves suspect and in the wrong. Would you eliminate heresy, then you must devise a plan to pluck it from the heart and root it out of the desires. With force you will merely entrench, not expel. What have you accomplished if you confirm heresy in the heart and weaken it only on the tongue and drive men to lies? But if you strive with the Word of God, this will enlighten the heart and all heresy and error will vanish of itself.

The prophet Isaiah had in mind this method of exterminating heresy when he wrote in the eleventh chapter: [52] "He shall smite the earth with the rod of his mouth, and with the breath of his lips shall he slay the wicked." He teaches here that the controversy of the godless should be settled by the Word and the force of the Spirit.[53]

In a word, the princes and tyrants of this world do not understand that to fight heresy is nothing other than to fight the devil, who has possessed hearts with error, as St. Paul says, "For we wrestle not against flesh and blood, but against principalities, against powers, against the rulers of the darkness of this world, against spiritual wickedness in high places." [54] If, then, Satan is not expelled from the heart I do as much good by destroying his vessel with the sword and fire as if I were to fight lightning with straw. As Job testifies in the forty-first chapter,[55] the devil "esteemeth iron as straw" and has no fear of its violence. If all the

[51] Luther: "spiritual."
[52] Isa. 11: 4.
[53] Luther: "that the godless should be killed and converted by the mouth."
[54] Eph. 6: 12.
[55] Job 41: 27.

Jews and Turks were killed or tormented none thereby would be overcome and converted to Christ.

What a spectacle it is to see the princes of the world. Neither part performs its office. Bishops exercise themselves to condemn the Word of God and commit the cure of souls to secular princes, while the spiritual lords rule by the sword rather than by the Word of God. The civil rulers in turn overlook, or themselves commit, usury, theft, adultery, robbery [56] and the like and leave it to the bishops to punish these offenses by excommunication. The shoe is on the wrong foot. Souls are governed by swords and bodies with bulls. Secular lords govern spiritual matters, and spiritual lords the secular. What better Halloween pranks could the devil play on earth? These are our Christian princes who defend the faith and devour the Turk! To these lords we must commit the state whose wisdom turns things upside down and involves their people in ruin.

I should like, however, to give a word of counsel to the poor blind people. Let them remember the little sentence of David in Psalm one hundred and seven,[57] "He poureth contempt upon princes." I swear solemnly before God that if this saying applies to you, princes, you are lost, though each one of you be as mighty as the Turk. Your snorting and cruelty will do you no good. Already this begins to be fulfilled. There are few princes who are not regarded as fools and knaves, and rightly so. The common man is waking up. The scourge of the princes, which God calls "contempt" [58] is gathering momentum among the common people, and there is grave danger that insurrection cannot be avoided unless the princes begin to show themselves to be truly such by ruling justly in the fear of God with mercy and mildness. Men will not and cannot longer endure your tyranny and hardness of heart. Be wise, princes, consider and amend, for God will no longer suffer your iniquity. The world is not as it used to be that you should stalk and hunt the people like game. Leave off your outrage and force; remember to deal justly. Give free course to the Word of

[56] Luther: "murder." [57] Ps. 107: 40. [58] *Ibid.*

God, else it will take it in spite of you. Should heresy arise, let it be overcome by the Word of Almighty God. If you use the sword more than is meet, beware lest someone come who will tell you to put it up, and that not in the name of Christ.[59]

You may object: If the sword has no place among Christians how can there be outward government? Even among Christians there must be government. I answer: Among Christians there can be no higher power. Each is subject to the other as St. Paul says in Romans twelve,[60] "In honor preferring one another," and in the first Epistle of St. Peter in the fifth chapter,[61] "Be subject one to another." Christ also confirms this teaching, ["The princes of the Gentiles exercise dominion over them . . . but it shall not be so among you"];[62] and again, "When you are bidden of any man to a wedding . . . go and sit down in the lowest room."[63] Among Christians no one is more eminent than Christ Himself, for what preëminence can there be among those who are equal and equally enjoy the same right, power, goods, and honor; among whom no one seeks to be greater, but rather to be less? Among such men authority cannot be used, even if desired, because their nature and character forbid it. Where men like this are not to be found there are no true Christians.

What place is there, then, for priests and bishops? I answer: Their rule does not consist in authority and force, but in service and ministry, for they are not higher nor better than other Christians. They should not impose laws and statutes upon others without their will and consent. The office of spiritual rulers is to preach purely the Word of God and with it to govern [and feed the flock of Christ], and drive away heresies [and wolves], for Christians, as we have said, cannot be led nor governed by anything other than the Word of God, as St. Paul says, "So then faith cometh by hearing, and hearing by the Word of God."[64] Those who have no faith are not Christians and do not belong in the kingdom of Christ, but in the kingdom of the world, where they must be ruled and

[59] Luther: "in the name of God."
[60] Rom. 12: 10.
[61] I Pet. 5: 5.
[62] Matt. 20: 25-26; Luke 22: 25-26.
[63] Luke 14: 8-10.
[64] Rom. 10: 17.

constrained by the sword and outward administration. But Christians, on their own initiative, do their duty, moved only by the Word of God [and His Spirit]. But of this I have written elsewhere, much and often.

The Same, in His Postills on the Gospel of the Tares for the Fifth Sunday After Epiphany on the Twenty-fourth Chapter of Saint Matthew [65]

We learn from this text . . . how we should treat heretics and false teachers. We are not to root them out nor put them to death. Christ makes this perfectly plain, when he says, "Let both grow together." [66] Combat them only with the Word of God, for he who is astray today, may return tomorrow to the right path. Who knows when the Word of God may move his heart? But if he is burned, or otherwise destroyed, his conversion is rendered impossible. He is cut off from the Word of God, and he who might otherwise have been saved is of necessity lost.

There is, besides, another grave danger of which Christ warns us in this passage, namely, that the wheat be rooted out with the tares. This is atrocious in God's eyes and absolutely indefensible.

See, then, what mad folk we have so long been, who have wished to force the Turk to the faith with the sword, the heretic with fire, and the Jews with death, to root out the tares with our own power, as if we were the people who could rule over hearts and spirits and make them religious and good, which God's Word alone must do. But by death we cut them off from the Word, so that it cannot operate, and we do our best to bring upon our heads the responsibility for two deaths, in that we destroy at once the body temporally and the spirit eternally, and we say afterwards that we have rendered God a service and have earned some credit in heaven. Wherefore the inquisitors and murderers, if their brows be not iron, might well be terrified by this parable, if they had genuine heretics before them. As it is, they burn true saints and are

[65] WA XVII, II, 125.1-27, "Fastenpostille" (1525). In the French of Castellio only. The Biblical reference should be Matt. 13: 24 ff.

[66] Matt. 13: 30.

themselves heretics. What does this come to, if not that, like imbeciles, they are rooting out the wheat and calling it the tares?

Another Passage from Dr. Martin Luther from the Sermon on the Gospel for the Fourth Sunday After Trinity, Luke 6[67]

If the poor hardened Papists were not such bitter enemies of the truth, and of us on account of the truth, they could see by our lives that we have well kept the injunction of Christ to be merciful, for, praise God, we have taken vengeance on no man who has done us wrong, nor have we driven any from house, castle, wife, and child. We have thrown no one into prison because of his faith, much less on this account have we beheaded, drowned, burned, or hanged anyone, as these gentle saints have done, shedding innocent blood, and still do. Rather we have kept this teaching and injunction of Christ. We honor the magistrate with our teaching in so far as he does right. We pray for him in public and in private and administer to him in writings friendly and earnest admonitions as to his office, as God has commanded and enjoined upon us, etc.

THE OPINION OF JOHN BRENZ WHETHER THE MAGISTRATE HAS AUTHORITY TO PUT TO DEATH ANABAPTISTS AND OTHER HERETICS[1]

Among the divisive errors, which have arisen in our time on account of the Christian faith, not the least is that of the Anabaptists so called, who through a misunderstanding of baptism teach that no children should be baptized before the age of reason. Infant baptism is of no avail. For that reason they baptize themselves over again in their maturity. They also practice community of goods, carry no sword, refuse to take an oath to the civil govern-

[67] WA XLI, 327.6-19, sermon no. 32, first printed in 1535 as of June 20. The editors are in doubt as to the year in which it was preached (*ibid.*, pp. xxiv, xxvi). This passage appears in the German version of our work.

[1] *Bedencken Iohann. Brentij. Ob ein Weltliche Obrigkeit in Göttlichen und billichen Rechten die Widertäuffer durch Fewer oder Schwerdt vom Leben zum todt richten lassen möge?* I have used the edition of Felix Bidembach, *Consiliorum theologicorum*, Decas IV (Franckfurt am Meyn, 1608), No. 1, pp. 429 (incorrect pagination 529) to 444. For an account of other editions and of the circumstances see the introduction, p. 53.

Johannes Brentius der H. Schrifft 77
Probst zu Studgard.
WEil mein Heimmat/Hall in Schwaben
Zum Predigr macht mich/durch Gotts gabn/
Zu Tübingn Schul vnd Kirch anricht/
Zu Studgard Probst stirb/nach Gotts gricht.
Starb im Jar. 1570. K v

John Brenz

ment, and declare that no Christian can bear the sword of the magistrate, and other like articles are deduced from an ignorance of Scripture.

Inasmuch as the Bible abundantly demonstrates that repetition of baptism is a disparagement of the sacrament and the teaching of the Anabaptists is a new, pharasaical and monkish seduction [2] the question then arises as to what is to be done to ward off and wipe out this fanatical heresy. Some magistrates think that fire and sword are the appropriate means for the extermination of heresy, and they appeal to the imperial law which prescribes the death penalty for Anabaptism.[3]

The first question then for our consideration is whether according to the imperial law all Anabaptists without distinction should be put to death.

Now, to begin with, we must distinguish two kinds of offenses, spiritual and civil. To the spiritual belong unbelief, despair, despondency, misunderstanding of Scripture, heresy, secret hate and envy, covetousness of another's goods or wife or anything else which offends God, but does not disturb the public peace. Among the civil offenses are treason, murder, robbery, theft, adultery, and whatever else destroys social tranquillity.

For these two types of offense God has ordained two types of swords and punishments. The spiritual are punished by the Word of God, the civil by the sword of the emperor. Each offense should be handled with that weapon only which is effective in suppression. Now spiritual sin is so subtle and the sword of the magistrate is so crass and carnal that it serves rather to erect than to eradicate. Spiritual sins do not reveal themselves with an evil countenance like murder and robbery, but appear adorned with respectability and prudence. No unbelief is so bad as to be bereft of plausibility, and no heresy so false as to lack Scriptural warrant. If, then, with the civil sword we attempt to punish unbelief and mere heresy, we simply entrench the devil and drive things from bad to worse. To Satan applies the passage in Job 41,[4] "The sword of him that layeth

[2] "Sedition" in Brenz.

[3] *Codex Theod.*, XVI, 6, 6; *Codex Iust.*, I, 6, 2. [4] Job 41: 26-28.

at him cannot hold: the spear, the dart, nor the habergeon. He esteemeth iron as straw, and brass as rotten wood. The arrow cannot make him flee." But the Word of God puts him to flight when his impostures and lies are disclosed. Then he can no longer stand. For when the devil fights with unbelief and heresy no other resistance is necessary than to drag him to the light and disclose his wiles. He is the father of lies,[5] and hateth the light.[6] As soon as the Prince of Darkness comes to the light of the truth he must cringe and fail.

The civil sword is not so mighty that it can disclose a secret sin in the same manner as a public offense, or strip hidden injustice of its alluring disguise. Such constraint only makes it the more intriguing. Unbelief and heresy are the more confirmed in their error by mere civil persecution. So long as the grace of God is lacking for the conviction of heretics, and they continue to defend their position from Scripture, however wrongly interpreted, prosecution must look like persecution for the Word of God. Torture but hardens their obstinacy to their own corruption and the readier seduction of those who see their steadfastness. For this reason the best way is to let the Gospel and the Holy Scripture only fight with heresy that by their revelation it may be exposed and denuded of its fair display.

Before the world heretics may perfectly well appear as upright, if not orthodox. So long, then, as they do not commit murder, adultery, and theft, do violence to no man and keep the civil peace; so long as they "render to all their dues: tribute to whom tribute is due; custom to whom custom; fear to whom fear; honor to whom honor," as St. Paul writes to the Romans,[7] civil punishment has no jurisdiction over them. Paul says that the magistrate is a "minister of God . . . a revenger to execute wrath upon him that doeth evil.[8] This text is by all means to be referred to civil offense and not to spiritual unbelief. Murderers, criminals, and public enemies are subject to civil punishment. Unbelievers and heretics, who live uprightly before the world, are subject to the

[5] John 8: 44. [6] John 3: 20. [7] Rom. 13: 7. [8] Rom. 13: 4.

Gospel and to God in the next world. This was the command of Christ to his disciples in the thirteenth chapter of Matthew that they should not root out the tares, but "let both grow together until the harvest, etc." [9] Christ means that Christians should not root out unbelievers and heretics—these are the tares—with the bodily sword, but should fight only with spiritual weapons until the harvest. Then the heretics will receive their punishment, if they have not changed. If unbelievers and heretics are put to death they are deprived not only of their bodies here, but also of their souls hereafter, because they might have turned from unbelief and error to the true faith, from which they have been prevented by the tyranny of the magistrate.

Again, Paul wrote, "A man that is an heretic after the first and second admonition reject." [10] Here Paul says not that heretics are to be burned or judged with the sword, but that, if they do not walk in the right way they are to be rejected.

The objection may be raised that Christ and Paul, by virtue of their office, put no one to death, whether the sin were great or small, but restored even penitent murderers and adulterers. I answer, It is true that the Gospel puts no one to death. Public offenders are excluded from the Christian congregation by the ban and treated as the heathen and the publican.[11] If they change their lives, they are restored to communion and declared to be Christians. At the same time the Gospel does not interfere with the office of the magistrate, provided he keeps within his proper bounds and punishes what he has authority to punish, namely, civil offenses, which disturb the public peace. If the sword intrudes into that which has been committed to the Gospel and God's Word, such as unbelief and heresy, then disturbance rather than peace will result, and the sword will be blunted through usurpation of an alien office. [This is to put one's sickle into another's harvest, as the proverb says.] [12] The heresy of the Anabaptists, if I judge correctly, has been fostered by nothing so much as by a tyrannical use

[9] Matt. 13: 30. [10] Titus 3: 10. [11] Matt. 18: 17.

[12] Karl F. W. Wander, *Deutsches Sprichwörter-Lexikon*, 5 vols. (Leipzig, 1867-1880), "Sichel," 4, 5, 10, 15.

of the sword wielded against them without the authority of the Word of God and the instruction of the Holy Scripture. God is angered because of this misappropriation of the civil sword for spiritual offenses and, to punish men, has given the devil free range to rage and establish his error. Civil punishment has produced no improvement among the common people, but has merely confirmed error precisely because the affair of the Anabaptists is not a public offense but a hidden illusion supported by Scripture.

This shows plainly and abundantly that unbelief and heresy, so long as nothing else is involved, are subject only to the punishment of the Word of God. If they break loose and commit sedition, murder, or some other crime, then, and then only, are they subject to the correction of the civil sword. The fact of unbelief and heresy, in such cases, is irrelevant. These offenses are punished in the case of heretics and unbelievers on precisely the same grounds as when committed by those of apparent orthodoxy. In a word, unbelief and heresy belong not to the civil, but to the spiritual, sphere. Otherwise, if unbelief were subject to the sword of the magistrate, then would the magistrate himself be as amenable to the sword as his subject, and if heresy were to be expelled by force what point would there be in studying Scripture? The hangman would be the most learned doctor.

In favor of the contrary view, appeal is made to Deuteronomy thirteen:[13] "If there arise among you a prophet, or a dreamer of dreams, and giveth thee a sign or a wonder, and the sign or the wonder come to pass, whereof he spake unto thee, saying, Let us go after other gods, which thou hast not known, and let us serve them; thou shalt not hearken unto the words of that prophet, or that dreamer of dreams, etc., but that prophet, or that dreamer of dreams, shall be put to death; because he hath spoken to turn you away from the Lord your God, etc."

And again in the same chapter: "If thy brother, the son of thy mother, or thy son, or thy daughter, or the wife of thy bosom, or thy friend, which is as thine own soul, entice thee secretly, say-

[13] Brenz quotes the whole of Deut. 13: 1-10. Castellio condenses.

ing, Let us go and serve other gods, which thou hast not known, thou, nor thy fathers, etc., thou shalt not consent unto him, nor hearken unto him; neither shall thine eye pity him, neither shalt thou spare, neither shalt thou conceal him: But thou shalt surely kill him; thine hand shall be the first upon him to put him to death, and afterwards the hand of all the people. And thou shalt stone him with stones that he die."

These are the two laws of Moses, which are adduced to prove that heretics should be put to death by the civil sword, because we are told that the introduction of heresy is equivalent to leading men away from the true God and His Word to another god and lies.

But Christianity is fundamentally different from Judaism. Among the Jews there were physical promises, physical blessings, a physical land, a physical kingdom, and priesthood: there was also a physical slaughter of enemies. These were but types of the truth to be manifested in Christianity. And the physical blessing of the Jews corresponds to the spiritual blessing of Christians, and the physical kingdom to the spiritual kingdom. The physical extermination of the Canaanites, Jebusites, and false teachers foreshadowed the spiritual extermination of the enemies of the Christian, that is, his sins and also false teachers. Sin in the body is to be repressed by the Spirit of God, and false teachers are not to be followed in the faith, but, as Paul said, are to be rejected.[14]

Christ taught the same thing in the eighteenth chapter of St. Matthew,[15] "Wherefore if thy hand or thy foot offend thee cut them off and cast them from thee." This saying has reference not merely to the corporal hand or foot, but also to the spiritual, to teachers, friends, and companions. Nor is the cutting off corporal, but rather spiritual. The meaning is this. If you have a minister, friend, or helper who offends you by false teaching or seduces you with an evil life you are not to obey him, but cut him off, that is, avoid his company and let him be as a heathen and a publican.[16] This spiritual avoidance or separation was signified in the law by the physical slaughter of the false prophets.

[14] Titus 3: 10. [15] Matt. 18: 8. [16] Matt. 18: 17.

The law of Moses exercised corporal punishment also with regard to the outward ceremonies, and physical penalties were inflicted. In the first book of Moses in the seventeenth chapter we read:[17] "And the uncircumcised man whose flesh of his foreskin is not circumcised, that soul shall be cut off from his people; he hath broken my covenant." And in the fourth book in the fifteenth chapter[18] Moses caused a man to be stoned to death for having gathered sticks on the Sabbath day. But in the Gospel there is freedom with regard to physical penalty or enjoyment, belief or unbelief, and the use or penalty is spiritual as Christ says, "He that believeth . . . shall be saved, but he that believeth not shall be damned."[19]

The objection is made that the corporal punishment of heretics is not committed to the Gospel and to preachers whose office is purely spiritual, but rather to the civil magistrate. I answer, as I have done above, that each office must stay within the prescribed limits. So long as the unbeliever or heretic conducts himself in civil matters in an upright and irreproachable fashion, the civil sword has no jurisdiction over him. What has it to do with unbelief or heresy? The function of the civil sword is to maintain the civil peace and not exceed the appointed bounds. The magistrate sets a highly dangerous precedent when he introduces the custom of suppressing any faith with the sword. He may indeed attack an erroneous faith, but his successors, having acquired the method, may turn against the true faith. This happened in the Arian controversy. The bishops accustomed the Roman emperors to persecute the Arian heretics. Then some of the emperors, already indoctrinated with this technique, were converted to the Arian position and began to persecute the orthodox bishops and to treat them as heretics. For this reason the safest course is for the civil government to adhere rigidly to its own domain and to suffer spiritual sins to receive a spiritual punishment, for it were four times or ten times better that an erroneous faith be tolerated than that the true faith be persecuted.

[17] Gen. 17: 14. [18] Num. 15: 32-36. [19] Mark 16: 16.

But now to leave heresy in general and to take up the Anabaptists again. The contention is made that Anabaptism is not simple heresy, but has accompaniments which fall within the sphere of the civil government, for the Anabaptists teach that goods should be held in common. Now this tenet might perhaps produce an insurrection. Very well, but one cannot legitimately put the Anabaptists to death on this score. They do not teach that others should be forced to practice community of goods, and they themselves constrain no one. Neither should we proceed against them with constraint.

Until now the monks and nuns have taught and held that anyone joining their orders must renounce private property and hold all things in common with them. How, then, does it come about that because of this very teaching the monks have been reputed as learned, saintly, God-fearing, and perfect Christians, but now, for precisely the same doctrine, the poor Anabaptists are strangled and put to death? Their hypocritical monastic position is not the fruit of baseness or malice, but of simplicity and ignorance in the understanding of certain passages of Holy Scripture. But if a man is immediately to be put to death because he misunderstands one or two passages of Holy Scripture, who would be secure from the sword? We find that almost all the saintly doctors failed on one passage or another. Ought they then to have been killed? What injustice?

The proper treatment for the misunderstanding [of the Anabaptists] is friendly and Christian instruction and not the sword of the magistrate. If they receive our teaching we have gained some for Christ and our side is increased. If they will not be instructed, then let them go and treat them as the heathen and the publican,[20] but the magistrate should not meddle, unless in addition to erroneous belief there is also a civil offense.

Again, the objection is made that there will be an insurrection if the Anabaptists become sufficiently numerous and use force against others. I answer: How does it happen that we have grown

[20] Matt. 18: 17.

so captious and fear an insurrection because of the Anabaptist doctrine of community of goods when we entertain no like fear because of the monks. Would it not have been possible formerly to say, "The monks teach and practice community of goods. When, then, they are grown numerous they will commence an insurrection and attempt to compel everyone to deposit his goods in their common fund? Even without an insurrection, by the leaven of their teaching and the hyprocrisy of their lives, they have drawn to themselves the goods of almost the whole world and have instituted a venal traffic in heaven and eternal life." If one, rather than another, should be put to death for teaching communism the bishops and the monks should have the preference rather than the poor Anabaptists who have not commercialized heaven and the life to come. If everything out of which sedition might conceivably at some time arise were to be suppressed with the sword, we should have to prohibit rigorously all banquets and business, assemblies and fairs and church gatherings, for experience shows that insurrection has been hatched at many a banquet, and many a fair has issued in a riot, and in many a church a conspiracy has been conceived. David would have had to suppress all sacrifice among the Jews because his son, Absalom, began the revolt at the sacrifice at Hebron,[21] and one would have to tear out the hearts of men because insurrection has its beginning in the heart.

The Anabaptists may well have some knaves among them who meditate revolt or other crimes, but we are discussing the genius of the movement and not particular black sheep. There is no faith and no profession without its discreditable representatives. If there is to be punishment, let it apply to them and not to the simple and ignorant. Time and again men, women, and maidens, though all their lives opposed to dissension, have nevertheless fallen into error. Ought they, then, to be put to death as disturbers of the peace?

A further objection is raised that even if the Anabaptists are not amenable to civil correction because of their communism, neverthe-

[21] II Sam. 15: 7 ff.

less they are because of their other tenet that no Christian can be a magistrate, and because they refuse to take an oath of allegiance to the government for civil protection.

Very well! This is their teaching and practice; but if they are to be put to death on this account, a beginning should be made with the priests and monks, for the "religious," to use the name which has been applied peculiarly to them, have been preëminently guilty on this score. They are the ones who have taught that no religious should pass a judgment of blood, and that no one who had done so should be received into their orders without a dispensation. Does not this mean that the office of the magistrate is forbidden to genuine Christians seeing that all genuine Christians ought to be religious, and the office of the magistrate cannot be conducted without the shedding of blood? There have been those who, on the basis of their constitutions and without any special examination, have presumed to take no oath of allegiance to the government, and if any of their members were constrained to swear, the magistrates were put under the ban. All this appears plainly in the papal decretals.[22] If then anyone were to be put to death on this account, who might be punished more appropriately than the religious, inasmuch as they have erred as grievously as the Anabaptists? They are both wrong in their interpretation that the Christian, as a Christian, may not wield the sword of the magistrate and shed blood because the Christian must be meek, forgiving, long-suffering, leaving vengeance to the Lord. The Anabaptists are wrong that the Christian in the rôle of the magistrate may not use the sword. God has instituted the magistracy and a Christian may better exercise this institution or office than a non-Christian. Equally is it true that the spiritual officer, the bishop, priest, or preacher, may not wear the sword because of his spiritual office. In committing the Gospel to the apostles and preachers, Christ at the same time instructed them not to use the sword as does the civil magistrate. They were not to suppose that the commission to preach the Gospel and to bind and loose carried with it authority

[22] Brenz may have in mind the passages which occur in *Corpus iuris canonici,* ed. Friedberg, I, 339-41.

to employ the civil sword. The prohibition of Christ applied not to their person in case they should be elected to the government or drafted by the government, but to their office. The apostles and their successors have no civil authority because they have received a spiritual commission, as the pope recognizes in his decretals. The religious were mistaken in that they associated the prohibition of bloodshed and of the exercise of civil authority not to the office, but to the consecrated person. If men are to be put to death on account of one error, who would be left alive? There would be no end to extermination.

But what then is to be done, seeing that the Anabaptists will neither promise nor swear to the civil government? The answer is that the Anabaptists should receive precisely the same treatment as the religious. If they will not swear civil obedience deprive them of civil rights. Treat them as foreigners who, on coming into a town, refuse to swear, on the pretense that they have done so elsewhere. The maximum penalty which can properly be inflicted is the denial of civil privileges. Anything beyond that is tyranny. Why then should the Anabaptists receive a harsher sentence?

Inasmuch as the imperial law is the prime authority to which appeal is made to justify the corporal punishment of the Anabaptists, the text of this law must now be cited that we may arrive at its meaning. The passage is found in the first book of the Codex, the second law, "That Holy Baptism is not to be repeated." [23] The Emperors Honorius and Theodosius to the Pretorian Prefect Anthemius.

"If anyone is discovered rebaptizing a minister [24] of the Catholic sect the penalty shall be death both for him who commits, and for him who suffers, the offense, if he be of the age of discretion."

This is the imperial law, word for word. First of all we observe

[23] *Codex Theod.*, XVI, 6, 6; *Codex Iust.*, I, 6, 2.

[24] The text which Brenz used and which prevailed in his day, read, "Si quis rebaptizare quempiam de Ministris Catholicae sectae," etc. The text of *Codex Iust.*, I, 6, 2 (p. 60), published by Mommsen and Krüger, reads, "Si quis rebaptizasse, ex quo lex lata est, quempiam de *mysteriis* catholicae sectae," etc. (Italics mine).

that it applies not to all Christians, who are rebaptized, but only to the ministers of the Christian Church, that is, to the acolytes, readers, exorcists, doorkeepers, subdeacons, priests, and bishops. The rebaptism of an ordinary Christian is not an offense, only that of a minister. In the second place, the law applies only to those who are caught in the act of rebaptizing and not to those who have already allowed themselves to be rebaptized. From this one may infer that the law was more of an intimidation to deter rebaptism than to kill rebaptists. Since rebaptism, though common, was secret, the law sought to prevent the offense by applying the penalty to him who was caught in the act, just as in the law of Moses [25] a householder was permitted to kill a thief who was caught red-handed, but lost the right if sunrise intervened.

In the third place, even if these considerations were irrelevant, the law cannot be applied to Anabaptism pure and simple, for we read in the histories [26] that this prefect Anthemius, to whom the law is addressed, was the wisest man of his day and a trusted counsellor of the Emperor Theodosius, who did and decreed nothing without his advice. We read also farther on [27] that the Emperor was a most God-fearing man whose court resembled a cloister and that he knew Scripture by heart. We may assume, therefore, that this law contemplated nothing imprudent or ungodly. But it would have been highly imprudent and ungodly to kill those who err simply because they err, when they might be reclaimed; if not, they ought in any case to be punished only by the Gospel. We may surely infer that this law contemplated in addition to mere rebaptism other circumstances which are not named. This imperial law as we have it consists merely of excerpts from works no longer extant. On this account great controversies have arisen among the jurists not only as to this law, but as to many other laws, because the primary sources are not

[25] Exod. 22: 2.

[26] In the margin Castellio supplies the reference and gives it incorrectly as Lib. I. The full reference is Cassiodorus, "Hist. Tripart." XI, 1: Migne, PL LXIX, 1187.

[27] Cassiodorus, "Hist. Tripart." XII, 17 (Migne, PL LXIX, 1199), from Socrates, HE, VII, 22 (Migne, PG LXVII, 784-88; PNF 2 II, 164).

available and there is no context to throw light on the meaning.

That this law does not contemplate mere Anabaptism may be inferred from the one immediately preceding in which the two Emperors Valentinian and Gratian say: [28] "We deem a bishop, who practices rebaptism unworthy of his priesthood and we condemn the error of those who rend the apostolic faith, and we condemn those who, having once received the sacrament of the Christian name, contaminate rather than purify it by rebaptism under the guise of baptism."

The two emperors, we see, were content to deem an Anabaptist bishop unworthy of his office and to condemn his errors. How, then, shall the other two emperors have been such tyrants as to put the poor people to death for mere Anabaptism?

The meaning may also be better understood in the light of the following law, in Book I, the section "On Apostates": [29] "If anyone has adhered to the venerable law and then from Christianity relapses into Judaism and joins himself to the blasphemous synagogue, his goods shall be confiscated."

This is the imperial law on apostasy. Now which is greater, to abuse one law, or to fall away from the faith entirely? Any fool can see that it is a greater offense to abandon the whole Christian faith than through misunderstanding to abuse one sacrament. Why, then, should the misuse of one sacrament be punished more severely than apostasy from the entire faith? If we are going to apply corporal punishment to all those who unworthily receive one sacrament, how many would be burned every year for unworthily receiving the Lord's Supper! Not even he [30] nor the bishops would escape, because they have forbidden communion in both kinds, which is not merely an abuse, but an abrogation of the whole ordinance of Christ.

Again, the imperial law punishes the greater heretics with noth-

[28] *Codex Theod.* XVI, 6, 1 and 2; *Codex Iust.*, I, 6, 1.

[29] *Codex Iust.* I, 7, 1, "De apostatis;" *Codex Theod.*, XVI, 8, 7, "De Ivdaeis, Caelicolis et Samaritanis."

[30] Castellio has substituted "he" for "the pope."

ing more severe than the loss of civil rights. Why, then, should it have applied a harsher punishment to the Anabaptists?

And if for rebaptism people are to be killed, the pope and the priests are subject to the penalty, because they both have rebaptized and still do. If an infant is baptized at home in urgent necessity by the women, then the child is baptized again in the church. Is not that rebaptism quite as much as the practice of the Anabaptists? The priests say, "If thou hast been baptized, I will not baptize thee again, but if thou hast not been baptized, then I baptize thee in the name of the Father, etc." [31] What is the point of this addition? They know from the testimony of the women that the child has been baptized. Why do they not leave it there? The Anabaptists also say that they do not baptize over again. They simply baptize for the first time, for they consider that infant baptism is no baptism, just as the priests regard that administered by the women, though there is no external defect.

In this connection it is not irrelevant to point out that Saint Cyprian, the martyr, the notable bishop of Carthage, and a whole church council [32] decreed that those who had been baptized by the heretics, and afterward became true Christians, should be baptized again. Although all the members of this council erred, they were not consigned to the devil, let alone put to death, and Cyprian, though he was the head of the council, is to this day esteemed as one of the holy martyrs. Since the Anabaptists have their error in common with such a learned and godly martyr, why are the Christians so bloodthirsty against them?

[31] Edmond Martène, *De antiquis ecclesiae ritibus libri tres*, Tom. I (Venetiis, 1788), Lib. I, Cap. I, Art. xvi, p. 59, traces the custom back to the fifth council of Carthage. The form is commonly supposed to have originated with John XXII in 1333, but Martène gives several earlier examples. For the survival in present usage, see *Catechismus Romanus* (1566), II, 2, 55, cited in Carl Mirbt, *Quellen zur Geschichte des Papsttums und des römischen Katholizismus* (4th ed. Tübingen, 1924), p. 346.

[32] *Sacrorum conciliorum nova et amplissima collectio*, ed. Joannes Dominicus Mansi, I (Florence, 1759), pp. 951-965: "Sub Cypriano episcopo sententiae episcoporum de haereticis baptizandis." ANF V, 565-72. Erasmus published the acts at the end of his edition of Cyprian, P. S. Allen, *Opvs epistolarvm Des. Erasmi*, IV (Oxford, 1922), Ep. 1000, p. 27.127.

All of these considerations indicate that the imperial law which condemned the Anabaptists to death had reference not to mere rebaptism, but to some associated civil offense which is not mentioned. Otherwise so Christian an emperor would have overstepped all humanity and justice.

But if this law does apply to rebaptism pure and simple, then it is certainly due to the instigation of the bloodthirsty bishops of whom there were many in the time of the Emperor Theodosius, to whom the emperors, being but newly converted to Christianity, accorded a docile adherence and regarded what fell from the bishops' mouths as the Word of God. We read in trustworthy accounts [33] that in the days of Emperor Theodosius there was a bishop of Synada who persecuted the Macedonian heretics so fiercely that he deprived them of their goods and went to Constantinople to stir up the whole court against them. In the histories his conduct is severely reproved as unbecoming a Christian.

A little farther on [34] we read that when Nestorius was consecrated bishop of Constantinople, in his first sermon to Emperor Theodosius, he said, "Give me, my Prince, the earth purged of heretics, I will give you heaven as a recompense. Assist me in destroying heretics, and I will assist you in vanquishing the Persians." This speech offended many upright men. No one favored heresy, but no one approved of the flippant and bloodthirsty address of the bishop to the emperor. If, then, the bishops led Emperor Theodosius like a bull by the nose and promised him heaven, little wonder that in his time such a law should be passed against the Anabaptists. Should we regard as a holy law one which was promulgated at the instigation of bloodthirsty bishops? Were it not more appropriate in such an instance to consider what is befit-

[33] Cassiodorus, "Hist. Tripart." XI, 3 (Migne, PL LXIX, 1189), from Socrates HE VII, 3 (Migne PG LXVII, 741-44; PNF [2] II, 154-55). Castellio omits Brenz's reference to "Nicephori Callisti ecclesiasticae historiae" Lib. XIV, Cap. 11: Migne, PG CXLVI, 1092.

[34] Cassiodorus, "Hist. Tripart." XII, 4 (Migne, PL LXIX, 1204), from Socrates HE VII, 29 (Migne, PG LXVII, 804; PNF [2] II, 169). Castellio omits the reference to "Nicephori Callisti ecclesiasticae historiae" Lib. XIV, Cap. 29 (which is a mistake for Cap. 31): Migne, PG CXLVI, 1157.

ting to a Christian government rather than what the violence of tyranny can extort?

It befits a Christian magistrate that he be not as bloodthirsty as a heathen. It befits him that, as a Christian, he have regard to the cure of souls and not merely to vengeance like a tyrant. But what sort of cure is this, to teach and instruct with the sword of the executioner the poor Anabaptists, who have fallen into error because of a mere misunderstanding of Scripture? No insurrection were to be feared from these people if the civil sword were otherwise properly employed. Let the magistrate attend to his office, oppress not the poor, forget not to protect the unfortunate, to guard widows and orphans, to give justice without respect of person according to the requirement of his office. Then he need fear no insurrection.

Rebellion is not so much the work of evil men as it is the consequence of the evil lives of rulers and subjects. Here is the principal cause of insurrection, as we plainly see in the case of King David. If he had not committed adultery, if he had not shed the innocent blood of Uriah,[35] and had accorded perfect justice to his subjects, then his son, however bad he might have been, would not have been able to hatch a conspiracy against his father and the poor subjects would not have suffered so miserably.[36]

The magistrates, therefore, should restrain the hand of correction from the simple Anabaptists and leave them to the chastisement of the Gospel. Let the rulers exert every effort to maintain peace and concord. Let anyone who disturbs the peace, be he Baptist or Anabaptist, receive the appropriate penalty.

ERASMUS

The Reckoning of the Errors in the Censure of Beda[1]

(Proposition XXXII.) The householder, that is, God, does not desire that the false prophets and heretics be rooted out, but that they be tolerated, if perchance they may repent and from tares be turned into wheat. If they do not repent they are to be reserved for

[35] II Sam. 11. [36] II Sam. 15. [1] *Opera,* IX, 580D-582F.

the judgment of Him to whom eventually they will pay the penalty. ⟦Castellio omits the initial dilatory expostulation, but fails to bridge the gap smoothly.⟧

First of all I should like to know whether Beda approves of our Lord's parable of the tares and the wheat. If he does, as I suppose he does, then I should like to know whether he approves of the interpretation of the orthodox Fathers, especially Jerome and Chrysostom. The latter copiously teaches that the Lord forbade putting heretics to death. Among other things Chrysostom says this: "The Lord did not forbid us to dissolve the assemblies of the heretics, to stop their mouths, and to take away their freedom of speech. He forbade us merely to kill and slay." [2] If I have correctly interpreted the passage in accord with the Gospel and the explanation of the ancient scholars, that the field is the Church, the seed is the evangelical doctrine, the householder is the Heavenly Father, or, if you like, Christ, the servants are the apostles and the leaders of the Church, the enemy is the devil, the tares are the doctrine of the heretics, the harvest is the end of the world, and the harvesters are the angels of God; if this is correct, why throw up at us the Wyclifites, Bohemians, the damned Lutherans, schisms of the Empire, and laws of the Church? Do I take away the sword of the magistrate, which is ordained of God even for the Gentiles for the vengeance of the bad and commendation of the good? [3] Although Christian princes should be slow to kill if there is any other way to save sinners. Do I take away the authority of bishops to teach, correct, excommunicate, and the like? What laws of the Church do you cite to me here? Is it a law of the Church to cast anyone into vengeful flames? For the ancient bishops the extreme penalty was excommunication. Augustine pleaded with the imperial prefects not to put to death the Donatists who were more than heretics. They were seditious brigands. He assigned as his reason that some among them might be saved, and he showed that the obstinacy of the heretics is advantageous to the Church. He confesses also that many who err in

[2] "In Matthaeum homil. XLVI": Migne, PG LVIII, 477, PNF [1] X, 289.

[3] Rom. 13: 3-4.

the faith are tolerated in the Church because they do not propagate their views. He does not object if God stirs up the minds of princes to the coercion of those who disturb the tranquillity of the Church. But who ever heard of orthodox bishops inciting kings to butcher heretics who were nothing more than heretics? Augustine would not suffer a heretic who through lust of power or goods should enlist a following. If riots ensue and each side claims to be the Catholic Church, and the question has not been sufficiently aired, the prince should curb both sides. What shall hinder the prince from killing heretics who disturb the public peace, seeing that even the rulers of the Gentiles have this right as well as our own princes against the orthodox? The Emperor commands that heretics be punished, but he adds, those who are lawfully convicted and are obstinate.[4] The task of the bishops, in so far as in them lies, is to teach, correct, and cure. What sort of bishop is he who can do nothing more than constrain, torture, and commit to the flames? If those who exercise this office are of the sort that Beda portrays in this book, if they have such a spirit of hate, such impudence, such zeal for calumny, such corrupt judgment that they would sooner drive ten men into heresy than reclaim one, can we say that the accused are accorded decent treatment? If I am not mistaken the inquisitor first singles out one against whom he has a grudge, lodges an accusation and secretly hurries the victim to prison where he is cross-examined on articles like those which Beda throws at me, some false, and some corrupt. If there is any discussion, it takes place in prison. If the accused mutter a defense, three picked monks are promptly called in to pronounce the final sentence. Where the theologian accuses, imprisons, prosecutes, and turns the victim over to the secular judge, and where the judge commits to the flames not on his own motion, but in accord with the sentence of the theologian, where the theologian acts as the

[4] This policy might be inferred from the edict of the Diet of Worms against Luther. *Deutsche Reichstagsakten unter Kaiser Karl V*, ed. Adolf Wrede (Gotha, 1896), No. 92 (May 8, 1521), p. 649. Deutsche Reichstagsakten, jüngere reihe. . . . Auf Veranlassung Seiner Majestät des Königs von Bayern, hrsg. durch die Historische Kommission bei der Königlichen Akademie der Wissenschaften (Gotha, 1893-), Bd. II.

author and executor of the penalty, how much, I ask you, does this differ from the shedding of blood, especially if the motive be hate, ambition, or avarice? Perhaps Beda is not the same in other matters as he is in this book. Nevertheless, I do know one whose name I spare because he has gone to his own place—I pity him if he receives from God, the Judge, the treatment which he has meted out to others.[5] I say this not because I favor the heretics. I hate them if anyone does. I will not favor a milder treatment of one whom I know to be a heretic, that is, one who errs maliciously, who is factious and incurable. I do not urge clemency for heretics to the point that I become one myself. With Augustine I say, "I am able to be in error. I am not able to be a heretic." [6] I have conducted myself in the present dissension so that both the Emperor and the Pope are persuaded of my sincerity, for both have thanked me, even though that which I did I could not have left undone without sin. The time may come when many will approve of my zeal and temper in this schism. The congeries of accusations assembled by Beda to the effect that I would tolerate any sort of criminal and other still more atrocious charges, these are mere calumnies. As a paraphraser I rendered the meaning of the Gospel in good faith. I did not digress from the footsteps of the ancient doctors, nor did I dare to add to the words of the evangelists the comment which Beda proposes. The discourse is conducted under the person of Christ. What appendix has the paraphraser a right to affix? Shall he add this: "Take up the tares, provided there is no danger to the wheat, and cast them into the fire?" Beda insists that this is what Christ meant, but this is precisely what He plainly forbade the servants to do. How nicely

[5] The reference is probably to Erasmus's troublesome opponent, the inquisitor Nicholas Baechem of Egmont (Ecmondanus), who died Aug. 23/24, 1526. P. S. Allen, *Opvs epistolarvm Des. Erasmi*, III (Oxford, 1913), Ep. 878.13, p. 416. The "Prologus in supputationem calumniarum N. Bedae" was dated Aug. 1526. *Bibliotheca Erasmiana* (Gand, 1893), I, 178. On a later occasion Erasmus did not hesitate to make this same remark about him by name. *Opera*, X, 1575 F.

[6] The thought but not the words in Ep. XLIII, 1: CSEL XXXIV, 85; PNF[1] I, 276.

Beda's comment fits in, "provided there is no danger." Why, then, did the Lord himself say to wait until the harvest? And he himself identified the harvest with the end of the world. Why did he tell the servants not to do anything before the harvest? Why did he give the reason for his prohibition? What are the angels to do if in the meantime the heretics have been removed by the servants? unless perhaps Beda would apply to all criminals a passage which I have expressly restricted to false prophets and heretics.

But the Church, he says, does otherwise now, and so also do the decrees of the popes. That has nothing to do with my paraphrase. Nor were these things said in the person of Erasmus, but in the person of Christ, nor of the present time, but of that in which the infant Church was planted by the martyrs and watered by blood. Nor was the parable addressed to the multitude, nor to princes, but to a select group of disciples to whom it was given to know the mystery of the kingdom.[7] Then Beda calumniously treats these words as if they were uttered by me, as if I taught that heretics should not be punished.

Nor, in the meantime, does he distinguish between ecclesiastical censures and capital punishment inflicted by civil law. Quite irrelevantly he appeals to the decree in Deuteronomy on putting the prophet to death,[8] as if the Church now wielded both swords. The Gospel says, "Tell it unto the Church, but if he neglect to hear the Church, let him be unto thee as an heathen man and a publican," [9] as if there were any mention here of burning at the stake. The disciples were commanded to avoid, not to burn. Again the Apostle says, "After the first and second admonition, reject." [10] Is to reject the same as to cast into the fire? Again he says, "Therefore put away from among yourselves that wicked person." [11] Does "put away" mean to kill? If this had been done he would not in the Second Epistle to these same Corinthians have commended the man who was corrected.[12]

The next text cited by Beda, "The weapons of our warfare are

[7] Mark 4: 11; Matt. 13: 11; Luke 8: 10. [8] Deut. 13.
[9] Matt. 18: 17. [10] Titus 3: 10. [11] I Cor. 5: 13. [12] II Cor. 2: 7-8.

not carnal"[13] but spiritual, militates against his own position, unless he should be so impudent as to suggest that I deprive ecclesiastics of all office and authority. Moreover, Peter did not pronounce sentence on Ananias and Sapphira, but through inspiration of the Spirit announced the vindication of God.[14] If this instance is to be regarded as an example, take also the case in which Peter raised the dead, healed the sick with his shadow, and opened closed doors with a word.[15] These things he did often, the other but once.

At this point they chant to us the celebrated dictum, "Repel force with force."[16] How much more should this saying be celebrated among theologians at least, "Resist not evil,"[17] and "Dearly beloved avenge not yourselves"?[18] In all of the passages cited by Beda in favor of his opinion from St. Augustine, and which we have thus far passed over, there is no mention of killing, only of punishment. The Donatists were punished by the transfer of their ecclesiastical property to the Catholics and by the exile of those who disturbed the public peace. I might examine Augustine's letter to Count Boniface[19] where many arguments are used which if understood with reference to capital punishment would require us to force the Turks and the Jews to the faith by the fear of death. That this was not the opinion of Augustine appears from his statement that the tractable are to be recalled, the intractable first cowed, then instructed. He adduces the example of Paul who was thrown to the ground, then commanded to go to Ananias. Who can teach those who have been killed? Who can raise up the slain? In the Epistle to Marcellinus, which is the 157th, he sings a song vastly different from that taught by Beda. With great solicitude he pleads that those who had committed crimes worthy of death against Christians, should be punished with some penalty other than death. His words read in part: "If the Count is not persuaded

[13] II Cor. 10: 4. [14] Acts 5. [15] Acts 9: 40; 5: 15; 12: 1-11.

[16] Karl F. W. Wander, Deutsches Sprichwörter-Lexikon, I, "Gewalt," 47. Cf. Erasmus, *Opera*, II, "Adagiorum," Chil. III, Cent. III, XLVII, 792E, and Chil. I, Cent. X, LXVII, 385 C-D.

[17] Matt. 5: 39. [18] Rom. 12: 19.

[19] Ep. CLXXXV: CSEL LVII, 1-44; PNF[1] IV, 633-51.

by my letters let him at least grant that the culprits be kept in prison until we have time to petition the Emperor, lest the sufferings of the servants of God, which should be glorious in the Church, be sullied by the blood of their enemies. I know that in the case of the clergy in the valley of Anaunia, who were killed by the pagans and are now honored as martyrs, the Emperor readily granted the petition that there be no retaliation in kind upon the murderers, who were caught and imprisoned."[20] Did, then, Augustine, who would spare the Donatist assassins, Augustine, who thought that the honor of the martyrs of God was stained by the blood of their enemies, did he think that the simple heretic, even though obstinate, should be burned in the flames?

[Castellio closes at just the right point. Erasmus continues. "However, I neither urge nor discourage princes from butchering heretics. I am talking about the office of an ecclesiastic. . . . Beda's reiterated accusation, that I agree with the ancient heretics and the modern Lutherans that heretics are not to be punished, is an unwarranted statement and a manifest calumny. I never thought or taught this. In my paraphrase I was giving not my opinion but that of Christ. . . . Beda could have maintained the papal constitutions without blasphemy against Christ, insult to the holy doctors of the Church, and calumny of a neighbor, had he referred the parable to apostolic men, that is, to those administrators of the Church whose office it is to cure souls not to take life. The parable, moreover, applies more particularly to the early days, when the Church was subject to pagan rulers and did not as yet enjoy the right to shed blood, but according to the dispensation of God was exercised and strengthened by persecutions, afflictions, and deaths, by the attacks of princes and heretics. This interpretation I think is true and sound, and I followed it in my paraphrase. In this way Beda could have harmonized his comment with the constitutions of the Roman pontiffs, but he passed this over in order to find room for calumny, and what the Lord said in former

[20] Ep. CXXXIX, 2: CSEL XLIV, 151; PNF[1] I, 489.

times to a handful of select apostles, instructing them against the adverse storms to be raised by the heretics, this Beda imagines Erasmus saying to the Lutherans, that I may condone them."]

The Same Erasmus in His Reply to the Inquisition [21]

[The objection of the monks reads: "In the *Paraphrase on Matthew XIII*," Erasmus has said that "the servants are those who wish to root out the tares before the time, that is, those who think that false prophets and heretics should be removed before the time by sword and death, whereas the householder desires that they be not rooted out, but tolerated, if perchance they may repent and from tares be turned into wheat, and if they do not repent, let them be reserved for their Judge to whom they will some day pay the penalty."

Erasmus, in his reply, says that he has sufficiently explained himself on this point in his replies to Beda and Latomus, and there is no need to repeat. Castellio picks up the reply at this point.]

As often as I consider within myself how execrable are heresy and schism I cannot condemn the cautery of the law, however severe. Yet again, when I reflect with what mercy Christ planted, nourished, advanced, and established his Church throughout the centuries, I scarcely see how I can approve of the example of those who today, on account of scholastic opinions, drag men to prison and the stake, as now we see priests burned because they would rather call a girl with whom they live a wife than a concubine. Such priests I mean to cure, not to condone. The reproach that I wish them to escape with impunity is not applicable here. I merely wonder whether such severity comports with the mercy of the Church. It is not for me to approve or disapprove of the laws of secular princes. They have their justice and their councils; they have their judge to whom they shall render an account. My paraphrase explains the meaning of the parable in the Gospel. If the explanation is true and worthy of Christ and in accord with

[21] *Opera* IX, "Adversus monachos quosdam Hispanos, titulus IV, Contra sanctam haereticorum inquisitionem, objectio XXII," 1054D-1055D.

the approved orthodox interpreters, why should it be rejected? Or if it is to be rejected, why are they not equally to be condemned? Up to the time of Augustine, that is, more than four hundred years after the birth of Christ, we never read that the orthodox bishops besought the aid of the emperors against the heretics, although the heretics themselves frequently did so.[22] Nevertheless the orthodox were unwilling to imitate their example until the headstrong, incurable, and utterly insufferable fury of the Donatists and Circumcellions drove them to it. In this case there was not only an unprecedented schism, but the Donatists even put out the eyes of the orthodox with lime and acid,[23] and some they killed and others they forced to commit homicide[24] under threat of death. Nor were the schismatics kinder to themselves than to others, for they took their own lives with the sword, or if swords were not available by leaping over precipices.[25] What more? Things had come to such a pass that the Donatists could not be suffered by any princes, pagan or Christian, even though neither heresy nor schism had been involved. Consequently when there was no tranquillity and no end of violence, the bishops agreed to ask the aid of the Emperor against the intolerable savagery of the Donatists. But the more merciful, among whom was Augustine, were displeased with this appeal to the secular authority in an ecclesiastical affair.[26] Bishops, they thought, should use no arms save the Word of God and prayer and as a last resort anathema, that is, exclusion from communion. This was then the extreme penalty of the Church. Just as in legal parlance exile is called civil death, so among the apostles and their successors separation from the fellowship of the Church was capital punishment. Not only the examples of Christ, the apostles, and the martyrs support this opinion, but even fear of the danger that if such severity be exercised, heretics will be replaced by feigned Christians to the

[22] This statement is not accurate. See the Introduction.

[23] Augustine, Ep. LXXXVIII: CSEL XXXIV, § 8, p. 414; PNF [1] I, 372.

[24] Castellio in the French has "suicide."

[25] Augustine, Ep. CLXXXV, II, 12: CSEL LVII, 10-12; PNF [1] IV, 637.

[26] *Ibid.*, VII, 25: CSEL LVII, 23-25; PNF [1] IV, 643.

great detriment of the flock of Christ. But when the contrary opinion prevailed, and things quieted down, many having been corrected by severity who had been detained against their will in the Donatist camp, or had been in doubt or seduced by error, then Augustine strongly approved of the course which previously he had condemned. Nevertheless even against such furious brigands and assassins a law all too mild, in my judgment, was passed which touched the goods and life of no individual, but merely transferred the property of the heretical churches to the orthodox,[27] and gave the Donatists the privilege of enjoying their former possessions if they would but transfer their membership. Such was the clemency that neither priests nor bishops, if repentant, were deprived of their station. A slight fine was imposed upon a small group of recalcitrants; but nothing was done about killing such beasts. When, then, for the first time an edict of the Prefect Macedonius,[28] if I recall, seemed ambiguously to menace unrepentant heretics with death, Augustine vigorously admonished him not to inflict capital punishment, which was not authorized by the imperial constitution, and commended a later edict which cleared up the ambiguity. Likewise he admonished the Prefect Dulcinius [29] to behead no one. From these statements it is sufficiently evident how he shrank from this cruelty of confiscations, imprisonments, executions, and burnings, which now are all too pleasing to some and particularly to those who profess the perfection of Christian piety. They should seek to heal rather than to destroy and to mitigate the severity of the law by their intercession. But now these masters of mercy exceed the edicts of princes in cruelty.

[Castellio breaks off here. Erasmus goes on to say that shifting the responsibility from the ecclesiastical to the civil authority is a mere subterfuge, since the civil proceeds at the instance of the

[27] *Codex Theod.*, XVI, 5, 43 (Nov. 15, 408 [407]). *Codex Iust.*, I, 9, 12.

[28] Marcellinus. Augustine, Epp. CXXXIII and CXXXIX, from which extracts are given below under Augustine.

[29] Dulcitius. Ep. CCIV, § 3: CSEL LVII, 318-19.

ecclesiastical. Then comes a comparison between the severity of the present time in comparison with the comparative mildness of the days of Augustine and Theodosius. "I do not condemn the surgeon's knife, but I regret that the sins of Christians should have deserved so severe a remedy. I am grieved at the punishment of parricides, though I assuage my grief by the consideration of the public peace. I feel the same way toward those who cannot be cured, but must of necessity be removed lest they lead others to destruction; but although the law must perhaps of necessity be severe, certainly the office of priests and monks is to strive to save rather than to destroy." This point is further elaborated. Then Erasmus complains of the triviality of the doctrines for which men in his day were prosecuted. He turns back to the Theodosian Code and to the Decretals to show that not every error was subject to penalty, but only those of real moment. "But now a man is dragged to the flames if he doubt whether the Roman pontiff has authority over purgatory." Here Castellio takes up the thread (1057 D-E)⟧.

Likewise a little further on: Formerly heretics, who were brought before a synod of bishops had the privilege of defending themselves. Those who were convicted had the option of pronouncing an anathema on their teaching or of being anathematized themselves along with their teaching, that is, excluded from communion. This was then the maximum penalty imposed by the Church. Berengarius [30] who was accused not because of his opinion on the origin of confession or of purgatory, but because of his view of the truth of the body of Christ, was not constrained, even though after having been once dismissed he relapsed into the same error. But now monks disseminate unfounded rumors, and then drag suspects to prison where debate is conducted in monkish fashion. Articles are noted and fagots prepared. But all of this is irrelevant to my purpose though perhaps of some use to others.

[30] Berengarius of Tours, who died A.D. 1088. See the article in RE [3] II, 607-12.

⟦Here Castellio again breaks off. Erasmus continues. "Someone may say that if I do not approve of the law for putting heretics to death, which is not the case, what will this mean for the Inquisition? Was there, then, no Holy Office in the days of Athanasius, Jerome, and Augustine because there was as yet no constitution for the burning of heretics?" Erasmus then says that his purpose in the *Paraphrases* was to follow the interpretation of the ancient doctors. It will not be amiss, therefore, to glance at their opinions on the parable of the tares, bearing in mind that their views are quite diverse. Here Castellio continues the citation. (1058A-1059B.)⟧

Again a little later on: John Chrysostom, a godly man and most learned in the Scriptures, in his Forty-seventh Homily on Matthew 13 [31] interprets the parable of the Lord to mean simply that heretics are not to be put to death, and assigns several reasons for this opinion. But lest anyone should suppose that he would grant heretics complete impunity, he adds this qualification, "The Lord," he says, "does not forbid us to restrain heretics, to stop their mouths and take away their freedom of speech, to break up their assemblies and societies; he forbids us merely to kill and slay." If anyone wishes the rest of the passage he can look up the reference which I have given.

Theophylactus took the same position: "The servants," he said, "are the angels, who were distressed at the presence of heresies and evil in the soul and desired to pull up and kill the heretics and evil minded. But God did not suffer the destruction of the heretics by wars lest the righteous also suffer and be destroyed," [32] etc.

St. Jerome interpreted the rooting up of the tares as the separation of the heretics from the Church: "Lest," he says, "in pulling up the tares you root out the grain at the same time. Give room for repentance, and let us be advised not to cut off a brother hastily, for it may come about that he who today is depraved by noxious

[31] Migne, PG LVIII, 477-78; PNF [1] X, 288-89.
[32] "Enarratio in Ev. Matt. XIII," Migne, PG CXXIII, 283-86.

doctrine may turn tomorrow and begin to defend the truth."[33] At this point, Jerome modifies his assertion in view of the fact that Paul plainly taught and acted otherwise, since he advised not so much as to eat with a brother who is a fornicator or avaricious, and himself delivered some to Satan.[34] Jerome says, therefore, that in a case of unmistakable error we should not cut off hastily, and where the matter is dubious, never, but should reserve the examination of such cases for the Lord. "Between the wheat and tares," he says, "while they are in the blade, there is a great likeness and either no difference, or one scarcely perceptible. For this reason the Lord says that in doubtful cases we should not pass hasty judgment, but should leave the decision to God, so that, when the day of judgment comes, He may eject from the company of the saints, not the suspicion of crime, but one manifestly guilty." This is Jerome's opinion.

⟦Castellio omits a few lines directed against those who cry "Heresy! Heresy!" without having read a book.⟧

Again a little farther on: "What point is there in recounting the opinions of Remigius, Anselm, and Bede? [35] I prefer St. Augustine, who is the fount and father of all scholastic theology, by which the authors of these tragedies especially swear. He gives his opinion in many places and with particular minuteness explains this parable in the book called *Gospel Questions* in the section on

[33] "Comment. in Ev. Matt.," Lib. II, Cap. XIII: Migne, PL XXVI, 93-94.

[34] I Cor. 5: 11, 5: 5; I Tim. 1: 20.

[35] Erasmus probably found the statements of Remigius and Bede in the *Catena aurea* of Thomas Aquinas, which is available in English translation, *Catena aurea. Commentary on the Four Gospels Collected out of the Works of the Fathers by S. Thomas Aquinas.* St. Matthew, Vol. II (Oxford, first ed. 1841, new ed. 1874). The original of Bede is in Migne, PL XCII, 68-69. The translators of the *Catena aurea* say that in their day the commentary of Remigius was unpublished. For his opinion see my article, "The Parable of the Tares as the Proof Text for Religious Liberty to the End of the Sixteenth Century," *Church History*, I (June, 1932), 74, n. 24. From what source Erasmus drew the reference to Anselm I do not know. There is nothing on the parable in Migne's edition, PL CLVIII and CLIX.

the 11th and 12th chapters of Matthew.[36] He adds to the comments of others that this parable applies not only to the heretics, but also to those who cause offense to the Church by their evil lives. Augustine adds that the saying of the Lord, "lest while ye gather up the tares, ye root up also the wheat with them," applies not only to those who think and live well, but also to those who might be converted to better things and from tares become wheat, for he destroys the good who casts out the bad, which was on the point of becoming good. With regard to killing the bad he has this:[37] "Our Lord did not say 'in the time of the harvest I will say to *you*, Gather ye together first the tares,' but he says, 'I will say this to the harvesters.' Whence it is evident that the task of gathering the tares for burning does not fall to the office of the sons of the Church." A little farther on, dealing with the case of the righteous man who is inclined to smite heretics, Augustine says, "The inclination may arise in him to make away with such men, if the opportunity presents itself, but he consults God's Justice as to whether he ought. Does it command or permit this and does it wish men to exercise this office? Here applies the question of the servants, 'Wilt thou then that we go and gather them up?' To whom the Truth itself replied, 'Man is not so constituted in this life as to be certain what one may become who is now in error, or what good may come of his error. Such persons are not to be killed, lest with the bad, the good be destroyed, or those who will become good. The separation should be made at the end, when there is no further opportunity of change or profit from the mistakes of others. The task also falls not to men, but to angels.' This is the meaning of the reply of the householder, 'Lest while ye gather up the tares, ye root up also the wheat with them. But in the time of the harvest I will speak to the reapers.' In this way the Lord made his disciples most patient and serene, etc." This is all from Augustine.

[In the remainder of the passage Erasmus reiterates his conten-

[36] Pseudo-Augustine, "Quaestionum septemdecim in evangelium secundum Matth. I, Quaest. XI, XII," Migne, PL XXXV, 1367-69.
[37] *Ibid.*, col. 1370.

tion that in the *Paraphrase* he was speaking, not in his own name, but in that of Christ. The conclusion is that princes should exercise moderation in the use of the sword and theologians should be concerned to heal and not to destroy. Then Erasmus discusses criticisms levelled against his dialogue on the Inquisition in the *Colloquies* and against a passage in the "Prologue" of the *Paraphrase on Matthew.*]

AUGUSTINE ELEUTHERIUS [SEBASTIAN FRANCK]

Heresy Not Lightly to Be Believed of Those Against Whom the World Brings the Charge!—From the Book on Heretics[1]

There is danger lest Jerome's statement be true that the bodies of many are revered on earth whose souls are tormented in Hell,[2] since the judgments of God and men are as far apart as heaven and earth, for that which is esteemed among men is an abomination in the sight of God[3] (Luke 16 and Isaiah 25). We clearly observe what the world has canonized until now and still does [canonize]. And on the other hand the world pronounces as heretics all those who are opposed to its truth, light, and Gospel, which is nevertheless itself a lie, darkness, and abomination; inasmuch as the world regards as saints only those whom it has itself hallowed, and again proclaims, publishes, and heralds its darkness and lies as light and truth, and holds as heretical anything, no matter how right and true, which opposes its abomination. Thus was it always, witness the treatment of Christ and the apostles, and before them, of the prophets, who were condemned as heretics. In like manner Waldo in 1158, Dolcino in 1307, Rockenzan in 1361, Wiclif in 1364, and Hus in 1414 were condemned as heretics.[4] The same thing com-

[1] Sebastian Franck, *Chronica, Zeÿtbuch und Geschÿchtbibel* (Strassburg, 1531), cccxxxiiij verso, line 8 from bottom, to cccxxxvj verso, line 24; ccccliiij, line 7, to verso, line 1; ccccclx, line 28, to ccccclxj verso, the entire page.

[2] This does not sound like Jerome who defends the veneration of relics. Ep. CIX: Migne, PL XXII, 906-909, and XXIII, 343-47.

[3] Luke 16: 15.

[4] Waldo embraced poverty in 1176 and was refused permission to preach by the Lateran Council in 1179. Dolcino was a leader of the Apostolic Brethren,

monly happens in our own day and will happen, that many are regarded as heretics and punished, whom future generations will revere as saints. Wherefore I fear that many good Christians have been numbered among the heretics. This was plainly true in the case of the prophets, Christ, and the apostles, among whom Christ is an outstanding example. Subsequent generations always build and garnish the tombs of the prophets, Christ, and the apostles and yet ever, like the Jews, fill up the measure of their fathers.[5] As the Lamb was slain from the foundation of the world[6] so to the end will it be slaughtered. Wherever Christ is present, there are found Judas, Annas, Caiaphas, Pilate, and the whole passion. The world has not become better, nor more wholesome,[7] that it should not do the like again, but rather worse, so that the truth must be severely persecuted as heresy by everyone. For this reason there should be very careful consideration as to what should be done and why, for commonly Christians called heretics are not understood [unless after it is too late] or are deliberately calumniated. Thus Christ and the truth were always condemned by the world and held for heresy and a lie.[8] [Christ had this in mind

---

a group similar to the Spiritual Franciscans, and like them inspired by the prophecies of Joachim of Fiore. Dolcino led an armed revolt, was captured and burned in 1307. Rokyczana was an Utraquist archbishop of Prague, who attended the Council of Basel in 1433. Hence Franck's date is out of the question. Wiclif died in 1384. The date, 1364, has no point. Hus was burned in 1416. Articles on all will be found under their names in the RE [3], except on Rokyczana for whom see II, 429 and III, 447. On Dolcino see, in addition to the article, I, 701-703. Castellio has omitted what immediately follows in Franck, namely: "Erasmus, Martin Luther, and Huldrich Zwingli in 1530. On the other hand, what the pope carries in his hands and that which supports and hallows his side, that is canonized."

[5] Matt. 23:29-32; Luke 11:47-48. [6] Rev. 13:8.

[7] Castellio has rendered "frömmer" by "sanior." "Fromm" in the sixteenth century was closer to "tüchtig" or "brav." Hajo Holborn, *Ulrich von Hutten* (Leipzig, 1929), p. 20.

[8] Castellio omits: "For this reason I am afraid that there are many destined for the outer darkness at the judgment who are now announced in the calendar of the saints and their bones held in honor, such as Thomas Aquinas, Scotus, and many popes, who are nearly all saints. Since their judgment is false, it must follow that everything deduced from it is incorrect."

Das verbüthschiert
mit siben Sigeln verschlossen Büch/
das recht niemandt auffthün/verstehen/oder lesen kan/
dann das lamb/vnd die mit dem Thaw bezaichnet/das lamb angehö-
ren/sampt einer vorred von den siben Sigeln/was die seyen/vnd
wie die auffthon werden. Zu letst ein klain einlaitung vnd
anweysung in die Hailigen Schrifft/wie man sich inn
Mosen richten/die Propheten lesen/vñ Christum
das büch des lebens verstehen soll/allen schü-
leren Christi/zur Christlichen vbung/
vñ Götlichen räterschafft/von
Sebastian Francken
fürgestellet.

Es werden euch aller Propheten gesicht sein / wie die wort
eines versigelten büchs / das man gibt einem der lesen kan / vnd spricht: Lieber lise das/
Vnd er spricht: Ich kans nicht / dann es ist versigelt. Esaie 29.

Es ist Gottes ehre sein wort verbergen / aber der Künig glori dem
selbigen nach zu fragen/ Prouerb. xxv.
Wa jr nit glaubt/so werdt jr fälen/vnd es nit verstehen/ Isai. vij.
M. D. XXXIX.

The Book Sealed with Seven Seals
by
Sebastian Franck

when he said, in John 7,[9] "The world cannot hate you; me it hateth, because I testify of it, that the works thereof are evil."] Herein is confirmed the saying of Luke 16,[10] "That which is highly esteemed among men is an abomination in the sight of God." And that you may prove all things,[11] God remains true,[12] and the holiness, righteousness, and wisdom of the world belong to the devil (Matthew 7, John 16, I Corinthians 13, and Isaiah 64). The Scriptures powerfully declare the works of God, which daily increase, if one has but the eyes to see. In a word, if I had the choice I should prefer to be among those whom the world[13] condemned as heretics rather than among those who have been esteemed as saints. One sees clearly enough in our own day what the world calls heresy and how maliciously and captiously words are snared and distorted and pronounced heretical, if they seem to diverge one iota from the truth, or rather from the world's legends and lusts [for the world proclaims as truth that which it approves and condemns without mercy all those who dissent]. Why should I not believe that Wessel,[14] Wiclif, John Hus, and some of the ancient heretics as well, though the Church was not yet so depraved, were unfairly and underhandedly oppressed and their words maliciously distorted, inasmuch as this is precisely what we see done today?

In truth those who today boast that they have the true orthodox religion as taught by the Catholic doctors,[15] and who so boldly condemn others as heretics, as a matter of fact are no more in accord with these doctors than with the Gospel, as we shall presently show, and really regard the doctors themselves as heretics in spite

[9] John 7: 7. [10] Luke 16: 15. [11] I Thess. 5: 21. [12] Rom. 3: 4.

[13] Throughout this paragraph Castellio has substituted "the world" for "the pope" and has omitted a reference to Erasmus.

[14] Wessel Gansfort, on whom see *Wessel Gansfort, Life and Writings*, by Edward Waite Miller . . . *Principal works*, translated by Jared Waterbury Scudder (2 vols., New York, 1917).

[15] Castellio paraphrases in this way Franck's reference to the Roman Church and omits his account of her false judgments not only upon Arius, Sabellius, Marcion, Luther, Zwingli, and the Anabaptists, but also upon the early fathers themselves.

of all garnishing of their tombs[16] and profession of discipleship. I well perceive with what discrimination such men are able to judge of spiritual things, for truth is of such a character that no one is able to judge of it or understand it [even though he have all human knowledge at his finger tips], unless he is himself in the truth (I Corinthians 2) since the world is not only incapable of such things, but rather loves and seeks the contrary, namely, a lie (Psalm 4).[17] How is he able to pass and pronounce judgment on these matters, who not only has no natural knowledge of them, but if anyone speaks of them, scoffs, maligns, and perverts the truth, however much he may profess it?

This I say because I know that the whole wide world is not able to understand a Christian, much less to speak and judge of his way, though the blind world daily does judge of this color, to be sure after its own fashion, and no better than flesh judges of spirit and darkness of light. This all appears clearly in the case of Christ. Nicodemus, the master in Israel, did not understand Him (John 3), and all the Scribes and Pharisees failed so completely that they considered his doctrine to be puerile, foolish, and a dreadful lie, and they judged him to be possessed of a devil and a heretic. Likewise today the truth which the world cannot understand nor grasp is considered heresy. The world fails as lamentably in judging the spiritual as does an ass in playing on a harp.[18] All is perverted and truth turned into a lie. The world can speak only falsehood of Christians.

For this reason Scripture is called a book sealed with seven seals,[19] and is so composed of the words of God that none may understand it save His children with whom He speaks in parables and mysteries, in order that they only may perceive who are born of Him.[20] This obscure speech is sealed to all who are without, that is, to all the world.[21]

[16] Matt. 23: 29. [17] Ps. 4: 2.

[18] Franck adds: "or a cow in playing checkers." Cf. Karl F. W. Wander, *Sprichwörter-Lexikon*, I, "Esel," 524, 568, 569; II, "Kuh," 399.

[19] Rev. 5: 1. [20] Reminiscences of Mark 4: 11-12, and John 3: 3.

[21] Castellio omits the statement that the philosophers learned the folly of a promiscuous proclamation of the truth and of God.

Hence Truth desires her time and pupils, so that it is better to be silent than to cast Truth unseasonably before a cruel world, as pearls before swine (Matthew 7 and Amos 5).[22] I see most clearly in our day how the spiritual are calumniated, and I infer that it was ever so, since true godliness has always been hateful to the ungodly. Evil and malicious writers in positions of authority have perverted everything and have not written sincerely and honestly about those whom they hate. From such the truth is not to be learned. If the Scribes and Pharisees had written the Gospel of Christ, we should find his words marvelously perverted and distorted. He would be called a revolutionary, seducer, fanatic, diabolical blasphemer, sorcerer, arch-heretic, chief of scoundrels, mortal enemy of God and of the law of Moses, as well as the son of a harlot, as he is called in their Talmud.[23]

If, then, in our own day men like these, cruel, false, and mighty (such men always are mighty with the blind world),[24] if such men were to give their opinion of the heretics precisely that would happen which we see happening. One sect would persecute another with deadly hatred. Neither would understand the other, and the very same thing would be condemned by the one and commended by the other. The defeated—and the godly are always defeated—would be universally maligned, both alive and dead, and the mighty would be praised. Such is the world; it always favors the powerful and hates the godly, because by their life it is condemned (Wisdom 2,[25] Matthew 10) [26] [but it is not able to hate the ungodly, John 7].[27]

Christ employed parables and obscure words, when, with his own mouth he addressed the learned, because they were unable to grasp his meaning, for the world is never able to grasp and com-

[22] Matt. 7: 6; Amos 5: 13.

[23] R. Travers Herford, *Christianity in Talmud and Midrash* (London, 1903), the opening section and especially pp. 43-45.

[24] Franck, in place of this, has: "the pope and the so-called Evangelicals."

[25] Wisdom 2: 12-16.

[26] Matt. 10: 16 f.

[27] John 14: 17. Castellio has paraphrased and expanded a great deal in this paragraph.

prehend the spirit of truth (John, 14) [28] that this mystery should be to them no more than a closed book. They then perverted all his words, and did not understand in the least, though they heard him speaking while yet alive. This is the reason for my belief that many were regarded as heretics either because the world condemned them, or because no one understood them and all manner of falsehood was said and written about them, just as we see it daily happening now. For that reason I very much wish that we had the copies and true originals of the works of the heretics, as we do of John Hus. No book is so bad that a Christian may not profit from it [for a Christian cannot be beguiled and corrupted]. Truth, when set over against error, shines forth only the more clearly and steadily. That is why God permitted heresies to arise, and it is expedient that there should be lies for the proving and establishing of the truth, for every proposition carries with it and demands its contrary.

I wish especially that we had their books that we might discern the falsehood or truth of their "errors." Those first heretics, in the days of the apostles, must have presented a plausible case, since they persuaded many, even though the apostles were still alive,[29] so much so in fact that on account of these heretics a council was held (Acts 15) which would never have been done, if they had not been able to give their assertions the color of probability from Sacred Scripture. Of the later heretics nothing is recorded but sheer perversity and abominable blasphemy with neither plausibility nor Scripture, as of Simon, Manes, Menander, etc.,[30] some of whom gave themselves out to be God and Christ and taught such nonsense that I cannot believe those first Christians would have been deceived by them had their heresy been so crass. It looks to me very much as if Eusebius had omitted passages, as we do. When we begin to hate someone we say nothing but evil of him, as the proverb has it, "The mouth of an enemy speaks

[28] John 14: 17.

[29] Castellio omits a reference to Cerinthus and Ebion, the Christological heretics, and to those who wished to perpetuate the law of Moses.

[30] Castellio omits Montanus.

well of no one." [31] Historians sometimes recorded popular rumors long after the event, and we may well conceive that the heretics themselves were altogether different. Many of their sayings were distorted, and many things were falsely attributed to them. The good was omitted, the bad accentuated or increased. Today if ten men listen to the same sermon they are no sooner out of the door but they debate as to what was said and there as as many opinions as heads. The very books which are treasured and widely circulated are nevertheless sometimes corrupted,[32] as Erasmus frankly confesses in his *Annotations*,[33] Tertullian in *Against Marcion*,[34] and Origen *On Matthew, Homily XXVI*.[35] Is it then incredible that the like should have happened to the words and writings of the heretics, who were the enemies of all? [Since often we observe that upright and highly esteemed men are so blackened by the calumnies of the Scribes and Pharisees as to be rendered hateful to all.] The like, I think, has happened to the heretics. If they had taught nothing but horrible blasphemies, as the Anabaptists are accused of doing, it would be a marvel that they should succeed in persuading one man.

These are the words of Eleutherius.[36] And again in the same book, *On Not Punishing Heretics with the Sword*,[37] he says:

Some think that when Christ forbade pulling up the tares before the harvest He did so because the world is blind and has no

[31] Karl F. W. Wander, *Sprichwörter-Lexikon*, I, "Feind," 88. From Franck's collection I, 78b.

[32] Castellio has blunted the point of the following citations by omitting the words of Franck: "Holy Scripture is not exempt."

[33] The "Adnotationes" in *Opera*, VI, are preceded by a list of "Loca manifeste depravata." Cf. IX, 1070C, where he says there is not a single codex without error.

[34] The entire work brings the charge that Marcion has corrupted the Gospel of Luke and the Epistles of Paul.

[35] Homily XXVI on Matthew is in Migne, PG XIII, 1868-69, but has nothing to the point. The passage which Franck had in mind I think is "Comment. in Matthaeum," XV: Migne, PG XIII, 1293A.

[36] Franck continues the Preface for little more than a folio page. He explains in greater detail the character of his chronicle of heretics and closes with his characteristic contrast between the spirit and the letter of Scripture.

[37] ccccliiij recto, line 7, to verso, line 1.

knowledge of the truth, especially its scribes [that is, the learned] and the leaders of the blind, because, if authority were given to the world to pull up the tares, since it is itself a tare, it would pull up the wheat for the tares, that it might occupy the field alone, just as it has always done, not only against the prophets and Christ and the apostles, but also today against many. For this reason authority is rightly denied to us and reserved for God alone, as Augustine says,[38] "They are not to be deprived of life, lest, if we wish to destroy the bad, we kill the good for the bad," and the same thing he says again clearly that this is not the duty of men, but of the angels.[39]

Moreover, not only Augustine took this view of the parable in Matthew 13, but also Chrysostom and others, as well as Bede, Remigius, and Anselm,[40] namely, that no force is to be used against heretics, nor is anyone to be compelled to a free faith, because God desires a willing and unconstrained heart, and Christians are called free and independent because their state proceeds from the compulsion of no law, but from the free leading of the Spirit which works and teaches in them faith and infuses love. Augustine in his book entitled, *Questions on the Gospel of Matthew*, Chaps. XI and XII,[41] explains the parable of the tares at length, and more than all other commentators he says that this parable is to be understood not only of the heretics, but also of moral delinquents. Such is his opinion. He goes on to say that the command to gather up the tares at the time of the harvest was not directed to the Church, but to the harvesters, that is, the angels, from which it is to be understood that this is not the business of the Church, but of the angels. Moreover that heretics should be punished only by excommunication is shown not only by the teaching of Christ and the example of the early Church, but also by the

[38] Pseudo-Augustine, "Quaestionum septemdecim in evangelium secundum Matth. 1, Quaest. XII": Migne, PL XXXV, 1370.

[39] Further testimony of Augustine is omitted.

[40] Franck probably borrowed these references from Erasmus, *Opera*, IX, 1058; see p. 181, n. 35, above.

[41] Pseudo-Augustine. See p. 29.

ancient doctors, such as St. Ambrose, c. II, Quaest. I, "Quae dignior," [42] and likewise Origen on Leviticus, "Cum aliquis." [43]

[Citations follow from Erasmus, Brenz, Melanchthon, and Odenbach's *Ain Sendbrieff vnd Ratschlag, an verordnete Richter über die armen gefangnen zu Altzey, so man nennet Widerteuffer,* 1528. (Copy at Cornell.) Castellio takes up the translation again on f. ccccIx recto, line 28, and carries it to the end of ccccIxj verso.]

The Same Eleutherius in the Same Chapter

In this connection all the works on Christian liberty and on the difference between the Old Testament and the New are relevant. Some formerly wrote well on the subject because they were in peril, but now that this liberty has become an embarrassment to them, they put on again the worn shoe and sing again the old song. From Christ they return to Moses, from the sun to the shadow, and would restore the force, sword, and law of Moses, although there is One here who is greater than Moses, Solomon, Jonah, and the prophets,[44] who has established a new covenant in the spirit which supersedes the old in the letter,[45] namely, Jesus Christ, whom the Father has commanded us to obey.[46]

On this subject Luther wrote excellently, in my judgment, on "How Moses should be read, and how far the Old Testament is valid, and how far it is now abrogated," [47] against those who bring forth Moses from the darkness, shadows, and figures and set him in truth in the place of Christ. This is going backwards from the

[42] *Decreti*, Pars II, Causa XXIV, Quaest. I, c. xxvj, "Quae dignior," Ambrosius in commentariis ad c. 9 Lucae: Friedberg I, 976; Migne, PL CLXXXVII, 1277. Ambrose, in this passage, is insisting on the duty of avoiding the heretic.

[43] *Decreti*, Pars II, Causa XXIV, Quaest. III, c. vij, "Cum aliquis," Origenes super Leviticum hom. XIV, ad c. 24: Friedberg I, 992; Migne, PL CLXXXVII, 1298. Origen is pointing out that an evil life really excommunicates whether the Church does so or not, and *vice versa.*

[44] Cf. Matt. 12: 41-42; Luke 11: 31-32. [45] Jer. 31: 31-34; Heb. 8: 8-11.

[46] Franck's word is "hear," alluding to the voice at the transfiguration, "This is my beloved Son: hear him." Mark 9: 7; Matt. 17: 5; Luke 9: 35.

[47] *Unterrichtung wie sich die Christen in Mose sollen schicken* (1525), WA XVI, 363-93.

promised land to Egypt, from the desert to Babylon, from sonship to servitude, etc.[48]

To turn now from these contemporary opinions, would that we had many like Emperor Constantine, who, in the first session of the Council of Constantinople, wrote plainly to Pope Agatho that he would constrain no one, force no one to the faith, but would merely exhort and leave the judgment to God.[49] He acted like a wise and prudent prince, and not like some of his successors, who seduced, bewitched, and induced by false doctors,[50] as Theodosius by Nestorius,[51] constantly enlarged their decrees, until at the Council of Constance, they arrived at chains, crosses, fires, and wheels.

The decree of Valentinian and Marcian, promulgated against the Manichean heretics, after the council of Chalcedon, orders that their books should be burned and they should be sent into exile. Their hearers or readers, however, should merely be fined ten gold marks.[52]

Another edict of the Emperor Marcian ordered that the heretics should suffer the confiscation of their goods and should be sent into exile. They should be deprived of the right to make a will or to appoint a guardian of their property, and any who gave them lodging should be beaten. If the heretics were rich and honorable they should be fined ten gold marks as an example and their books should be burned. This decree was directed solely against the Apollinarians and Eutychians, in the same manner as the former applied only to the Manicheans.[53]

[48] Castellio omits a reference to Luther's tract, *On Civil Government*, from which there is an extensive citation elsewhere in the *De haereticis*.

[49] The reference is to the Emperor Constantine Pogonatus who, at the time of the Third Council of Constantinople (A.D. 680-681), wrote a letter to Donus, the bishop of Rome, which was delivered to his successor Agatho (A.D. 678-681). Franck cites the letter *in extenso*. The original is to be found in Mansi, XI, 195-200.

[50] Franck: "by the popes." The reference to "successors" would indicate that Franck confused Constantine IV with Constantine I.

[51] Socrates, HE VII, 29: Migne, PG LXVII, 804; PNF ² II, 169.

[52] See the next note.

[53] Franck appears to have made two laws out of one. In the *Codex Iust.*, I, 5, 8, is a law of Valentinian and Marcian against the Eutychians and Apol-

Now indeed, although these decrees are not so objectionable as those passed at the Council of Constance, nor as those which now call for beheadings, burnings, and hangings, in which the bloodthirsty devil so obviously reveals himself—he would like to behead everybody at a blow—nevertheless both these decrees go beyond, and are contrary to, all the Scriptures and the early fathers and even to the decretals of the persecutors, witness Decret. XXIIJ, Quaest. IIJ, cap. IIJ, "Si ecclesia," [54] where it is plainly stated that the true Church is the one which endures persecution, not that which inflicts it. Such was the Church of Christ and the apostles.

In his sermon on *All the Saints,* Augustine says that the Church is always strengthened by the cross, not in resisting, but in suffering.[55] The Damascene teaches the same thing in 3 Sent., cap. 32,[56] namely, that the Gospel was preached to the whole world and overcame its adversaries, not by weapons, arms, and war, but the wise men of the world were put to shame by a handful of the

---

linarians. The previous law (I, 5, 5) of Theodosius and Valentinian against the Manicheans adds to the text of the Theodosian Code the words, *et ultimo supplicio tradendis* (and they are to suffer capital punishment).

[54] *Decreti,* Pars II, Causa XXIIJ, Quaest. IV, c. xlij, "Si ecclesia vera ipsa": Friedberg, I, 922; Migne, PL CLXXXVII, 1204, from Augustine Ep. 185 (in English translation in PNF [1] IV, 633-651). The statement that the true Church is the one which suffers persecution emanates from the Donatists and is cited by Augustine merely that he may refute it.

[55] I do not find the exact words, but the thought is expressed in "Sermones, Classis III De Sanctis," CCLXIII, cap. 9, and CCLXXVI, cap. 4: Migne, PL XXXVIII, 1252 and 1257.

[56] Professor S. Harrison Thomson writes me that the works of John of Damascus were never so divided in the Greek, but only in medieval Latin translations which have never been published. The reference is to the *De fide orthodoxa* divided into 101 "Sentencie." There were two translations. The more common was that of Burgundio of Pisa (c. 1150), the other that of Robert Grosseteste of Lincoln. Copies of both manuscripts are in the Bodleian. The reference in Burgundio's translation is MS. Canon. Patr. Lat. (Bodley, Oxford), 97. f. 30 A (ca. 1300), Cap. 31 in Bk. III. The reference in Grosseteste's translation is MS. Pembroke, Coll. Camb. 20, f. 20 B, XIII 2, Cap. 79 of the whole book = MS. Ashmole, Bodley, 1526, f. 156 A1, XIII 2. The original is to be found in "S. Joannis Damasceni de fide orthodoxa," Lib. IV, Cap. IV: Migne, PG XCIV, 1109.

naked, poor, unlearned, and afflicted. How is the Church able to have martyrs, if she makes martyrs?

Likewise Hilary, writing against the Arian Auxentius,[57] warmly deplores the perverted opinion that the Gospel should be advanced with the sword. Here are his words: "The utter folly of our time [58] is lamentable, that men should think to assist God with human help and to protect the Church of Christ by worldly ambition. I ask you bishops, you who think you are bishops, what help did the apostles have to proclaim the Gospel? With what assistance from the magistrate did they preach Christ and convert almost all the heathen from idols to God? As they lay imprisoned, chained [and scourged], did they praise God that they had received some honor from the court? Did Paul [when he was a spectacle in the theater] [59] or did Christ gather a Church at the command of a king? Did they enjoy the favor and protection of Nero, Vespasian, and Decius, under whose envy and hate the Gospel blossomed? The early Christians, living by the labor of their hands, assembling in upper rooms and secret places, yet traversed nearly all lands and peoples by land and sea in defiance of the prohibitions of senates and the edicts of kings. Shall I not believe that they had the keys of the kingdom of heaven? Was not the power of God made manifest against the hate of man in that Christ was only the more preached in proportion to the prohibition of preaching? But now, alas, divine faith is commended by earthly suffrages. The power has gone out from Christ, while ambition is advanced in His name.[60] The Church terrifies by exile and imprisonment and forces men to the faith, whereas the true Church is recognized by the endurance of exile and imprisonment. The Church now depends upon the favor of the world, she who was hallowed by the terror of the persecutor. She exiles the priests, she who was propagated

[57] "Sancti Hilarii contra Arianios vel Auxentium Mediolanensem liber unus, scriptus anno 364." Migne, PL X, 610, § 3.

[58] Franck inserts, "Anno 353."

[59] These words are covered by Franck with an *et cetera.* They are in Hilary whose text Castellio has reproduced verbatim instead of translating Franck. The Biblical reference is perhaps to I Cor. 4: 9 or 15: 32.

[60] Franck: "since help from the magistrate is sought in his name."

by exiled priests. She glories that the world loves her, she who cannot be the Church of Christ unless she is hated of the world." These are the words of Hilary.

Little by little things have grown worse. The devil was at first ashamed to go to such length of impudence among the faithful as to compel anyone to the faith and to introduce force into the affairs of the Church and the faith. This would have been too absurd, not to say ridiculous, not only in the sight of believers, but also in the eyes of the world, that anyone should attempt to bring the unwilling to faith against their hearts, and should try to employ coercion in the affairs of God, who desires the heart and the consent of His worshippers, a truth which is written in the hearts of all men and will be approved by all as just.

But one thing was introduced after another and the world grew daily more ignorant and estranged from the truth,[61] until Pope Pelagius in 553, being impelled and sent by the father of all the Pharisees (John 8) shamelessly promulgated a decree that heretics who would not suffer themselves to be persuaded by reasoning to the Roman faith (which he called the Christian faith), should be turned over to the civil arm to be constrained and forced.[62]

See what we have come to. More and more we have degenerated, until now there is no dealing or disputing with a heretic save by the gallows, sword, and fire. Faith is not kept with the heretic, but he is treated as was John Hus at the Council of Constance. Nor have the persecutors enough sense of justice to recognize that if faith is not to be kept with a heretic, neither should it be given, that he be thus tricked out of his life.

But the best of the ancient canons are opposed to this insolence

[61] Franck: "more external."

[62] Franck's source, I take it, is the *Historia B. Platinae de vitis pontificvm Romanorvm.* The account of Pelagius I in the edition of Lyons (1512) is on f. lxxxi verso to lxxxii verso. The passage reads: *Pelagius autem ecclesiam Dei in tantis perturbationibus non deserens, constituit, vt haeretici & schismatici coërceri etiam saecularium manu possent, quando ad sanitatem rationibus non deducerentur* (Pelagius, moreover, not deserting the Church of God in such trials, decreed that heretics and schismatics might be coerced by the secular arm if they were not brought to sanity by reasons).

in that they forbid the clergy for any reason whatever, let alone for faith or heresy, to kill or lay violent hands on anyone either directly or indirectly. Neither should they give consent, assistance, nor advice to this end, and should judge and punish others who so acted: XXIII, Quaest. ult. cap., "His a quibus"; "De re jud.," *Lib. VI,* "Quod"; *De peniten.,* Dist. I, "Periculose"; Augustinus, XIIII, Q. III, "Plerique".[63] If then, indeed, heretics are to be put to death according to the new law of the persecutors and contrary to the decrees given above, and inasmuch as, according to their law, Simoniacs are the worst heretics and have the chief place, I, Quaest. I, "Eos qui,"[64] and again since no one should suffer Mass to be said by a fornicator under penalty of excommunication and of the sin of idolatry, XJ. XIJ. Dist. J. "Verum,"[65] I ask what could be done with such a crowd of heretics? Where would one find executioners and wood enough to burn them all? etc.

But certainly not only Scripture but the canon law as well in many places shows that heretics should suffer no penalty beyond banishment, XXIIIJ. Quaest. I, "Quae dignior, verba Ambrosii."[66] Likewise in the same chapter, "Cum aliquis, Origenes,"[67] etc.

With these plainly accord the canons of the first ancient councils

[63] *Decreti,* Pars II, Causa XXXIII, Quaest. VIII, c. xxx, "His a quibus": Friedberg I, 964; Migne, PL CLXXXVII, 1260; *Liber sextus decretalium D. Bonifacii papae* VIII, Lib. II, Tit. XIV, "De sententia et de re iudicata" (*Quod* appears to be a false incipit for *Quum*): Friedberg II, 1007; *Decreti,* Pars II, Causa XXXIII, Quaest. III, "De poenit.," Dist. I, c. xxiij, "Periculose": Friedberg I, 1163 (the incipit is "Perniciose" in Migne, PL CLXXXVII, 1526); *Decreti,* Pars II, Causa XIV, Quaest. III, c. iij, "Plerique": Friedberg I, 735; Migne, PL CLXXXVII, 957.

[64] *Decreti,* Pars II, Causa I, Quaest. I, c. xxj, "Eos, qui pecunias." Friedberg I, 364; Migne, PL CLXXXVII, 488.

[65] *Decreti* Pars I, Dist. XXXIJ, c. vj (XJ. XIJ is a misprint for XXXIJ and J should be VJ). The incipit is "Non est audienda"; the comment of Gratian begins "Verum principia." Friedberg I, 118; Migne, PL CLXXXVII, 177-78.

[66] *Decreti,* Pars II, Causa XXIV, Quaest. I, c. xxvj, "Quae dignior": Friedberg I, 976; Migne, PL CLXXXVII, 1277.

[67] *Decreti,* Pars II, Causa XXIV, Quaest. IIJ, c. vij, "Cum aliquis": Friedberg I, 992; Migne, PL CLXXXVII, 1298.

and of the popes, who did not go beyond excommunication, until they began to banish and finally to seize and deliver heretics to the sword and the secular arm. Moreover, no one should be condemned or excommunicated except one who has been justly and legally convicted, IJ, Quaest. J,[68] in many places.

Again the punishment of such is plainly set forth by Augustine in Canon XXIIJ, Quaest. V, "Circumcel.," [69] where he says that heretics are not to be put to death. Such conduct does not befit a Christian. Although certain Donatists were criminals as well as heretics, using violence and even inflicting death upon some of the Christians, nevertheless Augustine advised the judge, Marcellinus, not to put them to death, but to be mindful of the conscience and office of a Christian. These decrees, and especially Augustine, ought to be of weight among those [70] who esteem him so highly.

Again, that no Jew or anyone else ought to be compelled to the faith or dragged away from his rites and ceremonies, but should rather be drawn to the faith by good counsels and admonitions, is clearly expressed in Dist. XIV, "Quid autem," "In calce," "Qui sinceram." [71] Thus far Eleutherius.

LACTANTIUS

Book Five, Chapter Twenty [1]

⟦Let the heathen prove their case by divine testimonies as we do.⟧

[68] *Decreti,* Pars II, Causa II, Quaest. I: Friedberg I, 438-49; Migne, PL CLXXXVII, 582-96.

[69] *Decreti,* Pars II, Causa XXIIJ, Quaest. V, c. 1, "Circumcelliones illos." Augustine Ep. 133: Friedberg I, 928; Migne, PL CLXXXVII, 1214.

[70] Franck: "the Papists."

[71] *Decreti,* Pars I, Dist. XLV, c. j, "Quid autem de episcopis"; Dist. XLV, c. iij, "Qui sincera intentione": Friedberg I, 160; Migne, PL CLXXXVII, 233. I do not find "In calce."

[1] "Lucii Caecilii Firmianii Lactantii divinarum institutionum liber V de justitia": CSEL XIX, Lib. V, 19, § 11-13, pp. 463.19-464.6; § 16-17, pp. 464.17-465.1; § 21-24, pp. 465.11-466.3: Migne, PL VI, 614A-615B; ANF VII, 156-57.

There is no room for force and violence because religion cannot be compelled. Let words be used rather than blows, that the decision may be free. Let them engage the edge of their understanding. If their reason is true let it be presented. We are prepared to hear, if they teach. We certainly do not credit those who maintain silence, nor do we yield to those who exercise cruelty against us. Let them imitate us and give a reason of the whole matter. We do not entangle [our converts] as they charge, but we teach, we prove, we explain. Therefore no one is held by us against his will, for he who lacks devotion and faith is useless to God. Nevertheless no one withdraws, because truth itself holds.

And a little farther on he says: ⟦Even a boy could refute their claim that they are gods who cannot be denied to have been mortals.⟧ From these instances, then, let them know the difference between the true and the false, since with all their eloquence they are not able to persuade, whereas the unlearned and rude produce conviction because the thing itself and truth speak. Why, then, are they so cruel? That they may increase their folly while they seek to diminish it? There is a great difference between carnage and piety. Truth cannot be joined with violence, nor justice with cruelty.

Again a little farther on: For they know that there is nothing more excellent in life than religion and that it ought to be defended with the greatest energy, but as they are deceived with regard to religion so also as to the manner of the defense. Religion is to be defended not by killing, but by dying; not by cruelty, but by patience; not by crime, but by faith. The first are the characteristics of the evil, the second of the good, and in religion the good is to be employed and not the bad. If you wish to defend religion with blood, with torments, with evil, then is she not defended but defiled. Nothing is so free as religion. If the heart is averse to sacrifice, then religion is taken away, is naught. The proper method is to defend religion by patience or death in which faith is conserved and is pleasing to God and enhances religion.

Again in Chapter Twenty-four [2]

God permits whatever evil princes inflict upon us. Nevertheless, let not the most unjust persecutors, who have made mockery of the name of God, suppose that they will escape with impunity because they have been the ministers of His wrath against us. They will be punished by the judgment of God because they have abused the power which was conferred upon them above the ordinary measure, because they have insulted God in their pride and have trampled His eternal name under their feet. For this reason He promises to take vengeance upon them speedily and to exterminate the evil beasts from the earth. Yet although He will vindicate His people for their present vexations, nevertheless He commands us to wait in patience the day of heavenly judgment when He will reward each according to his deserts. But let not sacrilegious souls suppose that those whom they thus crush will go unavenged. The savage and voracious wolves who torture just, simple, and innocent souls, shall have their reward. Let us, however, take care that men punish us only for justice. Let us strive with all our might to merit at God's hands the vindication and the reward of our suffering.

CASPAR HEDIO, MINISTER OF THE WORD IN THE CHURCH OF STRASSBURG

In Explanation of the Fifth Chapter of the Gospel According to Saint Luke, Which Is Read on the Sixth Sunday After Trinity, in the Little Book Called Outlines on the Gospels and Epistles to Be Read in the Churches [1]

Observe diligently what Christ said to Peter to whom he committed the sheep after a threefold profession of love. Here he says, "fisher of men," that is, You shall take men alive. This is directed against the cruelty of those who prefer to kill the Jews, the Turks,

[2] CSEL XIX, Lib. V, 23, pp. 477.15-478.8: Migne, PL VI, 630 A-B; ANF VII, 161.

[1] This citation appears only in the French and German versions. The passage is taken from Hedio's *Epitome in Evangelia et Epistolas quae leguntur in templis per circuitū anni, totius doctrinae pietatis medullam & nucleum seu Cornucopiae citra cuiuspiam morsum in se complectens, in usum Ministrorum Ecclesiae,* per D. Casparē Hedionem, Concionatorem Argentoratē̄

and the infidels and send them to hell rather than to gain them for God.

The Same Hedio in the Exposition of the Seventh Chapter of Saint Matthew on the Passage, "Beware of False Prophets," Which Is Read on the Eighth Sunday After Trinity [2]

Here we are to observe the moderation of Christ. He does not say, "Punish such men," nor, "Kill them," but, "Beware lest you be harmed by them and lest, incautious and defenseless, you fall into their snares."

JOHANN AGRICOLA OF EISLEBEN

Annotations on the Epistle to Titus, Commenting on the Verse Concerning the Heretic in the Third Chapter [1]

A heretic, as we learn from the Epistle to the Corinthians, is one who teaches contrary to the Gospel of Christ and follows his own reasonings [2] and opinions which exclude from the kingdom of heaven,[3] for they are works of the flesh (Galatians 5).[4] We see how this precept of Paul has grown cold in the Church.[5] Instead of *devita,* which means "avoid," they [6] read two words, *de vita,* and add *ad ignem,* which means "from life into the fire," [7] that is, kill, burn, cleave, hang, and drown. Thus far are they removed

---

conscripta anno MDXXXVII [Argentorati]. This is no. 18 in Adam's bibliography. There is a copy in the Preussische Staatsbibliothek at Berlin. The following passage is translated from p. M viij verso, "Dominica V. post trinitatis . . . evangelium Lucae V. cap."

[2] From the work cited above, signature N ij verso.

---

[1] *Epistola S. Pauli ad Titum, iam recens per J. Agricolam scholiis novis illustrata. . . .* Per I. Secerium Haganovae, 1530. This is bound with works of Melanchthon and Luther. There is a copy at the British Museum. The following citation, which happens only in the French and German versions, is from pp. 45 and verso.

[2] I Cor. 3: 20. [3] I Cor. 6: 9-10.

[4] Gal. 5: 19-21. Castellio here passes over the attempt of Agricola to define the heretic with the aid of citations from Jerome and Chrysostom.

[5] Agricola: "the Church of Rome." [6] Agricola has in mind the Papists.

[7] Erasmus was fond of telling this story which he heard from John Colet. *Opera* VI, 973 (on Titus 3: 10), and *Opera* IV, 495 (Ep. No. 2045, VII, 482).

from the footsteps of St. Paul, who boast to be the vicars of God and the true successors of the apostles.

JAKOB SCHENCK

Comment on the Verse About the Heretic in the Same Epistle the Third Chapter [1]

[Heretics] are not to be avoided when they attack us, but they should be instructed, reproved, and corrected by the Word of God with the greatest gentleness and mildness, without anger, reviling, and wrangling, and we should pray to God on their behalf. By this course alone are they either converted or [convicted] and avoided. Christ overcame and put to flight the Tempter in the wilderness, on the pinnacle of the temple, and on the high mountain not by reviling, murmuring, and wrangling, but by the Word and power of God.

CHRISTOPH HOFFMANN

Commentary on the Same Passage [1]

[The comment on Titus 3: 10 commences on p. 242. Hoffmann defines a heretic as one who obstinately opposes the teaching of Christ and endeavors to seduce others. Such heretics are the Roman pontiffs and bishops. Castellio omits this statement, but the "such" in the first sentence of the translation refers to them. The passage is in the French edition of Castellio only.]

[1] *In epistolam Divi Pauli ad Titum enarratio*, 1542, on the word *devita*, sig., N5-N6. A part of N6 appears in the French of Castellio only. There is a copy of the book at the British Museum. Schenck says that Titus was doubtless one of those who neglect their flocks in order to convert impious teachers. Paul wished to recall him to his pastoral duties. Too much time should not be wasted over such men who are captious and seldom converted. "Nevertheless," Schenck continues, a word which Castellio omits because he has left out the preceding passage.

---

[1] The passage is taken from the *Commentarii in ep. Pauli ad Tit. in quibus agitur copiose de universa doctrina Christiana et de corrigendis abusibus, qui in Ecclesiam, conniventibus episcopis et doctoribus, irrepserunt* (Frankfurt, March, 1541), p. 242 verso, sig. I i 2 verso. There are copies in the Staatsbibliothek, Berlin, and in the Königsberg Universitäts-Bibliothek, Germany.

Nevertheless, such heretics ought not to be burned, nor indeed should they be regarded as heretics unless they have first been admonished and convicted of error and impiety in opinion and doctrine, and have refused to retract their ungodly belief and purpose, and to change their impious dogmas. Then they may be punished as the magistrate deems fit. Yet they are not to be put to death unless they excite sedition against the civil State by their impious doctrines, since the punishment of heretics is spiritual and belongs to the judgment of Christ. For that reason Paul prescribes that they are to be admonished and corrected once and again. If they will not change their impious counsels, purposes, and doctrines and prefer to be obstinate rather than submit to the Church and to sound admonitions, then they are to be shunned and avoided. Yet if the penalty of fire were meet for heretics, certainly the Papists and the monks would have been, and would now be, subject to it.

JOHN CALVIN

Preface to the Acts of the Apostles [1]

This contemplation alone [of the kingdom of Christ as exemplified in the book of Acts] will preserve us from the fate which, as experience abundantly shows, Ennius only too truly declared to overtake most men, that "Wisdom vanishes when force is introduced." [2] For if the music of the flutes could so calm the warlike Spartans in the midst of the conflict, when even the mildest are stirred up above measure, how much more efficaciously should the kingdom of Christ excel through the celestial harmony of the Holy Spirit, whereby not only are wild beasts tamed, but wolves, lions, and bears turned into lambs, spears into pruning hooks, and swords into ploughshares? [3]

[1] Dedicated to Christian III of Denmark. *Calvini opera,* XIV, 293-4, Ep. 1607.

[2] *Ennianae poesis reliquiae,* Annalium Lib. VIII, III. 268, ed. Johannes Vahlen (Leipzig, 1903).

[3] Is. 11:6-8 and 2:4.

The Same John Calvin in the First Edition of the Institutes, Chapter II [4]

Although eccelesiastical discipline does not permit familiarity and intimacy with the excommunicated, nevertheless we should try by every means, whether by exhortation and teaching, clemency and mildness, or by our prayers to God, to bring them to a better mind that they may return to the society and unity of the Church. Not only are they to be treated in this fashion, but even the Turks and the Saracens and other enemies of the true religion. Far be it that we should approve of the means which many have employed hitherto to force them to our faith by denying them fire and the common elements and all the offices of humanity and persecuting them with the sword and arms.

OTTO BRUNFELS

In the Pandects: [1] to Burn Heretics, Is Against the Will of the Spirit

"They shall beat their swords into ploughshares and their spears into pruning hooks." [2]

"They shall not hurt nor destroy in all my holy mountain." [3]

"But if he neglect to hear the Church, let him be unto thee as a heathen man," etc.[4]

"Ye know not what manner of Spirit ye are of." [5]

"For the Son of Man is not come to destroy men's lives but to save them." [6]

[4] *Calvini opera*, I, 77, "Institutio Rel. Christ." 1536, Cap. II, "De fide." In the *Traité des hérétiques* Castellio translated directly from the Latin, instead of using Calvin's translation of 1541. See Jacques Pannier, *Quelques remarques bibliographiques sur le Traité des hérétiques à propos d'une nouvelle édition.* BSHPF LXII (1913), 551-56.

[1] *Pandectarum Veteris et Novi Testamenti. Libri XII. Othonis Brunfelsii.* Argentorati apud Joannem Schottium 1527. "Liber Quartus de Evangelio." *Haereticos combvri est contra uoluntatem spiritus.* In the edition of Bartholomew Westheimer (Basileae, 1547) the passage is on p. 119. There is a copy at the British Museum. Brunfels gives partial and not always correct Scripture references. Castellio omits some in the French, and all in the Latin, version.

[2] Is. 2: 4. [3] Is. 11: 9. [4] Matt. 18: 17.

[5] Luke 9: 55. [6] Luke 9: 56; Luke 19: 10.

"Beware of the leaven of the Pharisees." [7] He does not say, "Kill heretics, Pharisees," etc.

Moreover Christ never forced anyone to the faith with the sword or fire.

Christ, again, tolerated the Pharisees when he said, "Beware of the false prophets." [8] He does not say, "Kill the false prophets."

Here applies the parable of the tares and the wheat.[9]

Paul was a blasphemer, but nevertheless he obtained mercy.[10]

"A man that is a heretic . . . reject." [11] He does not say, "Kill."

CONRAD PELLICAN

Commentary on St. Matthew, Chapter Thirteen: On the Parable of the Tares [1]

The Lord was not vexed by the request of the disciples for a detailed explanation of the parable of the tares. The good householder, he said, who sowed the good seed, is the Heavenly Father. The field, in which he sowed, is the whole world and not simply Judaea. The wheat which sprang from the good seed stands for those who, from the planting of the Gospel, showed themselves worthy of the kingdom of heaven by living up to their profession in life and deeds. The evil tares, mingled with them from the bad seed, are the evil ones who do not sincerely profess the Gospel teaching. The enemy, who secretly by night introduced the bad seed from which perverse doctrine arises, is the devil. The servants, who wish to root out the tares before the time, are those who think that false prophets and heresiarchs should be removed

[7] Matt. 16: 6; Mark 8: 15; Luke 12: 1. [8] Matt. 7: 15.
[9] Matt. 13: 24-30, 36-43. [10] I Cor. 7: 25. [11] Tit. 3: 10.

[1] *In qvatvor evangelistas, Matthaeum, Marcum, Lucam & Ioannem, item in Acta Apostolorum commentarij Conradi Pellicani sacrae linguae in schola Tigurina professoris.* Tigvri excudebat Christophorus Froschoverus anno M. D. LXXXII, pp. 43-44. In the copy at Yale this work is bound with and preceded by *In libros qvos vocant Apocryphos vel potivs ecclesiasticos,* etc. Tigvri excudebat Christophorvs Froschovervs anno M. D. LXXXII. Castellio has reproduced Pellican word for word. He in turn has borrowed the entire passage, word for word, except for the recasting of the introductory sentence, from Erasmus, "Paraphrasis in Evang. Matthaei, Cap. XIII," *Opera,* VII, 80D-81B.

Conrad Pellican

by swords and death; whereas the Father is unwilling that they be destroyed. They are to be tolerated, if perchance they may repent and from tares be turned into wheat. If they do not repent they are reserved for their Judge to whom they will some day pay the penalty. The time of the harvest is the end of the world; the harvesters are the angels. In the meantime, therefore, the bad, mixed with the good, are to be endured, since there is less danger from suffrance than from severance. Moreover, at the last day, when the good shall be separated from the bad and each shall be rewarded according to his deserts, then the Son of Man, the judge of all, will send his angels, who will purge his kingdom, lest any offense remain. Then, when the good can no longer profit the bad, nor the bad be permitted to have anything more to do with the good, he will separate from the rest those who while among the good preferred to molest them, rather than to be improved by them, and will cast all such into the fire of hell. There they will suffer eternal punishments because of fleeting and false delights. They will be removed from the threshing floor of the Church and cast into the pit of Tartarus, that is, the kingdom of their father, the devil, where a belated and futile repentance will extort from those in misery weeping, wailing, and gnashing of teeth.

URBANUS RHEGIUS

The Theological Topics at the End of the Chapter on Heretics [1]

The spirit of Christians is clement and burns only with the fire of love (Luke 9) "Ye know not what manner of spirit ye are of." It seeks not vengeance, but the repentance of sinners. The godly dispute not obstinately, but with a mind humble and desirous of the truth after the manner of Acts seventeen, "They searched the Scriptures daily, whether those things were so," and sought not their own victory, but that of the truth.

God does not teach us to burn erring sheep but, in Ezekiel 34, to heal the weak and feed the lean, etc.

[1] "Loci communes," in *Opera Vrbani Regii Latine edita Cum eius Vita, ac Praefatione Ernesti Regii, F*[*ilii*], Impressa Noribergae, in Officina Ioannis Montani & Vlrici Neuberi M. D. LXII, f. cccxxxvij verso, sig. lij verso.

See Jerome on the second chapter of Hosea where he takes up the treatment of heretics.[2]

SAINT AUGUSTINE

Against the Grammarian Cresconius[1]

Good Catholics are not pleased that even a heretic should be prosecuted to the death. . . . The faithful do not abandon the granary of Christ because of the tares, nor the threshing floor because of the chaff, nor the mansion of Christ because of vessels of dishonor, nor the nets of Christ on account of the bad fish.

On Faith and Works, Chapter V[2]

[Augustine has been saying that some would tolerate no tares in the Church, others would exercise no ecclesiastical discipline.]

We think, indeed, that the sound course is to modify conduct and opinion in accord with the testimony of both sides, to tolerate the dogs in the Church on account of the peace of the Church, but not to give that which is holy to the dogs when the peace of the Church is secure.

The rest of the passage you may read in Saint Augustine.

In the 158th Letter to Marcellinus[3]

With regard to the doubt entertained by your Excellency whether you should order the edicts to be published in Theoprepia, let this be done if the people can be assembled. Otherwise choose a more frequented spot, but by no means leave the matter undone. But I beg that the death penalty be not inflicted upon them, for the sake of both your conscience and Catholic clemency, no matter how great the crimes which they have confessed.

[2] "S. Eusebii Hieronymi commentariorum in Osee," Lib. II, Cap. VI, Vers. 4-5, Migne, PL XXV, 869. See p. 21 of the introduction.

[1] "Contra Cresconium," III, 50 (55): CSEL LII, 462.6-7, 16-19 (A.D. 406/7).

[2] "De fide et operibus," V, 7: CSEL XLI, 42.10-13 (A.D. 412/13).

[3] Ep. CXXXIX, 1-2: CSEL XLIV, 149.16-20; 150.1-3; PNF[1] I, 488 (A.D. 412).

From the 159th Letter to Marcellinus [4]

Christian Judge, fulfill the office of a good father. In your wrath against iniquity be mindful of humanity. Do not give way to the desire for vengeance against the atrocities of evildoers, but endeavor to cure the wounds of sinners. Do not give up the paternal diligence which you have thus far exercised during the trial in that you have extracted confessions of such crimes not by the wrack, nor the scraping iron, nor the flame, but only by the rod.

In the 150th Letter to Apringius [5]

We have read what the Apostle says to you that you bear not the sword in vain and that you are a minister of God to punish those who do ill.[6] But there is a difference between the civil and the ecclesiastical sphere; the one cultivates severity, the other mercy. If I were speaking to a non-Christian judge I should make a different appeal, though without deserting the cause of the Church, and insofar as he would let me, I should insist that the sufferings of the Catholic servants of God, which should be examples of patience, be not sullied by the blood of their enemies, and if he would not agree I should suspect him of resisting through evil intent. But now, indeed, that the case comes up before you, I have a different reason and a different approach. We see you in an exalted position, but we recognize in you a son of the Christian religion. Let your Sublimity bow, let your faith submit, etc.

The Same from the Book of the Questions on the Gospel of Matthew, Chapter XIII [7]

⟦The servants moreover said to him⟧: "Do you desire that we go and gather them?" Are those who are called servants here the same as those who a little further on are called the harvesters? Since in the explanation of the parable He calls the harvesters angels, and no one would venture to say that the angels did not

[4] Ep. CXXXIII, 2: CSEL XLIV, 82.1-8; PNF [1] I, 470-71 (A.D. 412).
[5] Ep. CXXXIV, 3: CSEL XLIV, 86.3-17. [6] Rom. 13:4.
[7] "Quaestionum septemdecim in Matthaeum" I, 12, 1: Migne, PL XXXV, 1369-70.

know who sowed the tares, or that the tares would be evident to the angels only after the grain appeared, for these reasons it is better to assume that the faithful servants in this passage are men, whom also He calls the good seed. We need not be surprised that He calls them both the good seed and the servants of the Father, just as He calls Himself both the door and the Good Shepherd,[8] for the same thing is subject to diverse comparisons because of diverse meanings, especially because when He speaks to the servants He does not say, "In the time of the harvest I will say to you, 'Gather first the tares,' " but He says, "I will say to the harvesters." Whence we may infer that the office of collecting the tares to be burned belongs to another, and no son of the Church should think it his business.

In the Same Passage [9]

Hence the servants ask, "Do you wish us to gather them?" Since the Truth Himself told them that man is so constituted in this life that he cannot tell how anyone now in error may turn out in the future, nor how profitable the error may be to the good, for this reason such men are not to be deprived of life, lest in the attempt to destroy the evil, the good be killed, for they may prove to be good, and the good may suffer loss, since the bad may be of unintentional use to them. The weeding out may be done opportunely at the end, when no time remains for the improvement of life or the correction of opinion through comparison with the error of another.

Against the Letter of Manichaeus Called Fundamental [10]

I have prayed and I do pray God Almighty, from whom and through whom and in whom are all things, that in refuting and conquering the heresy to which you Manichaeans adhere, perhaps more through imprudence than malice, He may give me a calm and tranquil mind, concerned rather for your correction than for your overthrow, for although the Lord by His servants overcomes

[8] John 10: 7, 11. [9] I, 12, 2: Migne, PL XXXV, 1370.
[10] "Contra epistulam quam vocant Fundamenti," I: CSEL XXV, 193.4-12; PNF [1] IV, 129 (A.D. 396/7).

kingdoms of error, yet He commands that men, in so far as they are men, be corrected rather than destroyed.

CHRYSOSTOM

In Homily Forty-seven on Matthew Thirteen [1]

"Wilt thou then that we go and gather them up?" But the Lord forbade them lest in gathering up the tares they root up the wheat. This He said that He might prohibit wars and effusion of blood. For if heretics were put to death a truceless war would be let loose upon the world. By two reasons He restrained the servants, first, lest the wheat be hurt, and second, that the tares will be punished eventually if incurable. If, then, you wish to punish them without hurt to the wheat, wait until the proper time. And what is the meaning of this, "Lest you root out the wheat with them?" Either He means that if you resort to arms and slay the heretics many of the saints also will necessarily be slain with them, or else He means that in all probability many of the tares may change and become wheat. If then you root them up prematurely the wheat will perish which would have been produced by a change in the tares. He does not, therefore, forbid us to restrain heretics, to stop their mouths, to take away their freedom of speech, to break up their assemblies and societies; He forbids us merely to kill and slay.

From Homily Eight on Genesis One [2]

Heretics are like sick men and those whose eyes are weak. For as the latter cannot look upon the sun because of the defect in their eyesight and as the sick cannot touch even the most wholesome food because of the infirmity of their health, even so the heretics, being sick in soul and blinded in their understanding, are not able to behold the light of the truth. Let us then discharge the office of friendship, extend a helping hand, and address them with great gentleness, as the blessed Paul admonished us, saying, "We

[1] "In Matthaeum Homil. XLVI (al. XLVII)": Migne, PG LVIII, 477-78; PNF [1] (Chrysostom) X, 288-89.

[2] "In Cap. 1 Genes. Homil VIII," § 3: Migne, PG LIII, 72.

should be gentle towards all, apt to teach, forbearing, in meekness correcting them that oppose themselves; if peradventure God may give them repentance unto the knowledge of the truth, and they [may be sober and] [3] pull themselves out of the snare of the devil, having been taken captive by the Lord's servant unto the will of God." [4] Do you observe how he speaks of them as if they were drunk? And when he says, "Pull themselves out," he indicates that they have been submerged. And again when he says "ensnared by the devil" he implies that they have been caught in a net. Great gentleness and long-suffering are necessary to extricate them from the snares of the devil. Let us then say to them, "Be sober, pull yourselves out, look to the light of righteousness, etc."

The Same Chrysostom in His Homily on the Name of Abraham [5]

For impious doctrines and those set forth by the heretics we ought to refute and anathematize; but we should spare men and pray for their salvation.

JEROME

On Matthew: [1] Cited by Bartholomew Westheimer

A bruised reed He will not break, that is, He will extend a hand to the sinner and will bear his brother's burdens, and a smoking flax He will not quench, that is, He will not extinguish the least spark of faith in the little ones. Jerome thus shows whether those who rage and fume and introduce flames, fire, and death are imita-

[3] These words of the text of Chrysostom are omitted by Castellio, though plainly called for by the questions which follow. The Revised Version renders this passage, "and they may recover themselves out of the snare of the devil." A note says that the Greek means "return to soberness."

[4] II Tim. 2: 24-26.

[5] Castellio has given the title incorrectly. The passage is found in "De non anathematizandis vivis vel defunctis," § 4: Migne, PG XLVIII, 952. Castellio's translation is loose.

[1] Buisson (*Sébastien Castellion* I, 393, n. 3) was not able to locate the passage in Westheimer nor have I had the opportunity. The first two sentences are a free reworking of Jerome's commentary on Matthew 12: 20-21 (Migne, PL XXVI, 79).

tors of Christ or Antichrist. Hence, it ill befits a Christian to display a more than warlike ferocity, a more than canine rabies, a more than tryannical severity against a wandering sheep, to be hard on the unfortunate and savage toward the man who is despaired of and rejected by God. The Lord remonstrates in Ezekiel (the 34th chapter) [2] with the shepherds who ought to feed and not kill, "Woe to the shepherds of Israel that do feed themselves! etc. You have not bound up that which was broken, etc."

COELIUS SECUNDUS CURIO[1]

Against Anthony Florebell

They [the Anabaptists] were therefore to be coerced and reduced to order, not on account of religion, if they had any hid in their minds, but on account of sedition.

Again: Who does not know that he [2] has arrogated to himself both swords and that what he cannot do with the sword of the mouth he cuts with the sword of the hand? In this matter he imitates not merely Sabellius, but also Arius, Macedonius, and Mohammed, the three greatest pests of the world, for all these vexed and variously tormented those who would not accept their insane doctrine, but those who accepted it and sought death in its defense were regarded as martyrs and exalted to heaven.

[2] Ez. 34: 2-4.

---

[1] *C. S. Curionis pro vera et antiqua Ecclesiae Christi autoritate in A. Florebellum Mutinensem Oratio*, etc. Basileae [1550?]. There is a copy at the British Museum. The first citation is on p. 187, the second on p. 237. There is an English translation, "A Defense of the True and old Authority of Christ's Church, An Oration of Coelius, the Second Curio, for the True and Ancient Authority of Christ His Church, against Antony Florebell of Mutiny," translated out of Latin into English by Ihon Philpott. Printed in *The Examinations and Writings of John Philpot* . . . edited for the Parker Society (Cambridge, 1842), pp. 325-432. The first citation occurs on p. 402, the second on p. 422.

[2] Curio: "the pope."

SEBASTIAN CASTELLIO[1]

In the Preface to the Bible, Dedicated to Edward VI

[The initial portion of the Preface, which is omitted in the *De haereticis,* is essential to the argument. The whole point is to show that there is much in Scripture which we do not understand and hence about which we should not persecute. One proof of our ignorance is the very fact of controversy. A further proof is that the predictions of the golden age in Scripture have not been fulfilled in the past, and are not being fulfilled in the present. This point is demonstrated in the first passage used in the *De haereticis.* The next omitted section argues that the fulfillment of the predictions must be reserved for the future. But the future cannot be known. The moral is that we should not pass hasty judgments, but should rather wait for further light. This point is elaborated in the second passage used in the *De haereticis.* The closing section of the Preface, omitted in our compilation, is merely a direct address to Edward VI, for whom the author wishes the clemency of Moses, the piety of David, and the wisdom of Solomon.]

. . . Whence so many and such grave controversies which have not been composed during so many centuries, nor by so many disputations, controversies which have nearly always cost the blood of the weakest, while there is none who questions his own judgment, none who does not condemn others? We envy and revile and return not merely evil for evil, but often evil for good, and if anyone disagrees with us on a single point of religion we condemn him and pursue him to the corners of the earth with the dart of tongue and pen. We exercise cruelty with the sword, flame, and water and exterminate the destitute and defenseless. We declare that we are not allowed to kill anyone, yet we deliver men to Pilate and if he releases we say that he is no friend of Caesar.

[1] "Sebastianus Castalio Eduardo Sexto, Angliae Regi Clariss. Salutem," *Biblia, interprete Sebastiano Castalione, una cum ejusdem annotationibus* (Basel, 1551). For this and other editions see Buisson, *Sébastien Castellion,* II, 357 f. For copies in this country see my article, "Sebastian Castellio and the Toleration Controversy of the Sixteenth Century," in *Persecution and Liberty,* pp. 206-7.

And what is vastly worse we declare that all this is done through zeal for Christ and at His command and in His name. Thus we cover the cruelty of the wolf with sheep's clothing. What a time! We are bloodthirsty through zeal for Christ, who, rather than shed blood, poured forth His own. Through zeal for Christ we pull up the tares, though He commanded that they be left until the harvest lest the wheat be uprooted. Through zeal for Christ we persecute, though He told us when struck upon the right cheek to turn the left. Through zeal for Christ we render evil, in spite of His precept to return good for evil.

And a little farther on: If there are controversies in religion and there are many, we should, I think, follow the example of Judas Maccabeus and his men, who, not knowing what to do with the altar of burnt offerings, "laid up its stones in the mountain of the temple in a convenient place until there should come a prophet to say what should be done with them." [2] Or, better, let us follow Moses, who, although he had received an express command to kill anyone who transgressed the law, nevertheless, when a man was found gathering sticks on the Sabbath day, was unwilling to kill him without a special revelation on this point.[3] Yet Moses was a faithful servant of the Lord and singularly endowed with His Spirit. I need scarcely mention the advice of Gamaliel, who pointed out that if this "work be of men it will come to naught; but if it be of God ye cannot overthrow it; lest haply ye be found even to fight against God." [4] And if we think that we are better informed than Moses, for in these days no one admits error, we ought certainly not to be both judges and accusers, but should rather obey Paul, who said, "Him that is weak in the faith receive ye, but not to doubtful disputations. . . . Who art thou that judgest another man's servant? To his own master he standeth or falleth. Yea, he shall be holden up, for God is able to make him stand. . . . But why dost thou judge thy brother? Or why dost thou set at naught thy brother? For we shall all stand before the judgment seat of Christ." [5] Wherefore let us not judge one

[2] I Macc. 4: 44-46.
[3] Num. 15: 32-36.
[4] Acts 5: 38-39.
[5] Rom. 14: 1, 4, 10.

another, for with what measure we judge we shall be judged.[6] It were better, in my opinion to follow the Roman law on provisional status which reads like this: "If anyone who hitherto has been regarded as free is called into question by another and declared to be a slave, while the case is pending, he shall enjoy provisional freedom." [7] That is to say, he whose liberty is imperiled remains in the same condition of freedom until there is a judicial opinion as to whether he is slave or free. And rightly so, for in view of the doubt as to his condition, if it turn out that he was free, and in the meantime he had been treated as a slave, a grave injury would have been done to a free man. How much more does this principle apply in a capital case and especially in religion in which a sin is so serious. Let us wait for the sentence of the just judge and take pains not to condemn others, but rather look to ourselves that we may have no fear of condemnation. Let us obey the just judge and leave the tares until the harvest, lest by chance we root up the wheat through desiring to know more than the master, for the end of the world is not yet here and we are not the angels to whom this charge was committed. Add that it is absurd to wage spiritual war with earthly arms. The enemies of Christians are the vices which are to be cured by the virtues. Diseases are to be healed by contrary remedies; learning must drive out ignorance; patience overcome injury; modesty resist pride; diligence oppose laziness; clemency fight against cruelty; and insincerity is to be laid low by a mind transparent, religious, pure, and devoted to God. These are the true arms and the true victories of the Christian religion. The office of the doctor is not to be committed to the executioner, nor the outside of the cup to be cleansed before the inside.

[6] Matt. 7: 1-2.

[7] Castellio has phrased the law himself on the basis of *T. Livii historiarum libri* III, 44-48, from which we learn that the law belonged to the twelve tables. See *Fontes iuris Romani antiqui*, edidit Carolus Georgius Bruns (7th ed., Tübingen, 1909), p. 26. The law is discussed by Paul Frédéric Girard in his *Manuel élémentaire de droit romain* (2nd ed., Paris, 1898), pp. 97-98. A similar provision, though couched in different phraseology, is to be found in the *Codex Iust.*, VII, 16, 14.

This I say only with regard to religion; for when it comes to crimes, murder, adultery, theft, false witness, and the like, which God has commanded to be punished and for which He has prescribed the penalty, these are not called into controversy. God has spoken on these matters without obscurity and they pertain to the defense of the good, unless indeed we wish to have our throats cut in our beds, so depraved are the times. Nor is there any danger that the magistrate, who is ordained of God for the defense of the good, should in hanging a murderer put to death a good man. No one ever yet defended murder, not even the murderer. But the case of religion and of the knowledge of Sacred Scripture is altogether different, for the things contained in it are given obscurely and often in enigmas and inscrutable questions, which have been in dispute for more than a thousand years without any agreement, nor can there be agreement without love, which breaks and appeases all controversies and drives away ignorance. Yet for this cause the earth is filled with innocent blood. We ought certainly, however much we may think we know everything, we ought, I say, to fear lest in crucifying thieves justly, we crucify also Christ unjustly. If we suffer Turks and Jews to live among us, the former of whom scarcely love Christ and the latter dearly hate him, and if we suffer detractors, the proud, envious, avaricious, immodest, drunkards, and like plagues, if we live with them, eat with them, and make merry with them, we ought at least to concede the right to breathe the common air to those who confess with us the same Christ and harm no one, who are indeed of such a temper that they would rather die than say or do anything other than that which they think they ought to say and do, not to mention the fact that of all men this sort is the least to be feared. He who would rather die than say what he does not feel (for he would sin if he did and the one who forces him, compels him to sin),[8] such a man, I believe, need not be feared as open to bribery and corruption. I venture to say that there are no persons who are more obedient to princes and magistrates than those who fear God in simplicity and obey Him to the extent of their knowledge.

[8] In the Latin version only.

The obedience of the others is feigned and will not outlast intimidation or ulterior appeals. He who is moved by his conscience to obey and who is taught by God "to be subject to the higher powers" [9] even if they are unjust and how much more if they are just—the obedience of such a man is necessarily true and eternal, inasmuch as God, who is the cause of his obedience, remains true and eternal.

To come back to the point, this certainly is incontrovertible that he who judges too quickly makes haste to rue it. Many have been sorry to have judged, none to have deferred judgment, and he who is more inclined to clemency than to anger imitates the nature of God, who, though He knows us to be guilty, nevertheless postpones judgment and waits for us to correct our lives. He who kills hastily leaves no place for repentance and no time for amendment. If anyone dares to contradict these things he must confess that he strives to shed blood as we seek to staunch it. He will find out which cause is easier to maintain before God, the Judge. This I hold for certain that no one will regret clemency, patience, kindness, and obedience, whereas cruelty and rash judgments no one can but regret. And if the former road is perfectly safe and the latter full of peril, he is absolutely crazy who knowingly and willingly courts danger.

GEORGE KLEINBERG

On How Persecution Hurts the World

No one in his right mind doubts that our sins are the cause of the many calamities, discords, and wars with which the whole world today, especially Germany, is desolated. But few inquire as to the character of the sins which are the cause. I think they are cruelty and severity, and I will tell you why. God said, "Whoso sheddeth man's blood, by man shall his blood be shed," [1] for "in the image of God created He him." [2] Christ said, "All that take the sword shall perish by the sword." [3] James said, "He shall have judgment without mercy, that hath shewed no mercy." [4] There are

[9] Rom. 13: 1.
[1] Gen. 9: 6.
[2] Gen. 1: 27.
[3] Matt. 26: 52.
[4] James 2: 13.

many such passages which show that blood should be punished by blood. Examples prove the same thing. Abimelech, with the aid of the Shechemites, killed his brothers and God requited this cruelty by the death of both parties. Because Saul, in his zeal for Israel, slew the Gibeonites a famine came upon the land for three years, nor could it be staid until the line of Saul was destroyed. The Israelites were delivered to their enemies because of cruelty to the prophets. Innumerable are the examples of this sort which show that God not only punishes the cruel, but also those who either rejoice, or do not lament, over this rage. Tobit shows this when he relates that the tribes of Israel fell into calamity because they did not humble themselves before God and lament the disasters of their brethren, but instead made merry and gave themselves over to the delights of the flesh. The one hundred and thirty-seventh Psalm teaches the same thing in which the children of Edom were threatened because they insulted the Israelites who were wasting away,[5] not to mention the many passages in the prophets which make the same point. These things are all profitable for our instruction,[6] that when we are afflicted with the same penalties, we may recognize the same causes. Had we not been guilty of carnage, one might suppose that the causes were different, but inasmuch as the bloodshed in our day has been so great that I doubt whether there was ever more, there can be no question but that we are afflicted for the same cause. I speak not only of the blood which has been shed in wars, for which also an answer must be given if it was unjustly done, but chiefly of that which has been shed for religion, which is of such a nature that it stems and staunches the flow of blood, for "they shall beat their swords into ploughshares and their spears into pruning hooks." [7] Wherefore I cannot see by what perverse human reasoning it has come to pass that scarcely any shed so much blood as those who profess to have the true religion. I will pass over other nations and consider Germany alone. Here there have been so many changes of religion and so much human blood has been poured out that if

[5] Ps. 137: 7. [6] II Tim. 3: 16. [7] Is. 2: 4 and Micah 4: 3.

as many beasts had been killed men would lament. I have not much to say of lower Germany in which men have been drowned, not one by one nor two by two, but a hundred and a thousand at a time and even whole shiploads, and I dare not say (for the atrocity is almost incredible) that more than thirty thousand in about thirty years have been killed for religion at the command of one man. Other nations will scarcely believe this, but fires, swords, and seas are witnesses. If a prince had lost, I will not say so many horses, but even so many pigs, he would think that he had sustained great damage. What shall I say of the city of Münster in which, were we not blind as moles, we could see the evident displeasure of God with those who conduct religion by the sword.

From the cruelty first exercised against the Anabaptists arose a long succession of atrocities. They retaliated and slew many of their opponents. Thus blood was expiated by blood. Again the Anabaptists were miserably slain, even those who were not in arms, and what is still more cruel the suppression was carried on not only by the sword, but also in books which reach farther and last longer, or rather forever perpetuate this savagery. Let it be understood that I do not defend homicides, adulterers, or other like criminals. I know that against such the magistrate has received the sword from God. But I am talking about the understanding of Scriptural passages, the sense of which is not yet clear. If they were not obscure controversy would have ceased, for who is so demented that he would die for the denial of the obvious? I am talking about errors. If there is any offense here it must be due to error and ignorance. Certainly profit, pleasure, and honor are not involved, but rather the contrary. For error and ignorance, men now in our time and regions are put to death by the sword and afterwards their memory is defamed in books far and wide and for all time to come. He who does not deplore this, in my judgment, has not the heart of a man. God Himself seems to have manifested His displeasure against these murders in that the author of this policy, a learned man and famous throughout the world, shortly after he had put harmless folk to death, fell himself with many others at the edge of the sword.[8] In the eyes of many good folk this was a judgment of God upon his sin. So manifest an example ought at least to move us, but I fear that some have hardened their hearts. They continue in the same way to spread books of cruelty, that is of burnings, through the world, so that there is no end of this slaughter until the Lord, at His coming, overtakes us gory, battened, and fat with the blood of our brothers, and until He sets us among the hypocrites. The very persons who at first reproached their adversaries for resorting to the sword because of inability to debate with the truth, now, grown powerful, adopt the methods of their opponents. Having first burned the persons and the books of their critics at a slow fire, they then tilt against the ashes and vanquish in death those whom they could not overcome in life. Against even the ashes of books they argue to their sweet will now that no one is left to contradict. A just judgment indeed is this, to kill a man before we know whether he ought to be killed and not to premit even his books to plead his cause, at least, not after his death. We reproach those who cut out the tongues of their victims, while we cut off life and books in order that we may not prove all things and hold fast that which is good.[9] O heart of blood! O unheard-of cruelty! Who was ever so eager to save life as they are to destroy it? O Christ, O mighty God, O Father of the world to come! O Prince of Peace! O Light of the World! Enlighten the eyes of the princes that henceforth they may no longer serve the cruelty of Satan, but rather Thy mercy and meekness.

Princes and all rulers open your eyes, open your ears, fear God, and consider how you will render an account to Him of your administration. Many have been punished for cruelty, none for mercy. Many will be condemned in the last judgment for having killed the innocent, none for not having killed. Incline to the side of mercy, and do not obey those who incite you to murder. They will not help you when you give an account to God. They will have enough to do to look after themselves.

Believe me, if Christ were here he would not advise you to kill

[8] Zwingli. [9] Thess. 5: 21.

those who confess His name, however much they might err in certain respects, not to say that they merely seem to err. Take counsel with the merciful, who advise you to leave the tares until the harvest,[10] for those who wish to pull them up before, eradicate also the command of Christ, who directs that they be left. Those who order heretics to be killed thereby forbid that homicides and other criminals be executed, although the law requires that they be put to death. If this is not so, explain what is meant by the "tares." If the heretics are the tares, they are not to be killed, but are to be left to the harvest. If, however, not the heretics are the tares, but rather the homicides and other criminals, then these are to be left until the harvest and not to be put to death, which is false, for if criminals were not executed the world could not endure. Either, then, the heretics or the criminals are to be left until the harvest.

Hence it follows that he who wishes to kill heretics before the harvest is unwilling to kill criminals, and conversely, he who would kill criminals is unwilling to execute heretics, unless we repudiate the command of Christ to leave the tares. Wherefore, O Princes, do not heed those who counsel you to shed blood for religion. Do not serve as their hangmen. Believe me, if they were oppressed, they would advise otherwise, as indeed many of them did advise when they were suffering persecution, and as all true Christians always advise. St. Paul said that "all that will live godly in Christ Jesus shall suffer persecution." [11] Those who thus suffer will never advise others to persecute any more than did Christ and the apostles.

Be content with the sword which the Lord has given you. Punish brigands, punish traitors, false witnesses, and the like. But when it comes to religion protect the good from the injury of the bad. That is your office. The doctrine of theology cannot be defended by the sword. If theologians persuade you to defend their teaching by arms, the physician will have the right to ask that you defend his opinions against those of the other physicians, and likewise the dialectician, the orator, and the professors of the other

[10] Matt. 13: 30.

[11] II Tim. 3: 12.

arts. If these arts cannot be maintained by the sword, neither can theology which consists no less than the others in words and in spirit. If a good physician can defend his opinions without the aid of the magistrate, why cannot the theologian do the like? Christ could, the apostles could; surely their disciples can. Defend bodies with the bodily sword. This sword cannot touch the soul.

Be wise and follow the counsel of Christ, not of Antichrist. Otherwise, I assure you, there will never be an end of seditions and wars, until all of you who have lightly shed blood shall miserably perish. Think not that the exercise of cruelty will eliminate seditions, for if cruelty went so far that only two men were left in the world and these two differed, they would destroy one another as did the Midianites of yore.[12] There is danger that the like recur today, if we do not moderate our rage. If cruelty were the cure, these evils would long ago have been removed, for cruelty has been exercised for more than five thousand years. But this is certain that evil will never be overcome with evil. There is no remedy against murders other than to stop committing murder.

The Same Author in His Book on Religion

Those who persecute because of religion do so for a variety of reasons; some through envy, like Cain who slew Abel because of his superior piety,[13] and like the Scribes and Pharisees, who were envious of Christ; some persecute because of ambition, like these same Scribes and Pharisees, who hated Christ for disclosing their hypocrisy; [14] some again are actuated by avarice, like these same persons who devoured widows' houses,[15] and saw their gain gone through the exposure of Christ; or again, Demetrius, the silversmith, who persecuted Paul for doing away with the idols by the manufacture of which Demetrius made his living; [16] again, the motive may be voluptuousness as in the case of Herodias, who hated John for preventing her adultery.[17]

Others are actuated by zeal for God conjoined with ignorance like St. Paul, who before he was a Christian thought to do God

[12] Judges 7: 22. [13] Gen. 4. [14] Matt. 23. [15] Mark 12: 40; Luke 20: 47.
[16] Acts 19: 23 f. [17] Mark 6: 17-20; Matt. 14: 3-12.

a service in removing Christians from the world.[18] For men of this sort Christ asked forgiveness, saying, "Father, forgive them, for they know not what they do." [19]

Others sin through malice, and, what is worse, cover their envy, ambition, avarice, and luxury with the name of zeal, and by this spell bewitch the eyes of the people and perhaps even their own. The more these vices flourish the greater are the persecutions on account of religion. They will thrive especially in the last days when love is waxed cold and iniquities abound.[20] Wherefore, there will be great persecution in the last times on account of these vices.

If those who suffer persecution for the name of Christ are not the godly, then none are godly, as Paul says, "All that would live godly in Christ Jesus shall suffer persecution." [21]

If those who are killed as heretics are not martyrs (or at least some of them), then the Church has no martyrs: none were ever killed for Christ except with the title of heretic.

Whosoever believeth that Jesus is the Christ and is come in the flesh, is begotten of God.[22] Therefore, whosoever kills a man who believes that Jesus is the Christ, kills a man begotten of God.

If Christians persecuted the wicked persons in the world on account of the faith, then Christians would reign in the world and the kingdom of Christ would be of this world.[23]

"Fear not little flock." [24] "Behold I send you forth as sheep in the midst of wolves." [25] Will the little flock persecute the great herd, or the sheep the wolf?

"Ye shall weep and lament, but the world shall rejoice." [26] Who are those who rejoice? Are they not the persecutors? And who are those who weep? Are they not those who suffer persecution?

"Blessed are ye when men shall persecute you." [27] How then shall we be blessed if we persecute others?

"If any man would come after me let him take up his cross." [28]

[18] Acts 9; Gal. 1. [19] Luke 23: 34. [20] Matt. 24: 12. [21] II Tim. 3: 12.
[22] I John 4: 2, combined with 5: 1. [23] Cf. John 18: 36.
[24] Luke 12: 32. [25] Matt. 10: 16. [26] John 16: 20. [27] Matt. 5: 11.
[28] Matt. 16: 24; Mark 8: 34; Luke 9: 23.

How can we come after Christ if we crucify others? Shall we not be like the Jews who went after Christ not to be crucified with him, but to crucify him? Christ was crucified between two thieves. Therefore Christians will be held as thieves. Just as thieves take away the lives of men and are hated on that account, so Christians by word and example take away the life of the wicked, that is, their pleasures and desires without which they think life is not worth living.

The lioness pursues the wolf and the sheep. The wolf pursues the sheep, but not the lioness. The sheep is the last. It knows only how to suffer and help, not to hurt. There is nothing lower than the sheep. So it is among men. The great tyrants persecute the little tyrants and the Christians. The little tyrants persecute the Christians. The true Christian is the last. He is able only to help, not to hurt. There is none lower than he, for none is more humble than a Christian, more merciful, poor, and weak. In a word he is a worm, not a man, as David wrote of Jesus Christ.[29]

He who suffers persecution for the faith is either correct or mistaken. If he is correct he should not be harmed. If he is mistaken he should be forgiven. If Christ asked pardon for those who crucified Him on the ground that they knew not what they did,[30] how much more would He intercede for those who are ready to be crucified for Him? If the law of Moses pardons those who kill in ignorance,[31] how much more those who in ignorance are ready to be killed?

If someone found a stray sheep and brought it to your house supposing it to be yours, would you not love him for his good intent, even though it were not yours? If you who are so evil do this, what will God do? Will He not love those who with good intent defend that which they conceive to be true? If perchance they are wrong, will He not forgive them?

There are many other reasons which one might adduce in this matter, but these which we have given will content men of just judgment. The unreasonable are brought to sanity only by blows.

[29] Ps. 22: 6. [30] Luke 23: 34. [31] Lev. 4 and 5; Num. 15: 24-29.

If anyone is so bloodthirsty, so drunk with the cup of Antichrist that he wishes to refute these reasons, let him see to it that he refute them all and refute them truly. There are hairsplitting malicious sophists who, in opposing the truth according to their trade, make the worse argument appear the better. The attention of the hearer is diverted to the weaker considerations, while the stronger are beclouded, omitted, or dismissed with a casual allusion as if already refuted or unworthy of refutation, or again the treatment is so obscure that no one understands. And finally to oppress the truth they draw on all the arts of the Aristotles and the Ciceros to throw dust in the eyes of the judges, as their master Cicero somewhere or other boasts that he did.[32] Let them disabuse their minds. The perfect light, at its appearance, will dissipate these shadows. Though many should be killed and only three should remain, and wounded at that, yet would they storm and burn the fortresses and bring to light all the devices of the oppressors. Hypocrisy, drunk with the blood of the saints,[33] has already reigned long enough, her hour is at hand.

Of one thing would I warn princes and peoples that they beware of the seditions and tumults which always accompany persecutions, as the following examples demonstrate. In the time of the Maccabees there were great and long wars because of the persecutions of Antiochus Epiphanes, who molested the Jews because of their religion, nor could this evil cease until persecution ceased.

Later, in Jerusalem, there were very dangerous tumults because the Jews persecuted Christ. The like had not occurred before. The same thing happened in the time of St. Paul, who taught in Ephesus without disturbance until by persecution Demetrius the silversmith stirred up such a riot that the whole city was full of tumult.[34] Again, when the Jews persecuted Paul, who was making no disturbance in the temple, great tumults arose.[35] The same thing may be seen in our time. Wherever there are persecutions

[32] *M. Fabii Quintiliani institutionis oratoriae libri duodecim*, II, 17, 21. Professor O'Brien-Moore, who kindly supplied the reference, informs me that the statement is not to be found in any of the extant works of Cicero.

[33] Rev. 17: 6. [34] Acts 19: 23 f. [35] Acts 21: 26 f.

everything is full of disturbance. On the contrary where there are no persecutions, everything is tranquil in spite of diversity of religion. I know some cities in which there are almost as many opinions as heads, but because there is no persecution, there is no sedition, and should persecution commence all would be in disturbance. At Constantinople there are Turks, there are Christians, and there are also Jews, three peoples widely differing from one another in religion. Nevertheless they live together in peace, which certainly they could not do if there were persecution. A careful investigation will reveal that persecutors have always been the cause of great troubles.

Wherefore, Princes and Magistrates, if you desire peace and tranquillity, do not listen to those who incite you to persecution, for they are seditious, however much they accuse others of sedition, as the Jews accused Christ, though they were themselves responsible. The dwelling of Christ must be built by love. The persecutors wish to build it by hate and blood. If you do not beware of them they will forever wipe out your kingdoms, republics, cities, souls, and bodies and will reduce you to that ruin and misery to which the Jewish people were brought by the persecutions and bloody counsels of the Scribes and Pharisees.

BASIL MONTFORT

Refutation of the Reasons Commonly Alleged in Favor of Persecution

Some wish to see all heretics put to death, that is, all those who disagree with them, of whatever condition or nation they may be, provided this can be done. Others think that foreigners should be exempt, since the Israelites were not commanded to persecute foreigners, but to punish only those of their own sect. This is the subterfuge of the wolf, who does not attack the lion, but rather the lamb because there is less danger. In order to persuade princes and rulers, the persecutors collect all the passages of Sacred Scripture which may enflame princes to bloodshed. Although not a few authors have refuted these opinions, nevertheless, the persecutors persevere and listen to no one unless he is also a persecutor. Such conduct is not actuated by Christ, as it seems to me, for He did not defend Himself by arms, though He might readily have done so, since He had at His disposal ten legions of angels. The oppressors are actuated rather by the desire to defend their power and worldly kingdom by the arms of the world. This appears from the fact that when they were poor and powerless they detested persecutors, but now, having become strong, imitate them. Abandoning the arms of Christ they take the arms of the Pharisees, without which they would not be able to defend or retain their power. When I see how much blood has been shed since the creation of the world under color of religion and how the just have always been slain before they were recognized, I fear lest the same thing happen in our day, that we kill as unjust those whom our descendants will revere as just. For this reason I have here endeavored to answer the arguments of the persecutors. I have done so with good and ardent intent to open their eyes, if may be, that if they err in ignorance they may err no longer—better to repent late than never—and also that others may not be deceived by their authority. Wherefore I beg them to take my labor in good part, as true Christians ought, and not to resent opposition in the interests of the truth. If they so act, the time will come when they will thank God. I would gladly have listened to them in turn and conferred with them in an amicable and Christian manner, but inasmuch as they dispute with steel, flames, and water, and we are not so armed, for Christ has forbidden steel in this war, we shall therefore debate the question with them from afar and by words as did Jotham, the son of Jerubbaal.[1] This is the battle of Christ; we must use the arms of Christ. Let Him be judge and defend the persecuted, as He was persecuted. Let Him open the eyes of the oppressors to see that their sacrifices are not pleasing to God. May they turn again and be healed and saved.

Now let us come to the point. They cite the law in Exodus, "He that sacrificeth unto any god save unto the Lord only, he shall be utterly destroyed."[2] I ask you whether this destruction is cor-

[1] Judges 9. [2] Exod. 22:20.

poral or spiritual. If it is corporal, then must they first revive the whole law of Moses and inflict corporal punishment upon those who sacrifice. But to do this is to seek to be justified by works of the law,[3] and to be cut off from Christ, in whom the former things are passed away and all things are made new.[4]

Furthermore no one should be punished for this law, because no one sacrifices physically to strange gods, not even the Turks sacrifice to Jupiter or Mercury, to the Sun or the Moon, but rather to the God of Moses. If, on the other hand, the passage is interpreted spiritually, as Paul intended when he spoke of the "reasonable sacrifice," [5] then those who sacrifice to their god Maussim [6] are the first to be killed, that is, those who sacrifice to violence and cruelty. For this sacrifice they will certainly be killed if they do not amend, but this death shall be spiritual through the word and fire of Christ, so also the avaricious whose avarice is idolatry, and the gluttons whose god is their belly,[7] who, accordng to Paul, shall not inherit the kingdom of God.[8] Again, those who sacrifice to their belly, living in contention and debate, do not serve Christ but rather their bellies, as Paul says.[9] This is the true idolatry of the New Testament, of which that of the Old Testament is but a shadow and a figure. Hence it follows that the punishment of the Old Testament is a figure of that punishment which is not temporal but eternal.

The persecutors appeal also to Deuteronomy 13 where it is commanded that the false prophet be put to death. I ask, to begin with, who is a false prophet? Moses teaches in this passage that the false prophet is one who predicts something that does not come

[3] Gal. 2: 16; 5: 3. [4] Rev. 21: 4, 5.

[5] Rom. 12: 1. "I beseech you therefore, brethren, by the mercies of God, that ye present your bodies a living sacrifice, holy, acceptable unto God, which is your reasonable service."

[6] Dan. 11: 38. The Vulgate makes a proper noun of the Hebrew word which the King James version translates "God of forces." The Latin Bible of Castellio reads: *Ceterum Maozim deum vice eius colet.* Luther repeatedly called Maozim the god of the Mass. See the note in *Works of Martin Luther* published by the A. J. Holman Company and the Castle Press, III, 369, n. 1.

[7] Phil. 3: 19. [8] I Cor. 6: 10. [9] Phil. 3: 19.

to pass, and also one who teaches the people to serve strange gods. But today false prophets or heretics are not judged by these tests, but by their opinions. Now it is extremely difficult to pass judgment in view of the diversity of opinions and the animosity engendered even against one who errs on some minor matter of religion, though he retains the fundamentals. For, if every error of faith and every misinterpretation of Scripture obstinately defended makes a man a heretic or a false prophet, who ought to be put to death, none would be more subject to this law than those who teach others. Scarcely will you find in one city two who entirely agree, though they may conceal the disagreement in the interests of the common peace, and to avoid scandal and envy.

But let us suppose that it is possible to judge of the false prophet, nevertheless the heretic is not to be put to death according to this law, unless, like the false prophet, he predicts events which do not come to pass, for the false prophet and the heretic are not identical, and unless he exhorts to the worship of strange gods, who are no longer found among Christians. The persecutors say that those who falsely interpret the Scriptures lead others from the worship of the true God and thus exhort to the worship of strange gods; but this is a false and a diabolical device for the shedding of blood, for if any man build upon the foundation of Christ, even though he build hay and stubble, he shall nevertheless be saved himself, though his work perish.[10] Paul says that Christ died for him who thinks it wrong to eat meat,[11] even though he wrongly understands the Scriptures. God forgives his ignorance. I say nothing of the fact that in view of the innumerable sects, not one of which agrees with the other as to the interpretation of Scripture, all would have to be killed except one, and that the smallest, for the flock of Christ is always small. Who does not see that this is absurd and impossible? Nevertheless, should we grant it, this slaughter would have to be with the sword of the Spirit, as we have shown above.

Again the persecutors adduce the case of the blasphemer from

[10] I Cor. 3: 12-15. [11] Rom. 14: 15.

Leviticus.[12] Yet we have whole cities full of drunkards, and it is hard to tell whether they are more addicted to drink or to blasphemy. Certainly there is no doubt that they are genuine blasphemers, but we do not put them to death. Yet the persecutors wish to execute the so-called heretics, who are convicted of blasphemy neither by the voice of conscience, which is a primary witness, nor out of the mouths of two or three witnesses, unless we wish to accept the testimony of the accusers, that is, of our masters. But Christ said to leave them until the harvest.[13] Before that time uncertainty cannot be entirely removed. I say nothing of the fact that the greatest blasphemers, who should be punished according to this law, are those who confess God with their lips and deny him with their lives. This is why the name of God is blasphemed among the Gentiles.[14] Read the second chapter of Romans and you will see that these are the true blasphemers, all of whom, however, neither can, nor should, be put to death.

Then the persecutors introduce the case of the man who violated the Sabbath.[15] But if this is applied to the Jewish Sabbath, then ought all to be killed except the Jews. If, on the other hand, this is thc Sabbath which the Epistle to the Hebrews mentions, then it does not apply here, because in this passage the corporal sin is transferred to the spiritual. Hence the punishment also must be spiritual, not corporal.

Appeal is then made to the Levites who killed the makers of the golden calf.[16] To arguments of this sort I have sufficiently

[12] Lev. 24: 16. "He that blasphemeth the name of the Lord, he shall surely be put to death and all the congregation shall certainly stone him."

[13] Matt. 13: 28. [14] Rom. 2: 24. "Thou who gloriest in the law, through thy transgression of the law dishonorest thou God? For the name of God is blasphemed among the Gentiles because of you."

[15] Num. 15: 32-36. "And while the children of Israel were in the wilderness, they found a man that gathered sticks upon the sabbath day. And they that found him gathering sticks brought him unto Moses and Aaron, and unto all the congregation. And they put him in ward, because it was not declared what should be done to him. And the Lord said unto Moses, The man shall be surely put to death: all the congregation shall stone him with stones without the camp. And all the congregation brought him without the camp, and stoned him with stones, and he died; as the Lord commanded Moses."

[16] Exod. 32: 28.

replied. The corporal calf received corporal punishment. A spiritual offense is to receive a spiritual penalty.

One might quite as well adduce the case of Achan, who for his sacrilege was stoned with his family and his cattle.[17] If we wish to imitate this example let us kill the entire families of the heretics, or rather let us return to Moses and be circumcised. Let us reject Christ and with the Jews await another under the shadow of the law. For as Moses did not pass over Jordan nor enter into the promised land,[18] so those who live under the law of Moses shall not enter into the blessedness of Christ. If only the persecutors would select the finer portions of Moses, those which better accord with the mercy of Christ. If only they would imitate Moses, who even though the children of Israel wished to stone him,[19] nevertheless appeased the anger of the Lord against them and desired to be blotted out of the book of life rather than that they should perish.[20] But the persecutors select the harsher portions of the law and by every means seek blood. This is utterly contrary to the mercy of Christ. To please the mighty [21] they adduce also the case of the prophet Elijah, who slew the priests of Baal.[22] This is highly relevant! [23] Hereby our adversaries disclose their bad faith because they omit another instance of this same Elijah, who brought down fire from heaven and destroyed the officers of the king.[24] Our opponents would certainly not have passed over this passage if Christ had not reproved his disciples when they wished to follow the example of Elijah, "Ye know not what spirit ye are of," said Christ, "for the Son of Man is not come to destroy men's lives but to save them." [25] The persecutors think that we ought to do what Christ forbade to the apostles. We are given to understand that they were come not to save, but to destroy. Our adversaries wish to put to death the priests of Baal, although it is not yet apparent who they are. In the days of Elijah there was no un-

[17] Josh. 7: 24-25. [18] Deut. 3: 25-26; 34. [19] Num. 14: 10.
[20] Exod. 32: 31-32; Deut. 9: 12-22, combined with Rev. 3: 5.
[21] In the Latin version only. [22] I Kings 18.
[23] In the French version only. [24] II Kings 1.
[25] Luke 9: 56. In the Revised Version these texts appear in a footnote.

certainty. The priests themselves made profession of Baal. Today, on the contrary, none of the heretics professes to believe in strange gods. Moreover Elijah brought down fire from heaven to consume the sacrifice which had been wet with water three days. The priests of Baal were unable to do this. Elijah, having achieved the victory, enjoyed the triumph and slew them. But our persecutors wish to triumph without victory. What fire have they ever brought down from heaven? "The sacrifices of God are a broken spirit: a broken and a contrite heart," [26] "a living sacrifice, holy, acceptable unto God," [27] a people obedient unto God, who "worship him in spirit and in truth." [28] If the oppressors have such a people, and if they have brought down from heaven the fire of love and the Holy Spirit to burn the sacrifice, then they have a perfect right to triumph over the priests of Baal, and to kill them, not with the physical sword, but with the two-edged sword of the Spirit, which is the living word of God.[29] But if they have a people who are rebellious and obstinate, who spend their nights in gluttony—our opponents themselves proclaim this from the pulpits—if they have cried until evening without being able to bring down any fire of love, if, on the contrary things have gone from bad to worse and have come to such a pass that the pastors have often been exiled by their own flocks, then let them cease to imitate the triumph of Elijah, whose victory they have been unable to reproduce. As for the references to Jehu, Jehoiada, and Nebuchadnezzar, these allusions reveal an insufficient consideration of the reasons marshaled by Brenz, who has replied to this sort of thing once and for all. Our opponents make the kingdom of Christ worldly, although He said, "My kingdom is not of this world." [30] They are debtors to do the whole law [31] because they wish to remain under the law. It is surprising that they do not appeal to the case of Phineas, who with his own hands slew those who were not condemned.[32] This is not permissible, they say, for we are not authorized to kill anyone. Yet Phineas and Samuel did.

[26] Ps. 51: 17. [27] Rom. 12: 1. [28] John 4: 23.
[29] Eph. 6: 17, combined with Rev. 2: 12.
[30] John 18: 36. [31] Gal. 5: 3. [32] Num. 25.

If we really wish to imitate the ancients let us do the same as they. Let us abandon the New Testament and return to the Old Testament. Let us kill all those whom God has commanded to be killed, namely, the adulterers,[33] children who curse their parents,[34] the uncircumcised,[35] those who do not keep the Passover,[36] and the like.

The persecutors adduce also some passages from the New Testament. Which do they cite? Is it this? "I send you forth as sheep in the midst of wolves." [37] No. Is it this? "Blessed are ye when men shall persecute you." [38] Is it this? "The world shall rejoice: ye shall be sorrowful." [39] No. They introduce nothing of the sort, but rather this that Peter killed Ananias and Sapphira for their hypocrisy and lying or for their false religion,[40] that Paul blinded Elymas the sorcerer,[41] as if he had dug the eyes out of his head. O these blind men! They do not see that they cut their throats with their own sword, for Peter killed him who had lied against the Holy Spirit, if indeed Peter did it, and not the Lord. They, on the contrary, put to death only those who will not lie, for if anyone gives a verbal and outward conformity to their religion he is not killed even though he dissent in his heart. Whereby we perceive that a lie is more esteemed among them than the truth, seeing that if anyone says what he feels, he is put to death. But if they retort that they are unable to judge of the heart and look rather to a man's words, then the example of Peter does not apply. He was instructed by none other than the Holy Spirit, and he did judge the heart of Ananias, which they cannot do because they do not have the Holy Spirit. Moreover Ananias was not punished for heresy, but because he made a division with the Lord, instead of giving everything or nothing. Peter makes this plain when he says: "Whiles ⟦the land⟧ remained, did it not remain thine own? And after it was sold, was it not in thine own power?" [42] Which is as if he had said, "Nobody compelled you to sell it or bring the money, and we do not constrain those who bring nothing." But

[33] Lev. 20: 10. [34] Lev. 20: 9. [35] Gen. 17: 14. [36] Num. 9: 13.
[37] Matt. 10: 16. [38] Matt. 5: 11. [39] John 16: 20. [40] Acts 5.
[41] Acts 13: 1. [42] Acts 5: 4.

the persecutors wish to punish those who are not of their religion.

Why do they not say with Peter, "We compel no one to sell his goods and offer them to Christ"? That is to say, we compel no one to renounce himself, but if anyone makes a renunciation then he must do so utterly, presenting himself to God a complete sacrifice without blemish,[43] for our Savior will have the whole man, as the husband his wife.

If anyone does not give his whole heart to God, but makes reservations, this man truly follows Ananias. Besides, to attribute to the sword what Peter accomplished with the word is highly absurd, and they seem to realize the absurdity when they endeavor to escape by the subterfuge that there is no great difference in killing with the sword, poison, or words. To kill is to kill, no matter what the method, and what God did then through the apostles, he does now through the magistrate, since vengeance is of the Lord,[44] who has empowered magistrates and sovereigns to exercise authority and punish malefactors. This is what the persecutors say. Is there, then, no difference in killing by the sword, poison, or words? Why in that case, does Christ not destroy Antichrist with the sword instead of with the spirit of His mouth? [45] Why were the weapons of Paul not carnal? [46] Why did Peter not use the sword as he would like to have done in the case of Malchus,[47] and as Moses and Phineas formerly did? Is it not because the sword of the Old Testament is but a figure of the sword of the Spirit of God, which is to be used in the New Testament? That is why Christ told Peter to put up his sword,[48] that is, the carnal sword, and to use the spiritual, as he did in the case of Ananias. What shall we say? Are these statements true? Or can they be refuted? Shall we confuse the symbol with the thing symbolized and treat the sword, poison, and words as the same things? What did Jesus mean by these words, "When thou wast young thou girdest thyself, and walkest whither thou wouldst: but when thou shalt be old, thou shalt stretch forth they hands, and another

[43] Cf. Eph. 5: 27.
[44] Rom. 12: 19.
[45] II Thess. 2: 8.
[46] II Cor. 10: 4.
[47] John 18: 10.
[48] John 18: 11.

shall gird thee, and carry thee whither thou wouldst not."[49] Did he not mean that Peter should not kill by the sword, but should himself be killed?

But to kill is to kill, you say, no matter what the method. Very well. Then to cure is to cure, no matter what the method. Will you say that it is all the same whether Peter's wife's mother was cured by the words of Christ,[50] or by the medicine of Galen? If you wish to kill Ananias, raise Dorcas.[51] If the magistrate kills by the sword in the same way as Peter by words, why cannot the magistrate raise the dead with the sword as Peter did with a word? To kill with the sword—a brigand can do that, but he cannot with words. Show that you can do more than brigands, more than the Scribes and Pharisees, who killed Jesus by the sword. Kill with a word, use the sword of Saint Peter. Then we shall confess that you are the disciples of Saint Peter. Otherwise, who will not believe that your word has turned into a dagger, that you have beaten your ploughshares into swords and your pruning hooks into spears?[52] You say that the magistrate is authorized to punish malefactors. Right you are. But what malefactors? Was Ananias a malefactor? If you had been the magistrate, would you have punished Ananias as a malefactor? By what law? What had he done? He had lied against the Holy Spirit. And how many are there today who lie against the Holy Spirit, when they repeat after you these words, "Our Father who art in heaven?" How many are there who conduct themselves as becomes the children of God? Who desire that His name be hallowed, that His kingdom come, that His will be done? Who is there who does not wish that his own will be done instead of God's; that his own kingdom come? Do not all spend night and day to acquire riches and power? But would you wish that the magistrate put them all to death? And do you not see that the office of the magistrate and the minister are absolutely different? Come now, if you were the magistrate, would you have killed the children who mocked Elisha?[53] You would have no

[49] John 21: 18.
[50] Mark 1: 29-31; Matt. 8: 14-15; Luke 4: 38, 39.
[51] Acts 9: 36-43.
[52] Joel 3: 10, reversing Isa. 2: 4 and Mic. 4: 3.
[53] II Kings 2: 23, 24.

right to, for you have no law which commands that mockers be killed, and the magistrate can execute only in accord with the law.

I say the same thing of the officers upon whom Elijah brought down fire from heaven and consumed them.[54] They had committed no crime save that they had obeyed the magistrate himself, that is, the king, who told them to go and call Elijah. Here we observe that the office of the minister is vastly different from that of the magistrate, as an author, with whom you are well acquainted, has written in these words, "The Church does not assume the office of the magistrate, nor does the magistrate meddle with the affairs of the Church." [55] If you confess these words, then the magistrate would have no right to kill Ananias, nor any heretics, nor those who ought to be punished by the word. Otherwise the magistrate would take from the apostles their sword, for if the magistrate may kill by the sword those whom the minister ought to kill by the word, then the minister in turn may kill by the word those whom the magistrate ought to kill by the sword. The magistrate has no more right to perform the office of the minister than has the minister to assume that of the magistrate. Why do we confuse everything? If you have the word, be content with it and punish with the word heretics, hypocrites, the avaricious, etc., and let the magistrate punish criminals with the sword, let him take an eye for an eye, a tooth for a tooth, a life for a life, and money for money. If your word is weak then let them live whom you cannot overcome with this weapon, that you may not be like children at school, who when they cannot worst their companions by arguments, begin to pull their hair.

God wished to show in the case of Ananias what happens to those who do not dedicate themselves completely to the divine service and who lie against the Holy Spirit when they say that they cannot do more than they are doing. This was said in a figure

[54] II Kings 1:10-12.

[55] *Calvini opera,* I, 648, Instit. VIII (IV), 170 (the passage first appears in the edition of 1543 and thereafter in this form through the edition of 1554); II, 894, Instit. IV, XI, 3 (edition of 1559).

as was also the crucifixion of Christ when Paul said, "They that are Christ's have crucified the flesh with the affections and lusts thereof." [56]

Paul did not know Christ after the flesh, but after the Spirit,[57] and shall we know Peter and Paul after the flesh? Why do we not follow them, then, in curing the sick and raising the dead? Or if we are unable to do so, let us not take life away from those to whom we cannot give it, especially in view of the prohibition of Christ, before whom we stand or fall.

Paul did not desire that we despise the Jews, even though they deny and utterly detest Christ,[58] and shall we kill those who confess Christ and interpret certain passages of Scripture differently than we do? Just as if we were perfectly agreed among ourselves, when sometimes we cite ten opinions on a single passage. What sort of reasoning is this: adulterers, homicides, impostors, and blasphemers are rightly punished; therefore with equal right false prophets and heretics are to be put to death? This is as if you should say, "He who hates his brother is a murderer and should be put to death." Indeed he should, but with the sword of the Spirit, because he has committed a spiritual offense. I say the same thing of heretics. Otherwise, if you wish to kill all who hate another, who covet a neighbor's wife,[59] who call a brother fool or Raca,[60] beware lest your cities be depopulated.

The persecutors adduce also the examples and decrees of the emperors for the punishment of heretics. The oppressors do not observe that in so doing they place the sword in the hands of the tyrants against themselves, for they are considered heretics by the emperors, and Christ scarcely has had martyrs who were not killed by emperors or their successors. As soon as the gentiles ceased to persecute the Christians, they began to do the like, that we might never lack tyrants.

But we shall be told that there were formerly emperors who were more just. True, if they acted more justly. If they granted freedom of religion, their examples and decrees may be cited

[56] Gal. 5: 24. [57] II Cor. 5: 16. [58] Rom. 9.
[59] Exod. 20: 17. [60] Matt. 5: 22.

against the cruelty of those who do the contrary. We may easily show that often they did grant religious liberty. Gratian, after his recall from exile, passed a universal decree in conjunction with the younger Valentinian, that each religion might celebrate its own rights. The Church was closed only to the Eunomians, Photinians, and Manicheans.[61]

Sozomen, Tripartite History, Book Seven, Chapter Twelve

Valentinian, although he took the position of the Nicene fathers and favored those who upheld the same sentiments, nevertheless did not molest those who held other opinions.[62]

The Same, Book Eight, Chapter One

Valentinian framed a law and caused it to be published throughout all the cities, by which any man was permitted to have two lawful wives.[63]

The Same, Book Eight, Chapter Twelve

Themistius, the philosopher, recalled Valens from the slaughter of the orthodox by the following reasons: a prince ought not to exercise cruelty on account of discord in ecclesiastical dogma. Inasmuch as among the pagans there appear more than three hundred sects, each should be allowed to maintain his diverse opinion with regard to the dogma of Christ. Perhaps God is the better pleased not to be easily known and to be glorified in different ways, so that each may fear the more in proportion as his knowledge falls short of the perfection of God and of an understanding of what nature

[61] Socrates, HE V, 2: Migne, PG LXVII, 568; PNF [2] II, 118-19.

[62] Cassiodorus, "Hist. Trip." VII, 12: Migne, PL LXIX, 1078. Taken from Sozomen, HE VI, 6: Migne, PG LXVII, 1309; PNF [2] II, 350.

[63] The reference should be to Book 8, Chapter 11 of Cassiodorus, "Hist. Trip.": Migne, PL LXIX, 1118 (from Socrates, HE IV, 31: Migne, PG LXVII, 549; PNF [2] II, 114). A footnote in the last named work gives cogent reasons for regarding the statement as false. Why Castellio should have introduced the passage at all is a matter for conjecture. Perhaps he was pleading for a more tolerant attitude toward Anabaptists of the Münster type. Perhaps he wished merely to point out to his opponents that an appeal to the imperial law would involve them in more than they relished.

and how great He is. By these reasons the Emperor was rendered somewhat more mild.[64]

Socrates, Book Nine, Chapter Nineteen

Theodosius, having adopted the dogma of the consubstantial, expelled from Constantinople all the other sects except the Novatians, whom he permitted to hold their own churches in the city and to enjoy the privilege of their Church and faith.[65] The same statement is found in another place of the *Ecclesiastical History*.[66]

Sozomen

The Emperor promulgated a law that the heretics should neither hold churches, nor teach concerning the faith, nor ordain bishops or others. Some were expelled from the cities; others were allowed to remain, but were deprived of honor. He permitted them to enjoy civil rights and although in the law he prescribed cruel penalties against them these were not executed. He hoped in this way to promote concord, and did not actually inflict penalties.[67]

The Same in Book Nine, Chapter Thirty-six

The Church was divided into the Consubstantials, the Arians, the Novatians, the Macedonians, and the Eunomians. Be it observed that Emperor Theodosius persecuted none of them except

[64] Cassiodorus, "Hist. Trip." VIII, 12: Migne, PL LXIX, 1118 (from Socrates, HE IV, 32: Migne, PG LXVII, 552; PNF [2] II, 115). Castellio in the Latin version (p. 155.20) reads *scientia* instead of *scientiae* as in Migne. The French translation shows that this is not a misprint. On Themistius consult p. 18, above.

[65] Cassiodorus, "Hist. Trip." IX, 19: Migne, PL LXIX, 1136-38 (from Socrates, HE V, 10: Migne, PG LXVII, 583-94; PNF [2] II, 122-23). Castellio's summary is not accurate. Socrates says that the leaders withdrew discomfited from a conference with the Emperor.

[66] Socrates, HE V, 20: Migne, PG LXVII, 621; PNF [2] II, 129.

[67] Cassiodorus, "Hist. Trip." IX, 19: Migne, PL LXIX, 1138 (from Sozomen, HE VII, 12: Migne, PG LXVII, 1445; PNF [2] II, 383). Castellio in the Latin version (p. 154, line 7) reads *atque* instead of *neque*. The original says that Theodosius did not permit them to enjoy civil rights. The Latin of Cassiodorus is itself a condensation which does not give the full sense of the Greek.

Eunomius, who, by reading his own books in private assemblies, corrupted many with his doctrines. On this account he was exiled, but no one else was molested and the Emperor compelled none to communicate with him, but permitted all to meet in their several conventicles, and to observe the Christian faith as each saw fit. Some were allowed to construct churches outside of the city. The Novatians, who agreed with him in the faith, were permitted to meet within the city. Agelius was bishop of the Novatians for forty years, from the reign of Constantine to the sixth year of Theodosius.

The Novatians held a synod in Sangatium of Bythinia in which they passed a canon that each should be permitted to observe Easter as he chose, and that the Church should not be divided because of a difference as to the celebration, since the ancients who lived nearest to the days of the apostles communicated with one another in spite of a difference on this point.[68]

Sozomen, Book Ten, Chapter Twenty-two

In order to enforce conformity with Arsacius ⟦of Constantinople⟧, and Porphyry ⟦of Antioch⟧, as well as with Theophilus of Alexandria, the leading men at court secured a law that all the people must worship in church and that those who did not communicate should be banished, but since many opposed the party of John Chrysostom there was again great division, so that many took communion apart and great scandal arose.[69]

[68] Cassiodorus, "Hist. Trip." IX, 36 and 37: Migne, PL LXIX, 1152-53. These passages are taken from Socrates, HE V, 20 and 21: Migne, PG LXVII, 619-25; PNF [2] II, 128-29. Castellio has condensed Cassiodorus and has changed Sangarium into Sangatium. Socrates has Angarum, which the editors of the PNF identify with Angora.

[69] Cassiodorus, "Hist. Trip." X, 23: Migne, PL LXIX, 1181 (from Sozomen, HE VIII, 24: Migne PG LXVII, 1580; PNF [2] II, 415). Cassiodorus has misunderstood Sozomen and has placed the commission at Constantinople instead of at Antioch. Castellio has inverted the order of both Cassiodorus and Sozomen, who record first the division and then the order of conformity. The citation does not occur in the French version of Castellio.

The Same, Book Eleven, Chapter Two

In the year 411 during the reign of Honorius, Annas [70] was the bishop of Constantinople, a man distinguished and learned, venerable and prudent, during whose episcopate the churches prospered greatly. He was gracious not only to those of his own faith, but displayed the marvel of his wisdom even to the heretics, whom he was unwilling to molest. Although he had attempted to intimidate them, yet again he showed his magnanimity.[71]

And Chapter Three [72]

A certain Theodosius was the bishop in Synada of Phrygia Pacata. He violently persecuted the Macedonians of whom there were many, and with undue severity expelled them, not only from the cities, but even from the country, although the orthodox Church was not accustomed to inflict persecution. He even armed the clergy and the provincial judges against the heretics and in particular molested their bishop, Agapetus. Since the provincial judges were not invested with sufficient authority to inflict the torments which he desired, he made off to Constantinople to enlist the assistance of the prefects. While he was gone Agapetus adopted the dogma of the consubstantial and was received as bishop by the constituency of Theodosius himself, who, on his return, was rejected and expelled.[73]

These are the ancient examples of justice and clemency which we should imitate.

And if sometimes the men of old acted as men do now, in that case they were no better. But if you appeal to their violence toward the weak in justification of your own, suffer the clement to appeal also to their clemency. If you reject clemency, permit us to reject violence, which is not to be found in the camp of Christ, but rather in that of Antichrist.

[70] Both Cassiodorus and Socrates call him Atticus.

[71] Cassiodorus, "Hist. Trip." XI, 2: Migne, PL LXIX, 1188 (from Socrates, HE VII, 2: Migne, PG LXVII, 741; PNF [2] II, 154).

[72] This heading is in Castellio's Latin version only.

[73] Cassiodorus, "Hist. Trip." XI, 3: Migne, PL LXIX, 1189 (from Socrates, HE VII, 3: Migne, PG LXVII, 741-44; PNF [2] II, 155).

I grow weary of refuting all of the inane arguments which are brought forward to stir up persecutions. The oppressors sedulously collect all that has been said or done from the foundation of the world in favor of shedding blood, which ought by every consideration to be assuaged. They reject the advice of Paul to Titus that a heretic after a first and second admonition should be avoided.[74] Paul was writing to an apostle, we are told. Had he been addressing Sergius Paulus or some magistrate, undoubtedly he would have explained his duties. I think so too. He would have told Sergius to hang all the Jews, heretics, and enemies of Christ.

Dost thou hear this, O Paul? And what dost thou reply? "I could wish that myself were accursed from Christ" [75] for the Jews. Dost thou then desire that they be slain for whose salvation thou wert content to lose salvation?

Let us cease to imagine such absurdities about Paul and to make him like ourselves. He struck Elymas with physical blindness in order to illustrate for Sergius the duties of the magistrate. Yes, he did: if the principle which we formulated above be true that the magistrate is not to do that which pertains to the Church. Paul wished to show that the false prophet is not to be punished by the magistrate but by the apostle. We do not object if all the false prophets be killed in this way, for thereby the will of God will clearly appear.

But we are told that the heretics blaspheme. To this I reply, in the first place, that everybody blasphemes. All confess God in words and deny him in deeds and in the heart. "The fool hath said in his heart, 'There is no God.' " [76] What blasphemy could be greater? But this is secret, you say. On the contrary, it is quite manifest. The fools, like the Sodomites, clearly display their folly and publicly boast of their misdeeds, as their own masters testify. Moreover, as we pointed out above, we do not perfectly know who are the true heretics. Christ and his disciples were esteemed heretics according to the judgment of the Scribes and Pharisees, and if our churches have no Scribes and Pharisees, I marvel that

[74] Titus 3: 10. [75] Rom. 9: 3. [76] Ps. 14: 1.

the tares have been eradicated before the harvest.[77] But if the churches do have Scribes and Pharisees, then let Christ come when He will and they will say again as of yore, "He has blasphemed." [78] They will always have power and be approved of the people as they formerly were. Thus the truth will be repudiated until the light of the Lord discloses them. If we pass a law to put false prophets to death, certainly Christ Himself will be killed with His followers. They will be done to death before they are recognized. But they ought to be known before they are killed.

But heretics hurt others. I know it, and I should be glad to see all real heretics and enemies of the truth dead, if they do not amend. But what shall we do? The tares hurt the wheat, but to pull them up before the harvest is to pull also the harvest. The avaricious also and other bad folk hurt and corrupt people not only by example, but by words, but there is no law which commands that the avaricious, flatterers, or the envious be put to death, even if they are recognized.

You say that the father can compel his child to go to school. You do well to say the father. The father of Christians is not the magistrate, but he who teaches them as Paul taught the Galatians, whom for that reason he could constrain, but only by that instrument through which he had begotten them, namely, the Word. Are the preachers the children of the magistrate in view of the fact that they teach the magistrate? Certainly not. They are the fathers of the magistrate, who must obey them as fathers in the affairs of Christ. Just as the preachers in turn must obey the magistrate as their protector in worldly affairs. But if in religion the magistrate commands something unjust, we must obey God rather than men.[79] In Christ there is neither father, son, nor brother, but a new creature. He is a spiritual father, who has begotten another, and has spiritual authority over him.

Petilian cried, "Far be it from our conscience to compel anyone to embrace our faith." [80] Is he for that reason to be considered a

[77] Matt. 13: 28 ff. [78] John 10: 33-36. [79] Acts 4: 19.

[80] In Augustine's "Contra litteras Petiliani," II, 83 (183): CSEL LII, 112. 21-24; PNF [1] IV, 572.

heretic? How many there have been of genuine insight who have been condemned as heretics by heretics. Take, for example, Vigilantius, who was condemned by St. Jerome because of his criticism of the abuse of candles and of prayers for the dead.[81] Today we agree with Vigilantius and condemn Jerome. Do we suppose for a moment that Vigilantius was the only one to be unjustly condemned? Believe me, the judgment of God will be different from that of men.

The other arguments which are adduced for the coercion of faith I pass over as irrelevant. The persecutors wish to constrain by force those whom God wishes to draw by spiritual exhortation and ardent impulse. They cite Augustine, who at first thought that no one should be constrained to the unity of Christ, that men should be opposed by the Word, combated by disputation, and vanquished by reason, lest those who were known to be manifest heretics should turn into false Catholics. Augustine changed his mind, persuaded not by words, but by example. The city of Augustine, named Hippo, was converted to the Catholic faith by the imperial laws. To which I reply, first of all, "Ho, everyone that thirsteth, come ye to the waters." [82] If Hippo had no thirst she would not have come to the waters and would not have drunk. Thirst had to be created. Augustine perhaps thought they were true Christians who professed Christ with the mouth. He did not perceive that he had fallen into the very calamity which he at first feared. What good is it to be a pretended Catholic? If the sultan of Turkey gave the order, all his subjects would embrace the Evangel at once. Would they, therefore, be real Evangelicals? "This people honoreth me with their lips, but their heart is far from me." [83] Augustine saw but a feigned profession which lasted as long as the coercion and the fear of punishment. He did not consider what a poor guarantee of endurance is fear. We find that shortly afterward Augustine himself and his church and the whole of Africa were subject to that same cruelty which, by his approbation or dissimulation toward others, he had brought upon his own. When

[81] "Contra Vigilantium": Migne, PL XXIII, 337-52; PNF [2] VI, 417-23.
[82] Isa. 55: 1.
[83] Mark 7: 6; Matt. 15: 8; Isa. 29: 13.

the Vandals, steeped in the Arian faith by the Gothic bishops, broke into that part of Africa in which St. Augustine dwelt, they constrained the Catholic bishops either to abjure that form of religion which they professed or to abandon their churches. Great cruelty was inflicted on the true Catholics, as the Vandals vented their fury under the pretext of religion. In that very night on which Hippo was besieged, Augustine died, as it is written in the history of Victor.[84]

Socrates likewise testifies in the *Tripartite History*, Book 11, Chapter 9,[85] that at the very time when Pope Innocent at Rome began to persecute the Novatians and other evil sects and to dissipate and destroy their churches, the Goths invaded Italy, captured Rome, and sacked all. The same Socrates testified in the same place that up to this time the Novatians at Rome had their own churches, their own bishops, deacons, councils, etc.,[86] that never before this time were they molested by any of the bishops at Rome, nor were they troubled even at Constantinople, for here, he says, the Novatians were so cherished that they were allowed to hold their services within the city.[87]

In the time of Justinian already the bishops of Rome obtained their urgent requests to the emperors that those called heretics be expelled from Constantinople and that their churches be scattered. Justinian it was who, after many importunate exhortations, granted to Agapetus, the bishop of Rome, that the heretics be driven out and that their churches be destroyed. Such was the lust of the Roman bishops for power and such their zeal to banish those who did not agree with them, that Vigilius (the third from Agapetus) suffered himself to be bound and maltreated by Justinian, the emperor (otherwise held in high esteem by the bishops), rather

[84] "Victoris Vitensis historia persecutionis Africae provinciae," I, 10-11: CSEL VII, 6; Migne, PL LVIII, 185.

[85] Cassiodorus, "Hist. Trip." XI, 9: Migne, PL LXIX, 1192 (from Socrates, HE VII, 9-10: Migne, PG LXVII, 756-57; PNF [2] II, 157).

[86] Castellio is combining references to the Novatians here and there in Socrates, for which see the index in PNF [2] II.

[87] Cassiodorus, "Hist. Trip." XI, 10: Migne, PL LXIX, 1193 (from Socrates, HE VII, 11: Migne, PG LXVII, 757; PNF [2] II, 158).

than consent to the restoration of certain exiled heretics.[88]

The fruit of harsh persecution and of the cruelty of the Church was manifest first of all in the case of the Arians, who, having suffered from the emperors at the instigation of the Catholics, exercised a like cruelty against the Catholics so soon as the emperor took the Arian side. I refrain for the moment from recounting how Mohammed immediately leveled at the Christians the persecution exercised by the Catholics, so that the evil which our side introduced rebounded against them. Similarly in our own day we observe that the Church which was formerly flourishing is now overwhelmed with confusion, mutilation, corruption, and the murders of so many thousands of men. Likewise recently, under the boy king, Edward, England favored the Gospel and was entirely on our side. If anyone had told us then that the profession of this people was insincere we should have despised him as malicious. But the issue showed what sort of Evangelicals they were who had received the Evangel by force. Those who have but barely escaped with their lives know well, and they say that nothing could be more alien to the Evangel. Little wonder that measure is given for measure and that those who do violence suffer violence. What need is there to mention the cities which formerly seemed to be well grounded in the Gospel, but now the pioneer reformers think that only with difficulty could one or two be found in any city who really favor the Gospel, whereas there is scarcely a city among the outsiders which does not have several, for the strength of Christ

[88] Castellio probably derived his information from the *Historia B. Platinae de vitis pontificum Romanorvm* (Lugduni, 1512, Venetiis, 1515). In the edition of Lyons Agapetus I is treated on fol. lxxviiib-lxxix and Vigilius I on fol. lxxx-lxxxib. Platina says that Justinian was moved by the intrepidity of Agapetus and by the divine impulse to embrace the Catholic faith and remove Anthemius, the Eutychian, from the patriarchate at Constantinople and put in his place Menas, the Catholic, who was consecrated by Agapetus. The Empress Theodora wished to reinstate Anthemius, and removed Silverius, the next pope, because he would not consent. Vigilius was appointed as pope on the promise to comply, but when brought to Constantinople, he proved obdurate in spite of severe persecution. Castellio has exaggerated the rôle of the bishops in making a bigot out of Justinian. See J. B. Bury, *History of the Later Roman Empire from the Death of Theodosius I to the Death of Justinian* II (London, 1923), Chap. XXII.

is made perfect in weakness.[89] Many preachers confess that after long years of instruction there is not one among their people who would lose so much as a little money for the truth. And even those who have engaged in persecution now frankly confess that they did so unwillingly, giving place to violence, but always at heart they adhered to their first opinion.

I have heard that there is in England one who previously preached the Gospel diligently, but who now opposes it with a bitterness exceeding his former zeal. He says that before he was under constraint; now he is declaring his heart of his own accord. Augustine had good reason to fear the production of hypocritical Christians. Better one who is genuine than thousands who make a pretense. To be brief, if men could be constrained to the faith, Christ would have constrained them and would have taught us to do the like. "How often would I have gathered thy children together, even as a hen gathereth her chickens under her wings, and ye would not!"[90] Christ himself could not save an unwilling Jerusalem, and are we stronger than he?

Our opponents quote the text, "Compel them to come in."[91] Yes, but with the sword of the Spirit (at least if the marriage is spiritual), that is, with powerful, living, divine words. By the Word the heavens visible and invisible were made.[92] To seek to create a new creature with anything other than the Word of God is to turn upside down the creation of the world.

Again we are told that Christ compelled Paul by corporal punishment to embrace the Gospel. Let us all be constrained in this way by Christ that we may say, "Lord, what wilt Thou have me to do?"[93] But to assign this constraint to the magistrate is to drag heaven down to earth. The persecutors dare to assert that the apostles asked no aid of the magistrates against opponents in religion because the magistrates were not Christian. Consider well what this implies. Christ said that His kingdom was not of this world, else would His servants fight[94] that He be not delivered to Pilate. The magistrate should protect the good against force

[89] II Cor. 12: 9. [90] Matt. 23: 37; Luke 13: 34. [91] Luke 14: 23.
[92] Cf. John 1: 3. [93] Acts 9: 6. [94] John 18: 36.

and injury, but the magistrate cannot make men good by force, nor handle religion by the sword. Otherwise Christ was not adequately armed, nor were the apostles. Nevertheless, though poor, powerless, and persecuted by all the princes in the world, the apostles accomplished more than we are able to do with the aid of all the princes, now that we have grown strong and violent. No wonder! They built the tabernacle from the free gifts of the people. But we employ forced gifts, if indeed they be gifts which are not given from the heart. We need not be surprised if we have the experience of tyrants who force their soldiers to take an oath of allegiance. In battle such commanders are deserted or betrayed by their troops, who either flee or are captured. "The weapons of our warfare," says Paul, "are not carnal, but mighty through God to the pulling down of strongholds; casting down imaginations, and every high thing that exalteth itself against the knowledge of God, and bringing into captivity every thought to the obedience of Christ." [95] If the sword takes captive the imaginations of men, and if St. Paul used one, we will certainly do so, but if he used none, let us be content with the weapons which Christ gave to the apostles, especially in view of our repeated assertions that the Holy Scriptures are perfect and nothing must be added nor taken away, lest we turn the heavenly into an earthly battle and build the house of God with unworthy material and implements.

These are the arguments in favor of persecution adduced by some even after the publication of the books of Luther and Brenz, whose replies suffice in general. But inasmuch as there are still those who prefer the authority of others, I have seen fit to examine the question in greater detail in order to serve the salvation of men as much as possible and to remedy this effusion of blood. I have done so, not with the intent of withdrawing princes and peoples from the instruction of their pastors and teachers, but since there are two kinds of pastors I say that the better should be obeyed. Some are violent, fierce, hard, irritable, impatient, who condemn all teaching except their own and wish to put to death

[95] II Cor. 10: 4, 5.

all who disagree with them. The others are meek, humane, merciful, slow to anger, patient, who bear all things, endure all things, hope all things.[96] They have no desire to coerce religion. I say that these should be followed as the better. The former assert that the latter, who will not constrain religion, are nourishing monsters and giving them the liberty to sow their poison. The meek reply that, on the contrary, the persecutors are rather those who nourish monsters by making religion servile and destroying men on account of it. This violence brings it about that men are constrained to approve of whatever the violent assert. Nothing is too monstrous to teach the people when to doubt is prohibited, since if you doubt or do not believe, you are put to death. Hence the power of the Scribes and Pharisees, who exclude from their synagogue those who dare to speak of Christ. Hence the tyranny of him who in our day has been unmasked and is rightly held in detestation. He could never have attained to this tyranny if he had left religion free, nor would he have introduced so many errors had he not deprived men of the power of judgment.

Finally, to resort to force even in civil matters is a confession of guilt and of a lack of confidence in the justice of one's case. Christ says, "I will give you a mouth and wisdom, which all your adversaries shall not be able to gainsay nor resist." [97] Those who are armed with this wisdom desire no other weapons. They fear not to fight openly and to withstand all comers, provided there be a just and legitimate discussion. They know that truth is an invincible weapon and that light prevails over darkness. The others, on the contrary, fear the light and seek to hide. They employ the sword after the manner of the world, and conclude with iron the discussion which began with words, for they well know that without the sword they would be defenseless and would not be able to resist their adversaries. Thus the wolf fights with teeth, the bull with horns, the mule with hoofs: each animal uses his own mode of defense, except the sheep, which, not knowing how to fight, is entirely dependent on the shepherd.

To conclude, if you are not yet able to distinguish the true

[96] I Cor. 13: 7.

[97] Luke 21: 15.

shepherds from the false, employ this test: paint a picture of an army, of the good and of the bad. On the left portray an elder and powerful prince, named "Cain," with a red banner and a wolf as emblem. The device is, "Let us lay wait for blood." [98] The watchword is "Crucify"; the escutcheon, unbelief; the girdle, a lie; the breastplate, injustice; the greaves, swiftness to shed blood; and the sword, violence. Let this figure be followed by his progeny with fire and sword, the giants, the Sodomites, Ishmael, Esau, the Egyptians, Saul, the false prophets, the Babylonians, Scribes, Pharisees, tyrants, and all the host of the powerful of the world. Paint then on the right side a younger and weaker prince, by name Abel, with a white banner and a sheep as emblem. The motto is, "All that will live godly in Christ Jesus shall suffer persecution"; [99] the watchword, "patience"; the escutcheon, faith; the girdle, truth; the breastplate, justice; the greaves, swiftness to aid a neighbor; and the sword, the Word of God.

Above the two armies place a judge. Inscribe on his left in letters of fire these words, "O Cain, where is thy brother?" [100] "Woe to thee that spoilest. Shalt thou not be spoiled?" [101] "With what measure ye mete it shall be measured to you again." [102] "All that take the sword shall perish with the sword." [103] "He that leadeth into captivity shall go into captivity." [104] "Woe to the bloody city." [105] "Woe unto you that are rich! for ye have received your consolation. Woe unto you that are full! for ye shall hunger. Woe unto you that laugh now! for ye shall mourn and weep. Woe unto you, when all men shall speak well of you! for so did their fathers to the false prophets." [106] "Woe unto you Scribes and Pharisees, hypocrites!" [107] "O thou wicked servant, I forgave thee all that debt, because thou desirest me: Shouldest not thou also have had compassion on thy fellowservant, even as I had pity on thee?" [108] "Depart from me, ye cursed, into everlasting fire." [109]

But on the right side let these words be written: "Blessed is he

[98] Prov. 1: 11. [99] II Tim. 3: 12. [100] Gen. 4: 9. [101] Isa. 33: 1.
[102] Matt. 7: 2; Mark 4: 24. [103] Matt. 26: 52. [104] Rev. 13: 10.
[105] Ezek. 24: 6; Nahum 3: 1. [106] Luke 6: 24-26.
[107] Luke 11: 44; Matt. 23: 23. [108] Matt. 18: 32, 33. [109] Matt. 25: 41.

that considereth the poor."[110] "Blessed are the poor in spirit. Blessed are they that mourn. Blessed are the meek. Blessed are they which do hunger and thirst after righteousness. Blessed are the pure in heart. Blessed are the peacemakers. Blessed are they which are persecuted for righteousness' sake. Blessed are ye, when men shall revile you, and persecute you, and shall say all manner of evil against you falsely, for my sake. Rejoice, and be exceeding glad: for great is your reward in heaven: for so persecuted they the prophets which were before you."[111] "Come, ye blessed of my Father."[112] Let these pictures be called, "The Shepherds," "The Meek," and "The Cruel." The arms and the insignia, the mottoes and manners will readily show which designation applies. The same description cannot apply to both sides for "no man can serve two masters."[113]

To this picture add, if you will, the description of the warfare of Christ from Esdras. "And behold," he says, "all who were gathered together to wage war with him were seized with great fear; yet they dared to fight. And lo! when he [that is, the Son of God] saw the assault of the multitude as they came, he neither lifted his hand, nor held spear nor any warlike weapon; but I saw only how he sent out of his mouth as it were a fiery stream, and out of his lips a flaming breath, and out of his tongue he shot forth a storm of sparks. And these were all mingled—the fiery stream, the flaming breath, and . . . the storm, and fell upon the assault of the multitude which was prepared to fight, and burned them all up, so that suddenly nothing more was to be seen of the innumerable multitude save only dust of ashes and smell of smoke."[114]

From these passages it is sufficiently clear what are the weapons of Christ and of Antichrist, and who are the persecutors, and who those who endure persecution. If there is anyone who is not satisfied with these considerations I do not know what would satisfy him.

Arise, O Lord, and judge Thy cause.[115]

[110] Ps. 41: 1. [111] Matt. 5: 3-12. [112] Matt. 25: 34. [113] Matt. 7: 24.
[114] IV Ezra 13: 8-13. R. H. Charles, *Apocrypha and Pseudepigrapha of the Old Testament*, II (Oxford, 1913), 617.
[115] Cf. Ps. 7: 6.

CONCERNING THE CHILDREN OF THE FLESH AND THE CHILDREN OF THE SPIRIT

"But as then he that was born after the flesh persecuted him that was born after the Spirit, even so it is now. Nevertheless, what saith the Scripture? Cast out the bondwoman and her son: for the son of the bondwoman shall not be heir with the son of the free-woman." [1]

Consider these words of Paul, reader. Ishmael, born according to the flesh, was persecuting Isaac, born according to the Spirit. Even so now the carnal persecute the spiritual. It cannot be other-wise. Isaac, because he is younger and weaker, is not in a position to persecute Ishmael. Just so now the Christians, because they are born after the Antichrists, are weaker and are not able to perse-cute the Antichrists. And this has been signified by many examples. Abel did not persecute Cain; nor Noah, the giants; nor Lot, the Sodomites; nor David, Saul; nor the prophets, the false prophets; nor Christ or the apostles, the Scribes and Pharisees; but precisely the contrary. Even if they were able to do so, they did not, like David whom Saul persecuted as a flea or a partridge upon the mountains.[2] Yet when David came upon Saul defenseless once, and even twice, he might have killed him, but would not.[3] So today the godly are like a flea whom the ungodly persecute. And if some-times the godly are in a position to harm the ungodly, yet are they so far from doing so that rather they seek their good. This the godly have learned from their father David, as the others have learned from Saul their father to harm those from whom they have received good. These are the marks of the godly and of the ungodly. The latter are noble, rich, learned, powerful, mockers, persecutors, cruel, proud, famous, and ambitious like Cain, the giants, the Sodomites, Saul, the Egyptian magi, the false prophets, the Scribes and Pharisees, Herod, Pilate, Annas, Caiaphas, and the philosophers. The godly are ignoble, poor, unlearned, weak, mocked, harassed, peaceable, meek, humble, submissive, obscure, vile, abject, despised, and rejected,[4] the filth and offscouring of the

[1] Gal. 4: 29, 30.
[2] I Sam. 26: 20.
[3] I Sam. 24 and 26.
[4] Isa. 53: 3.

world,[5] who despise their own honor and seek the honor of God, who return good for evil, bless those that curse them,[6] and follow Christ, the lamb of God, in crosses, tribulations, adversities, and virtues.

Now, Christian reader, place such a people before your eyes and consider for a moment whether it is possible that these poor folk, dispersed throughout the world, should persecute the ungodly, that is the giants and the powerful of the earth who have banded and conspired together. And if this cannot be, as indeed it most certainly cannot, then rest assured that those who persecute for the faith are the Ishmaelites, because they follow the nature of Ishmael.

"Nevertheless what saith the Scripture? Cast out the bondwoman and her son: for the son of the bondwoman shall not be heir with the son of the freewoman." [7] Now who is the bondwoman? It is the law, according to St. Paul, and the sons of the bondwoman are under the law, that is, they wish to be under the letter and persecute those who wish to be under the Spirit, as Ishmael persecuted Isaac. Thus we see that they are utterly Ishmaelites who cite the letter of the law which commands that false prophets be put to death. The false prophets are the heretics. The heretics are those with whom the persecutors disagree. Herein they are the sons of those who say, "We have a law, and by our law he ought to die, because he made himself the Son of God." [8] You see that the sons of the law persecute the sons of the Spirit and cite the law in their favor. But how did Sarah act, that is, the free and spiritual Church? She did not herself cast out the son of the bondwoman, that is, the servant of the letter, nor did Isaac cast out Ishmael, for he could not, that is, the godly do not cast out the ungodly; they cannot. But Sarah asked her husband, that is, the Church asks God to cast out the law, the persecuting letter, and its persecuting sons, lest they be heirs of the kingdom of heaven. Thus the Church is not empowered to cast out the ungodly from the heavenly inheritance. She must leave this to Christ her spouse, who will cast them out

[5] I Cor. 4: 13. [6] Matt. 6: 44. [7] Gal. 4: 30. [8] John 19: 7.

with the rod of His mouth [9] when he says, "Depart from me, ye cursed, into everlasting fire." [10] To pronounce this sentence belongs neither to Sarah nor to Isaac, but to Christ. Wherefore let those who condemn heretics, beware what they do. Heretics are not usually condemned in the same way as brigands. Those who hang brigands often hope and pray for them and do not believe that they are damned to hell. But those who persecute heretics regard them as utterly rejected by God and adjudged to eternal fire. To pronounce this judgment is obviously to sit on the tribunal of Christ and pass the sentence, "Depart from me, ye cursed, into everlasting fire." [11] This verdict is not to be passed by any save by Christ and not before the day of judgment. Precisely on this account the judgment day is so called, because then and not before, judgment shall be passed on the elect and the reprobate, as Paul teaches when he says, "Therefore judge nothing before the time, until the Lord come, who both will bring to light the hidden things of darkness, and will make manifest the counsels of the hearts." [12] When I consider these words I find nothing to add save an admonition to all to consider seven times what they do when it comes to condemning anyone as a heretic to eternal pains as one forever rejected by God, for heretics are so esteemed. Again I will write in large letters this counsel that "he may run who readeth it." [13] JUDGE NOTHING BEFORE THE TIME, UNTIL THE LORD COME, WHO BOTH WILL BRING TO LIGHT THE HIDDEN THINGS OF DARKNESS, AND WILL MAKE MANIFEST THE COUNSELS OF THE HEARTS.[14]

[9] Isa. 11: 4. [10] Matt. 25: 41. [11] *Ibid.*
[12] I Cor. 4: 5. [13] Hab. 2: 2. [14] I Cor. 4: 5.

Excerpts from Other Works of Castellio and Joris

Excerpts from Other Works of Castellio and Joris

PREFACE TO THE FRENCH BIBLE [1]

To the most valiant and victorious Prince Henry of Valois, the second of that name, by the grace of God most Christian King of France from Sebastian Castellio, his subject, greeting.

When night falls upon the battle field the combatants wait for the day lest by chance friends be killed instead of enemies, for it is better to spare one's enemies than to kill some of one's friends. Likewise also in the day time, when the hand to hand combat begins the artillery ceases for fear of the aforesaid mischance. Here I should like to point a moral if your Majesty will deign to listen. The world today is embroiled in great disturbance principally touching the question of religion. There never were so many calamities and evils, from which we may well perceive the night of ignorance. If not all are enveloped, at least many are. If it were day there would never be such diverse and even contrary judgments about the same color. Or if it is day, at least the good and the evil are so confused in the matter of religion that if one wishes to disentangle those who are at variance as to the truth there is danger lest the wheat be rooted out with the tares. That would be an irreparable loss. Hitherto the world has always made this mistake. The prophets, the apostles, so many thousands of martyrs, and even the Son of God were put to death under color of religion. An account must be given for all this blood by those who have been striking at random in the night of ignorance. . . . Believe me,

[1] *La Bible nouvellement translatée* (Bâle, 1555). This Preface circulated in manuscript as early as 1553. *Calvini opera*, XIV, 586, n. 7, Ep. 1769 (Aug. 6, 1553). The first section of the following translation is from a photostat of signature 2 from the copy in the British Museum. The second paragraph is from the portion reprinted in *Calvini opera*, XIV, 737, No. 1889.

your Majesty, the world today is neither better nor wiser nor more enlightened than formerly. It were better, therefore, in view of so much doubt and confusion to wait before shooting until the dawn, or until things are better disentangled, lest in the darkness and confusion we do that of which afterwards we shall have to say, "I did not intend to."

When I have written that I do not understand such and such a passage I do not mean to imply that I do understand all the others. I mean that in the case of the others I have some glimmering of the sense, but in this, none whatever. I have noted the fact lest the reader unduly rely upon my translation at these points. But I have not recorded all that I do not understand. There would be no end of it.

COUNSEL TO FRANCE IN HER DISTRESS[1]

[The cause of the present civil war in France is the attempt to constrain religion. Some propose to settle the controversy by war to the end with the aid of foreigners. This will be the ruin of the land, for the foreigners will feather their own nests, and even if they are disinterested will shed blood. Already fifty thousand have fallen. Now I will address an appeal to each side, using not the names which they apply to each other of Papist and Huguenot, but those which they prefer for themselves of Catholic and Evangelical (3-12).]

To the Catholics.—(12) And first I address you, Catholics, you who say that you have the ancient true and Catholic faith and religion, (13) consider closely your case for a moment. It is high time that you did. Recall how you have treated the Evangelicals. You have pursued and imprisoned them and left them to be consumed of lice and rot in foul dungeons in hideous darkness and the shadow of death, and then you have roasted them alive at a slow fire to prolong their torture. And for what crime? Because

[1] Extracts from the *Conseil à la France désolée* (October, 1562). The numbers in parentheses refer to the pages of the original. There is a copy at Cornell.

Wie man die falschen Propheten erkennen ia greiffen mag/ Ein predig/ zu Mynden jnn Westphalen gethan/ durch

D. Vrbanum Rhegium.

Canonicus: Monachus.

Jeremie 10. Die Hirten sind zu narren worden/ vnd fragen nichts nach Gott/ Darumb können sie auch nichts rechts leren/ sondern zerstrewen die Herd.

How to Recognize and Seize
the False Prophets
by
Urbanus Rhegius

they did not believe in the pope, the mass, purgatory, and other things, which are so far from being based on Scripture that even the very names are not to be found there. Is that a good and just cause for burning men alive? Do you call yourselves Catholics and profess to maintain the Catholic faith contained in the sacred Scriptures and yet hold as heretics and burn alive those who wish to believe only that which is contained in the Scriptures? Wait now and weigh this carefully. Here is a point of great importance. Answer now, for you will have to answer (14) some day, whether you like it or not, before the just Judge whose name you bear. Answer this one question which undoubtedly will be asked of you at the judgment day. Would you wish that this be done unto you? . . . (15) You well know whether the wrong you have done to your brothers is small. It is so small indeed that they have preferred to endure all that your cruelty (I must call it by its proper name) could invent than to go counter to their conscience as you require, and this is a sign that to force the conscience of a man is worse than cruelly to take his life. . . .

To the Evangelicals.—(17) I turn now to you, Evangelicals. Formerly you suffered persecution for the Evangel with patience. You loved your enemies and returned good for evil. You blessed those that cursed you,[2] and offered no resistance save flight in case of necessity, and this you did in accord with the command of the Lord.[3] How does it happen that some of you are now so changed? . . . Has the Lord changed His commandment? . . . (18) and ordered you to return evil for evil? Or have you turned your backs on His commandment? . . . What else can one infer when you convert all resourses even to the substance of the poor into battle axes, and massacre your enemies at the edge of the sword until roads and byways, yes, houses and temples, are stained with the blood of those for whom Christ died as much as for you, and who are baptized in His name as are you? What more can I say than that you compel them to attend your sermons, and you even force brothers to take arms against brothers and those of their

[2] Matt. 5: 44.

[3] Matt. 10: 23.

own religion contrary to conscience? (19) You examine men as to your doctrine and are not content that they should agree on the main points of religion, which are clear and evident in sacred Scripture. . . . Here are the three remedies which you employ: to shed blood, to force consciences, and to condemn as infidels those who do not agree with your doctrine. I am at a loss to discover what has become of your intelligence if you do not see that in these three points you follow your enemies, those whom you commonly call Antichrist. I know well that some of you reply, "We are right and they are wrong." (20) . . . But rationalize as much as you please before men and draw as many fine distinctions as you please, nevertheless we know well, and I call your own consciences to witness, that you are doing to others what you would not have done unto you. . . .

To both the Catholics and the Evangelicals.—(25) When Jesus disputed with the Jews, though they were highly opinionated, he was sometimes able to reduce them to silence with a single word. . . . The world is not more obstinate today. I am sure, therefore, that this case can be settled by a single word of evident truth and none will be able to gainsay it. We need only ask those who force consciences, "Would you like to have yours forced?" and immediately their own conscience, which is worth more than a thousand witnesses, will convict and make them dumb. (27) . . . And do not begin to excuse yourselves and say as someone once did, "If I were an adulterer I should not wish to be punished, but it does not follow that if I were the judge I should not punish an adulterer." To which I reply, "If you were an adulterer and you were punished, you would admit that you had been done no injustice. So, also, a thief when punished confesses that he deserves it, or if his mouth denies it, his conscience, whether he will or no, confesses and gives him the lie." (28) Here we see the invincible force of truth and rectitude which cannot be extinguished in the heart of a man, no matter how bad he is. The case of one whose conscience is forced and who is persecuted for the faith is precisely the reverse. Though he may be constrained to confess with his mouth that no wrong is done, yet in his heart he will always say, "You have done me an injustice, and you would not have wished the like done to you." See how we ought to understand this rule, "Do not unto others what you would not that they do unto you." [4] This is a rule, so true, so just, so natural, and so written by the finger of God in the hearts of all men that there is no one so degenerate, so estranged from discipline and enlightenment, but that he will confess this rule to be right and reasonable the moment it is proposed to him. Hence we can easily see that when the Truth judges us it will be in accord with this rule. And in fact Christ, who is the Truth, has confirmed it when He not only forbade us to do to others what we would not have done unto us, but, even more, commanded that we should do unto others as we would that they do unto us. . . .[5]

(33) Take the case of a man who has scruples against going to Mass or hearing a minister whom he considers a heretic or supporting by money and arms a church which he regards as heretical against one which he holds as Catholic, and you tell him that if he does not comply he will be banished, or disinherited or miserably put to death. What do you want him to do? Advise him, for he is in extreme anguish like a piece of bread roasted on the end of a knife. If it moves forward it is burned and if backward it is pierced. So the poor man, if he does what you desire he will be damned for going against his conscience; if he withstands you he will lose goods and life. . . . I ask you, you Inquisitors (34) . . . you who egg on princes . . . what advice would you give to such a man? Would you counsel him to go against his conscience? Then he will lose his soul. Or would you advise him to follow his conscience? Then he will be put to death. . . . (35) If a sick man does not wish to eat meat, will you ram it down his throat, or if a donkey will not drink, will you drown him to make him drink?

⟦(36-39) Examples of constraint in the Old Testament are not valid for us, partly because the patriarchs had a special command from God, but more particularly because the Old Testament has been superseded by Christ.⟧

[4] Tobit 4: 15.

[5] Matt. 7: 12; Luke 6: 31.

When we come to examples outside of Scripture . . . (40) the Saracens were forced to be baptized and the Jews in Spain. . . . But the Saracens never became true Christians as they showed when they later returned to their first religion, and the Jews in Spain baptized by force are no more Christians than they were before. . . .

(47) Those who have regard to numbers and for that reason constrain men, gain nothing, but rather lose. They are like a fool who having a barrel containing a little wine fills it full of water to get more; instead of increasing the wine he spoils what he had. . . .

(49) ⟦By constraint⟧ you engender mortal enmities and make hypocritical Christians who have no other purpose than to ruin that which they have embraced through constraint. . . . At the first opportunity they revolt. These are the evils which result from your good intentions and your exercise of force. It is a marvel if you do not see that instead of advancing your religion you have set it back. Stop and examine. First, you Catholics, when Luther arose you started to persecute his sect and to burn his followers . . . and subsequently you have never ceased to make every attempt to eradicate his party. (50) And what have you gained? You have rendered yourselves suspect, you have provoked revolt, and things have come to such a pass that for one you have burned, a hundred have arisen and now there are thousands in place of tens, so that, as you see, they dare even to make war upon you.

And you Evangelicals, when you fought with spiritual arms, as you learned from Christ and the apostles, namely, with faith, love, patience, and the like, God blessed you and strengthened you and you increased as drops of dew at break of day. And now that you have abandoned the spiritual arms for the carnal, everything has gone wrong.

⟦(51) Then Castellio cites the case of the Protestant Zwingli who, having taken the sword, perished by the sword, and of the Catholic Charles V who, having led captive the princes of Germany, was himself undone chiefly by the Catholic king of France.

(52-62) As the only alternative to mutual extermination or the tyranny of one party over the other Castellio proposes that both religions be free and cites by way of support a tract of one of the *Politiques* in France.

(63-71) A heretic is defined in the etymological sense as the member of a bad sect. There is no law of God that he be put to death, for the penalties of the Old Testament apply to blasphemers and false prophets, and a blasphemer is one who consciously reviles God. To extend the law of Moses to cover those who err in the interpretation of Scripture is to be too ingenious in shedding blood.

(72-73) Even if princes are subject to the law of Moses they may let heretics live, since Moses has nothing against heretics. But even the persecutors are forced to confess that we are not subject to Moses. The law of Moses against idolatry in Deuteronomy 13 calls for the total destruction of goods, cattle, and infants. Would the persecutors go so far?

(76) It were better to refer disputed points to the prophet predicted in Deuteronomy 18: 15 and 18. (77) Now this prophet is Christ.

(78) The only ways of knowing His will are by His written word, by the example of His life, by the nature of His spirit dwelling in His own or by a new revelation. In the Word we find nothing beyond avoiding a heretic. (79) As for Christ's example we find Him as a lamb before the wolf. The spirit in His disciples is that of the followers of the lamb. (80) A new revelation need not be considered, for the persecutors pretend to none and if they did it would have to be subjected to the mind of Christ. You say that disobedience to the priest is punishable by death. (81-82) Very well, in that case moral offenders should suffer. (83) You say that moral offenders at least confess Christ with their lips. So do the heretics, but both are the worse for it. They are hypocrites. It were better that they should deny Christ with their lips as well as with their lives, so as not to seduce others.]

(84) I come now to the dangers which might ensue if heretics were suffered to live. There are two: sedition might be engendered, and false doctrine disseminated. To the first I say that the fools cause the evil which they seek to avoid. Seditions arise from the attempt to force and kill heretics rather than from leaving them

alone, because tyranny engenders sedition. . . . (85) I admit the danger of the dissemination of false doctrine, but . . . the remedy must not be worse . . . than the disease. . . . When people see the constancy of the heretics in martyrdom, many begin to esteem them and join their party until there are seven for one. (86) This is the issue of your foolish wisdom. Then, too, there is the danger that in persecuting a heretic a Christian be persecuted by mistake. Christ foresaw this when he said, "The time cometh that whosoever killeth you will think that he doeth God service."[6] This has constantly happened from the time of Christ to our own. First, Christ and his apostles were persecuted as heretics and after them the martyrs. And ever since, if there have been simple and true Christians, they have been persecuted as heretics. Today when we garnish the sepulchres of the martyrs killed by our fathers,[7] I fear lest we are following our fathers and making new martyrs to be honored by our sons. Usually truth is disregarded and unrecognized, and in this regard we are no better than our fathers. . . . (87) The wise doctor will not kill the patient to cure the disease, nor will the wise husbandman destroy the wheat in pulling up the tares. . . . The parable is relevant whether or no the tares are to be identified with the heretics—I say this because the question is controverted. The point is similar in any case. . . . (88) In a word, Christianity is today divided into so many sects that they cannot be counted. Each sect regards itself as Christian and the rest as heretical. If, then, we are to apply the law for the persecution of heretics we shall let loose a Midianite war of extermination. . . .[8]

⟦(90-96) Excommunication is the sole weapon to be used against heresy. The apostles guarded their Church by this means alone and the Anabaptists today are so successful without the aid of the sword of the magistrate that even the most learned theologians cannot divert their followers.

Final exhortations.⟧

[6] John 16: 2. [7] Matt. 23: 29. [8] Cf. p. 221, above.

REPLY TO CALVIN'S BOOK IN WHICH HE ENDEAVORS TO SHOW THAT HERETICS SHOULD BE COERCED BY THE RIGHT OF THE SWORD[1]

Calvin 1. [Aiij, p. 17] Defense of the Orthodox Faith Concerning the Sacred Trinity against the prodigious errors of the Spaniard Michael Servetus, where it is shown that heretics are to be punished with the sword and in particular that this so impious man was justly and properly punished at Geneva.

Vaticanus. Calvin defines heresy in terms of error, as if he said, I will write against the errors of Servetus and will show that those who err, that is, heretics, are to be punished with the sword as Servetus, who erred, was punished with the sword. We shall see that this is the mind of Calvin. He wishes all those who grievously err to be killed unless they endorse the opinion of Calvin. . . . If this were done, all who bear the Christian name would be killed, except Calvinists. . . .

Calvin 2. . . . I did not at first think it necessary to make a direct reply to this man. The absurdity of his delirium seemed to me so great that I hoped it would go up in smoke without opposition.

Vaticanus. [Aiij verso, p. 18] . . . And it would have gone up in smoke had it been absurd delirium.

Calvin 14. [B verso, p. 30] When warning and exhortation were

[1] *Contra libellum Calvini in quo ostendere conatur haereticos jure gladii coercendos esse. Anno Domini MDLCXII.* Printed in Holland. Buisson in his *Sébastien Castellion* II, 365, No. 16, quotes the interesting suggestion of Bordier that the date is a combination of the year of composition, 1562, and the year of publication, 1612. The paternity of Castellio was placed beyond question by Buisson's discovery of a portion of the manuscript at Basel in his hand, including portions which were not printed (*ibid.*, II, 32 and 477-479). The work is a *seriatim* reply to Calvin's *Defensio orthodoxae fidei de Sacra Trinitate, contra prodigiosos errores Michaelis Serveti Hispani* (Geneva, 1554, reprinted in the *Calvini opera*, VIII, 453-644). Excerpts from Calvin are followed by refutations under the pseudonym Vaticanus. There is no pagination. I have supplied it in the translation. The excerpts from Calvin are numbered, and the signatures indicated. The last four citations are from the letter of Zürich to Geneva quoted by Calvin. The seventh excerpt is from Calvin's *Institutes*.

of no avail I was unwilling to exceed the rule of our Lord to avoid a heretic who sins, being self-condemned, as the Apostle Paul puts it.[2]

Vaticanus. . . . The rule of our Lord is to admonish a sinner first in private, then to take with thee one or two witnesses, and finally to tell the Church.[3] Calvin's first admonition has been described above; the second was prison; and the third, the rod of the magistrate.

Calvin 17. [Bij verso, p. 32] What preposterous humanity is it, I ask you, to cover with silence the crime of one man and to prostitute a thousand souls to the snares of Satan?

Vaticanus. If the errors of Servetus are snares, then you prostitute a thousand souls to the wiles of Satan by stirring them up. . . . Although you misrepresent and mutilate much in Servetus, nevertheless many are seduced by the excerpts in your book. . . . I know a man who has been so taken by the reasoning of Servetus concerning infant baptism, cited by you on page 215,[4] as to assert that nothing could be more cogent. . . .

Calvin 18. Would that the errors of Servetus were buried, but when I see them circulating I cannot be silent without the guilt of perfidy.

Vaticanus. You have only yourself to blame. There was almost no mention of the first book of Servetus and the subsequent works could have been sold like the others without disturbance, [Biij, p. 33] but now that the man has been burned with his books, everybody is burning with a desire to read them.

Vaticanus ⟦in reply to Calvin 20⟧. [Biij verso, p. 34] . . . ⟦Calvin⟧ wishes to kill all heretics and wishes to hold as heretics all who disagree with him. His program would call for the extermination of all the Papists, Lutherans, Zwinglians, Anabaptists, and the rest. There would survive only Calvinists, Jews, and Turks, whom he excepts. . . .

Calvin 25. [Bv verso, p. 38]. Prove that the coming of Christ has mitigated the penalties against heresy.

[2] Titus 3: 10. [3] Matt. 18: 15-17.
[4] "Defensio orthodoxae fidei," pp. 215-23: *Calvini opera,* VIII, 613-18.

Vaticanus. How mitigated? Before the coming of Christ there is no mention of heretics in the whole law. . . . I do not deny that there were heretics, but I do not find that the law prescribes any penalty for them. In the New Testament I find that they are to be avoided. So the penalty is not mitigated, but altered. . . .

Calvin 26. Another fanatic . . . calls Servetus his best brother and for that reason denies that heretics are to be punished on the ground that each may forge the sense of Scripture to his liking, since the certain truth lies hidden in clouds.

Vaticanus. He is wroth that anyone should declare the Scriptures obscure. He thinks them clear. He contradicts Zwingli who considers them obscure,[5] and he contradicts himself who writes so many commentaries to explain what is so clear.

Calvin 28. [Bvj, p. 39] What will become of religion? By what marks will the true Church be discerned? What will Christ himself be if the doctrine of piety is uncertain and in suspense?

Vaticanus. Religion will be based on an assured faith concerning things which are hoped for, not known, as Abraham, when he was called to go out, obeyed not knowing whither he went.[6] [Bvj verso, p. 40] . . . The true Church will be known by love which proceeds from faith, whose precept is certain. "By this shall all men know that ye are my disciples if ye have love one to another."[7] . . . The doctrine of piety is to love your enemies, bless those that curse you, to hunger and thirst after righteousness, and endure persecution for righteousness' sake. . . .[8] These and similar matters are certain, however dubious may be the obscure questions about the Trinity, predestination, election, and the rest on account of which men are regarded as heretics. Many of the saints knew nothing about them. . . .

Vaticanus ⟦in reply to Calvin 29⟧. [Bvij, p. 41] . . . Christ spoke only in parables to those without, that is, obscurely, but privately he explained all things to his disciples.[9] From this we see

[5] *Huldreich Zwinglis sämtliche Werke* I (CR LXXXVIII), "Von Klarheit und Gewissheit des Wortes Gottes" (September 6, 1522), pp. 328-84, in particular the section "Von der klarheit des worts gottes," pp. 358-84.

[6] Heb. 11:8. [7] John 13:25. [8] Matt. 5. [9] Mark 4:33-34.

that the Scriptures can be properly understood only by Christ's disciples. They are His disciples who obey Him and have love. . . . They alone understand Scripture. Others, though learned in all knowledge, find the Bible a maze. The Apocalypse is a mere riddle which can be understood only by the wise, [Bvij verso, p. 42] that is, those who fear God. It is a book sealed, which only the Lamb can open. . . .[10] Is nothing then certain? No, indeed, all things are certain which are necessary for salvation, for obedience, and for duty. . . .

Calvin 41. [Cvj verso, p. 56] The fact that the sword has been used for persecution does not prevent the pious magistrate from using his rod to defend the afflicted Church, nor do the crosses of the martyrs impede the just aid of the laws that the faithful may worship God in tranquillity.

Vaticanus. . . . If Servetus had attacked you by arms, you had rightly been defended by the magistrate; but since he opposed you in writings, why did you oppose them with iron and flame? Do you call this the defense of the pious magistrate? Does your piety consist only in hurrying to the fire strangers passing peacefully through your city? And do you dare to upbraid the Papists? Produce a single instance in which the Papists dragged a Lutheran or Calvinist from Mass to prison as Servetus among you was dragged from a sermon.

Vaticanus ⟦in reply to Calvin 46⟧. [Cviij, p. 59] . . . To assert one's faith is not to burn a man, but rather to be burned. "He that shall endure unto the end, the same shall be saved." [11] How? By persecuting? Rather by suffering. This is the true assertion of faith which Calvin does not know.

Vaticanus ⟦in reply to Calvin 55⟧. [Dij, p. 63] . . . Calvin boasts that he did not cut out Servetus's tongue. But he did cut off his life and burn his books lest Servetus be able after his death to defend his cause before the world, even with books. [Dij verso, p. 64] Yet Calvin thinks that everyone should accept his judgment about Servetus and make no further inquiry after our master has made his pronouncement. Why did he burn the books? He

[10] Rev. 5. [11] Matt. 24: 13.

feared, I suppose, that men would be corrupted. Then why did he not entertain the same fear formerly, when he himself took care to print the *Interim* at Geneva in his refutation? [12] Why did he not do the same for Servetus, unless because Servetus exposed Calvin more successfully than did the *Interim?* Calvin may say that he was not in a position to suppress the *Interim.* Why did he not at least banish it from his city? Why does he not prohibit the printing and sale of other pernicious books at Geneva? Aristotle is allowed, though he denies the foremost article of the creed, the creation of the world. The Koran is permitted and Apuleius, Martial, Plautus, Terence, Horace, Catullus, Tibullus, Propertius, and other nefarious corrupters of morals. Ovid's *Art of Love*—that is, of Adultery—is allowed, as well as the works of his imitator Clement Marot.[13] A refugee from France wrote back from Geneva a few years ago: "I have escaped from Babylon. Please send me all the works of Ovid with commentaries." They call the papacy "Babylon." What is Jerusalem? What shall I say of the trash which is printed there? Beza's *Zoographia* [14] and *Passavant,*[15] or Viret's book *On the Death of His Wife?* [16] These books are full of nothing but scurrility and triviality. . . .

Calvin 63. [Diiij verso, p. 68] . . . ⟦Christ⟧ sent the apostles as lambs in the midst of wolves and did not equip them with the power of the flesh. . . . The Lord never commanded them to punish theft, rapine, adultery, murder, and poisoning. Are these offenses, then, to go unpunished?

Vaticanus. When theft, rapine, adultery, and murder are pun-

[12] "Interim adultero-Germanum: cui adiecta est vera Christianae pacificationis et ecclesiae reformandae ratio. Per Ioann. Calvinum, 1549, cum appendice 1550." *Calvini opera,* VII, 543-686. The reply to the *Interim* proper occupies pp. 543-90.

[13] On whom see: Ph. Aug. Becker, *Clement Marot, sein Leben und seine Dichtung* (München, 1926). Sächsische Forschungsinstitute in Leipzig. Forschungsinstitut für neuere Philologie, IV, Romantische Abtl. Heft 1.

[14] Reprinted in J. H. Baum, *Theodore Beza,* 2 vols. (Leipzig, 1843-51), I, 357-63.

[15] Reprinted by Isidore Liseux, *Le Passavant de Théodore de Bèze* (Paris, 1875).

[16] We have here an additional and hitherto unnoticed confirmation of the

ished they are not punished in order to establish the kingdom of Christ, to justify men, to save men, to generate a new creature, but to protect the bodies and possessions of the good. . . .

Calvin 67. [Dv verso, p. 70] There are few ⟦princes⟧ who freely submit their necks to the yoke and bear it as a delight.

Vaticanus. Yes, when it comes to voting on religion, as in the Servetus case, the larger part conquers the better and the few are always overcome by the many. . . .

Vaticanus ⟦replying to Calvin 70, which occupies Dvj and verso, pp. 71-72⟧. [Dvp verso, p. 72] . . . Inasmuch as Calvin said above that the good are few, it must follow that he is pleasing the larger, hence the worse, part in opposing Servetus; otherwise he would not be able to do it.

Calvin 72. [Dvij verso, p. 74] "God hath chosen the foolish things of the world to confound the wise. . . ."[17]

Vaticanus. And Calvin and his followers reject the foolish things of the world and extol the wise. They will not let a man teach and preach unless he be learned and skilled in languages, especially Latin. . . .

Calvin 75. [E, p. 77] Certainly Christ drew the wise men to himself by the star no less than the shepherds by the voice of the angel.

Vaticanus. And he would draw the Calvinists if they would condescend to enter the stable. God rejects not the learned, but the proud. . . .

Calvin 76. Wherefore the fact that Christ drew the first fruits

---

existence of this book. Pierrefleur asserted that the book was suppressed because of its ineptitudes and had entirely disappeared. *Mémoires de Pierrefleur, grand-banderet d'Orbe, où sont contenus les commencements de la réforme dans la ville d'Orbe et au pays de Vaud (1530-1561), publiés pour la première fois et accompagnés de notes historiques* par A. Verdeil (Lausanne, 1856), p. 185. J. Cart. Pasteur (*Pierre Viret*, Lausanne, 1864, p. 102) could not believe that Pierrefleur was correct. Jean Barnaud (*Pierre Viret*, Saint-Amans (Tarn), 1911, p. 314, n. 3) points out that Viret protested to the council at Geneva against the publication of a book concerning the death of his wife seven years after by a Dr. Hester. *Calvini opera*, XXI, 482 (June 9, 1551).

[17] I Cor. 1:27.

of the Church from a humble and obscure group does not prevent kings from offering themselves and their all, nor does it disqualify the power of the sword with which they are equipped from being a sacred oblation.

Vaticanus. Paul records that when Christ ascended on high "he gave some, apostles; and some, prophets; and some, evangelists; and some, pastors and teachers; for the perfecting of the saints, for the work of the ministry, for the edifying of the body of Christ," which is the Church.[18] These are the sacred oblations for this work. [E verso, p. 78] The sword is not admitted in Christ's kingdom save to kill Christ and His disciples. There are those who bear the sword as ministers of God, but to punish malefactors, not to erect the kingdom of Christ. The former, Christians have in common with all nations. Christians bear the same sword, but not to serve the kingdom of Christ.

Calvin 77. Now we see that the ministers of the Gospel must be prepared to bear the cross and enmity and whatever pleases the world, and the Lord equipped them with no other arms than patience. Nevertheless, kings are commanded to protect the doctrine of piety by their support.

Vaticanus. To kill a man is not to defend a doctrine, but to kill a man. When the Genevans killed Servetus they did not defend a doctrine; they killed a man. The defense of doctrine is not the affair of the magistrate but of the doctor. What has the sword to do with doctrine? . . .

Calvin 78. Our critics say that nothing is more inappropriate than to force men to the faith which consists in free obedience. . . .

Vaticanus. [Eij, p. 79] "No man can come to me, except the Father which hath sent me draw him." [19] These persecutors wish the magistrate to draw men who are unwilling to be drawn by God, as if the magistrate could accomplish more than God. . . .

Calvin 79. We grant that the magistrate is not in a position to penetrate the hearts of men by edicts that they should embrace the doctrine of salvation obediently and submit themselves to God, but the calling of the magistrate does require that impure and

[18] Eph. 4: 9-12.

[19] John 6: 44.

petulant tongues should not be allowed to lacerate the sacred name of God and trample upon His worship.

Vaticanus. [Eij verso, p. 80] . . . This is said in a captious and malicious spirit. An impure and petulant tongue is not to be ascribed to anyone who differs from Calvin on the Lord's Supper, infant baptism, predestination, and persecution, provided one believe in the truth of Sacred Scripture.

Calvin 80. A private man, who does not exercise the power of life and death, would not be guiltless if he suffered his home to be polluted by sacrilege. How much more craven would it be in the magistrate if he connived at the unbridled violation of piety? . . .

Vaticanus. This is more rhetorical than Christian. . . . What does Calvin consider "an unbridled violation of piety"? . . . Servetus denied that infants should be baptized. Did Servetus believe what he said or did he not? Calvin calls this an unbridled violation. By what right? An unbridled violation calls for conscious sin. But Servetus, if he sinned, sinned unconsciously. Did you then, Calvin, kill Servetus because he so believed or because he so spoke? If you killed him because he so spoke, you killed him on account of the truth, for the truth is to say what you believe, even though you are in error. . . . [Eiij, p. 81] But if you killed him because he so believed, then you should teach him to believe otherwise, and you should show from Scripture that those who err and believe incorrectly are to be killed.

Calvin 82. [Eiiij, p. 83] . . . If the Son of God drove out those who on the pretext of religion sold sacrifices in the temple court, why may not the pious magistrate use the sword committed to him to coerce perfidious apostates who profane and violate the temple of God with open contumely?

Vaticanus. We, too, may argue after Calvin's fashion: if the Son of God did not condemn the adulteress, why should the magistrate condemn adulterers? If Calvin replies that Christ was not the judge of adultery, we say the same with regard to the whip of cords. There was no law—and if Christ had acted as a magistrate He ought to have followed the law—there was no law that the whip of cords should be used on the money changers. [Eiiij verso, p. 84] Moreover, if Christ drove them out, He did not kill them; and if Christ did it with His own hand, the magistrate should do the like and not leave the office to the executioner. If Christ drove them out of a temple made with hands, the magistrate should do the same. If Calvin answers that the temple was a figure of the temple not made with hands, that is, of the heart of man . . . we say by the same right that the whip made by hand was a figure of the spiritual whip, that is, of the Word of God, which Word is given not to the magistrate, but to the minister. . . . If Christ did not command that the money changers be cast out of the temple of God by the magistrate, and did not make Himself an accuser against them, but with His own hand cast them out, then Calvin who wishes to be the vicar of Christ should not have sent Servetus to the magistrate to be cast out and killed, [Ev, p. 85] nor should he have employed his cook [20] as an accuser, but should have cast out Servetus with his own hand, his own weapon, that is, with the word. . . .

[Evj verso, p. 88] And why not cast out ⟦hypocrites⟧? Because they cannot be convicted? Conviction is easier than in the case of heretics. There is no controversy as to who are hypocrites, ambitious, avaricious: especially in the case of hypocrites, who come in sheep's clothing and are known by their fruits, that is, homicides, as the wolf is recognized by eating sheep. But concerning heretics there is controversy, and Calvin has not yet been able to show who is a heretic, although he writes about the very subject of killing heretics. [Evij, p. 89] Why has he never burned anyone for avarice and envy though he knows many culprits and could accuse and convict them? Why does not the proper severity of discipline thrive at Geneva? Calvin thinks it does. He shows above that only good magistrates may punish heretics. Since he incited his magistrate against Servetus, Calvin must hold his magistrate as good. Why does he not then urge him to kill hypocrites and the avaricious? Are hypocrites better than heretics? If not, why should

[20] His secretary rather, Nicolas de la Fontaine, on whom see Émile Doumergue, *Jean Calvin* (Neuilly-sur-Seine, 1926), VI, 312.

not the magistrate lend an ear to the heretics as well? But why do I press the point? Calvin does not hold those sins to be great which God regards as the greatest. This appears from the laws which Calvin drew up for the administration of the Church. Here vices are classified in two categories. In the first are those offenses which are *absolutely* insufferable in a minister. The foremost of these is heresy and among the others are card playing and dancing. The other group includes the tolerable offenses among which he places scurrility, lying, calumny, avarice, unruly temper, and wrangling.[21] These are tolerable offenses, though Sacred Scripture finds nothing worse than scurrility; Psalm 1 places it among the worst. As for avarice, Paul says that the love of money is the root of all evil.[22] . . . What can you do with a man who regards scurrility, avarice, and calumny as lighter sins than heresy, card playing, and dancing? . . .

[Evij verso, p. 90] Let me give but a single example from which the rest may be perceived. John Gast, the minister at Basel, relates in his *Book on the Anabaptists* that a certain Anabaptist was condemned to death at Basel, but on the intercession of Oecolampadius, the magistrate agreed to pardon him on condition that he recant. He did recant and thereafter lived an abominable life, but was not molested on that account. . . .[23]

The persecutors teach that correct doctrine and the proper use of the sacraments constitute the Church. Sin cannot be eradicated. We are and shall be carnal flesh until death. The people assent, and the magistrates, who have no knowledge of the matter, are incited against heretics . . . and are told that no crime is greater than heresy or worthy of a greater punishment. [Eviij, p. 91] Hence Anabaptism is regarded by them as an offense much worthier of death than adultery, envy, cursing, dicing, and wasting precious time. . . . Anabaptists are commanded to be killed not on the authority of Scripture, but of Zwingli, who ruled that those

[21] "Ordonnances ecclésiastiques" of 1541. *Calvini opera,* X, 17-19.

[22] I Tim. 6: 10.

[23] Joannes Gastius, *De Anabaptismi exordio, erroribus, historiis abominandis, confutationibus adjectis, libri duo* (Basileae, 1544), pp. 112-13.

who immerse should be drowned.[24] The persecutors clamor that they do all in accord with Scripture; yet they cannot produce a syllable which commands that men be put to death for an error on the Lord's Supper or baptism. O Magistrates, your leaders mislead you. This is truly the profane money changing of souls, for these men make alive souls which God does not make alive and kill those whom God does not kill. Wherefore, when the Son of God comes He will drive out these money changers, not with the whip which they use against us, for they think the whip of Christ is the axe of the executioner, but with His fiery, unconquerable word, because they have profaned and violated the whole sacred temple of God with open contumely and blasphemy.

Calvin 85. [Eviij verso, p. 92] The gentleness and mildness attributed to Christ have reference to his attitude to the weak. Hardy malice he did not harden.

Vaticanus. Yet he suffered the hardy malice of Judas and did not harden it. Nor would Calvin have hardened Servetus by bearing with him. Rather Calvin hardened him by not bearing. Men are not hardened by kindness, but rather are invited to repentance.

Calvin 87. [F, p. 93] He is long-suffering. The "smoking flax shall he not quench," [25] but will he not dissipate darkness?

Vaticanus. How? With the sword or with light?

Calvin 89. I know that Christ used no other weapon than the sword of the Word to bring swift judgment upon all the impious, but shall we say that Peter was not moved by the same spirit when he struck Ananias and Sapphira with sudden death? . . .

Vaticanus. This man is marvelously slippery. He uses an adversative where the sense calls for a conjunction. His "but," however, actually introduces nothing contrary to what he has said, for Peter used no weapon other than the sword of the Word. And

[24] Zwingli latinized the mandate of the Zürich council of March 7, 1526 (Emil Egli, *Actensammlung zur Geschichte der zürcher Reformation*, Zürich, 1879, I, 445, No. 936), in these words: *Decrevit autem clarissimus Senatus post eam collationem . . . aquis mergere, qui merserit baptismo eum qui prius emerserat*. In "Catabaptistarum strophas elenchus," *Huldrici Zuinglii opera*, ed. by Schuler und Schulthess, III (Zürich, 1832), 364.

[25] Matt. 12: 20, from Isa. 42: 3.

this is precisely what we contend, that the sword of Christ is the Word. [F verso, p. 94] That Peter was moved by the same spirit, who will deny? But show that he used the sword which you employed against Servetus. Moreover, Calvin falsely accuses Peter. He did not kill Ananias, but merely upbraided and reproved him. If Ananias was struck dead by the rebuke, the one who administered it is not responsible, but God the avenger. . . . Why did Calvin not smite Servetus with a word as Peter did Ananias? Why did Calvin delegate his authority to the executioner? . . .

[Fiij, p. 97] Peter upbraided Ananias and killed him, if you please (we will concede this to Calvin), but he did so with a word alone, without the help of anyone. Calvin killed Servetus with the sword alone and with the help of the magistrate. Peter killed Ananias because of falsehood, since he lied against the Holy Spirit. Calvin killed Servetus because of the truth, since he would not lie, for if Servetus had been willing to recant and speak against his conscience he might have escaped. Because he said what he believed, he died. Peter influenced others in the future to fear lying. Calvin influenced others in the future to fear to speak the truth through consideration of the penalty. Peter showed the power of his word to the glory of God. Calvin showed the weakness of his word to the glory of the sword, which is his god. Peter did nothing further, so far as we know. Calvin put out this book and wrote obstinately and implacably to stir up similar persecutions throughout the earth. Woe to you, blind leaders of the blind. . . .

Calvin 92. Cruel is the clemency which you laud, to expose the lambs to slaughter and to spare the wolves.

Vaticanus. . . . Wolves come in sheep's clothing, but within they are ravening. By their fruits ye shall know them.[26] The fruit of the wolf is to eat raw flesh. Hence, not those who are killed, but those who kill are wolves.

Calvin 93. [Fiij verso, p. 98] They infect souls with the poison of depraved dogma, and shall the sword be withheld from their bodies?

Vaticanus. The envious, avaricious, and proud infect souls and

[26] Matt. 7: 15, 16.

beget their like by words and example . . . but the sword has no power against their bodies.

Calvin 94. Shall the whole body of Christ be mangled that one putrid member remain intact?

Vaticanus. . . . To kill a man is not to amputate a member. . . . [Fiiij, p. 99] When a man is killed as a heretic he is not amputated from the body of Christ, but from the life of the body. Otherwise, if the death of the body were amputation, all who die would be amputated from the Church. . . .

Calvin 96. They adduce Scripture passages which do seem to favor them. Christ said, "Let the tares grow with the wheat lest the wheat be rooted out at the same time." [27] If the parable be taken strictly to the letter, not only would the sword of the magistrate be prohibited, but all discipline would be done away. . . .

Vaticanus. [Fv, p. 101] . . . To root out the tares is to pronounce someone to be reprobate and cut off forever from the body of Christ. This should not be done before the day of the Lord. As for Calvin's objection that the parable does not apply to the magistrate, I answer that when the magistrate kills robbers he does not cut them off from the body of Christ, but only from this life. Often the magistrate hopes for the souls of those whose bodies he severs. He kills them not because they are evil, but because they have done evil and caused harm. The case of heretics is different. Those who kill them regard them as reprobates damned forever. This is to anticipate the judgment of God for which Paul says we should wait.[28] [Fv verso, p. 102] . . . The tares are those whom the devil sowed by false doctrine after the coming of the Gospel. Of this sort are the heretics and hypocrites who deceive men through the guise of the Christian religion and lie concealed among the godly as the tares among the wheat until the fruit appears. Christ commands that they be left until the harvest lest perchance the good be destroyed with them, for it is better that all the bad live until the judgment than that one good man should be destroyed in keeping out the bad; just as a king [Fvj, p. 103] prefers that all the robbers in the kingdom should live

[27] Matt. 13: 28-30. [28] I Cor. 4: 5.

than that one of the king's sons should be killed with them. We may represent the case in this way. Suppose that the king of France has several sons scattered throughout his kingdom and clad in white robes, but unknown to the people. Some impostors mingle with them and to gain the honor of the king's son put on white robes. . . . The king, learning this, announces that no one wearing the white robe is to be killed or hurt on pain of death lest one of the king's sons be destroyed. After a year the king will gather all together and expose and kill the impostors, but will save his sons, on whose bodies, when the robe is removed, will appear stamped a lily. Would not the king punish anyone who killed a man in the white robe whether the king's son or not? Now Christ is this king. Those clad in white robes are his disciples. The hypocrites and heretics are those who mingle with them and assume white robes in order to be honored as sons of God, that is, they live to all appearances as saintly and godly men. Christ, observing this, commanded that both be left until the day of judgment when the robe of dissimulation will be stripped off, the hidden things of darkness brought to light, and the secrets of hearts revealed which now lie hid. Should we not await that day? Do we think that we have sufficient knowledge to read the secrets of hearts which Paul said would not be revealed before the day of the Lord? [29] Do we not go counter to this commandment of Christ if we kill hypocrites and heretics clad in white, that is, those who are guilty of no crime; for if they are guilty they are not clad in white, since crime is a black robe. [Fvj verso, p. 104] May it not happen that in killing such men we kill also some of the godly just as it has always happened hitherto? If we say that we cannot make a mistake, we are saying only what those who killed the godly have always said. . . . Are we better than they? Who ever thought that he held a false religion? The Jews erred in persecuting Christ and the apostles. The gentiles erred who persecuted the Christians. The pope erred in persecuting Lutherans and Zwinglians. Henry, king of England, erred in killing Papists, Lutherans, Zwinglians, and Anabaptists. Luther erred when he

[29] I Cor. 4: 5.

called the Zwinglians devils and damned them to hell. Will the Zwinglians and Calvinists alone be free from error? Will they alone sit in the tribunal of Christ and pass judgment on heretics and kill them? . . .

Calvin 101. [Fvij verso, p. 106] The authority of Gamaliel is incorrectly adduced by them. Gamaliel tried to pacify the Scribes by pointing out that that which is of men will fall of itself but that which is of God cannot be overthrown.[30] We can readily see that his advice is not sound because it destroys not only civil government, but also ecclesiastical discipline. We must have regard also to the person of the speaker. Gamaliel was uncertain as to the proper course and suspended judgment like a blind man in the dark. . . . From true premises he drew a false conclusion that no action is to be taken because God watches over His own and that which is of man perishes.

Vaticanus. [Fviij, p. 107] . . . Now let us ask [Fviij verso, p. 108] this keen Calvin what advice he would have given the Scribes had he been in their council. He would have told them to kill the apostles. Since he describes the man who tried to dissuade them as blind, we must infer that Calvin would have given the contrary advice, that is, death. . . . [G, p. 109] Calvin's statement that the counsel of Gamaliel would destroy not only civil government, but also ecclesiastical discipline is not true. The discipline of the apostles was not spineless, though lacking Calvin's spine, and civil government applies to certain and uncontroverted sins. . . .

Calvin 112. [Giiij, p. 115] What is more absurd than for a judge to punish theft severely and give license to sacrilege? When each is jealous for his own honor, shall we suffer the glory of God to be exposed to mangling by the impious?

Vaticanus. [Giiij verso, p. 116] . . . You might as well argue: If ministers have authority over the souls of magistrates, how much more over their bodies? If with a word Peter struck Ananias, how much more Malchus with a sword? If Elias was permitted to bring down fire from heaven to destroy the king's messengers, how much more might the apostles burn the Samaritans? If Moses

[30] Acts 5: 34-40.

might kill the Egyptian, how much more might Christ? These are the fallacies devised by the sophists to impel men to shed blood. [Gv, p. 117] One might also argue: "If theft is punished, how much more hypocrisy, avarice, and envy? etc." And rightly. But theft is punished by man and hypocrisy by God. . . . "O ye sons of men, how long will ye turn my glory into shame? How long will ye love vanity and seek after leasing?" [31] To love vanity is to mangle the glory of God. Nevertheless, if Calvin wished all the lovers of vanity to be punished by the magistrates no one would be left to punish the magistrate himself. These offenses are to be punished by God, not by men. . . .

Calvin 116. [Gvj, p. 119] The Spirit of God gives us an excellent example in the case of Nebuchadnezzar. For Daniel celebrates his edict whereby he visited the death penalty upon any who should blaspheme the God of Israel. . . .[32]

Vaticanus. Why Calvin, in the above passage, so fastidiously rejected the advice of Gamaliel and now so avidly appropriates the example of Nebuchadnezzar, I do not see, unless because the one was milder, the other harder, not to say more cruel. . . . [Gvij, p. 121] But let us concede these cruel examples to Calvin. Grant that the tyrant should be imitated. What follows? All who blaspheme the God of Israel should be killed. By this law no one would be killed, for all confess God. If we transfer this to Christ, then the Jews would have to be killed because they blaspheme Christ. This does not apply to the heretics who confess Christ even though they may err. To err is not to blaspheme, as if, for example, someone should say in error that Calvin is clad in white instead of red, that would not be blasphemy. If we are to imitate the edicts of kings, let us take Cyrus who is lauded by Ezra [33] more than Nebuchadnezzar by Daniel. Cyrus stirred by the prompting of the divine spirit decreed that the Jews in his kingdom might go up to Jerusalem, but he compelled none. So we should compel none to godliness. A man cannot be made good against his will. Those who would force men to the faith make the mistake of one who

[31] Ps. 4: 2. [32] Dan. 3: 29. [33] Ezra 1.

would ram food down the mouth of an unwilling invalid with a stick. . . .

Calvin 117. [Gvij verso, p. 122] . . . God commanded: "If thy brother, the son of thy mother, or thy son or thy daughter, or the wife of thy bosom, or thy friend, which is as thine own soul, entice thee secretly, saying, Let us go and serve other gods . . . thou shalt not consent unto him . . . but thou shalt surely kill him. . . . And thou shalt stone him with stones, that he die." [34]

Vaticanus. This does not apply to heretics, for none of them says, "Let us go and serve other gods" . . . If Calvin says that those who corrupt Scripture serve other gods he is wrong. The Sadducees corrupted Scripture when they denied the resurrection and their error was greater than any of Servetus. And again when they thought carnally about marriage in the kingdom of God. . . . Nevertheless they were never charged with this crime. Christ did not accuse them of serving other gods. He said they were mistaken. . . . [Gviij, p. 123] And if Calvin wished to follow the law he ought not to have burned Servetus, but should have had him stoned by the people, and Calvin as the most innocent should have cast the first stone. . . .

Calvin 119. [Gviij verso, p. 124] Before going further two things are worth pointing out, that God is not thus jealous of any religion whatsoever, but only of that which He has instituted by His Word. Secondly, that the penalty of stoning does not apply to outsiders, but only to those who have accepted the teaching of the law and then fallen away. This removes the scruple of the uninstructed who fear lest the pope's butchers would be armed for cruelty by this pretext. . . .

Vaticanus. [H, p. 125] All sects hold their religion as established by the Word of God and call it certain. Therefore all sects are armed by Calvin's rule for mutual persecution. Calvin says he is certain, and they say the same. He says they are mistaken, and they say the same of him. Calvin wishes to be judge, and so do they. Who will be judge? Who made Calvin judge of all the

[34] Deut. 13: 6-10.

sects, that he alone should kill? How can he prove that he alone knows? He has the Word of God, so have they. If the matter is so certain, to whom is it certain? To Calvin? . . . Why does no one write a book to show that homicide and adultery are crimes? Because this is certain. Why does no one suffer himself to be burned for a denial that Scripture is true? Because everyone is agreed on this point. Why, then, do some men, who accept and revere Scripture, suffer themselves to be killed on account of rebaptism and the like? Is it not because these questions are controversial? And if Calvin is so sure, why does he not wait until others see as well? Why does he prevent them by death from learning? There are twelve hours in the day. One might learn in the eleventh. . . .

Calvin 121. [H verso, p. 126] This answers the objection of those who ask whether the Turks, Jews, and the like are to be compelled to the faith. [Hij, p. 127] God does not command that the sword be used promiscuously against all; only upon apostates who impiously alienate themselves from the true worship and try to seduce others to a like defection is just punishment to be inflicted.

Vaticanus. . . . But the Turks and others in Asia are apostates, since the Gospel was preached and believed there. They, especially, should therefore be persecuted. What shall I say of the Jews to whom it was promised that God would raise up a prophet, and that whoever would not hearken to his words should die? [35] Stephen shows that this prophet is Christ.[36] Since the Jews rejected him they are especially worthy of punishment. If Calvin regards heretics as apostates and considers the Papists to be heretics he should raise an army in Geneva and invade France, which has fallen away from the true religion of the apostles. If he objects that he is not strong enough, the answer is: "Fear not, one of you shall put to flight a hundred and a hundred shall put to flight ten thousand." [37] And if Calvin does not dare, he ought at least to have apprehended the Cardinal Tournon when shortly before the death of Servetus he went through Geneva, on his way, as all

[35] Deut. 18: 15-19. [36] Acts 7: 37. [37] Cf. Lev. 26: 8.

know, to burn the godly men who lay in chains at Lyons, and whom not long after he did burn. . . .[38]

Calvin 129. [Iiiij verso, p. 148] Whence it follows that the sword is placed in the hands of the magistrate to protect sound doctrine. . . .

Vaticanus. Paul calls sound doctrine that which makes men sound, which endows them with love, real and not fictitious faith, and a good conscience. . . .

[Iviiij verso, p. 156] When there is a dispute among the medical men and the people cannot judge because each side is plausible and cites the authority of Hypocrates and Galen, the only recourse for the people is to drop the arguments and look at the fruits and to award the palm to the one which cures the most and the worst diseases. So with regard to the medicine of souls. The common man cannot judge of the disputes of the doctors, but he can tell which is the best by the fruit, that is which makes the best men, which cures the diseases of the soul, that is the vices, and changes the greatest number from drunk to sober, [K, p. 157] from intemperate to continent, from greedy to generous, making them patient instead of impatient, kind instead of cruel, instead of impure, chaste. . . . By such fruits it is possible to judge which sects are the best, namely those which believe and obey Christ and imitate his life, be they called Papist, Lutheran, Zwinglian, Anabaptist or anything else. This is not a question of names but of truth. . . .

[Kij, p. 159] A distinction is to be made, I think, between the impious and the erring. Why does Calvin in disputing about heretics confound everything and apply to the heretics the invidious names of blasphemer, worshipper of strange gods, and false prophets? I will show that those who are regarded as heretics are not such. I do not classify under the name of heretic the impious, the despisers of sacred Scripture and blasphemers. These in my judgment are to be treated as impious. If they deny God, if they blaspheme, if they openly revile the sacred teaching of Christianity,

[38] The Cardinal went through Geneva on September 19, 1552. *Calvini opera*, XIV, Ep. 1647, p. 355.

if they detest the holy lives of godly men, I leave such offenders to be punished by the magistrate, not on account of religion—they have none—but on account of irreligion. If the magistrate keeps them in chains in the hope of correction, for great is the mercy of God, it does not seem to me that the magistrate goes counter to Christian clemency.

When it comes to heretics let us see who today are commonly regarded as such. The Papists are considered heretics, the Waldenses, Lutherans, Zwinglians, Anabaptists, and Schwenckfelders and the like. I see no reason for calling any of them impious even though they all err. They all believe in the same God, in the same Lord and Savior Christ. I know with how many and what prodigious errors the pope filled the world so that these sects rightly seceded from him. I recognize that in other matters there remain errors [Kij verso, p. 160] which greater light may dissipate. I recognize also that in these sects there are many masters who are no better than the pope. But I have in mind those who live religiously in their sects. Take a good Papist, one who fears God and does not swear, commit adultery, bear false witness, or do to another what he would not have done to him. I say that such a man should by no means be called impious and killed. He worships idols. Well? He does so in error and not with malice, just as we all worship. If you urge the words of the law, we should have to kill all. But it is not so. God in His mercy desires to teach not to kill the erring. "But the man is obstinate in his error," you say. Well? The apostles were not able to cure the demoniac because the demon was obstinate. Should they have killed him because they could not cure? Should they not rather have blamed their own lack of faith as the Lord chided them, saying, "This kind can come forth by nothing save by prayer and fasting." [39] What if we, like the apostles, have not sufficient faith and have not fasted enough from our sins nor given ourselves sufficiently to prayer? . . .

Calvin 138. [Kvij verso, p. 170] . . . This I wish to testify in public that I should not have so pressed the death penalty that

[39] Mark 9: 29.

he could not have saved himself by modesty alone had he not been out of his mind.

Vaticanus. So he was not put to death for heresy, but for immodesty. Heretics then are not to be killed unless they are immodest. Why did not Calvin give us this rule before? And if modesty will save the lives of heretics, why not of homicides? For heresy is a graver offense than homicide at Geneva. . . .

Calvin 140. [Kviij, p. 171] Someone may object that I went beyond the injunction of Paul to Timothy to merely avoid desperate heretics.[40] My defense is ready. It was enough for me to avoid and to advise others to avoid a man whose abandoned heresy was evident. But this avoiding did not prevent me or anyone else from taking care that the godly magistrate, by virtue of the authority committed to him, should coerce the heretic.

Vaticanus. The excuse of the Sorbonne! . . . [Kviij verso, p. 172] Bring water for Calvin to wash his hands. He is innocent of his blood. "It is not lawful for us to put any man to death,"[41] but "If thou release this man, thou are not Caesar's friend."[42] O Calvin, Calvin, do you think God is like a man to be beguiled by these sophisms of the Sorbonne? . . .

Calvin 143. [Lij verso, p. 176] . . . Let not these savage scoundrels glory in the perversity of this madman as a martyr. In his death he showed a beastlike stupidity from which it is easy to judge that he never took anything seriously in religion.

Vaticanus. Calvin displays his modesty.

Calvin 144. When the death sentence was announced to Servetus he was now stunned, now he would sigh deeply, now wail like a lunatic.

Vaticanus. Although I believe that Calvin has related this in bad faith, nevertheless I see no beastlike stupidity. . . . To be moved is not beastlike, but human. Hezekiah sighed at the announcement of a death much milder than that of Servetus. . . .[43] [Liij, p. 177] Job, that model of patience, was as if stunned for seven days when his friends brought him no news so sad as en-

[40] II Tim. 2: 16, unless this is a slip for Titus 3: 10.
[41] John 18: 31. [42] John 19: 12. [43] II Kings 20: 1-3.

emies broke to Servetus.[44] Christ Himself sweat blood,[45] and His soul was exceeding sorrowful even unto death,[46] and on the cross He cried out as if deserted, "My God, my God, why hast thou forsaken me?" [47] . . . If Servetus is moved by death, they say he shows a beastlike stupidity. If an Anabaptist dies with constancy—and the Anabaptists show an incredible constancy—they call it obstinacy and the power of the devil. In this they are the disciples of the Jews who were satisfied neither with John's austerity nor with Jesus' good cheer. . . .

[Liij verso, p. 178] I do not know what Calvin would have done had he been in the place of the dead man whom he so petulantly insults. If anyone criticizes him too freely he has an immediate attack of his hemicrania. . . . Believe me, reader, it is one thing to write about the fire in the shade and another to see the executioner sprinkle sulphur and put the fire in your face. O Calvin, Calvin, beware lest in this life, which were better, or in the next, you be called on to give an eye for an eye.

Vaticanus. [Lv, p. 181] ⟦commenting on Calvin 147, which begins on Liiij, p. 179⟧ If Servetus had said that God is a devil that would have been real blasphemy and I should rejoice to see him punished. But if he said that the Calvinists do not know what God is and therefore worship a false god, he spoke not against God but against men. Otherwise by the same token the Jews might accuse Christ when he said they had made the house of God into a den of thieves. . . .[48] The people was persuaded that Servetus called the Trinity a Cerberus, which is not so. He believed in the Father, Son, and Holy Spirit, that is, in the Trinity, but he interpreted it differently from them. This interpretation was invidiously exaggerated before the people until they thought that Servetus [Lv verso, p. 182] was like Rabelais, or Dolet, or Villanovanus, who believe neither in God nor Christ.[49]

[44] Job 2: 13. [45] Luke 22: 44. [46] Matt. 26: 38; Mark 14: 34.
[47] Matt. 27: 46; Mark 15: 34. [48] Matt. 21: 13; Mark 11: 17.
[49] Castellio may well have taken these names from Calvin's "De scandalis" (*Calvini opera*, VIII, 44-45), without knowing anything more about them. He may not have known whether Villanovanus was Arnold or Simon. On the latter, see R. C. Christie, *Etienne Dolet* (London, 1899).

Calvin 148. Servetus gave no sign of repentance and made absolutely no defense of his teaching. What did he mean when in the hands of the executioner he steadfastly refused to call upon the eternal Son of God and would not excuse himself even in a word, as he might have done, for he was free? Who will call this the death of a martyr? . . .

Vaticanus. The same may be said of Christ. I do not say that Servetus was like Christ, but the calumny is similar. Christ in the hands of the executioner refused to dispute. . . . Why should Servetus dispute when the executioner had the last word? Could Servetus have persuaded the people who held him for a devil? I think he was discreet to be silent. In the midst of the flames he called upon the Son of the eternal God. He would not say "the eternal Son," because he reserved the title of sonship until after the nativity. Before the virgin birth Christ was not the Son but the Word. If this was an error, was it a just cause of death? [Lvj, p. 183] Servetus defended it with his blood because words were futile.

CONCERNING DOUBT AND BELIEF IGNORANCE AND KNOWLEDGE [1]

BOOK ONE

[The work begins (Bk. I, Chaps. 1-4) with the arguments for belief in a good God. The problem of evil is taken care of by immortality. The next section (Chaps. 5-11) takes up the proof that Christianity is the best religion, because it makes the best men. The superiority of Judaism cannot be inferred from the antiquity of Moses, for if we believe in Moses only because of his antiquity we should not have believed in him had we lived in his day. Biblical difficulties are examined (Chaps. 7-11).

[1] MS. No. 505, Bibliotheek der Remonstrantschgereformeerde Gemeente te Rotterdam. The manuscript is described by Ferdinand Buisson, *op. cit.*, II, 379-80, No. 40. The first book of the manuscript contains 33 chapters, the second 46 by actual count, though 44 is the highest number, the number 43 having been used three times. Etienne Giran kindly placed a transcript at my disposal, which I collated with the original. My readings in turn have been revised by Elizabeth Feist of Berlin, who is planning soon to bring out an edition of the whole work.

The succeeding section takes up the inspiration of the Scriptures (Chaps. 12-17). Most of this is reproduced in *Novum Testamentum Graecum opera et studio Joannis Jacobi Wetstenii*, 2 vols. (Amsterdam, 1751-52), II, 856-57 and 884-89. Scripture, says Castellio, contains discrepancies both in word and thought. Scribal errors need not trouble us, for the authority of Scripture does not reside in a few words. Discrepancies as to the subject matter are more disconcerting. Here, with Paul (I Cor. 14: 6), we must distinguish revelation, knowledge, prophecy, and doctrine. Revelation and prophecy are directly of God, but knowledge is based on human testimonies and doctrine on human opinions. The evangelists did not write everything under direct inspiration, but partly from memory and imagination.⟧

Chap. 16. Someone may say that if these statements be true the authority of Scripture will be undermined and confidence in it destroyed. To which I reply: even if the inference be correct the statements are not, therefore, false. . . . But I do not admit the inference. The authority of Scripture does not reside in a few passages to be squeezed into a rigid conformity, but in the tenor and body of the thought. . . . I do not know how it appeals to others, but my confidence in the authority of the sacred authors is confirmed when I see them so intent upon the salvation of men as to be unconcerned for words. Their reliability is thereby manifested. Those who tell the truth do not strain at words. It is precisely liars who aim at a meticulous verbal consistency to hide their deception.

⟦The rigid harmonists make the Scriptures suspect. For example Andreas Osiander is compelled to conclude that Peter must have denied Christ eight times because the four gospels each have a prediction and an account of the denial in slightly variant form.

Chapter 18 commences the discussion proper of the limits of doubt and belief, ignorance and knowledge.⟧

Chap. 18. [f. 80b] First we must know what matters are to be doubted and what to be known without doubt; further, what matters, I will not say ought to remain unknown, but may remain unknown and are not essential, whereas others can and ought to be known. These questions must all be answered. But first let me make myself clear as a precaution against possible contradiction. There are some who are unwilling to doubt anything, to be in ignorance of anything. They assert everything unreservedly, and if you dissent from them they damn you without hesitation. Not only do they doubt nothing themselves, but they will not permit others to doubt and, if you do doubt, they do not hesitate to call you an Academician, who thinks nothing certain and assured. As a matter of fact I hold more for certain and assured than they like. Not to mention other matters, I hold it for certain and assured that they are altogether rash when they affirm all things and so boldly damn dissenters, and with God's help I believe I shall make them certain and assured of that which now they do not know, if only they will hear and consider as they ought with patience and without self-confidence. [f. 81] Solomon says in Ecclesiastes, "To every thing there is a season, and a time and purpose under heaven: a time to be born, and a time to die; a time to plant, and a time to pluck up that which is planted," [2] and so on. In the same way, I say, there is a time to doubt and a time to believe; a time to be ignorant and a time to know. There is no need, however, to discuss further knowing and believing, for no one will disagree with me on that point. But I must go into the matter of doubting and not knowing because of those who contradict. I will endeavor to establish the point both by reason and authority.

The reason for doubting is this. To hold the uncertain for certain and to entertain no doubt on the point is rash and dangerous. That no one will deny. Is there any need to prove that some matters are uncertain? This is abundantly demonstrated by the innumerable books and disputations, and by the daily and perpetual contentions of the most learned. Obviously, so long as men are in their right minds, they do not contend about matters which are certain and assured. Hence, I conclude that there should be doubt about uncertain matters.

I will cite also the authority of God Himself, who prescribed in Leviticus with regard to leprosy that anyone suspected of the disease be brought to the priest, and if the malady is clear he is to

[2] Eccl. 3: 1-2.

be pronounced unclean, but if the matter is doubtful he shall be shut up seven days, and if at the end of that time it is still impossible to judge, he shall be shut up seven days more until the priest can be sure.[3] The rule prescribed by God in this one instance should apply in all similar cases, that is, in all matters which are uncertain.

[f. 81b] Concerning not knowing I say this. We may be ignorant of those matters which man does not need to know for salvation. No intelligent man will deny that there are many. Here I will cite Christ. When the disciples after His resurrection asked of Him, saying, " 'Lord, wilt thou at this time restore again the kingdom to Israel?' He said unto them, 'It is not for you to know the times or the seasons, which the Father hath put in his own power. But ye shall receive power, after that the Holy Ghost is come upon you: and ye shall be witnesses unto me both in Jerusalem, and in all Judaea, and in Samaria, and unto the uttermost part of the earth.' "[4] These are the words of Christ by which He showed that neither the apostles nor others need to know everything, but each should attend to his own business. That is why I say that some matters need not be known.

Not without great cause do I assert that some things ought to be doubted, for I see no fewer evils arising from not doubting where there should be doubt than from not believing where there should be belief. Examples are abundant. . . . [f. 82] Today in the Christian churches some of the most saintly persons are put to death indiscriminately. If the Christians entertained a doubt about what they are doing they would not perpetrate such dreadful homicides for which they will have to repent very soon after.

Chap. 19. Now we must consider what matters are dubious and to be doubted, what certain and to be believed, what may be unknown and what can and should be known. Dubious are conjectures which have probability, but cannot be determined by the senses or the intellect, nor are they handed down in clear and certain fashion by authors worthy of credence. Of this sort is the question in John's gospel, whether John should never die because Christ said to Peter,

[3] Lev. 13: 1-8. [4] Acts 1: 6-8.

"If I will that he tarry till I come, what is that to thee?" [5] Certain are those matters which are handed down clearly and plainly by authorities worthy of credence and are not contradicted by the senses nor the intellect, nor by reliable authorities. Of this sort is the statement of Paul, "Be not deceived. Neither fornicators, nor idolators, nor covetous shall inherit the kingdom of God." [6] [f. 82b] We may be ignorant of those matters which are not prescribed by God and are not necessary to man for the knowledge of God and the proper performance of duty, as, for example, whether, after the virgin birth of Jesus, Mary had other sons by Joseph. We are able to know that which falls under the testimony of the senses of the body or mind. The Jews who were present were able to know that Jesus raised Lazarus, and that he turned water into wine was known to those who drew or saw the water drawn and then tasted wine. Those matters ought to be known which are necessary for the knowledge of God or the duty of man, as, for example, the works of God which have or do confer benefit upon man and whatever in turn is required by duty.

And now we must consider what it is to believe and to know and what is the difference between them. This being determined, it will appear by the contrary what it is to doubt and what not to know. The necessity of making clear the distinction, which is obvious to the unlearned, arises from the ignorance of the learned (I speak frankly) who obscure, if they do not extinguish, the clearest light with darkness, for they say that faith is acquaintance or knowledge by which they demonstrate that they do not know as much as the illiterate, as women or even boys. These all know what it is to believe, and faith is the same thing. In conversation they distinguish faith from knowledge. Boys talk in this fashion when something is related:

"What does he say?"

"His father has returned."

"Do you believe that he has returned?"

"I believe."

"Do you know for sure?"

[5] John 21: 22.

[6] I Cor. 6: 9-10.

"I do not know."

"Why do you believe?"

"Because he who told me is always trustworthy."

To believe then is to give credence to what is told whether true or false. Sometimes the false is believed no less [f. 83] than the true. But the same cannot be said of knowing. The false cannot be known, though it may be believed. That is why Christian faith is a virtue, as no one will deny. But I cannot see how knowledge is a virtue. I do not find it praised as such in Scripture unless in a metaphorical sense which is not under discussion. To be brief, where knowledge begins faith ends. He who once said, "I believe," now says, "I know." This is the common mode of speech among authors sacred and profane. . . . [f. 83b] Judges believe witnesses. Witnesses do not believe. They know.

Chap. 20. [f. 84] ⟦The nature of knowledge is sufficiently clear. We said above that we must know that which is necessary for the knowledge of God and duty. But this does not mean that we must know every detail. To admire a building we do not need to know the minutiae. The citizen need not know all the laws, but only those which apply to him. [f. 84b] The tailor need not know the laws of agriculture, nor the celibate the laws of marriage.⟧

Wherefore, with regard to knowledge I say that the duty of man is to know God and His precepts, that is, a man must know what is his duty. If he knows this and does his duty, blessed is he, even though he is ignorant of much else. Now this can easily be known. The world, which is the work of God, is unknown to no man and the precepts of love on which hang all the law and the prophets and which are fulfilled in Christ; these are so plain, so natural, and so known to man that even the wicked know them, whether they will or not, and cannot withhold their assent. This point is demonstrated by the fact that if you tell a perfect scoundrel he should love God and his neighbor as himself, he will agree. These rules are inscribed as it were by the finger of God in the hearts of all, and can no more be erased that the other common notions of men. That is why I assert so confidently that what needs to be known can be known with perfect ease. This is the way of salvation. . . . Christ taught this way. The publicans and sinners were saved in it. They became Christians through one or two sermons of Christ in which he spoke of duty. They did their duty. They were so ignorant of many of the questions which now rend the Church that they had not even heard of them. [f. 85] So today there are no better Christians than those who do not occupy themselves with subtle questions and do their duty according to Christ's precepts. And Christ himself, the Judge at the last day, will disregard these questions and pass sentence according to the performance of duty. "I was thirsty. I was hungry. Ye fed me. Ye fed me not." This will be the end of the debate. . . .

Chap. 21. Now I hasten to consider what may be known for certain in these questions in order that lovers of the truth may occupy themselves wholly with the clear and assured truth and with what God requires of man.

First let me point out that if men draw from Scripture with as much bitterness as heretofore they will derive from it no more than in time past. [f. 85b] Mutually biting, mutually we consume each other. . . .

[f. 86] All opinions are defended out of Scripture. Each defends his views tenaciously and will not be dislodged. Nor is the rule adequate which some propose of interpreting one passage in the light of another. All the sects do this without reaching an agreement. He who cites one passage incorrectly can easily find others to cite incorrectly by way of support. Unless some other rule is discovered I see no way here of attaining concord. . . .

Chap. 22. [f. 86b] When it comes to knowledge we must make plain to the reader that we are not discussing the authority of Scripture which is held on faith, but that we are talking of the mind or sense of which there is knowledge. All the Christian sects are agreed as to the authority. The question is not whether Scripture is true, but how it is to be understood. All agree that it is true, but contend as to the meaning. Learned men have not been so blind as to debate for centuries about matters which are perfectly plain. . . .

[f. 87] But the questions commonly controverted are obscure.

This point can be readily established. No one doubts whether there is a God, whether He is good and just, whether He should be loved and worshipped, whether vice should be avoided and virtue followed. Why? Because these points are clear. But concerning baptism, the Lord's Supper, justification, predestination and many other questions there are capital dissensions. Why? Because these points are not cleared up in Scripture. I could cite a thousand examples to show that God has desired [f. 87b] to leave some obscurity in the Bible. If anyone asks why, I will answer that I do not know. There is nothing absurd in this reply. . . . Why did not God put food in birds' nests as He put food in the ground for trees? Why did He give birds wings to go and get their food? Because He did not wish them to be lazy in exercising the resources of their intelligence. Now if this is plain in the works of nature, all who have not degenerated from nature will confess that the same principle holds in Sacred Scripture and doctrine. God desired to leave obscurity [f. 88] as an exercise to human industry that the mind, like the body, might gain its bread by the sweat of its brow.

Chap. 23. Now since Scripture is obscure on controverted points . . . we must consider where lies the plain incontrovertible and unshakable truth. Then when this is discovered we can see which side of the controversy accords with Scripture and with the plain incontrovertible truth as above determined, for this must decide. Nor is there doubt that a double support is preferable to a single. I am thinking of the support of sense and intellect. These are the instruments of judging. . . . But first we must note that there are two kinds of controversies, one which falls under sense and intellect and another which is above sense and intellect. The latter we shall take up by and by; and now for the former, which falls within the scope of sense and intellect. . . .

[f. 88b] At this point there are those who clamor that Christ used parables in order that he might not be understood by the common man. The natural man, according to Paul, receiveth not the things of the Spirit [7] . . . Others, again, assert that the very

[7] I Cor. 2: 14.

characteristic of the Christian faith is to credit the incredible. They take this example. God said: "This is my body. This is my blood." This saying is not impossible for God, and is to be believed solely because God said so without any other reason, even though eyes, ears, nostrils, taste, touch, and universal reason and the very nature of things object. We must do this especial honor to God and His Son, we are told, that we believe His word, however incredible, against all of our senses and those of other men.

[f. 89] These and similar arguments . . . are calculated to deceive. When men have been persuaded to shut their eyes and reject the evidence of the senses of the body and of the mind, to believe words, though all the senses refute the words, then nothing is so absurd, impossible, or false as not to be accepted. Why not believe that the white which you see is not white? . . . That what you perceive with the mind is not what you perceive? And then do we wonder that such monstrous errors survive until now among those who are persuaded of the like, or that today such stubborn controversies flourish among theologians? When each adheres tenaciously to words and words disagree, how can you decide if the judgment of the senses is rejected? . . . One says that you must eat Christ's flesh to be saved, and he has the plain words of Christ, "Except ye eat the flesh of the Son of Man," [8] etc. Another denies that Christ's flesh profits a man for salvation and he, too, cites the plain words of Christ, "The flesh profiteth nothing." [9] What will you do? . . .

[f. 89b] I will fight with all my might against this monster. If I cannot kill it I hope at least to wound it severely.

Chap. 24. We must make it clear, however, that in denying what is contrary to the senses we do not deny that which is above the senses. There is a vast distinction. In human and divine things we say that those matters are above the senses, which cannot be perceived by the senses, for example the questions what God is and whether He created the world; in how many days He made it; whether the souls of men sleep with their bodies, to rise with them. Then there are those things which belong in the same category

[8] John 6: 53.

[9] John 6: 63.

because, though perceptible by the senses when present, in this life, which is alone under discussion, they are not and cannot be present; such as, for example, the questions whether the stars are solid bodies, whether there is a vacuum in the center of the earth, whether the just shall live in heaven or on earth after the resurrection. We must confess that there are many such questions which cannot be subject to the judgment of the senses. They are to be believed if clearly set forth in Scripture. [f. 90] They are to be doubted if ambiguously explained, and to be left in ignorance if there is nothing recorded about them. Contrary to the senses are those matters which, falling within the scope of the senses, contradict them, as if one should say that fire is cold, when the touch pronounces it hot; or that snow is black, when the eyes indicate that it is white; or that absinthe is sweet, when the palate declares it bitter. Such matters, when handed down in opinions, we shall resolutely proclaim false. I hope to establish the case by the testimony of nature, and of authorities both sacred and profane, as well as of the very persons who reject them so fastidiously.

⟦Then follow citations from the Greeks and from Christ.⟧

[f. 90b] I never find that Christ did anything contrary to the senses and intellect, and rightly, for the senses and intellect are the works of the Father, and Christ came to destroy not the works of the Father, but of the devil. [f. 91] No wonder then that he did not deprive men of sense and intellect. . . .

Chap. 25. I come now to those who want us to close our eyes and repudiate the testimony of the senses. First I should like to know whether they give this counsel with their eyes closed, that is without judgment, intellect, and reason, or whether with reason. If they have no reason, we rightly reject their advice; but if they ground their position on reason they do ill to use their reason to persuade us to surrender ours. . . .

[f. 91b] Then I should like to know why they do use their reason against the plain words of God. . . . Christ said, "Resist not evil." [10] Why then do they, contrary to the Anabaptists, approve of the magistrate when he resists evil? Why do they not

[10] Matt. 5:39.

rather twist the passages favorable to the magistrate into accord with the plain words of Christ? I do not see what they can answer, nor do they answer anything, to my knowledge, [f. 92] in their sermons and books, other than that reason is to be followed against these words lest an absurdity be admitted. They are right. But if, then, the judgment of reason is to be admitted in this and other matters and is to be preferred to the words, where the case falls within the scope of reason, then they should grant us the same privilege elsewhere if we can show that the case is subject to the judgment and reason and sense.[11] Let them not deny to us, who are endowed with reason, what they claim for themselves, who are endowed with reason. For reason is, so to speak, the daughter of God. She was before letters and ceremonies, before the world was made; and she is after letters and ceremonies, and after the world is changed and renewed she will endure and can no more be abolished than God Himself. Reason, I say, is a sort of eternal word of God, much older and surer than letters and ceremonies, according to which God taught His people before there were letters and ceremonies, and after these have passed away He will still so teach that men may be truly taught of God. According to reason Abel, Enoch, Noah, and Abraham and many others lived before the letters of Moses, and after these many have lived and will continue to live. According to reason Jesus Christ himself, the Son of the living God, lived and taught. In the Greek he is called *logos,* which means reason or word. They are the same, for reason is a sort of interior and eternal word of truth always speaking. By reason Jesus refuted the Jews who placed greater trust in letters and ceremonies. Reason worked upon the Sabbath day and taught the Jews that they might remove a sheep from the ditch on the Sabbath without offense. . . .

Chap. 26. [f. 93] ⟦Cites passages from classical authors on reason.⟧

Chap. 27. [f. 94] We have still to consider some objections. We are told that man's sense and judgment were corrupted in

[11] The text of the remainder of this paragraph is printed in Buisson, *op. cit.,* II, 495.

Adam and that the taint has been transmitted to posterity. . . . ⟦Biblical passages.⟧

[f. 94b] First we must inquire whether man's sense and intellect were corrupted by the sin of Adam. Then we must ask what is the meaning of these Biblical passages. As for the first, I fear that we are dealing with a general and hoary error, rather than with the truth. There is neither authority nor reason for it. Someone rashly proposed it and then it was kept as an oracle by a blind posterity following the blind. Let our opponents tell which sacred author hands this down? None. What reason teaches it? None. Experience and history teach the contrary. As for experience, we find man's senses of mind and body whole and sound as we have abundantly shown. History, that is, Moses, records that men's eyes were opened after tasting of the fruit of the tree of knowledge and they became aware of their hitherto unnoticed nakedness. And rightly; for the tree was properly and not inappropriately called the tree of knowledge. I am positively astounded as to what has come into men's minds, that they should make out of the tree of knowledge a tree of ignorance. What sense was corrupted? Of the body or of the mind? Not of the body. With their eyes our first parents saw that they were naked and with their ears heard the voice of God. Had their senses been corrupted they would not have seen nor heard or would have seen and heard incorrectly, [f. 95] which was not the case. Nor were the senses of the mind corrupted. The judgment that they were naked was a judgment of the mind, seeing and judging through the eyes. . . .

Chap. 28. We have still to consider certain passages which are cited to the contrary. They fall into two classes. Some transcend sense and intellect. These we do not discuss. They cannot be comprehended by human powers whether of the bad or even of the good. Some persons may know these things if God grants a revelation. Others, whether good or bad, remain in ignorance. But if the passages do not transcend the senses, then they may be referred to the test of sense and reason.

We must acknowledge, however, that there are obstacles to sound judgment. Some lie in man and some outside. Take first the senses of the body. Here there are two impediments, namely, will and disease. The impediment of will is man's unwillingness to apply his senses to something. . . . The impediment of disease is the corruption of the senses. [f. 96b] Those who persist in a voluntary aversion to the truth become diseased. . . . Because they are unwilling to see, they are deprived of sight so that they cannot see even if they wish. . . .

Chap. 29. Reason is said to be corrupted by disease when a man is blind and cannot see nor discern the truth. This sometimes happens from the mother's womb. Some are born defective and throughout life have no use of reason. They can no more reason nor judge than beasts, and can neither learn nor commit sin. For this reason Christ neither teaches nor reproves such men, for there would be no point in reproving or teaching one who could not feel reproof or instruction. . . . Sometimes the defect comes after birth. . . . [f. 97] So much for defects which are in man.[12]

[f. 100] We turn now to impediments which are outside man. They are of this sort. If we look at snow through a red glass it appears red, or if sunlight falls through a red glass on white paper it seems red. If you look at one man through a many-faced prism you seem to see several men. . . . There are lenses which make things smaller and others which make things larger, which invert left and right, top and bottom. . . . Objects seen from a distance appear small and round even though square. A mountain in the distance seems small and blue and swiftly moving objects appear to be stationary as do the stars. A straight stick half immersed in water looks broken, and clear water if sufficiently deep seems green. In a mist the sun appears bloody. There are a thousand such external factors which vitiate the judgment of perfectly sound eyes. Other factors prevent judgment. A stone cannot be seen in water which is disturbed or too deep, and the parts of a louse are too small for examination. So it is also for the other senses. Man endowed with reason must meet these impediments by recourse to reason, and by reason he must correct the judgment of the senses

[12] The pagination of the manuscript is irregular from f. 97 to f. 101.

and believe other than the senses indicate. . . . [f. 100b] So much for the impediments outside man and the senses of the body.

Chap. 30. Now we must consider the mind, and that in many ways which I cannot take up in detail. A few examples must suffice by way of illustration. Sometimes the matter is as it were far off. When we begin to learn a subject such as medicine or mathematics we cannot see far, even though we have the capacity for understanding. Sometimes it is not so much that the question is far off as that it is elusive, as when we inquire why ashes make the ground more fertile or as to the cause of the ocean waves or of vision and hearing or the other senses. Sometimes a question is neither far off nor elusive, but confused and mixed, such as the dispute about faith and works in justification. Here both Scripture and reason have to be taken into account, and judgment is difficult. Sometimes a matter has been handed down with the obscurity of an oracle so that to judge of it is as difficult as to appraise colors in a poor light. These and many other difficulties beset the sound mind. Thus far we have been considering the impediments to the senses of body or mind which lie within or without man. If these are removed we assert that man is able to judge of those matters which fall within the scope of the senses and reason. ⟦Replies to objection.⟧

Chap. 31. ⟦Discussion of Biblical passages.⟧

Chap. 32. [f. 99b] ⟦Summary.⟧

[f. 101] Above all you must remove those impediments which are in your mind, that is, the carnal affections. Where these are strong you cannot but judge incorrectly. I say this not as if the judgment were corrupted at every point by a particular vice. An avaricious man can pass a sound judgment about drunkenness or luxury, and a drunkard or a spendthrift in turn can judge of avarice or other vices from which he does not suffer. But what good is it to be able to judge well in one matter if you are deceived in another? Of what advantage is it to the avaricious to be able to judge of drunkenness if he is blind as to avarice and worthy of punishment on account of that vice? What can a bird do with free beak, neck, and wings if its foot is held? What does it profit a man to be free from all diseases except the one from which he dies? [f. 101b] Or to be innocent of all offenses save the one for which he is beheaded? To judge rightly of all matters we must renounce all disturbances of the mind. These disturbances are like bribes which corrupt judges. . . .

[f. 102] For example, if a Lutheran is wedded to his opinion on the Lord's Supper he will scarcely be able to weigh dispassionately his opponent's opinion, or even to follow it. The same is true of other opinions. The judgment is beclouded by mental disturbances and above all by a closed mind, for this impedes judgment not of one only but of all matters. . . . A man whose mind is closed holds tenaciously to his opinion and prefers to give the lie to God Himself and all the saints and angels if they are on the other side rather than to alter his opinion. Flee this vice as you would death itself. . . . And do not be ashamed to confess your error. . . . It were better to swallow a small and brief shame [f. 102b] before men in the present than to incur an eternal reproach before God and all men hereafter. . . .

[f. 103] Since the matter is very important and man is slow to learn that which is necessary for his salvation and in the meantime must be goaded like an ass and supplied with premasticated food like a child, it is well to explain what is meant by an affection of the flesh and to give a few examples of how it blinds a man.

Chap. 33. ⟦An affection of the flesh is defined as a sickness or sin and intemperance or disturbance of the mind contrary to nature, and nature is the state in which God created man before the fall, and to which man is restored by Christ.⟧

Now let me offer some examples of how these disturbances blind the mind and interfere with its duty.

We see, then, two parties contending. Each is absolutely certain that right is on his side. . . . What is the reason? Too much self-love and carnal affection of the mind by which each looks to his own rights and does not consider the others. This is plainly apparent because neither errs or strays on the right side, that is, neither errs so that the other has a little more, and he a little less, than justice. Now unless these mistakes proceeded from love of self the error would be to the left as often as to the right, and each would make a mistake to his own advantage as often as to the other's.

So, likewise, in disputes, a man will cling to an opinion which is false, absurd, and silly, and everyone sees it but himself. Nevertheless he adheres to it tenaciously and would rather die than give it up. The cause here [f. 104] is the desire of victory which is ambition. This prevents him from seeing the arguments of the other.

A foolish and indulgent mother so loves her children that she thinks them perfect, though the whole neighborhood knows the contrary, and she would rather give all the neighbors the lie than to examine the conduct of her children dispassionately. One so loves his wife that he can excuse any fault; and another hates his wife so that he can disparage and even make a vice of the greatest virtue. In a word, in all contentions and wars we always find a blindness and obstinacy without love. Those who have these faults see them not, while others see most clearly. . . . In short, the judgment of the world is blinded by the love of itself. In the mind, as in the body, no one is distressed by his own impurity. . . .

[f. 104b] The love of self blinds men. For this reason a man must learn to hate himself. Otherwise he is incurable. This is absolutely true. Put away your impurity. Then it will be as objectionable to you as to another. . . . If you will do this with a mind desirous of truth and prepared to follow it whether it square with your opinion or not, you will, I hope, discover some light of truth and give thanks to God, the Father of light. Let this be the end of this book.

BOOK TWO

Chap. 1. ⟦Introduction.⟧

Chap. 2. [f. 105b] ⟦This book, like the preceding, begins with God; the Trinity is first discussed. [f. 106] The existence of God may be discerned by reason, for all nations following reason—unless they were savage and akin to the brute—have agreed on this. But whether God is one or many, either cannot be discerned by reason or can be discovered only with difficulty, for the heathen, endowed with reason but lacking revelation, have worshipped many gods. After the advent of Christ, the light of the world, Asia, Europe, and Africa have confessed that there is one God only.]]

This assumption that there is but one God, which no one will deny, is to be taken on faith, and from this point of departure reason may consider whether there is a Trinity and of what sort. The question is difficult and to assert anything for certain is precarious. For that reason I will affirm nothing, but I will record for consideration the following unpublished anonymous discussion of which the reader may judge for himself. It seems to me worthy of consideration. The author represents himself as debating with the Athanasian Creed in these words:[13]

Athanasius. "Whosoever will be saved: before all things it is necessary that he hold the Catholic Faith. Which Faith except everyone do keep whole and undefiled: without doubt he shall perish everlastingly."

[f. 106b] *Anonymous.* Yes, but the Catholic faith must be such that everyone can hold it; the publicans and sinners and the thief upon the cross believed and were saved. Otherwise they would have perished.

Athanasius. "And the Catholic Faith is this: That we worship one God in Trinity, and Trinity in Unity."

Anonymous. I do not think the publicans and the sinners know this faith. If you think so, prove it. There is not a word about it in Scripture. If you are right they are undoubtedly damned unless perhaps you are speaking of the future instead of the past, but it is not in your power, Athanasius, to change the times and to make necessary for faith what was formerly not necessary. . . . [f. 107] If you hold that there is one substance in three persons and three persons in one substance you are certainly speaking in a most obscure and enigmatic fashion, which is not appropriate for a creed which is to be held by all. What everyone must know must be expressed in a way which everyone can understand. . . .

[13] The citations from the Athanasian Creed are taken from the translation of Philip Schaff, *The Creeds of Christendom*, II (New York, 1890), 66-70.

[f. 107b] *Athanasius.* "And yet they are not three eternals: but one eternal. . . . The Father is Almighty: the Son, Almighty: and the Holy Ghost, Almighty. And yet they are not three Almighties: but one Almighty. So the Father is God; the Son is God; and the Holy Ghost is God. And yet they are not three Gods, but one God. . . ."

Anonymous. This is as if you should say, "Abraham is an old man, Isaac is an old man, and Jacob is an old man; yet they are not three old men, but one old man." If I were to believe this, Athanasius, I should have to say farewell to reason, the noblest gift of God, by which man most markedly differs from the beasts, and I should have to return to the nature and sense of the brute and should lack the capacity for belief. One cannot believe without reason. Those who are devoid of reason cannot believe anything. . . . For myself I believe in "God the Father Almighty, Maker of heaven and earth, and in Jesus Christ His only Son our Lord and in the Holy Ghost." In this faith I will live and die, God willing, and I think that this simple faith, given to us by the apostles, is sufficient for salvation, even if one neither knows nor believes inexplicable enigmas introduced by the curious after the days of apostolic simplicity. If some are acute enough to understand what I and those like me cannot grasp, well and good, but to demand the same acumen of everybody, as a condition of salvation, means that the majority will be excluded.

⟦Chapters 3-6 discuss faith, chapters 7-29 justification. This portion is printed as the section "De justificatione" in the edition of Castellio's works at Gouda, 1613. See Buisson, *op. cit.*, II, No. 31, 373. Chapter 30 commences a discussion of the atonement.⟧

Chap. 31 [f. 150] There are those who think that God was not placated toward man by Christ, but that man having falsely supposed God to be angry was converted and reconciled to God by the teaching of Christ. . . . [f. 151] The question is, whether God being angry and wrathful against sinners restrained His wrath through the propititation of Christ, or whether God was placated simply because sinners returned to a better way. To which I reply that according to Scripture both are true. God forgives men sometimes for the sake of Christ and sometimes because of the correction of their lives. Reason, authority, and examples point in the same direction. . . . We sometimes forgive others for their own sakes and sometimes because of the requests of our friends.

⟦Chapter 38 to the end is a discussion of the Lord's Supper. The words of institution are taken figuratively.⟧

Chap. 43. [f. 165] Would that today there were not such violence. I see some who impose opinions, often false, like oracles upon their disciples. New articles of faith are forged and thrown like a snare about the conscience of posterity, sowing thereby the seeds of persecution. The disciples without doubt if they become powerful . . . will think that heretics are to be persecuted and will persecute those whom they hold as heretics, that is, those who reject their interpretations. O God, the Father of light, avert this sequel. Be appeased by the punishments visited upon our fathers and ourselves and enlighten posterity. And thou, Posterity, beware of this outcome. Be warned by our example and do not so adhere to the interpretations of men as not to put them to the test of reason, sense, and Scripture. And you, scholars, avoid this course. Do not arrogate so much to yourselves that you bring the souls and bodies of many into peril by your authority.

THE PLEA OF DAVID JORIS FOR SERVETUS[1]

Most noble, just, worthy, gracious, dear Lords, now that I, your friend and brother in the Lord Jesus Christ, have heard what has happened to the good, worthy Servetus, how that he was delivered into your hands and power by no friendliness and love but through envy and hate, as will be made manifest in the day of judgment to those whose eyes are now blinded by cunning so that they cannot understand the ground of the truth. God give them to

[1] *Sendbrieven*, Boek I, Deel 4, Brief 9, of which there is a copy in the Bibliotheek der vereenigde Doopsgezinde Gemeente to Amsterdam. This letter is reproduced in Johann Lorenz von Mosheim, *Anderweitiger Versuch einer vollständigen und unpartheyischen Ketzergeschichte* (Helmstaedt, 1748), pp. 421-25. The letter is dated July 1, 1553, which must be incorrect because it contains a reference to the letters of the Swiss cities of September, 1553.

understand. The report has gone everywhere abroad, and even to my ears, that the learned preachers or shepherds of souls have taken counsel and written to certain cities who have resolved to pass sentence to put him to death. This news has so stirred me that I can have no peace on behalf of our religion and the holy churches far and near, which stand fast in the love and unity of Christ, until I have raised my voice as a member of the body of Christ, until I have opened my heart humbly before your Highnesses and freed my conscience. I trust that the learned, perverted, carnal, and bloodthirsty may have no weight and make no impression upon you, and if they should ingratiate themselves with you as did the Scribes and Pharisees with Pilate in the case of our Lord Jesus, they will displease the King of Kings and the teacher of all, namely, Christ, who taught not only in the Scripture according to the letter, but also in divine fashion, that no one should be crucified or put to death for his teaching. He himself was rather crucified and put to death. Yes, not only that, but He has severely forbidden persecution. Will it not then be a great perversion, blindness, evil, and darkness to indulge in impudent disobedience through hate and envy? They must first themselves have been deranged before they could bring a life to death, damn a soul forever, and hasten it to hell. Is that a Christian procedure or a true spirit? I say eternally no, however plausible it may appear. If the preachers are not of this mind and wish to avoid the sin against the Holy Ghost, let them be wary of seizing and killing men for their good intentions and belief according to their understanding, especially when these ministers stand so badly in other people's books that they dare not go out of their own city and land. Let them remember that they are called, sent, and anointed of God to save souls, to bring men to right and truth—that is, to make alive the dead, and not to destroy, offend, and corrupt, let alone to take life. This belongs to Him alone to whom it is given, who was crucified, who died, and who suffered. The government is ordained of God to inflict bodily punishment upon those who sin in the body against the love of the truth and the law of God's Christ. The magistrate is to punish the bad and protect the good, lest they be dispossessed and killed by the evil. But, as Dr. Martin Luther says,[2] the servants of the temple have incited the magistrates to dispossess and kill good, upright folk who were not subservient to the clergy. Yet Christ, our Lord, neither did nor taught this, but endured and suffered to the end. Wherefore he declared, "They shall put you out of the synagogues: yea, the time cometh, that whosoever killeth you will think that he doeth God service. And these things will they do unto you, because they have not known the Father, nor me." [3] Does this apply to those who inflict or to those who endure suffering? . . . The persecutors have not made man and should not destroy him apart from the true law of our Lord Christ. Let those who thirst for blood kill their own sons and daughters, if they be in error. Yet no godly father will do that, but rather the devil who is a murderer and a liar from the beginning.[4]

Noble, wise, and prudent Lords, consider what would happen if free rein were given to our opponents to kill heretics. How many men would be left on earth if each had this power over the other, inasmuch as each considers the other a heretic? The Jews so regard the Christians, so do the Saracens and the Turks, and the Christians reciprocate. The Papists and the Lutherans, the Zwinglians and the Anabaptists, the Calvinists and the Adiaphorists, mutually ban each other. Because of these differences of opinion should men hate and kill each other? . . . "Whoso sheddeth man's blood, by man shall his blood be shed," [5] as Scripture says. Let us, then, not take the sword, and if anyone is of an erroneous and evil mind and understanding let us pray for him and awaken him to love, peace, and unity. . . .

And if the aforesaid Servetus is a heretic or a sectary before God . . . we should inflict on him no harm in any of his members, but admonish him in a friendly way and at most banish him from the city, if he will not give up his obstinacy and stop disturbing the peace by his teaching . . . that he may come to a better mind

[2] The reference is probably to Luther's tract "Von weltlicher Obrigkeit." See above, p. 144.

[3] John 16: 2-3. [4] John 8: 44. [5] Gen. 9: 6.

and no longer molest your territory. No one should go beyond this. . . .

The Lord himself will judge of soul and spirit and will separate the good from the bad. He will speedily come, according to Scripture, against the rebellious, bad, hidden evildoers, such as hypocrites, liars, envious, haters, deceivers, betrayers, persecutors of the truth, and Antichrist himself (what does that signify?), to slay them with the "spirit of his mouth" [6] and "the breath of his lips," [7] that is, with no worldly sword, for He "maketh his sun to rise on the evil and the good" and wills that we should imitate Him in His long-suffering, graciousness, and mercy.[8] He instructed the servants, who wished to anticipate the harvest [9] as the apostles wished to call down fire from heaven,[10] to leave the tares with the wheat. At the harvest He will send His angels who have knowledge and understanding to separate the good from the bad, the lies from the truth, the pure from the impure, the new from the old, light from darkness, righteousness from sin, and flesh from spirit, and to give each his place in spirit and truth, for God's judgments are true and eternal and cannot fail . . . but great insufficiency shall be found in men when the day of light and the spirit of perfection shall appear. . . .

Those who have an evil spirit should be instructed, not put to death in the time of their ignorance and blindness similar to Paul's. That no one should assume judgment, the Lord has given us a new commandment in love that we do unto others as we would that they should do unto us. So be merciful, kind, and good, doing as it has been done to your Honors, and as the Lord wishes. "Judge not that ye be not judged." [11] Condemn no man that ye be not condemned. Shed no blood and do no violence, my dear Lords. Understand whose disciples you are, for nothing has the Lord punished more and forgiven less than the shedding of innocent blood and idolatry. Follow no one and believe in no one above God or Christ, who is Lord in spirit and truth. That you may look to this I have trusted to your good intentions and have not been

[6] II Thess. 2: 8. [7] Isa. 11: 4. [8] Matt. 5: 45-48; Luke 6: 35-36.
[9] Matt. 13: 24 ff. [10] Luke 9: 54. [11] Matt. 7: 1.

able to refrain from writing to you according to my knowledge. Although I have withheld my name, you should not give this communication less consideration. In these days one cannot write everything because the pen is not to be trusted.

As best I may, I present myself most submissively to your Highnesses as your brother and friend in the Lord always.

Appendix

A Finding List of the Works of Sebastian Franck in Some Libraries of the United States

There is a bibliography of Franck's works in Karl Gödeke, *Grundriss der deutschen Dichtung*, Vol. II [2] (Dresden, 1886), § 105, pp. 8-14. His order and spelling are followed here for convenience in reference. He placed the *Sprichwörter* first, because of his interest in German literature. The other works are arranged in chronological order. The numbers in parentheses are those of his list; the letters in parentheses are the abbreviations employed in the section on Franck in our introduction. The Dutch translations of Franck's works are discussed by Bruno Becker, "Nederlandsche Vertalingen van Sebastiaan Franck's Geschriften," *Nederlandsch Archief voor Kerkgeschiedenis*, N. S., XXI (1928), 149-60. There are further notes by C. P. Burger, Jr., in his article, "De Nederlandsche Vertalingen van de Werken van Sebastiaan Franck," *Het Boek*, XVII (1928), 215-17.

Sprüchwörter Gemeiner Tütscher nation . . . 2 pts.
[Froschower's preface, 1545], Zürich. (2) Harvard.
Frankfurt a. M., 1548. (Not in Gödeke.) University of Chicago.
Latendorf, Friedrich, hrsg., Sebastian Franck's erste namenlose Sprichwörtersammlung vom Jahre 1532 in getreuem Abdruck. Poesneck, 1876, vii + 367 [1] pp.

Von dem grewlichen laster der trunckenheit. . . .
At the end of the dedication, "Justenfeld, 1531." (7) Harvard.

Cronica, Abconterfaytung vnd entwerffung der Türkey . . . von einem Sybenburger . . . inn Latein beschryben. Durch Sebastianũ Franck verteütscht. . . . Newlich widerumb vberlesen Corigiert vnd gebessert. [Nuremberg?] 1530. Gödeke has Augsburg, 1530, and Zwickau, 1530. (10b) Harvard.

Chronica Zeytbůch vnd geschycht bibel von anbegyn biss inn diss gegenwertig M. D. xxxj jar . . . 1531. At the end Strassburg. (12a; GB) Cornell, Hartford Seminary, Yale.
——— n. p., 1536. (12b) University of Pennsylvania.

Chronica/Tytboeck eñ gheschiet/bibel, van aenbegin/der Werelt, tot den Jare M. D. XXXVI. verlengt. 3 pts., to which is added, as a fourth part, the Werelt-boeck, Spieghel en-/de Beeltenisse des gheheelen Aerdtbodems. Leyden, 1583. New York Public Library. The same title, Delft, 1583. Schwenkfelder Historical Library (Pennsburg, Pa.). Reprint, Amsterdam, 1595. Columbia. Of the Dutch translations Gödeke knew only that of 1558.

Dass Gott dass ainig ain vnd höchstes gut sein allmächtigs, wars, lebendigs Wort. . . . n. p., 1534. (16) Cornell.

Weltbuch: spiegel vñ bildtniss des gantzen erdbodens in vier bücher. . . . Tübingen, 1534. (17a; WB) Columbia, Cornell, Hartford Seminary, Harvard.

Weltbuch, spiegel vnd bildtnis des gantzen Erdtbodens. . . . n. p., 1542. (17b) Columbia, New York Public Library.

Dat wereltboeck, spiegel ende Beelteniss des gheheelen Aertbodems. Bound as a fourth part with the Dutch translations of the Chronica, Leyden, 1583, Delft, 1583, and Amsterdam, 1595. See above.

Des grossen Nothelffers vnnd Weltheiligen Sant Gelts oder S. Pfennings Lobgesang. . . . Facsimile durch Hermann Aupperle (n. d., Gmünd, Schwäb.), 16 pages (no pagination), from the first edition of Ulm, 1537. (19) Library of R. H. Bainton.

Erasmus von Rotterdam, das Lob der Thorheit (Encomion moriae) verdeutscht von Frank. Mit Vorwort von Götzinger. Leipzig, 1884. xxiv u. 163 pp. (21c; ME) University of Chicago, Columbia, Library of R. H. Bainton.

Unfortunately Götzinger reprinted only one out of the three tracts originally printed together. According to Gödeke (21) the title of the entire work reads: Das Theür vnd Künstlich | Büchlin Morie Encomion | das ist. Ein Lob der Thorhait, von | Erasmo Roterodamo schimpfflich | gespilt, zů lesen nit weniger nützlich | dann lieblich, verteütscht. || Von der Haylossigkaitt: Eytelkaytt: vnd vngewisshait aller Menschlichen Künst vñd weysshait. Zů ende mit angehefft Ein Lob des Esels auss Heinrico Cor | nelio Agrippa, De Vanitate, etc. verteutscht. || Von dem Bam dess wissens Gůtz vnd böss | Dauon Adam den Todt hat gessen, vnd noch heüt alle | Menschen den Todt essen, Was der sei, vnd wie er noch heüt ieder | man verbotten. Was dargegen der Bawm des Lebens sei. || Encomion: Ein lob des Thorechten Götlichen worts, was das sei, von des selben Ma | iestät, vnd was für vnderschaid zwisschen der Schrifft, eüssern | vnd innern Worts sei. Alles zum tail verteutscht, zum tail | beschrieben durch Sebastian Francken von Wörd. . . . Am Schl., Hans Varnir zu Vlm, n. d. Inasmuch as the pagination is consecutive most writers refer to all of the tracts as *Morie encomium*. I have preferred to reserve the abbreviation ME for the first tract reprinted by Götzinger. The third tract, *Von dem*

Bam dess wissens (BM) appeared also separately (Gödeke, No. 24), but I have been unable to locate a copy in this country and have been compelled to rely on the excerpts in Erbkam, Hegler, and Koyré. Note that the Latin translation of this work, *De Arbore scientiae boni et mali . . . Augustino Eleutherio authore,* 1561 (Gödeke, No. 24), employs the pseudonym for Sebastian Franck already used in the *De haereticis.* I have been unable to discover any occurrence of the pseudonym prior to our compilation.

Paradoxa du- | centa octoginta, das ist, CC. LXXX. Wunderred. . . . n. p., n. d. Alfred Hegler (Geist und Schrift bei Sebastian Franck, Freiburg i. B., 1892, p. xi, n. 10), gives 1534 as the date of the first edition. (27a; Par.) Cornell, Hartford Seminary.

Ziegler, Heinrich, Sebastian Franck Paradoxa eingeleitet von W. Lehmann (Jena, 1919), xxxviii + 371 pp. Mennonite Historical Library (Scottdale, Pa.), Yale.

Van het Ryke Christi. Gouda, 1611. (28) Cornell.

Germaniae Chronicon. . . . Augsburg, 1538. (29b) Hartford Seminary, Union Theological Seminary (New York), Yale.

Germania. Von des gantzen Teütsch- || lands/aller Teutschen völcker herkom̄en Namen/Händeln/Gůten vnd bösen Thaten/Reden/ || Räthen/Kriegen/Sigen/Niderlagen/Stifftungen. . . . || Auffs new mercklich gemehret vnnd gebessert. || Durch Sebastian Francken/ von Wörd., n. p., Colophon, 1539, fol. 402. (Unknown to Gödeke.) Columbia.

Chronica des gantzen Teutschen lands . . . Ausz glaubwirdigen . . . Geschichtschreibern . . . zůsamen getragen . . . durch Sebastian Francken/von Wörd. Colophon, Getruckt zů Bern̄ inn Dechtlandt/ by Mathia Apiario/unnd vollendet uff den ersten tag Martii. Anno M. D. XXXIX. (Unknown to Gödeke.) Cornell.

Die Guldin Arch. . . . Augsburg, 1538. (32) Hartford Seminary, Mennonite Historical Library (Scottdale, Pa.), Yale.

Das verbüthschiert | mit siben Sigeln verschlossen Bůch. . . . n. p., 1539. (33; VB) Hartford Seminary, Mennonite Historical Library.

Von der Hoffnunge vnnd Liebe Gottes. . . . Frankfurt a. M., 1543. (34) This work is a separate printing of the Guldin Arch, fol. CCXXXV-CCXLVI verso. Schwenkfelder Historical Library.

Warhafftige/Zeügknusz der Schrifft/vom/Leiden/Angst/Trübsal/ vnd/allerley not/was nutzes mit/sich bringt/vnnd wie nott/es vns sei/zum Ewi-/gen Leben./Durch Sebastian Francken/zusa-/men gebracht./Getruckt zu Franckfurt am Meyn/bey Cyriaco Jacob./ MDXLIII. This is a separate printing from the Guldin Arch, fol. CCXLVI verso-CCLXVII verso. (Unknown to Gödeke.) Schwenkfelder Historical Library.

Das Kriegs-Büchlein des Friedes. . . . n. p., 1539. (35) Klink, V., hrsg., Sebastian Franck von Donauwörth Kriegbüchlein des Friedens. Schwäbisch-Gmünd [Introduction, 1929], pp. 17 (introduction), 18-76 + [1] (condensed reprint). Library of R. H. Bainton.

Bibliography

Bibliographie

[illegible]

Acton, John Emerich Edward Dalberg: The History of Freedom and Other Essays. London, [illegible].

Adam, Johann: Evangelische Kirchengeschichte der Stadt Straßburg [illegible]. Straßburg, [illegible].

Allen, Percy Stafford, ed.: Opus Epistolarum Des. Erasmi Roterodami. Oxford, [illegible].

Alverdes, [illegible]

Aquinas, Thomas: Catena aurea. [illegible] Oxford, [illegible].

Barnaud, Jean: Pierre Viret. [illegible]

Baron, Hans: Calvins Staatsanschauung und das konfessionelle Zeitalter. [illegible]

Baur, [illegible]

[illegible]

Bohatec, [illegible]

Bonnet, Jules: [illegible]

[illegible]

Bibliography

The following list is composed of the titles of the more important works referred to in the footnotes. The titles of sixteenth-century books are not repeated, nor are the titles of periodical articles. Bibliographies of nearly all of the sixteenth-century figures in the *De haereticis* can now be found in Karl Schottenloher, *Bibliographie zur deutschen Geschichte im Zeitalter der Glaubensspaltung, 1517-1585*, Leipzig, 1933- .

Acton, John Emerich Edward Dalberg, The History of Freedom and Other Essays. London, 1922.

Adam, Johann, Evangelische Kirchengeschichte der Stadt Strassburg. Strassburg, 1922.

Allen, Percy Stafford, Opvs epistolarvm Des. Erasmi Roterodami. Oxford, 1906- (in progress; 8 vols. have thus far appeared).

Altendorf, Erich, Einheit und Heiligkeit der Kirche. Berlin & Leipzig, 1932. Arbeiten zur Kirchengeschichte, XX.

Aquinas, Thomas, Catena aurea. Commentary on the four gospels collected out of the works of the Fathers by S. Thomas Aquinas. Oxford, 1841; new edition, 1874.

Barnaud, Jean, Pierre Viret. Saint-Amans (Tarn), 1911.

Baron, Hans, Calvin's Staatsanschauung und das konfessionelle Zeitalter. Berlin & München, 1924. Historische Zeitschrift, Beiheft I.

Baur, Chrysostomus, Der heilige Johannes Chrysostomus und seine Zeit. 2 vols., München, 1929-30.

Beyerhaus, Gisbert, Studien zur Staatsanschauung Calvins. Berlin, 1910. Neue Studien zur Geschichte der Theologie und der Kirche, VII.

Bibliotheca Erasmiana, edited by Ferdinand François Ernest van der Haeghen. 6 vols., Gand, 1897-1907.

Bidembach, Felix, Consiliorum theologicorum decas VII. Frankfurt a. M., 1608-11.

Bonnet, Jules, Récits du seizième siècle. Paris, 1864.

Bossert, Gustav, Quellen und Geschichte der Wiedertäufer: I, Herzogtum Württemberg. Leipzig, 1930. Quellen und Forschungen zur Reformationsgeschichte, XIII.

Buisson, Ferdinand, Sébastien Castellion. 2 vols., Paris, 1893.

Bury, John Bagnell, History of the Later Roman Empire from the Death of Theodosius I to the Death of Justinian. 2 vols., London, 1923.

Calvinstudien, Festschrift zum 400 Geburtstage Johann Calvins, unter Redaktion von Lic. Dr. Bohatec, hrsg. von der Ref. Gemeinde Elberfeld. Leipzig, 1909.

Charles, Robert Henry, Apocrypha and Pseudepigrapha of the Old Testament. 2 vols., Oxford, 1913.

Christie, Richard Copley, Etienne Dolet. London, 1899.

Combès, Gustave, La Doctrine politique de Saint Augustin. Paris, 1927.

Corpus Schwenckfeldianorum, eds., Chester David Hartranft (1907-16) and E. E. S. Johnson (1922-). Leipzig, 1907- (in progress; 12 vols. have thus far appeared).

Doumergue, Émile, Jean Calvin. 7 vols., Neuilly-sur-Seine, 1899-1927.

Egli, Emil, Actensammlung zur Geschichte der zürcher Reformation. 1 vol. in 2, Zürich, 1879.

Erbkam, H. W., Geschichte der protestantischen Sekten im Zeitalter der Reformation. Hamburg & Gotha, 1843.

Evans, Austin Patterson, An Episode in the Struggle for Religious Freedom. New York, 1924.

Förstemann, Karl Eduard, Neues Urkundenbuch zur Geschichte der evangelischen Kirchenreformation. Hamburg, 1842.

Fredericq, Paul, Corpus documentorum inquisitionis haereticae pravitatis Neerlandicae. 5 vols., Ghent, 1889-1906.

Füsslin, Johann Conrad, Beyträge zur Erläuterung der Kirchen-Reformations-Geschichten des Schweitzerlandes. 5 vols., Zürich, 1741-53.

Gansfort, Wessel, Wessel Gansfort, Life and Writings by Edward Waite Miller. . . . Principal works translated by Jared Waterbury Scudder. 2 vols., New York & London, 1917.

Giran, Etienne, Sébastien Castellion. Haarlem, 1914.

Gordon, Alexander, "Michael Servetus," in Addresses Biographical and Historical. London, 1922.

Hartmann, Julius, und Karl Jäger, Johann Brenz. 2 vols., Hamburg, 1840-42.

Hegler, Alfred, Geist und Schrift bei Sebastian Franck. Freiburg i. Br., 1892.

Hegler, Alfred, Beiträge zur Geschichte der Mystik in der Reformationszeit, ed. Walther Köhler. Berlin, 1906. ARG, Ergänzungsband I.

Heim, Karl, Das Gewissheitsproblem in der systematischen Theologie bis zu Schleiermacher. Leipzig, 1911.

Hermelink, Heinrich, Der Toleranzgedanke im Reformationszeitalter. Leipzig, 1908. SVRG XCVIII.

Hessels, Joannes Henricvs (Jan Hendrjk), Ecclesiae Londino-Batavae archivvm. 3 vols. in 4 (Vol. III has 2 parts), Cambridge, 1887-97.

Himmelheber, Emil, Caspar Hedio: Ein Lebensbild aus der Reformationsgeschichte. Karlsruhe, 1881. Studien der evangelisch- protestantischen Geistlichen des Grossherzogthums Baden, VII, 1.

Hoffmann, Heinrich, Reformation und Gewissensfreiheit. Giessen, 1932. Aus der Welt der Religion, Religionswissenschaftliche Reihe XVIII.

Holl, Karl, "Augustins innere Entwicklung," in Gesammelte Aufsätze zur Kirchengeschichte. 3 vols., Tübingen, 1923-28.

Horawitz, Adalbert, und Karl Hartfelder, Briefwechsel des Beatus Rhenanus. Leipzig, 1886.

Hottinger, Johann Heinrich, Historiae ecclesiasticae Novi Testamenti. . . . 9 vols., Hanover, 1655-67 (imprint varies, Vols. IV-IX, Zürich).

Humphrey, Edward Frank, Politics and Religion in the Days of Augustine. New York, 1912. Dissertation, Columbia.

Iongh, Wilhelmina de, Erasmus' Denkbeelden over Staat en Regiering. Amsterdam, 1927.

Jones, Rufus M., Spiritual Reformers in the Sixteenth and Seventeenth Centuries. London, 1914.

Jordan, Wilbur Kitchener, The Development of Religious Toleration in England from the Beginning of the English Reformation to the Death of Queen Elizabeth. Cambridge, Mass., 1932.

Kawerau, Gustav, Johann Agricola von Eisleben. Berlin, 1881.

Kidd, Beresford James, Documents Illustrative of the History of the Church. 2 vols., London, 1920-23.

——— A History of the Church to A.D. 461. 3 vols., Oxford, 1922.

Köhler, Walther, Reformation und Ketzerprozess. Tübingen, 1901. Sammlung gemeinverständlicher Vorträge und Schriften aus dem Gebiet der Theologie und Religionsgeschichte, XXII.

——— Bibliographia Brentiana. Berlin, 1904.

Köhler, Walther, Jacobi Acontii Satanae stratagematum libri octo . . . curavit Gualtherus Koehler. Monaci, 1927.

Kühn, Johannes, Toleranz und Offenbarung. Leipzig, 1923.

Löwenich, Walther von, Luthers Theologia crucis. München, 1929. Forschungen zur Geschichte und Lehre des Protestantismus, 2te Reihe, II.

Luther, Martin, The Works of Martin Luther. Published by the A. J. Holman Co. 6 vols., Philadelphia, 1915-32.

McNeill, John T., Unitive Protestantism. New York, 1930.

Mansi, Joannes Dominicus (Gian Domenico), Sacrorum conciliorum nova et amplissima collectio. 57 vols., Florence, 1759-1927.

Martène, Edmund, De antiquis ecclesiae ritibus libri tres. 4 vols. in 2, Bassani, 1788.

Matthes, Kurt, Das Corpus Christianum bei Luther im Lichte seiner Erforschung. Berlin, 1929. Studien zur Geschichte der Wirtschaft und Geisteskultur, hrsg. von Rudolf Häpke, V.

Mausbach, Joseph, Die Ethik des Hl. Augustinus. 2 vols., Freiburg i. Br., 1929.

Mestwerdt, Paul, Die Anfänge des Erasmus. Leipzig, 1917.

Mirbt, Carl, Quellen zur Geschichte des Papsttums und des römischen Katholizismus. 4th ed., Tübingen, 1924.

Mosheim, Johann Lorenz von, Anderweitiger Versuch einer vollständigen und unpartheyischen Ketzergeschichte. Helmstaedt, 1748.

Murray, Robert Henry, Erasmus und Luther: Their Attitude to Toleration. London & New York, 1920.

Nörregaard, Jens, Augustins Bekehrung. Tübingen, 1923.

Offergelt, Franz, Die Staatslehre des Hl. Augustinus. Bonn, 1914. Dissertation.

Otto, August, Die Sprichwörter und Sprichwörtlichen Redensarten der Römer. Leipzig, 1890.

Paulus, Nikolaus, Protestantismus und Toleranz im 16. Jahrhundert. Freiburg i. Br., 1911.

Persecution and Liberty: Essays in Honor of George Lincoln Burr. New York, 1931. The following essays have been directly utilized: Ernest W. Nelson, "The Theory of Persecution," pp. 3-20; Wallace K. Ferguson, "The Attitude of Erasmus toward Toleration," pp. 171-81; Roland H. Bainton, "Sebastian Castellio and the Toleration Controversy of the Sixteenth Century," pp. 183-209.

Pierrefleur, Mémoires de Pierrefleur, grand-banderet d'Orbe, où sont contenus les commencements de la réforme dans la ville d'Orbe et au pays de Vaud, 1530-1561, publiés pour la première fois et accompagnés de notes historiques par A. Verdeil. Lausanne, 1856.

Pressel, Theodore, Anecdota Brentiana. Tübingen, 1888.

Prinsen, J., Collectanea van Gerardus Geldenhauer Noviomagus. Amsterdam, 1901. Historisch Genootschap, III, 16.

Rembert, Karl, Die "Wiedertäufer" im Herzogtum Jülich. Berlin, 1899.

Richter, Aemilius Ludwig, Die evangelischen Kirchenordnungen des sechszehnten Jahrhunderts. 2 vols. in 1, Weimar, 1846; new edition, Leipzig, 1871.

Riggenbach, Bernhard, Das Chronikon des Konrad Pellikan zur vierten Säkularfeier der Universität Tübingen. Basel, 1877.

Röhrich, Timotheus Wilhelm, Geschichte der Reformation in Elsass und besonders Strassburg. 2 vols., Strassburg, 1830-32.

Romeis, Capistran, Das Heil der Christen ausserhalb der wahren Kirche nach der Lehre des Hl. Augustins. Paderborn, 1908. Forschungen zur christlichen Literatur- und Dogmengeschichte, VIII, 4.

Rommel, Christoph von, Philipp der Grossmüthige, Landgraf von Hessen. 3 vols., Giessen, 1830.

Ruffini, Francesco, La libertà religiosa. Turin, 1901. Tr. by J. Parker Heyes under the title, Religious Liberty. London & New York, 1912. Theological Translation Library, XXXII.

Salin, Edgar, Civitas Dei. Tübingen, 1926.

Schickler, Fernand de, Les Églises de refuge en Angleterre. 3 vols., Paris, 1892.

Schiess, Traugott, Bullingers Korrespondenz mit den Graubündnern. 3 vols., Basel, 1904-6. Quellen zur schweizer Geschichte, XXIII-XXV.

——— Briefwechsel der Brüder Ambrosius und Thomas Blaurer, hrsg. von der badischen historischen Kommission. 3 vols., Freiburg i. Br., 1908-12.

Schilling, Otto, Die Staats- und Soziallehre des Hl. Augustinus. Freiburg i. Br., 1910.

Schmid, Reinhold, Reformationsgeschichte Württembergs. Heilbronn, 1904.

Scholz, Heinrich, Glaube und Unglaube in der Weltgeschichte im Kommentar zu Augustins De civitate Dei. Leipzig, 1911.

Schwarz, Rudolf, Johannes Calvins Lebenswerk in seinen Briefen. 2 vols., Tübingen, 1909.

Seeberg, Erich, Gottfried Arnold. Meerane i. Sa., 1923.

Sehling, Emil, Die evangelischen Kirchenordnungen des XVI. Jahrhunderts. 5 vols., Leipzig, 1902-15.

Seidemann, Johann Karl, Dr. Jakob Schenk, der vermeintlicher Antinomer, Freibergs Reformator. Leipzig, 1875.

Seitz, Anton, Die Heilsnotwendigkeit der Kirche. Freiburg i. Br., 1903.

Shotwell, James T., and Louise Ropes Loomis, The See of Peter. New York, 1927. Records of Civilization, VII.

Smith, Preserved, Erasmus. New York, 1923.

Stadelmann, Rudolf, Vom Geist des ausgehenden Mittelalters: Studien zur Geschichte der Weltanschauung von Nicolaus Cusanus bis Sebastian Franck. Halle, 1929. Deutsche Vierteljahrsschrift für Literaturwissenschaft und Geistesgeschichte, XV.

Tausch, Edw., Sebastian Franck von Donauwörth und seine Lehre. Halle, 1893.

Thimme, Wilhelm, Augustins geistige Entwicklung in den ersten Jahren nach seiner "Bekehrung." Berlin, 1908.

——— Augustin: ein Lebens- und Characterbild auf Grund seiner Briefe. Göttingen, 1910.

Troeltsch, Ernst, Die Soziallehren der christlichen Kirchen und Gruppen. Tübingen, 1923. Tr. by Olive Wyon under the title, The Social Teaching of the Christian Churches. 2 vols., London, 1931. Halley Steward publications, 1.

Uhlhorn, Gerhard, Urbanus Rhegius. Elberfeld, 1861. Leben und ausgewählte Schriften der Väter und Begründer der lutherischen Kirche, VII.

Viénot, John, Histoire de la réforme dans le pays de Montbéliard depuis les origines jusqu'à la mort de P. Toussain, 1524-1573. 2 vols., Montbéliard, 1900.

Van Schelven, A. A., De Nederduitsche Vluchtelingenkerken der XVIe eeuw in Engeland en Duitschland. The Hague, 1909.

——— Kerkeraads-Protocollen der Nederduitsche Vluchtelingen Kerk te Londen, 1560-1563. Amsterdam, 1921. Historisch Genootschap, III, 43.

Völker, Karl, Toleranz und Intoleranz im Zeitalter der Reformation. Leipzig, 1912.

Vries de Heekelingen, H. de, Genève pepinière du Calvinisme hollondais. 2 vols., Vol. I, Fribourg, Suisse, 1918; Vol. II, The Hague, 1924.

Wander, Karl F. W., Deutsches Sprichwörter-Lexikon. 5 vols., Leipzig, 1867-80.

Wappler, Paul, Inquisition und Ketzerprozesse in Zwickau zur Reformationszeit dargestellt im Zusammenhang mit der Entwicklung der Ansichten Luthers und Melanchthons über Glaubens- und Gewissensfreiheit. Leipzig, 1908.

——— Die Stellung Kursachsens und des Landgrafen Philipp von Hessen zur Täuferbewegung. Münster i. W., 1910. Reformationsgeschichtliche Studien und Texte, XIII/XIV.

Wilbur, Earl Morse, "The Two Treatises of Servetus on the Trinity." Cambridge, Mass., 1932. Harvard Theological Studies, XVI.

Willis, Robert, Servetus and Calvin. London, 1877.

Wrede, Adolf, Die Einführung der Reformation im Lüneburgischen durch Herzog Ernst den Bekenner. Göttingen, 1887.

Index

Index

A

D

E

F

I

J

K

L

M

Q

R

T

U

V

W

Y

Z

RECORDS OF CIVILIZATION
SOURCES AND STUDIES
Edited under the auspices of the

DEPARTMENT OF HISTORY, COLUMBIA UNIVERSITY

I. HELLENIC CIVILIZATION. By G. W. Botsford and E. G. Sihler. xiii + 719 pages. $4.50.
II. HISTORY OF THE FRANKS, BY GREGORY, BISHOP OF TOURS. Selections, translated with notes by Ernest Brehaut. xxv + 284 pages, map. $3.50.
III. THE BOOK OF THE POPES (LIBER PONTIFICALIS). Translated with an introduction by Louise Ropes Loomis. xxii + 169 pages. $3.00.
IV. AN INTRODUCTION TO THE HISTORY OF HISTORY. By James T. Shotwell. xii + 339 pages. $4.50.
V. THE LITERATURE OF THE OLD TESTAMENT. By Julius A. Bewer. Revised edition. xiv + 464 pages. $3.00.
VI. A GUIDE TO THE PRINTED MATERIALS FOR ENGLISH SOCIAL AND ECONOMIC HISTORY, 1750–1850. By Judith Blow Williams. Two volumes. xxiii + 535, v + 653 pages. $10.00.
VII. THE SEE OF PETER. By James T. Shotwell and Louise Ropes Loomis. xxvi + 737 pages. $10.00.
VIII. THE HISTORY OF YABALLAHA III. Translated from the Syriac and annotated by James A. Montgomery. ix + 82 pages. $2.00.
IX. THE TWO CITIES, BY OTTO, BISHOP OF FREISING. Translated in full with introduction and notes by Charles Christopher Mierow. xv + 523 pages. $10.00.
X. AN ARAB-SYRIAN GENTLEMAN AND WARRIOR IN THE PERIOD OF THE CRUSADES: MEMOIRS OF USAMAH IBN-MUNQIDH. Translated from the original manuscript by Philip K. Hitti. xi + 265 pages, illustrations and map. $4.50.
XI. THE SOURCES FOR THE EARLY HISTORY OF IRELAND. VOLUME ONE: ECCLESIASTICAL. By James F. Kenney. xvi + 807 pages, maps. $12.50.
XII. ON THE GOVERNMENT OF GOD: A TREATISE BY SALVIAN. Translated with an introduction by Eva M. Sanford. viii + 241 pages, illustrations. $3.75.
XIII. PEASANT LIFE IN OLD GERMAN EPICS: MEIER HELMBRECHT AND DER ARME HEINRICH. Rhymed translations with introduction and notes by Clair Hayden Bell. ix + 184 pages, illustrations and map. $3.00.
XIV. THE CORRESPONDENCE OF POPE GREGORY VIII: SELECTED LETTERS FROM THE REGISTRUM. Translated with an introduction by Ephraim Emerton. xxxi + 212 pages. $3.50.
XV. THE LITERATURE OF THE NEW TESTAMENT. By Ernest Findlay Scott. xiii + 312 pages. $3.00.
XVI. THE BOOK OF DELIGHT, BY JOSEPH BEN MEIR ZABARA. Translated by Moses Hadas, with an introduction by Merriam Sherwood. xi + 203 pages. $3.25.
XVII. CATO THE CENSOR ON FARMING. Translated by Ernest Brehaut. xlvi + 156 pages, illustrations. $3.75.

XVIII. Tracts on Liberty in the Puritan Revolution, 1638–1647. Edited, with a commentary, by William Haller. In three volumes. Vol. I, xiv + 197 pages; Vol. II, 339 pages; Vol. III, 405 pages. $12.50.

XIX. Papal Revenues in the Middle Ages. By W. E. Lunt. In two volumes. Vol. I, x + 341 pages; Vol. II, v + 665 pages. $12.50.

XX. The Earliest Norwegian Laws. Translated, with introduction, annotations, and glossary, by Lawrence M. Larson. xi + 451 pages, maps. $5.00.

XXI. The Chronicle of the Slavs, by Helmold. Translated with introduction and notes by Francis Joseph Tschan. xii + 321 pages, map. $4.00.

XXII. Concerning Heretics; an Anonymous Work Attributed to Sebastian Castellio. Now first done into English by Roland H. Bainton. xiv + 342 pages. $4.00.

FORTHCOMING VOLUMES

Abelard: Sic et non. By Richard McKeon, Assistant Professor of Philosophy, and Mary Sweet, Columbia University.

The Conquest of Lisbon. By Charles Wendell David, Professor of History, Bryn Mawr College.

Correspondence of Bishop Boniface. By Ephraim Emerton, Professor Emeritus, Harvard University. To be published posthumously.

Erasmus: Education of a Christian Prince. By Lester K. Born, Assistant Professor of Classics, George Washington University.

Eudes of Rouen: The Diary of a Bishop. By Sidney M. Brown, Professor of History, Lehigh University.

Medieval Handbooks of Penance. By John T. McNeill, Professor of the History of European Christianity, University of Chicago, and Helena M. Gamer, Instructor in Latin, Mt. Holyoke College.

Medieval Universities and Intellectual Life. By Lynn Thorndike, Professor of History, Columbia University.

Orosius: Seven Books of History against the Pagans. By Irving W. Raymond, Assistant Professor of History, Columbia University.

Pascal: On the Equilibrium of Fluids. By A. G. H. Spires, Professor of French, and Frederick Barry, Associate Professor of the History of Science, Columbia University.

Philippe de Novare: History of the War between Frederick II and John d'Ibelin, Lord of Beirut. By John L. La Monte, Assistant Professor of History, University of Cincinnati.

Robert of Clari: Conquest of Constantinople. By Edgar H. McNeal, Professor of History, Ohio State University.

The Sources for the Early History of Ireland. Volume Two: Secular. By Dr. James F. Kenney.

William of Tyre: History of Things Done in the Lands beyond the Sea. By Mrs. Emily Atwater Babcock, Instructor in Latin, and A. C. Krey, Professor of History, University of Minnesota.

COLUMBIA UNIVERSITY PRESS
COLUMBIA UNIVERSITY
NEW YORK

FOREIGN AGENT
OXFORD UNIVERSITY PRESS
HUMPHREY MILFORD
AMEN HOUSE, LONDON, E. C. 4

XVIII. [illegible] with a commentary, by William [illegible]. Vol. I, [illegible] pages. Vol. II, [illegible] pages. [illegible]

XXIX. [illegible] Vol. [illegible] pages. [illegible]

XXX. THE [illegible] Translated with introduction, notes, and glossary, by [illegible] pages, maps. [illegible]

XXXI. THE CHRONICLE OF THE [illegible] Translated with introduction and notes by [illegible] Joseph [illegible] pages. [illegible]

XXXII. [illegible] By Robert H. [illegible] pages. [illegible]

MISCELLANEOUS VOLUMES

[illegible] By [illegible] Professor of Philosophy and [illegible] Columbia University.

THE [illegible] By [illegible] Professor of History, [illegible] College.

[illegible] By [illegible] Professor [illegible] Columbia University. To be published [illegible].

[illegible] By [illegible] Professor [illegible] Columbia University.

[illegible] By [illegible] Professor of History, [illegible].

[illegible] By John T. McNeill, Professor of the History of European Christianity, University of Chicago, and Helena M. Gamer, Instructor in Latin, Mount Holyoke College.

[illegible] By [illegible] Professor of [illegible].

[illegible] By Irving W. Raymond, Assistant Professor of History, Columbia University.

[illegible] By [illegible] Professor of French and [illegible] Associate [illegible] of Science, Columbia University.

[illegible] By [illegible] Associate Professor of History, University of [illegible].

[illegible] By Arthur [illegible] McNeal, Professor [illegible].

THE [illegible] By [illegible].

[illegible] By [illegible] Professor of [illegible] University of Minnesota.

COLUMBIA UNIVERSITY PRESS

COLUMBIA UNIVERSITY

NEW YORK

FOREIGN AGENT

OXFORD UNIVERSITY PRESS

HUMPHREY MILFORD

AMEN HOUSE, LONDON, E.C. 4